REDISCOVERING abundance

Catholic Social Tradition Series

Preface to the Series

In *Tertio millennio adveniente*, Pope John Paul II poses a hard question: "It must be asked how many Christians really know and put into practice the principles of the church's social doctrine." The American Catholic bishops share the pope's concern: "Catholic social teaching is central and essential element of our faith . . . [and yet] our social heritage is unknown by many Catholics. Sadly, our social doctrine is not shared or taught in a consistent and comprehensive way in too many of our schools." This lack is critical because the "sharing of our social tradition is a definite measure of Catholic education and formation." A United States Catholic Conference task force on social teaching and education noted that within Catholic higher education "there appears to be little consistent attention given to incorporating gospel values and Catholic social teaching into general education courses or into departmental majors."

In response to this problem, the volumes in the Catholic Social Tradition series aspire to impart the best of what this tradition has to offer not only to Catholics but to all who face the social issues of our times. The volumes examine a wide variety of issues and problems within the Catholic social tradition and contemporary society, yet they share several characteristics. They are theologically and philosophically grounded, examining the deep structure of thought in modern culture. They are publicly argued, enhancing dialogue with other religious and nonreligious traditions. They are comprehensively engaged by a wide variety of disciplines such as theology, philosophy, political science, economics, history, law, management, and finance. Finally, they examine how the Catholic social tradition can be integrated on a practical level and embodied in institutions in which people live much of their lives. The Catholic Social Tradition series is about faith in action in daily life, providing ways of thinking and acting to those seeking a more humane world.

Michael J. Naughton
University of St. Thomas
Minnesota, USA

REDISCOVERING abundance

Interdisciplinary Essays on
Wealth, Income, and Their Distribution
in the Catholic Social Tradition

edited by

HELEN ALFORD, O.P., CHARLES M. A. CLARK,
S. A. CORTRIGHT, & MICHAEL J. NAUGHTON

University of Notre Dame Press
Notre Dame, Indiana

Manufactured in the United States of America

Library of Congress Cataloging in-Publication Data

Rediscovering abundance : interdisciplinary essays on wealth, income,
and their distribution in the Catholic social tradition / Helen Alford . . . [et al].
  p.   cm.— (Catholic social tradition series)
Includes index.
ISBN 0-268-02027-2 (pbk. : alk. paper)
1. Wealth—Religious aspects—Catholic Church.   2. Income distribution.
3. Economic development—Religious aspects—Catholic Church.
I. Alford, Helen J., 1964–   II. Series.
BR115.W4R43   2006
261.8'5088282—dc22

2005029356

∞ *This book is printed on acid-free paper.*

In memory of
Cardinal François Xavier Nguyên Van Thuân,
former President of the Pontifical Council for Justice and Peace,
whose life and work embodied the heart of the gospel.

Contents

Preface

DANIEL FINN

Some sixteen hundred years ago, St. Augustine was urging his prosperous listeners to be generous toward the poor. Like the other Fathers of the early Church, he offered numerous reasons. Most important of these was that God as Creator gave the world to humanity in order that the needs of all be met. Another of the arguments he made is particularly telling. Augustine rebuked the wealthy by saying that they had "found" their wealth here; they did not "bring it with them" at birth. In Augustine's day, of course, as throughout the pre-modern world, the wealthy were largely those who owned land. This is what provided them with the lion's share of its annual produce and distinguished them from the ordinary working people of their era.

Today, we are aware that wealth is not simply "found" in the world, although it remains true that great wealth is frequently passed on in inheritance within families. In the modern world we are far more conscious of the role of human labor and ingenuity in the production of wealth. Farming, where the bounty of natural rather than human processes is most apparent, represented more than 80 percent of all the wealth produced in pre-modern nations. Today, in the industrialized world, less than 3 percent of annual production arises from agriculture. The moral questions surrounding wealth, its production, and its proper uses are now, if anything, more difficult than when there was good reason to say that wealth was more importantly found than produced.

Because the goods of this world were intended by God to meet human needs, the early Fathers of the Church shared a common understanding of the responsibilities of the owners of those goods. The classic patristic formulation was that if I have more than I need and you have less than you need, then I have an obligation to share with you from my surplus. Like the ancient Israelites, Christians are to understand ownership as stewardship, not as an absolute or ultimate control over the goods one possesses. This implicit obligation incurred by all who own goods has been named in various ways in the modern world. Pope John Paul II often spoke of the "social mortgage" on all property, a kind of moral lien on our goods that we must respect. In other terms he has referred to "the universal destination of goods," naming more directly this sense that we must respect God's intention that goods meet everyone's needs.

Throughout much of modern history, many defenders of markets and business have chided Christian teaching on economic life as unrealistic, pie-in-the-sky virtue. Analogously, those Christians who did speak religiously about business frequently condemned it for its encouragement of greed and self-interest, vices that contradict the mandate of the Gospel to love one's neighbor. In the last thirty years or so, a systematic effort has been made by Christians to provide a specifically religious defense of markets and the businesses that operate within them. In the work of Michael Novak, Robert Benne, Dennis McCann, and others, we find a concerted theological argument designed to show the moral attractiveness of capitalist business enterprise and wealth production.

Modern Catholic social thought has regularly both praised the wealth-creating strengths of market-based economic relations and criticized their weaknesses. Pope Leo XIII, in 1891, defended the right to private property; he cited in part the jobs that such property ownership can create. John Paul II's now classic encyclical, *Centesimus annus*, identifies clearly both the moral advantages and disadvantages of markets.

Although Christians today need to appreciate the moral defense of markets and business, we must also recognize the risks entailed in this undertaking. For all the importance of the production of wealth and prosperity that markets can make possible for a broad range of citizens, we must not forget that wealth itself is only a proxy for well-being. Economic well-being in particular is only a small portion of the broader notion of well-being for a Christian. Two hundred years before Augustine, Clement of Alexandria taught that self-sufficiency (being able to care for one's self and family) is crucial for a Christian, but he added that this is something "anyone can achieve by a few things."

Similarly, we should recall that in every age the economic "winners" articulate the moral legitimacy of the game that they play better than others. We now look back with a condescending smile at the self-serving assertions made by the nobility in France in the eighteenth century, or by the patricians of Rome two millennia ago. However, we who are among the economically most successful on the planet should remind ourselves that our beliefs about the moral legitimacy of our own world are held with no greater fervor or deeper conviction than were those of the privileged who came before us.

In addition, because these moral dangers of self-deception are great, those of us among the better off have an obligation to be extraordinarily active in efforts to reform the current system where it falls short. The social mortgage on our prosperity requires not simply that we comply with the moral requirements of an ideal economic system should it ever come into existence. That lien on our holdings requires us to attend both to unmet needs around us and to ongoing efforts at achieving an economic system more just than the one we have.

Unlike in Augustine's day, we may not have "found" our wealth here, but we did indeed find the market system in place when we arrived. This book takes seriously this system of wealth creation and the moral challenge of rendering it more humane. Unlike much contemporary neoliberal and neoconservative writing about business and the economy, the authors in this volume possess that self-critical edge required for moral authenticity. Combining that with a faith commitment and the savvy of thoughtful people of diverse experience, the book promises significant contributions to those who take it seriously.

The Nature of Wealth

Introduction

The rapid growth in wealth during the roaring 1990s, followed by the more rapid disappearance of much of these gains in the 2000–2002 stock market decline, has intensified interest in the topic of wealth.[1] While both the serious press and the general public are fascinated by, and inundated with information about, the creation and use of wealth, little attention is devoted to a moral and spiritual evaluation of this creation, distribution, and use. Wealth plays an important role in the economic life of any community, but it is also an important factor in its cultural, political, and religious life. If we would understand that impact, we must closely consider the ends toward which wealth is directed.

Thinking through the ends we aim to achieve through wealth creation and distribution is particularly important. All too often we see the ends-means relationship reversed, and wealth becomes an end in itself instead of a means to more excellent ends. Christian critiques of the prominence of wealth in contemporary culture, while cognizant of the potentially positive role that it can play in a well-ordered market economy, emphasize that wealth is ambivalent—whether it benefits or harms us depends entirely on how it is created, how it is distributed, and how it is used. Wealth can be created by promoting the good of the community (improving its productivity) or by retarding the community's pursuit of genuine goods (setting collusive limits on production to keep prices high, for instance). If wealth is created virtuously, it promotes the authentic development of persons, the prosperity of the firm, and the stability of society. If it is based on exploitation or on fraud, then wealth creation is damaging to persons, to the firm, and ultimately to society.

This collection of twelve essays considers what insights the Catholic social tradition can offer to our understanding of the creation and distribution of wealth. All of the essays are based on the assumption that this topic is too important to be left solely to economists and business professionals and that, similarly, ethical evaluations of wealth are not the domain of theologians and philosophers alone. To

1

understand the topic of wealth creation and distribution, we require an interdisciplinary investigation. Too often, universities divide knowledge into neat little com-
partments or academic departments, but, in practice, we must deal with problems
:as an integrated whole.

Wealth is not a natural phenomenon governed by impersonal laws of motion. It
results from human activity, serves human goals, and is regulated by human laws. If
wealth is a "phenomenon," it shares all the complexity of the human phenomenon.
Consequently, an examination of the question of wealth creation and distribution is
a complex and multifaceted undertaking. As a way to introduce the contents of this
volume, we present some of the various dimensions and levels of this undertaking.
We start with a brief discussion of the meaning of the word "wealth." We then look at
two dimensions of wealth, economic and moral, and at how wealth functions at three
different levels of society: that of the individual person, the productive organization,
and the nation and community of nations. We also look to the spiritual dimension of
the human person: how does wealth's functioning at each level—personal, organizational, national/international—bear on human spirituality? Only by examining all
these dimensions and levels can we begin to understand how wealth can either promote, or undermine, the common good and the dignity of persons.

Defining Wealth

A look at the history of the meaning of the word "wealth" reveals a multitude
of uses and meanings. The *Oxford English Dictionary* derives the word from the Old
English "welde," "[t]he condition of being happy and prosperous; well-being." The
second definition given is: "spiritual well-being. Often in the testamentary phrase *for
the wealth of (one's) soul.*" Only with the third definition do we get close to the contemporary meaning: "Prosperity consisting of abundance of possessions: 'worldly
goods,' valuable possessions, esp. in great abundance." And only with the fourth do
we arrive at an economic definition: "A collective term for those things an abundant
possession of which (by a person or a community) constitute riches."[2]

These definitions emphasize wealth's protean character. "Wealth" refers not
only to the economic value of things, of course, but also to other riches. It names that
enrichment of persons which is their growth in virtue, and the spiritual well-being of
those who, through the proper use of material wealth and by the grace of God, are
enabled to live out their vocation in society unstintingly. Catholic social thought
concentrates on economic wealth as a means to an end and evaluates its creation and
distribution based on its success in promoting final human ends. Economic and
business perspectives too often emphasize wealth as an end—a goal that rational

agents and businesses strive for—at the cost of neglecting the fact that it is a human instrument. The tendency to view wealth as if it were an end in itself is one of the major shortcomings of our modern perspective on business and the economy. It allows economic agencies to pursue shortsighted goals at the expense of the long-term well-being of their companies, their employees, their stockholders, and society as a whole. The corporate misdeeds of Enron are one example of what happens when a company mistakenly pursues wealth as an end, forgetting that it is also a means to a higher end.

Before we examine the moral and economic dimensions of wealth as it relates to the personal, organizational, and national/international levels, we need to lay out the controversies over, and complexities of the term "wealth." Particularly difficult is deciding how to measure it and how to distinguish wealth from the related concept of income.

Measuring Wealth

The "wealth" of a nation comes from three factors: its capital stock, the availability of resources, and the state of technological knowledge (which includes human capital). None of these factors is easily measured without complicated implications for the others.[3] Coupled with the influence of culture and the size and composition of the labor force, they determine the level of production of goods and services. When we measure wealth, we are in fact measuring the valuations of these factors— valuations that reflect many additional factors besides productivity and that are notoriously imprecise, both theoretically (as exposed in the Cambridge Capital Controversies of the 1950s, 1960s, and 1970s) and empirically.[4] Market valuations of these assets are often driven by expectations (as with the "dot-com" stocks in the late 1990s) and by manipulations (as with companies purchasing their own stock) and thus are not reliable indices of their real worth.

There is no precise theoretical definition of wealth (or of income, as we will see). Economists have adopted definitions of wealth (and income) that were developed by governments for the purposes of tax assessment and collection. Hence, when we measure wealth, we are implicitly adopting a very narrow, and to a large extent arbitrary, conception of it. Currently, personal or household marketable wealth typically includes: owner-occupied housing and other real estate and land; consumer durables; financial assets such as checking and savings accounts, cash and currency, bonds and financial securities, the cash surrender value of life insurance, and equities (stocks, mutual funds, unincorporated business equity, and trust equity); and miscellaneous assets, such as money owed by a family business or friends. Other measures make adjustments for how liquid the assets are, thus leading to more narrow definitions of household wealth (fungible wealth and financial wealth). Moreover, one can take a broader conception (based on what wealth provides in terms of financial security) and include Social Security and pension wealth (augmented wealth), which can increase the total "measure" by 50 percent or more. Personal or household income, which is usually important for discussions of income inequality, is defined as money one receives to support one's current well-being, and it typically includes: labor income (wages and benefits), proprietor's earnings, rental income, dividends, interest income, and transfer payments.[5]

Similarly, when governments differentiate between wealth and income, they have in view practical issues of measurement for tax assessment instead of the functional differences or interrelations between wealth and income. It is important at the outset to differentiate between wealth and income, for the failure to make such a distinction (even though in practice it can be difficult to make) is the source of much confusion and misunderstanding in economic and social analysis. Most discussions of economic inequality, especially from the perspective of social justice, fail to make this distinction and thus invite rejection for superficiality or for uninformed moralizing—even if, in many ways, this would be an unfair criticism, since the distinction between wealth and income, even at the highest levels of economic theory, is neither clearcut nor compelling.[6]

Wealth and Income

Just as the word "wealth" has an early spiritual connotation in its etymology, so too does the word "income," which originally referred to the coming in of divine influence. Eventually the meaning of "income" evolved from "entering in" to "the fee paid for entering" to "the payment for some service." As we noted above, unfortunately no commonly accepted definition of either wealth or income is both theoretically consistent with neoclassical economic theory and usable for empirical measurement and analysis. This is not for want of trying. Defining wealth and income was a key question for late-nineteenth–early-twentieth century economists, culminating in John Hicks's and Nicholas Kaldor's work in the midtwentieth century.[7] Attempts to treat income as the consumption of utility (which left one as well off at the end of the time period as one was at the beginning) and wealth as deferred consumption (savings) offered neither significant theoretical insights nor practical policy guidance.

The classical economists had a very useful approach to the understanding of the source of wealth (though clearly limited to their level of economic development).

Based on the insights of the eighteenth-century Irish economist Richard Cantillon and the French Physiocrats, the classical economists viewed the economic system as one of reproduction.[8] Everything that contributed to the reproduction of the material aspects of society was viewed as basic production, and everything above that was viewed as the social surplus.[9] If the social surplus were used productively—to purchase productive assets (capital or raw materials), to expand economic activities (invest in hiring more labor), or to develop new technology or skills—it would contribute to expanded reproduction (economic growth). If the surplus were used to support lavish spending and luxury, that is, on unproductive consumption, then it would not lead to economic growth. While there are limitations to the classical approach (one has to take into account the social structure of the accumulation process, as—we should state—is often done), it does provide a useful heuristic for the influence of wealth creation, distribution, and use on economic growth and development (topics sadly neglected in the neoclassical approach).

A theme common to both the classical and neoclassical explanations of wealth and income is the demarcation of income as a flow variable and wealth as a stock variable. Income is what is available for consumption and is produced in regular intervals (weeks, months, years), while wealth consists of those assets that are not being consumed (with the assumption that they are being used to promote future production) and are thus stored up. Income, if it is saved and invested, adds to the stock of wealth and is not available for current consumption, whereas wealth that is sold (made liquid) enters into the income stream and is available.

Adam Smith, David Ricardo, and John Stuart Mill (the principal classical economists) supported capitalism, that is, the private ownership of the creation and use of the social surplus, because they judged that individuals would naturally use the surplus for future profit-making activities. In turn these activities would, because of competition, promote expanded production, to the gain of all. Karl Marx adopted the classical economists' basic analysis of the social surplus, yet he argued that the surplus was based on exploitation of workers and that its use by private individuals would benefit only them and lead to wasteful economic activities. Marx's analysis of exploitation is well known, but the main point is worth noting. He argued that workers get paid less than the value they create, thus creating surplus value, the source of profits (or capital income in general). Marx knew that a surplus had to be created (to support not only expanded reproduction but also to replace worn-out capital goods), but he objected that the surplus's benefits were not reaching the masses and that private control of the surplus would lead to contradictions in the economy. Marx's second objection is in many ways the more telling one: he asserted that private individuals cannot make the best choices for the use of capital (leading to economic depressions and other economic problems). Accordingly, his call for state control over the nation's productive assets was a call for more "rational" use of those assets. History has shown that Marx was both right and wrong. Wealth, or the social surplus, has often been created through exploitation and used unproductively, frequently for the benefit of the few; but the state's control of these assets has not necessarily eliminated the exploitation of workers or the unproductive use of wealth. In fact, in many ways the opposite has happened.[10]

Likewise, the private control and use of the social surplus does not ensure that it will be employed for the common good, mostly because Adam Smith's invisible hand is weaker than the very visible hand of economic power and control, and because the market evokes materialist biases. From the perspective of Catholic social thought, mere ownership is not the problem. The problem is ownership based on a false sense of the social nature of the human person and on the denial of participation (see Charles Clark, chapter 6, "Wealth and Poverty"). Furthermore, when the classical economists thought of wealth, they thought in terms of material goods, such as factories and other means of production. One can present a reasonable argument in favor of private control of these assets, as we see below in our discussion of John Locke's theory of property. Private ownership can promote the efficient use of society's productive assets and reduce conflict over these assets. But the imperative of Catholic social teaching, that this wealth be used for the common good, is in no way nullified by the argument in favor of private property. The common good is not merely what is most profitable for property owners. Moreover, much of the wealth of a modern economy does not consist of ownership and use of factories or other physical assets for which competing usage would be problematic (just as two people cannot drive the same car). Instead, it consists of ownership and control of knowledge and organization, neither of which is necessarily scarce in an economic sense.[11] Hence, as we see in Charles Clark, chapter 1, such assets are artificially kept scarce to increase the value of the holdings of those who are already wealthy. This tactic makes sense only if wealth is an end; it is untenable if wealth is a means to other ends. The creation of social institutions that would ensure that the social surplus is created in a manner that protects the rights and dignity of all and is used in a manner that promotes the common good, and not merely the interests of the rich and powerful, is certainly one of the great challenges facing those who would promote a just economy. In addressing these issues, as this volume shows, Catholic social thought has much to offer.

The relationship between wealth and income goes well beyond the fact that each can be transformed into the other. Wealth can become income when it is sold; income can become wealth when it is used to purchase income-yielding assets. However, these superficial relations do not illuminate the complex interconnections between wealth and income at the economywide, social level or at the microeconomic level of the business firm. Wealth implies not only the ownership of income-yielding assets, namely, assets that society has deemed "productive" (that is, involved in generating profit whether or not they contribute to production), but also control of the assets, the determination of their usage, as well as the security that comes from owning them.

These interrelations carry implications for the determination of an individual's or a household's level of income and social class. To illustrate, the ownership of an income-yielding asset provides the owner with an income.[12] Thus, the distribution of capital income (as distinct from labor income) will go to those who own capital. Since the ownership of capital (that is, wealth distribution) is almost always very unequal, this situation will exacerbate the problem of economic inequality. As we see in table 1, the level of wealth inequality in the United States is much greater than the level of income inequality: the top 1 percent of American households receive 16.6 percent of all income yet hold 38.1 percent of all net worth and 47.3 percent of net financial assets (almost more than the other 99 percent of households). Since the ownership of assets yields an income (though not always a paid or measurable income), this inequality of wealth ownership translates into greater income inequality, as we see in table 2. Thus, while the top 1 percent of richest households receive 10.4 percent of aggregate labor income, they receive 47.8 percent of capital income. That, of course, is what makes them the top 1 percent.

Table 2 not only shows how unequal is the distribution of income from wealth, but it also gives us evidence of the influence of wealth on labor income. The top 20 percent of households receive not only 80.9 percent of income from capital but also 54.3 percent of income from labor. While the determination of labor incomes is a complex process, we know that human capital (skills, training, and education) and economic power are two of the most important determinants. We can see that there is a strong connection between wealth and earned labor income, and it is not too difficult further to see that the possession of past wealth allows for better educational opportunities and other avenues to the formation of human capital. The children of the rich can go to the best schools, with greater chances of becoming rich

TABLE 1.   Distribution of Income and Wealth in the USA, 1998 (percent)[13]

	Household Income	*Net Worth*	*Net Financial Assets*
All	100%	100%	100%
Top 1%	16.6	38.1	47.3
Next 9%	24.6	32.9	32.4
Bottom 90%	58.8	29.0	20.2

TABLE 2.   Sources of Household Income by Income Type for the USA, 1999[14]

Income Group	Labor Income	Capital Income	Govt. Income	Total Income
Bottom fifth	2.7%	0.9%	18.3%	3.3%
Second fifth	7.4	2.7	21.7	7.3
Middle fifth	12.9	6.1	23.0	12.1
Fourth fifth	22.7	10.0	20.6	19.8
Bottom four-fifths	45.7	19.7	83.6	42.5
Top fifth	54.3	80.9	16.7	57.6
81–90%	17.2	9.3	9.2	15.0
91–95%	12.0	7.5	3.9	10.5
96–99%	14.7	16.3	3.2	14.3
Top 1 %	10.4	47.8	0.4	17.8

themselves. As these schools often give them the best credentials (not to mention connections), they believe that they have earned their higher incomes. To quote Jesse Jackson, "they are born on third base and think they have hit a triple." It is thus much easier for them to reach home plate, that is, to capitalize on economic opportunities.

Furthermore, wealth provides economic power. Owners and managers of companies have considerable influence on their "wages," whether they are operators of small firms or executives positioned to cultivate cozy relationships with corporate compensation committees and boards of directors. Moreover, wealth provides political influence. The wealthy, both households and corporations, have a disproportionate influence on tax and spending policies of governments at all levels, as the move to reduce or eliminate the estate tax (which affects only a minute portion of the population) or the concentration of the benefits of tax cuts and tax subsidies toward the richest Americans clearly demonstrates. To give just two examples: the benefits of the home-mortgage deduction and the tax credit for dependents go disproportionately toward the most affluent households and are far in excess of government support for housing for the poor or income support for impoverished children. Moreover, tax cuts that favor the rich increase their disposable income, thus allowing them to accumulate more wealth. In fact, this is the whole logic of supply-side economics: cut taxes on the rich so that they will accumulate more wealth, which will lead to economic growth and job creation. While this can happen, it is not very likely, as most money is saved and not spent on job-creating activities (such as consumption or productive investments).[15]

The interconnections between wealth and income also go the other way. Wealth is augmented and increased when income is invested in productive assets rather

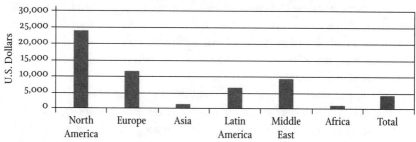

Source: World Wealth Report, 2002 and author's calculations

than consumed. While the idea that wealth is based solely on individual savings is more myth than reality, the fact is that only those whose incomes exceed their basic needs can purchase productive assets. Higher incomes lead to higher wealth accumulation. Moreover, as we note below, much of the wealth-creation process in advanced capitalist economies is created within the corporation, thus generating a cycle of wealth creation that excludes most of the population.

What is true on the national level is even more the case on the international or global level. The ownership of productive assets and of assets that have a claim on social output is even more unequally distributed than is income. This disparity is partly the result of past inequality, and it contributes to future inequality. It stems partly from rich societies taking, purchasing, or using the productive assets of poor ones, historically a common practice well before colonialism but one that became much more efficient under colonialism and neocolonialism. We see in the graph that the international distribution of wealth is grossly uneven. Looking at per capita wealth by continent, we find that North American and European economic prominence comes at least partly from past accumulation of wealth. However, we also see that the Middle East is surprisingly close to European levels of per capita wealth, while we know that regional standards of living are nowhere near those in Europe. Clearly, wealth is not the only factor. Middle Eastern wealth is mostly in the form of natural resources such as petroleum, and the benefits of these resources have not, for the most part, been used to promote other forms of economic development, nor have they trickled down to the masses.

Our inquiry into the various connotations of the term "wealth" and its relation to "income" shows that at both the level of popular discourse and at the highest levels of rigorous economic theory, these are amorphous terms used to indicate amorphous objects. Income can be transformed into wealth as easily as wealth can be transformed into income. The key distinction between wealth and income is not found in the fundamental characteristics of the objects we deem to be wealth (productive assets, stocks and bonds) or income (money). These can be otherwise: with my money, I can acquire stocks, but I can also purchase goods and services with stocks and bonds as long as the seller is willing to accept them. In fact, the situation gets more complicated when we consider that economists do not have an adequate definition of money, either.

The important distinction between "wealth" as wealth and "income" as income lies in the rights that society accords to their possessors. Income gives its owner legal right (that is, power) over goods and services that are placed on the market to be sold; wealth gives its owner control over its use, a right to a share of its output if it is used productively or by another. The latter right may last into the indefinite future, or theoretically forever, when the owner is a corporation. With this greater level of rights also comes greater moral responsibility, for the use of wealth has a wider, greater, and more lasting impact than the use of income.

DIMENSIONS AND LEVELS OF WEALTH

The nature of wealth is multifaceted and multilayered. When we talk about the wealth of a nation, we most often mean its annual production of goods and services or social product, usually measured as gross domestic product (GDP). By contrast, when we talk about the wealth of individuals, we are referring rather to their claims on the social product.[16] Organizations are somewhere in the middle between individuals and the nation. A corporation may be called "wealthy" based on its sales, on the value of its assets, or both. The market valuation of corporations, carried out daily in stock markets, attempts to combine both concepts by valuing both tangible and intangible assets and expected profits from current and future sales. The instability in stock prices attests to the difficulties inherent in such undertakings.

Our brief exploration has shown that wealth's multifaceted nature involves economic and personal or moral dimensions and is revealed at various levels of human activity. A like complexity is found in the Catholic social tradition's ongoing reflection on wealth. Wealth is described in terms of property and labor, land and knowledge, the material and the nonmaterial; it is referred to persons and to organizations; and it is divided into personal and social wealth.[17] The following matrix models the distinctions among levels and dimensions that we have so far identified and that we will observe as we discuss how the Catholic social tradition addresses the question of wealth. We gladly concede that the matrix, like the distinctions it models, is not comprehensive, but we think it will be found apposite and useful.

Levels and Dimensions of Wealth

	Economic	*Moral*
National/International	GDP/Capital formation	Global common good
Organizational	Revenue, capital, market valuation	Community of work
Personal	Income-generating property/Labor	Character of the person

Wealth of Individual Persons: Economic and Moral Dimensions

For individual persons, economic wealth consists primarily of the ownership of property (assets) that generate an income or can be exchanged for income. The legal and ideological structures of private property make individual property ownership possible. Modern thinking on private property largely responds to the liberal tradition, which in this connection stems from John Locke's theory of private property.[18] Locke affirms, and thus far the Christian tradition would agree with him, that nature's bounty is the gift of God to humankind in common. His theory of property therefore responds to the question: How can one acquire a private right to some part of what is open to all by a common right? It aims to show how the private right can come into being without injury to the antecedent common right.

Locke argues that private property derives from the "mixing" of an individual's labor with nature's bounty, a "mixing" that is necessary in order to appropriate or befit a thing for human use.[19] For Locke, then, private property is at root one's exclusive, natural right to what one appropriates by labor, from the bounty of nature, for the benefit of use. And it is essential to his conception that *to acquire property is to remove something from the purview of the common human right to sustenance by means of nature's bounty.*

Under certain conditions, according to Locke, the forging of private rights to property need not come at injury to the common right. One could not, he argues, appropriate perishables in quantities beyond what one could use without spoilage. To do otherwise would be to preclude, to the extent of one's power, the exercise of the common right by others. Concerning nonperishables (Locke mentions ores, and we might think of pottery clays or quarry stone), the rule is similar: no injury could accrue to the common right were one to appropriate only the quantities one needed, leaving "enough and as good in common for others."[20] One might, then, rightly acquire property in any quantity and kind that would not preclude others' similar acts of acquisition. This general condition, together with consideration of the labor that enters into improvement for tillage, would justify (as Locke argues) *original* property in land, especially when small populations and vast uncultivated tracts would ensure that "there was enough and as good left" to the common right.[21]

Locke's philosophical justification of private property belongs to a speculative "narrative" or "history" of humankind's emergence from a "state of nature" into social-political life. The story he tells (spiced with illustrations from the then contemporary "state of nature" in the Americas) bids to show that there is no inconsistency in supposing both: (1) that an original right to benefit from nature's bounty is the gift of God to humankind in common; and (2) that one expression of human nature as God ordains it is the forging of exclusive, private rights to the possession and use of natural things. But this justification supposes "elementary" or "original" property rights forged either in an indefinitely remote past or in a primitive present.[22] What does it have to do with the burgeoning money economy, the estates system, the mercantile practices, or the complex laws of inheritance and entailment that defined the "property" of Locke's day?

Locke's liberalism (and his enduring importance for modern liberalism) emerges as he makes the transition from the philosophical to the political justification of private property.[23] A right is, according to Locke, a liberty or permission for its holder and a duty, usually of noninterference, for rights regarders. Accordingly, the obverse of the natural right to withdraw goods from the common into the private weal is a liberty to "settle," in Locke's terms (that is, to institutionalize), ownership exclusively by consent (that is, by political deliberation resulting in positive law) among the owners. Laws of inheritance, for example, entail the tenure of land and the formation of estates. These are political innovations on the original liberty of property and are unexceptionable as such, whatever their effects on the tendency of property to accumulate and concentrate in more or fewer hands.[24]

Moreover, for Locke the emergence of money effects a twofold transformation in the forging of property. First, lacking any intrinsic use-value, money has value strictly by common consent. Second, it erases the natural limits to accumulation posed by the problems of spoilage (for perishable goods) and of disuse or wastage (for enduring goods, especially the land). The use of money allows anyone the limitless accumulation of property without the reproach of hoarding (withdrawing from use) or wasting usable goods. At the same time, the use of money is every user's tacit consent to the actual dimension and distribution assumed by the accumulations of property that money promotes.[25]

On Locke's account, then, the political inventions and social innovations that set accumulation free from natural constraints or promote unequal concentrations of property are no more than expressions of the liberty of action that is supposed in private property's elemental character, namely, a withdrawal of something from the common right (constrained by the wills of others) into the private right (unconstrained, subject to one's will only). Following Locke's lead, liberalism has historically regarded a right as an individual's power to compel the forbearance or performance of another, and it has regarded the right of private property as entailing a strict duty on the part of all others to forbear from interfering with an individual's liberty in regard to a thing owned.[26] Consistently therewith, liberalism has insisted that any constraint on the uses of property, its accumulation, or concentration can come only by consent—including, of course, consent mediated by broadly consensual political procedures. Historically, the liberal tradition gradually elaborated private property rights as the liberty to possess goods and use them without corresponding duties or social obligations on the part of owners. In nonowners, in this view, property rights create a perfect obligation to refrain from interfering with owners' possession and use of things.

While the Catholic social tradition affirms the importance of individual or private ownership, it does so for reasons very different from those advanced by the liberal tradition. In the Catholic tradition, individual ownership is seen as a means of implementing the common human right to be sustained by, and to flourish from, God's gift of natural goods: "ownership" means private *possession* of goods for the sake of making goods' *use* common to all. Far from *withdrawing* goods from the purview of the common right, private possession *implements* the common right. Owners have strict duties in justice to meet the needs of their dependents, their fellow citizens (including the poor among them), their political community, their co-religionists, and so on into ever-widening and overlapping circles of community.

Private possession (or stewardship) is preferred to common possession (collectivism or communism) in the Catholic tradition for reasons of efficacy: it encourages *personal initiative, productivity,* and *orderliness* (peace) in the making, management, and distribution of useful goods.[27] These are understood as comprehensive conditions for general prosperity. When people own something, they are most likely to manage it in a considered, enterprising way. This personal initiative tends in turn toward greater productivity and efficiency, and it militates against waste. Again, when people possess as their own the things they need to meet their responsibilities, keep their promises, and realize their ambitions, they are simply more disposed to treat others harmoniously than they are in the opposite case. Accordingly, in the Catholic social tradition, ownership is legitimated by its efficient promotion of a moral goal, the universal destination of material goods.[28] To drive this point home, John Paul II has coined the helpful phrase that private property is "under a 'social mortgage.'"[29] According to the Christian social tradition, the nature of rights over private property cannot be expressed by the popular idiom, "It's mine and I can do whatever I want with it." Owners have a moral responsibility to use their property in a way that is consonant with the promotion of the common good.

Wealth at all three of the levels we discuss here has economic and moral dimensions. But at the individual level, there is a further spiritual dimension to consider. At this level, we can speak of the "vocation" of a person and of the part that creating, distributing, and using wealth has in this vocation. For instance, when it comes to using our property, we are called to collaborate with the Creator so that all people can share in the dominion over creation that God has given to humankind as a whole. When individuals do not use their property with this aim in mind, they not only contribute to social problems such as consumerism, glaring wealth inequity, and environmental degradation, but they also corrupt their own souls. Our character is formed by how we act at work, in our business dealings, and in the management of our property no less than by how we act at home, at play, or in civic connections.

Wealth of Organizations: Economic and Moral Dimensions

It is often said that knowledge of work is critical to wealth creation, but for knowledge of individuals to create wealth in any sustained way, such knowledge needs to be embodied in organizational practices and policies that can generate profitable goods and services. This transfer of knowledge from individual minds to organizational practices is always complex and fragile. Terms such as "learning organization," "intellectual property rights," and "intellectual capital" point to the fact that knowledge has become the primary source of wealth creation and of sustainable competitive advantage.

Since most of the capital stock, or productive wealth, of the nation is in the hands of businesses, much of the creation, distribution, and use of wealth is carried out at the level of the firm. Material wealth—the productive assets used to pursue the objective of profitability—is the lifeblood of an organization. Profit and productivity are vital, necessary dimensions of the business enterprise. But the purposes of the enterprise extend also to human flourishing, the development of the organization's members and of the communities to which the organization itself belongs. As John Paul II puts it, profit is a "regulator" of the life of an organization, but "it is not the only one."[30] In an address to Italian managers and workers, the pope outlined how the social teachings of the Church make clear "that the sole criterion of profit is insufficient, especially when it is raised to the level of an absolute."[31] This absolutization of profit is expressed in the widely accepted financial principle of the "maximization of shareholder wealth."

We have raised elsewhere the problem of an organization being devoted to shareholder wealth maximization.[32] We will not rehearse those arguments here. What we focus on here is the process by which the assets of an organization are created and distributed. Jeff Gates has noted that the creation of wealth in an organization mostly takes place in a "closed distribution loop."[33] He argues that the owners of existing wealth provide the funds to generate increases in wealth (investment in plant and equipment and technological developments), which then go to those same owners. These funds do not come mostly from individual savings but instead are generated internally, within corporations. In 2000 total gross savings in the U.S. economy equaled $1.8 trillion, of which $201.5 billion (11.2 percent) was held as personal savings and $435.8 billion (24.1 percent) as gross government savings, with the remaining $1,170.6 billion (64.7 percent) coming from business.[34] As John Kenneth Galbraith pointed out in the 1960s, the business sector does not need personal savings to finance its investment activities.[35] These investment activities generate most of the additions to the productive stock of capital in the modern economy, and the income they generate goes to owners of the shares in the companies that undertake these activities. Despite the growth in pension funds and in similar financial instruments, the ownership of financial wealth remains concentrated in a few hands.

As we are often told, the majority of Americans, at least, are now stockholders. The fact of wider stock ownership is often cited to suggest that wealth is more equally and democratically distributed than is in reality the case. The vast majority of financial wealth is in the hands of a small percentage of the population (as we saw in table 1). According to Edward Wolff's analysis of wealth distribution in the United States, the bottom 80 percent of American households in 1998 owned 16.6 percent of the privately held wealth, leaving 83.4 percent to the top 20 percent. Furthermore, among the top 20 percent, the top 1 percent of households owned 38.1 percent of America's net worth, while the next 4 percent (96–99 percentiles) held 21.3 percent of the nation's net worth. Moreover, the top 1 percent owned 42.1 percent of the stocks, mutual funds, and retirement accounts, which gives this form of wealth a higher degree of inequality than overall wealth distribution.[36] The rise of these financial instruments has stimulated inequality in wealth ownership, not the reverse. If the mission of an organization is to maximize the share price for the current owners, then this process of concentrating ever-increasing wealth in their hands makes eminent sense. If, however, capital is subject in some meaningful way to a "social mortgage," then the huge gains in wealth that propertyholders have made is a scandal.

National and International Wealth: Economic and Moral Dimensions

Since Adam Smith's "Wealth of Nations," economists have noted the important role that capital accumulation plays in economic progress in general. Productive assets make for productive workers, and productive workers make for an affluent

country. In many ways the fundamental factor in the creation of wealth at the national and global level is the social context within which wealth is generated—
everything from the protection of property rights to the enforcement of contracts,
to public subsidies for research and development to the provision of free education,
social protection, and economic regulation, and finally to a vibrant and healthy
culture. All these social achievements—or, to use an older name, these common
goods—lay the groundwork for the conditions that promote wealth creation. Economic research shows that spending on research and development (both public and
private), on education, and on securing an orderly and safe society (social capital)
as well as on capital goods (private and public investment) all play a role in the economic health of a nation, and lead both to a higher flow of goods and services and
higher stocks of private wealth.

On the national and international level, one sees the particular importance of
the common good, that is, the sense that "the will of someone willing a particular
good is not ordered unless he refer it to the common good as to an end."[37] Take, for
example, "efficiency." Much of the wealth of a country consists of capital goods that
promote current and future production. It is very important that these assets be used
in an efficient manner. "Efficiency," however, is a term that derives its meaning from
the end in view. The Catholic social tradition holds that efficiency cannot be reduced
to economic variables alone but must be ordered to the common good, to fostering a culture of life. Too often, citing "efficiencies" is the mode of argument for
those who promote a culture of death. The importance of drawing this distinction
is brought out when one realizes that part of the economic growth in Western countries in recent years is really only social decay by another name. Divorce and construction of nursing homes and prisons contribute much more to measured economic output than do united families, in-home care for the elderly by unpaid family
members, and law-abiding citizens who have little use for the paid services of police,
law courts, child protection services, and so on. GDP goes up with the divorce rate,
with the building of nursing homes and prisons, and with increases in criminal justice services, but who wants increases in that kind of "efficiency"?

Efficiency at enhancing economic value is a concept that has meaning only in
terms of goals or ends, since it measures how successfully we achieve our goals or
ends. These ought to be defined in terms of the common good. Similarly, wealth is
a concept that must be understood as a means to an end. It does not make sense to
measure it in terms of means alone. A clear understanding of the common good
is necessary to any meaningful evaluation of efficiency and wealth. Moreover, the
common good reminds us that the size of the stock of capital is not the conclusion
of the story. How this wealth is distributed (or, more important, how ownership and
control of this wealth are distributed) and used has important political consequences
for the distribution of power in society. It also has sociological significance: social

status, class, and culture will be greatly affected by patterns of wealth accumulation as well as by its distribution and use.

An examination of the history of wealth and its creation shows the very strong connection between the wealth of individuals and organizations and their influence on the wealth of nations through the use of political power. In the past, the mere ownership of land gave one both individual and organizational wealth and political power. Even with the rise of democracy, a wealth requirement (not completely eliminated in the United States until the 1850s, and much later in other countries) was often attached to the right to vote. The connection between wealth and political power remains strong. Recent efforts at campaign finance reform and attempts to eliminate "corporate welfare" (business subsidies from the state) are only two examples of efforts to reduce the control that wealth has over the U.S. political system. The management of large corporations for the sole benefit of the shareholders, as if they were the only ones who had a stake in the company's performance, demonstrates the economic power that wealth can wield and underscores how fragile is our grip on the common good. The influence of these same corporations on the U.S. electoral process and on the management of the federal government's affairs demonstrates how wealth's influence extends to civil and political society.

The rise of globalization has extended the political influence of corporate wealth and corporations in the public square, for the globalization of markets has led to a decline in the economic and political power of the state. When economies were mostly national, the state could restrict the economic, political, and social power of wealth, though it often did the opposite. Today, most governments, having insufficient economic power to buck international markets, are less able to influence economic outcomes. Only a handful of countries have the possibility of effective economic policy, and often these have to be coordinated internationally. Globalization requires that the pursuit of the common good must be defined in global terms for the simple fact that it can only be carried out globally. Even the most environmentally responsible country needs to have its neighbors follow similar policies to have a positive effect on pollution. Furthermore, global markets have greatly reduced the ability of individual countries to follow independent economic policies; only international coordination can match the power of global markets.

CONCLUSION

The twelve essays that make up this volume explore the question of wealth creation and distribution by examining the various dimensions of this topic in light of the rich moral and spiritual insights of the Catholic social tradition. The Catholic social tradition is particularly adapted to help us comprehend these dimensions, since it offers a more complete vision of the person and society than economic theories alone can provide. Economists will address wealth creation, distribution, and use, but the modern economist avoids addressing the essence or nature of wealth and evaluating its impact on our culture, values, happiness, or politics.[38] The Catholic social tradition's understanding of wealth gives us a more holistic account of the role of wealth in our society, its social and historical context, and, most important, its impact on the dignity of the individual and on the common good. While the economic or business perspective often gives us insight into the use of wealth as a means, it hardly illuminates the legitimate ends toward which wealth should be employed. This lacuna regarding the "end or purpose of wealth" allows many people to make the means of wealth creation ends in themselves. This is nonsense in the fullest sense of the word. The creation of wealth merely so that one can create more wealth, so that one can then create even more wealth, is rightly described as irrational behavior.

Unfortunately, while the Catholic social tradition has much to contribute to an understanding of wealth, recent thinkers in this tradition have stinted consideration of it. In particular, they have neglected to develop the important work done on wealth through the first half of the twentieth century. This volume is one of the first in recent years to bring together a widely diverse collection of scholars from different academic fields to reflect on both the creation and the distribution of wealth in light of the insights of the Catholic social tradition. The hope is that a perspective from the vantage point of Catholic social thought will allow us to dig deeper into the nature of wealth and to see its importance in the economic, moral, and spiritual life of society.

Genesis of This Volume

Similar to the second book in this series, *Rethinking the Purpose of Business: Interdisciplinary Essays from the Catholic Social Tradition*, this volume is the result of a multistage process sponsored by the John A. Ryan Institute for Catholic Social Thought of the Center for Catholic Studies, University of St. Thomas, St. Paul, Minnesota; St. John's University Tobin College of Business, New York; and the Faculty of Social Sciences of the Pontifical University of St. Thomas Aquinas (Angelicum), Rome.

The first stage of this process began in Puebla, Mexico, in July 2000 at the Fourth International Symposium on Catholic Social Thought and Management Education on "Wealth Creation and Wealth Distribution" (papers from the Puebla symposium can be viewed at http://www.stthomas.edu/cathstudies/cst/mgmt/PUEBLA/INDEX. HTML). From among the scores of contributors to the Puebla proceedings, the organizers invited some fifteen authors to present revised versions of their papers at a further, intensive symposium held in Rome in November 2001.

Invitations to the follow-up symposium took into account the diversity of the disciplines represented, the authors' success in bringing fundamental principles of Catholic social teaching—the common good, primacy of labor over capital, the social nature of property, solidarity, subsidiarity, etc.—to bear on the question of wealth creation and distribution, and the tendency of each of the selected papers to speak to the others. At the follow-up symposium in November 2001 in Rome, we invited corporate executives and managers, economists, and business educators to join us in lively, critical exchanges. On the basis of these discussions, the twelve papers that form the present volume were selected, and the authors undertook further revisions in consultation with one another and with the editors. The result merits description as a volume of integrated, interdisciplinary essays. The contributors represent distinct disciplines: theology, philosophy, economics, finance, management, and production engineering, but they write in light of a common set of principles to address the critical question of wealth creation and distribution.

Acknowledgments

We are deeply indebted to the contributors for their collaboration in this work. The consulting participants in the crucial, follow-up symposium contributed much to the essays' final forms: Thomas Bausch, Luigino Bruni, Paul Dembinski, Jean-Loup Dherse, Pier Giorgio Gawronski, Ferruccio Marzano, Ernest Pierucci, Alessandro Pietrogiacomi, and Edward Wolff.

Several institutions provided significant financial support to make this volume possible: the University of St. Thomas's John A. Ryan Institute for Catholic Social Thought of the Center for Catholic Studies, the Aquinas Foundation, St. John's University Tobin College of Business, and an anonymous donor. In particular we would like to thank Charles Kronke, Larry Boone, and especially Peter J. Tobin, who served as deans at the Tobin College of Business. Special thanks go to Sara Freund, Lisa Rumpza, and Mary Kay O'Rourke, who helped edit this volume.

And finally, with special appreciation we would like to remember and acknowledge the generosity of Msgr. Terrence Murphy of St. Thomas, without whom this book would not have been possible. We find it strangely fitting that his death would occur on Ash Wednesday, February 25, 2004. May his soul, and the souls of the faithful departed, through the mercy of God, rest in peace. ✠

NOTES

1. According to the World Federation of Exchanges, the market capitalization of domestic exchanges totaled $9.4 trillion in 1990, rising to $21.7 trillion in 1997 and then to just under $35 trillion at the end of 1999. After reaching a peak in March 2000 at $36.3 trillion, market capitalizations of domestic markets have fallen considerably, to $31 trillion at year-end in 2000 to $26.7 trillion at year-end in 2001, and hitting bottom (so far) in October 2002 at $21.9 trillion (World Federation of Exchanges, "Market Capitalization of Shares of Domestic Exchanges," various years).

2. *The Compact Edition of the Oxford English Dictionary*, 1982, s.v. "wealth."

3. See Thorstein Veblen's essays, "On the Nature of Capital I and II," reprinted in *The Place of Science in Modern Civilization and Other Essays* (New Brunswick, N.J.: Transaction Publishers, 1990).

4. For an excellent and short overview of these debates in economic theory, and why they are fundamental, see Avi J. Cohen and G. C. Harcourt, "Whatever Happened to the Cambridge Capital Theory Controversies?" *Journal of Economic Perspectives* 17, no. 1 (Winter 2003): 199–214.

5. Edward N. Wolff, *Economics of Poverty, Inequality, and Distribution* (Cincinnati: South-Western College Publishing, 1997).

6. The fact that economists no longer try to define wealth and income in theoretical terms does not mean that they have settled the issue and moved on. Because they could not settle the issue, which exposed one of the many great weaknesses of neoclassical economic theory, they have instead decided to pretend that the theoretical problems do not exist.

7. See John Hicks, *Value and Capital* (Oxford: Oxford University Press, 1939), and "Maintaining Capital Intact: A Further Suggestion," *Economica* 9 (1942): 174–79; and Nicholas Kaldor, *An Expenditure Tax* (London: Allen and Unwin, 1955).

8. Richard Cantillon, *Essai sur la nature du commerce en général* (n.p., 1775). Cantillon (1680–1734) was an Irish banker (his family were from Kerry) who lived in Paris. The Physiocrats were the first real school of economic theory. Prominent members included François Quesnay, founder of the school and developer of the *Tableau économique,* the first economic model; Pierre Samuel du Pont de Nemours, who later moved to America (where his son founded gunpowder works that became today's prominent chemical company bearing the Du Pont name and who wrote the first history of economic theory); the Marquis de Mirabeau; and Anne-Robert-Jacques Turgot.

9. One of the great weaknesses of this approach, however, was the treatment of the surplus in physical terms and not as a social creation, which becomes clear in much of the post–Marx work in the "surplus tradition." Richard Cantillon highlighted the surplus by pointing out that agriculture produced greater outputs than it consumed in inputs. Yet, what is most important is the social construction of the surplus, the defining of part of the output as somehow special and important, and thus going to a special and important social class.

10. One is reminded of the Polish joke: "In capitalism you have man exploiting man, whereas in communism you have the opposite."

11. This theme is taken up by Robert Kennedy in chapter 2, this volume.

12. Capital income (rent, dividends, and interest) accounted for 20 percent of personal income in the United States in 2000, while proprietor's income, which combines the owner's work and his capital income, accounted for 9.4 percent. Labor's share has steadily fallen since the 1970s and capital's share has risen.

13. Unpublished analysis of 1998 Survey of Consumer Finances by Ed Wolff, in Lawrence Mischel, Jared Bernstein, and Heather Boushey, *The State of Working America 2002/2003* (Ithaca, N.Y.: Cornell University Press, 2003), 279.

14. Institute on Economic and Tax Policy as cited in ibid., 86.

15. We should also remember one of Keynes's main conclusions, that savings does not necessarily increase investment, as investment is demand determined (entrepreneurs invest based on expected profits and not on the availability of money to invest).

16. Comparisons between the two conceptions of wealth cause further confusion due to the fact that "wealth as goods and services (material well-being)" deals essentially with the flow of goods and services, whereas the individual view of wealth is based on the stock of assets. Even more confusion is added by the fact that the value of this stock of assets is continually measured by their exchange value in secondary markets, that is, on the ability to exchange the rights to the stock to purchase the flow. When Bill Gates was said to be worth $100 billion, it did not mean that he could purchase $100 billion in goods and services, as his net worth is based largely on a stock calculation and consumption is based mostly on flow. Any attempt by him to sell the stock to purchase the flow would have no doubt crashed the market valuation of the stock.

17. See, for example, John Paul II, *Centesimus annus*, 31, 32, 43.

18. John Locke, "Of Property," in *Second Treatise of Government*, ed. Thomas P. Peardon (Indianapolis: Bobbs-Merrill, 1952), 25–51.

19. A thing made fit for use by someone's labor cannot be, as Locke puts it, "within the right" of any other person. To seize another's body, or to compel or appropriate another's labor, is violence. When one's labor is incorporated in a second body, making it fit for use, that body is no more within the right of any other person than is the labor that went into it (see ibid., 27). Locke offers a number of supplementary and ancillary arguments in support of the conclusion that by labor, which renders a natural thing fit for use, the thing becomes a property of the laborer. For a review and evaluation of the range of Locke's arguments, see Lawrence C. Becker, *Property Rights: Philosophic Foundations* (Boston, London, and Henley: Routledge & Kegan Paul, 1977), 33–48.

20. See Locke, *Second Treatise*, 28, 31, 44.

21. See ibid., 32–33, 37.

22. See ibid., 38–41, 49.

23. Ibid., 45–51.

24. Ibid., 45.

25. Ibid., 46–48, 50.

26. See, for example, Jeremy Waldron, "Property Law," in *A Companion to Philosophy of Law and Legal Theory*, ed. Dennis Patterson (Oxford: Blackwell, 1996), 3–23.

27. St. Thomas Aquinas, *Summa Theologica* (New York: Benziger Brothers), IIa-IIae, q. 66, a. 2. Hernando de Soto has argued that when the poor are given assets that can be solidified in property law, an enormous formation of wealth can occur (see Hernando de Soto, *The Mystery of Capital* [New York: Basic Books, 2000]).

28. Ibid.

29. John Paul II, *Sollicitudo rei socialis*, 42.

30. John Paul II, *Centesimus annus*, 35.

31. He goes on to say: "Anyone who collaborates, at any level, possesses the rights that correspond to his role in the common enterprise, as well as the respective obligations. In particular, he enjoys those rights and duties which proceed from his dignity as a man or a woman called, indeed obliged, to live a life that is truly human in all its dimensions: affective, cultural, social, spiritual, religious. This, once again, is a consequence not merely of legal impositions, valid though they may be, but of the obligations of conscience, both human and Christian" (Robert Kennedy, Gary Atkinson, and Michael Naughton, eds., *The Dignity of Work: John Paul Speaks to Managers and Workers* [Lanham, Md.: University Press of America, 1994], 110).

32. S. A. Cortright and Michael J. Naughton, eds., *Rethinking the Purpose of Business: Interdisciplinary Essays from the Catholic Social Tradition* (Notre Dame, Ind.: University of Notre Dame Press, 2002).

33. Jeff Gates, "Reengineering Ownership for the Common Good," in *Rethinking the Purpose of Business*, 272. See also Jeff Gates, *The Ownership Solution* (Reading, Mass.: Addison-Wesley, 1998).

34. U.S. Census Bureau, *Statistical Abstract of the United States of America* (Washington, D.C.: GPO, 2001).

35. John Kenneth Galbraith, *The New Industrial State* (Boston: Houghton Mifflin, 1967).

36. Edward R. Wolff, "Recent Trends in Wealth Ownership, 1983–1998," Levy Working Paper no. 300, April 2000.

37. Aquinas, *Summa*, Ia-IIae, q. 2, a. 10.

38. This is a break with the illustrious past of economic theory, as all the great, and not so great, economists of the past would speak to these issues. Why they no longer do so is partially explained by Charles Clark and Stefano Zamagni (chapters 1 and 8, this volume).

PART ONE   Wealth Creation

Introduction

If, however, economic ambitions are good servants they are
bad masters. Harnessed to a social purpose they will turn
the mill and grind the corn. But the question—to what
end the wheels revolve—still remains.

—Richard Tawney

Richard Tawney's quote directs us to a fundamental insight of the Catholic social tradition: creating material wealth cannot be the final goal of any human activity because wealth itself is at best an instrumental good. In order to understand the creation of wealth as a human act—that is, a moral act—one has to ask, "What is wealth created for?" In more concrete terms, an increase in Gross Domestic Product (GDP), a jump in shareholder wealth, or the creation of another product or millionaire cannot be said to be "good" without qualification, simply on the basis that "more" has been produced and consumed. We need to know why and how that "more" has been produced before we can say that this "more" is a "good thing."

Recent experience as well as the witness of history attest to the ugly side of wealth creation. The collapse of speculative bubbles from the tulipmania of the seventeenth century to the "dot-coms" of the twenty-first, the extensive corruption within publicly traded companies, and the untold suffering from the iniquitous disparity in wealth in an era of globalization—these and other examples remind us of the kind of destructiveness that can result from so-called wealth creation. As Tawney indicates above, economic ambitions, and the impulse to create wealth, must be harnessed to an end that truly can create moral and spiritual well-being; otherwise, wealth corrupts its creator and hurts those around him.

Discussion of the meaning and end of wealth creation has been somewhat neglected among thinkers in the Catholic social tradition, though it has certainly not been absent. We could perhaps visualize our discussion of wealth creation and its relationship to distribution as the construction of bridges between various disciplines, particularly between ethics (seen philosophically and theologically) and economics. At present, there are important foundation stones laid by earlier thinkers, but the bridges are not finished, and in some places the whole construction has become overgrown because ongoing work has been suspended for so long. What is needed is to clear away the undergrowth, see what construction is there already, and then attempt to bridge the gaps left by previous thinkers in their consideration of the question of wealth from the perspective of the Christian social tradition.

This volume, and in particular Part I, represents an attempt to do some of this clearing away of the undergrowth, some of the surveying of the present construction, and some filling-in of the gaps. In so doing, the authors hope to build upon the thought of those popes, bishops, theologians, economists, and businesspersons who in the past have considered the question of wealth creation in light of the Catholic social tradition. Within this section of the volume, the authors make three significant contributions toward this goal. They examine the engagement between economic theory and Catholic social thought on the topic of wealth creation in order to suggest what further work needs to be done; they examine the relationship between virtue and wealth creation; and they explore the theological significance of wealth creation. In this short introduction, we summarize some of these points highlighted by the authors.

ENGAGEMENT OF ECONOMIC THEORY AND CATHOLIC SOCIAL THOUGHT ON WEALTH CREATION

In clearing away the undergrowth surrounding the construction of the bridge and in surveying the present situation, several of our authors note that the lack of key developments within their own disciplines vitiate interdisciplinary discussion on the nature, creation, and use of wealth. Charles Clark, an economist, makes a striking criticism of the gaps in economists' thinking. He argues that the fundamental problem is their unwillingness to incorporate any discussion of the ends of the economy into their theories, so that they all too often wind up turning the means of wealth creation into an end. Their reticence makes engagement with Catholic social thought well-nigh impossible.

Robert Kennedy and John Haughey, as a philosopher and theologian, respectively, are concerned that each of their disciplines holds a bias against wealth creation. They find that while the emphasis on the distribution of wealth in the Catholic social tradition is critically important, theologians have failed to evaluate properly the important and dynamic impulse of the person toward wealth creation. Kennedy argues that economics is too often misunderstood in the Catholic social tradition and that, for instance, theologians sometimes fail to understand the distinction between bounded and boundless goods. He maintains that some of the Fathers of the early Church were "mistaken in assuming that the distribution of wealth is like a zero-sum game, where an increase in benefits to one party can only come at the expense of another party."

The authors start from different disciplines and try to meet each other in a discussion over the whys and wherefores of the creation of wealth. While their backgrounds as theologians, philosophers, or economists color their analyses, their common interest in the Catholic social tradition allows them to launch a wide-ranging conversation on the means and ends of wealth creation. Despite the fact that the highly specialized environment of universities often does not encourage interdisciplinary work, the authors here have managed to offer a broad interdisciplinary examination of wealth creation on the basis of a common commitment to ideas born in tradition of Catholic social thought.

Virtues and Vices of Wealth Creation in the Catholic and Liberal Traditions

Another of the important contributions of this book is a reflection on the virtues and vices associated with wealth creation within Catholic social thought, and a comparison of this characterization of virtues and vices with that of the liberal tradition. In answering the question, "Is creating wealth a virtue?" the liberal tradition would immediately respond "yes," whereas the Catholic tradition, without more information, would need to say "perhaps." Such a difference in answers makes it clear that we are dealing with two different traditions of thought in regard to the nature of the virtues and their corresponding vices.

The influence of liberalism on business, and on the answer to the aforementioned question, can be demonstrated with an example. The CEO of RJR Nabisco, Steven Goldstone, once argued in an interview that the production of tobacco is virtuous because it increases people's choices. His responsibility as a CEO is not to dictate which choice one should make, since this would restrict another person's freedom, but rather to provide consumers with the option to smoke or not. For Goldstone, RJR Nabisco is not responsible for manufacturing a habit-forming product that kills, precisely because people choose to use it. The "choice" of consumers dictates whether goods or services are produced; no moral criterion on the part of the maker is allowed to intrude on the freedom of choice of the consumer. Otherwise the firm would be suffering from the vice of paternalism.

Underlying Goldstone's position is a liberal notion that choice is the highest good because what matters is not what you choose but rather your ability to choose. Such a position refuses to accept the fact that some choices are good and others are not and therefore implicitly treats anything that is wealth-generating, whatever its effects otherwise, as good. This failure to distinguish between good and bad choices releases wealth creators from any responsibility for the negative effects that their products and services may have on consumers.

Francis Hannafey, for example, explains that the popes have employed the language of virtues to examine wealth creation. He mentions, in particular, Pius XI's revival of Thomas's and Aristotle's use of "magnificence," a virtue that is particularly related to entrepreneurs and investors. Entrepreneurship practiced in a magnificent way is not about expanding choices but is rather about creating useful goods and services that supply the needs of others in society. As Hannafey explains, '[t]he virtues are at the center of papal teachings on entrepreneurship because they are the nexus between effective business activity, and thereby wealth creation, and effective and just forms of wealth distribution."

Liberalism and Catholicism offer radically different notions of virtue and correspondingly different understandings of vice. For the liberal tradition, any restriction on what the individual may want to produce or consume smacks of vice, of intolerance, self-righteousness, paternalism. Within the Catholic social tradition, wealth creation is never automatically a virtue, while the self-interested, profit-maximizing, and instrumental mentalities that sometimes accompany it are sources of vice: greed, manipulation, and antagonism. Moreover, such mentalities fuel self-important delusions not unlike those of Dennis Kozlowski, who, in defending his $170 million in total pay for 1999 as then CEO of Tyco, argued, "the way I calculate it, while I gained $139 million [in options], I created about $37 billion in wealth for our shareholders." Apart from his apparent disregard for the fact that many other people were involved in generating this wealth, his words "I created" carry a certain idolatrous tone. Many CEOs' multimillion-dollar salaries have contributed to a deluded overestimation of self not only in regard to their talents but also in regard to their place in creation.

THEOLOGICAL UNDERPINNINGS OF WEALTH CREATION

This overestimation of self that often develops in people responsible for generating large amounts of wealth leads us to the third contribution of Part I. Without a theological perspective on wealth creation, we fail to understand both the potential greatness and the pitfalls of a life devoted to creating wealth. Our capacity to deceive ourselves into thinking that we are more important than in fact we are is evidenced throughout history. At the same time, the vocation to creating wealth in a particular kind of way is essential for the proper functioning and success of human society.

While Kozlowski may have overestimated himself and his role in the world, the essays in this section point out that the Catholic social tradition must not underestimate the moral and spiritual responsibility of creating wealth. There is a very real sense that we are wealth *creators* in so far as we collaborate with *the Creator.* In the first chapter of Genesis, God commands that humans have dominion over the earth—a charge undoubtedly overemphasized in the past to justify exploiting the environment, but nevertheless a command to create, build, and transform what we have before us. The person, made in the image of God and given this command to have dominion over God's creation, is fundamentally a maker and builder of products and services—*homo faber.*

Yet, human wealth is not created *ex nihilo,* out of nothing. In one sense, we are not creators of wealth at all. We transform what already has been created and make it pass from one state to another. When this fundamental truth is applied to the wealth "creation" process, it becomes apparent that human beings are first of all *given* wealth and are therefore not the originators of wealth. This initial gift, as Simona Beretta explains, "generates a dynamic process of reciprocal gift-giving that expresses and substantiates personal or social relations. This process generates a story in which things and meanings circulate, a story that can either be freely nurtured (so that, at the end, we can say, 'We owe each other so much!'), or truncated ('I owe him nothing anymore')."

Beretta and the other authors argue through Part I that wealth originates from God's gift of creation to humanity, a gift we are called to use toward the integral human development of each individual person and of all persons. Through their capacity to do and to make, human beings, cast in the image of God, are involved in a project of advancing creation toward its destination, the kingdom of God. Wealth is first a gift, to be used not only on the basis of one's individual preference or autonomy but also as a means to forge stronger communion among persons, among peoples, and between the person and God and the peoples and God. This gift of creation by the Creator is not "some quaint theological assertion that sits on the sidelines of economic analysis," as Beretta ironically puts it, but rather is "a central concept in understanding wealth creation" as a means to human development.

Catholic social thought will not develop or be of much use to those involved in creating wealth if it is not engaged with the practice and theory of economics and business. Without a thorough interdisciplinary discourse on the relationship between the means and ends of wealth creation, we will not sufficiently understand the meaning of wealth creation. The essays in this section of the book form part of the bridge between social thought and economics, a bridge that must be built in order to ensure that such an interdisciplinary discourse may take place.

ONE   # Wealth as Abundance and Scarcity

Perspectives from Catholic Social Thought and Economic Theory

---

CHARLES M. A. CLARK

If you want to know what God thinks about money, just look at the people He gives it to.

—Old Irish saying

Wealth is a term overflowing with contradictions. On the one hand, it holds out the promise of abundance, while on the other hand its actualization (for individuals) is tied to a reality of scarcity. Furthermore, while it is linked to happiness and well-being on the one side, after a minimum level is acquired it bears very little correlation to either happiness or well-being.[1] Last, it can provide the individual with security against the uncertainties of the future and simultaneously be "the economic face of that political stratification, lodged in the hands of a class whose ability to grant or deny access to resources becomes the 'economic' basis for both prestige and power,"[2] and thus the cause of individual insecurity for those without prestige and power.[3] Such contradictions seem to call out for Harry Truman's proverbial one-handed economist.[4] The contradictions stem, as we saw in the introduction to this book, "The Nature of Wealth," from the competing notions of what wealth is, specifically concerning the differences between social and individual wealth.

This dual notion of wealth, as something that can either promote or retard the common good, is evident throughout the history of economic thought. It is also expressed within the Judeo-Christian social tradition, particularly within the Old and New Testaments and in the subsequent 2,000-year Catholic moral/social tradition. An examination of these two intellectual traditions' reflections on the nature of wealth shows that many of their positive and negative pronouncements are related, stemming from whether wealth is seen from a social or an individualistic perspective, whether wealth is understood as essentially the result of abundance or the result of scarcity, whether wealth is perceived as a means to an end or as a legitimate end in and of itself, and whether wealth is seen as a gift from God or due solely to human ingenuity.

There is a link between how wealth is conceptualized and how it is created, distributed, and used, as there is with all objects; thus, whether wealth is beneficial or harmful to the common good is presaged in how it is understood and explained. When wealth is understood in terms of promoting human flourishing, it will tend to promote the common good, for it will be a means to a legitimate end. When wealth is defined in any other terms, it will tend to counter the common good, to harm the individual, the economy, and society as a whole. When wealth is seen as having a social dimension and being a tool of social responsibility, it will promote the common good. However, when it is conceived solely in terms of individual ownership and use, it will tend to be employed in a manner that is contrary to the common good. And finally, when wealth is understood as a gift from God, it will tend to be used toward the common good. When it is understood in terms of scarcity, wealth cannot help but harm the common good. Ultimately, wealth is beneficial or harmful mostly as the result of how it is created, how it is distributed, and how it is used. Explanations of its nature are, in fact, usually efforts to legitimate and justify the practices and activities of those with power over wealth. Thus, through an examination of the meanings given to wealth we gain insights into the nature and logic of economic power.

In this chapter I will confine myself mostly to the intellectual history of how wealth has been conceptualized, based on the conviction that how we conceptualize things helps to determine our actions toward them. This approach is explicitly based on a rejection of the position that wealth—its causes, its distribution, and its use— is somehow ruled by physical laws (such as the laws of gravity) and is not within the realm of human discretionary action. While economic actions, like all human actions, fall under the purview of the natural law, we must remember Jacques Maritain's oft-stated point that the natural law is a moral code we are called to follow, not a set of physical laws we cannot disobey.[5]

Our primary interest is how wealth has been understood in the Catholic social tradition and economic theory. Our hope is that the wisdom common to both traditions will guide us in our understanding of wealth and the role it plays in contemporary society. We will first very briefly review why the topic of wealth is important. Next we will examine the treatment of wealth in the Catholic social tradition, starting with the foundations of this tradition in the Old and New Testaments, followed by the modern encyclical tradition. An examination of how economists and moral philosophers have viewed wealth comes next, with particular attention to Plato, Adam Smith, Karl Menger, Thorstein Veblen, and John Maynard Keynes. So that our analysis is not merely an exercise in the history of ideas, we take a brief look at how wealth is currently created and relate it to one of the perspectives covered in this chapter. Our final section looks at what a Christian perspective of wealth is, and how, when combined with the insights of the economists discussed here, this perspective can guide us in our individual actions and social institutions regarding the creation, distribution, and use of wealth in a manner that protects human dignity and promotes the common good. The major theme of this chapter is the contention that if wealth is to provide us with abundance, then its creation, distribution, and use need to be ordered toward the common good and the protection of human dignity. If it is viewed as primarily created by and for individuals, divorced from the common good and the social nature of property, and if people act on this view, then wealth will be the source of scarcity and will retard human flourishing. As Cicero noted, "Personal wealth draws us one way, humanity the other."[6] We will see that this observation is confirmed both by Christian theology and much economic theory.

WHY WEALTH MATTERS

Just about everyone has an interest in wealth as wealth itself, beyond even the normal concern that one has for one's personal means. All the social and human sciences have something to say about wealth and its role in human affairs. The reason for this pervasive interest is simple: wealth has widespread effects on most, if not all, aspects of human social life. The connection between wealth and well-being makes it an important topic for all citizens of a community. From the perspectives of economics and Christian theology, wealth is an important topic for two primary reasons: (1) it influences individual behavior; and (2) it affects aggregate outcomes. Both economists and theologians seek to understand and explain human behavior— economists from the perspective of how that behavior promotes or retards the solving of the economic problem (how societies provide for their material well-being), and theologians from the perspective of how human behavior moves us closer to, or farther away from, God.[7] Few would argue that wealth does not play an important role in individual decision-making, if only for its effect on the range of choices; thus, both disciplines need to consider its ramifications. Wealth also plays a role in determining social structures and institutions such as class divisions; income distribution; economic, political, and social power; status; economic enterprise; conceptions of what is good and valuable; modes of governance; and laws and customs. The list could go on and on. These structures and institutions play an important role in whether the common good of the community is being promoted or not, both in terms of the ability of the community to solve its economic problems and in terms of promoting virtuous behavior among the individuals who make up the community. The creation, distribution, and use of wealth can establish structures of virtue or structures of sin, each rife with economic and theological implications.

WEALTH IN CATHOLIC SOCIAL THOUGHT

Although the Catholic social tradition does not present an alternative economic theory, it does include reflections and observations on many of the same economic realities and actions that economists have considered. The Catholic social tradition differs from mainstream economic theory mostly in its philosophical foundations, specifically its philosophical anthropology and "vision" of society.[8] This tradition's richer understanding of the human person causes it to adopt a broader perspective on human affairs than modern economists typically do, thus frequently giving it a deeper understanding of economic activity than that offered by neoclassical economic theory.[9] The philosophical foundations of the Catholic social tradition come from its grounding in the Bible and in the natural law tradition best exemplified by St. Thomas Aquinas. To fully appreciate this view of wealth in Catholic social thought, it is useful to go back and look briefly at what the Old and New Testaments say about wealth. While the following two essays by Robert Kennedy and John Haughey (chapters 2 and 3) also examine wealth from a scriptural perspective, my purpose for covering this ground is to highlight its dual nature and, specifically, its abundance/scarcity and social/individual aspects.

Wealth in the Old Testament

The Old Testament has a few clear themes regarding wealth. First, wealth is conceived of as goods that promote material well-being. Second, wealth comes from God and is a gift to those who follow His ways.[10] This is the promise of abundance. Third, those who believe that their wealth is due to their own efforts (and not a gift from God) or who do not use it according to the Divine Plan will lose their wealth or worse (creation of scarcity).[11] Fourth, wealth and property are to be shared and not hoarded. Wealth is for the common good of all. Most societies throughout history have shared the trait of having some mechanism for redistributing hoards of wealth.[12] In fact, one of the main points of the Jubilee was to break up large accumulations of wealth and property. And last, hoarded wealth is a cause of poverty (by creating scarcity, a point I will develop further below). In terms of our taxonomy of wealth, the Old Testament tells us that social wealth is a gift from God; that the individualization of wealth, in the creation of actual property, must follow the laws of justice (and therefore not be at the expense of the poor). In other words, wealth needs to be used for all and thus must be widely distributed.

Most important, wealth needs to be employed for the promotion of the true ends of the children of God, namely, human flourishing and the glory of God, and not for individual aggrandizement. Wealth also needs to be kept in its proper place and not elevated to the same level as godliness. In Ecclesiastes we are warned:

> The man who loves money can never have enough, and the man who is in love with great wealth enjoys no return from it. This too is emptiness. When riches multiply, so do those who live off them; and what advantage has the owner, except to look at them? Sweet is the sleep of the labourer whether he eats little or much; but the rich man owns too much and cannot sleep. There is a singular evil here under the sun which I have seen: a man hoards wealth to his own hurt.[13]

And in Ezekiel, another, direr warning:

> Clever and shrewd as you are, you have amassed wealth for yourself, you have amassed gold and silver in your treasuries; by great cleverness in your trading you have heaped up riches, and with your riches your arrogance has grown. Therefore these are the words of the Lord God: Because you try to think the thoughts of a god I will bring strangers against you, the most ruthless of nations, who will draw their swords against your fine wisdom and lay your pride in the dust.[14]

Wealth can be a means for promoting human well-being, but it can also be a barrier to true happiness.

Wealth in the New Testament

Two central messages of the New Testament relate directly to our topic: (1) a message of hope and good news to the poor; and (2) a demand that the affluent take responsibility for helping the poor.[15] Both complement the views of wealth in the Old Testament. Wealth is the material production that sustains life. It is a means to an end, the good of each individual and the common good of the community. But when it becomes an end in itself, wealth serves as a barrier to following God. The New Testament carries forward the idea that wealth is a gift from God, but it presents a more developed analysis as to how wealth can be a barrier to understanding and following God.

In the New Testament the pursuit of wealth is seen as a distraction from the real goal of human life. Jesus tells us:

> Do not lay up for yourselves treasures on earth, where moth and rust consume and where thieves break in and steal, but lay up for yourselves treasures in heaven, where neither moth nor rust consumes and where thieves do not break in and steal. For where your treasure is, there will your heart be also. . . . No servant can be the slave of two masters; for either he will hate the first and love the second, or he will be devoted to the first and think nothing of the second. You cannot serve God and money.[16]

This passage from Matthew, which clearly demonstrates the dangerous aspects of wealth, is followed by an example of the promise of wealth as well-being. Here, Jesus tells us not to worry about material subsistence; that God will provide for us just as he does for the birds of the air and the lilies in the fields. This promise of abundance allows us to direct our efforts to more important pursuits. We are told not to strive for material wealth, as the heathens do, but instead to: "Set your mind on God's kingdom and His justice before everything else, and all the rest will come to you as well."[17] Abundance is promised for those who adhere to God's ways, and especially to the commands of justice, whereas those who pursue wealth instead of salvation are condemned. The major sin referred to here is greed—hoarding riches for oneself instead of sharing with the community. This causes two problems: (1) it distracts us from our true calling, which is to follow God; and (2) it causes scarcity for the poor (the hoarded-up wealth of the rich leaves less for the subsistence of the poor and contributes to their poverty). So important is the concern for the poor in Jesus' message that He tells us that we will be judged based on how we treat the "least of our brothers": the hungry, the sick, the thirsty, those in prison. In fact, we are told that in them we are to see Jesus. Thus, we are to share our material wealth with others.

Wealth in the Papal Encyclicals

From its biblical roots, as indicated in Kennedy's and Haughey's essays, the Catholic social tradition advances the idea that wealth consists of goods and services intended to meet human needs, and that these goods and services are derived from God's gift of creation to us (see Francis Hannafey's essay). This is the promise of abundance. Yet abundance does not come without effort, for we are called to be "collaborators" in creation through work. As John Paul II has noted, through work we produce the goods and services that form the social wealth of a nation, but, more important, through work we develop ourselves to our fullest potential. The value of work has more to do with the effect it has upon the authentic development of the worker (subjective dimension of work) than on the output produced by the worker (objective dimension of work).[18]

That the subjective dimension of work is more than the objective is seen in John XXIII's earlier encyclical, *Mater et magistra*, when he states:

> Justice is to be observed not merely in the distribution of wealth, but also in regard to the conditions under which men engaged in productive activity have an opportunity to assume responsibility and to perfect themselves by their efforts. Consequently, if the organization and structure of economic life be such that the dignity of workers is compromised, their sense of responsibility is weakened, or their freedom of action is removed, then we judge such an economic order to be unjust, even though it produces a vast amount of goods whose distribution conforms to the norms of justice and equity.[19]

Wealth is based on work and God's gift of nature, where work is seen as "collaboration" with God, to use the words of John Paul II.[20] However, the Catholic social tradition clearly sees that wealth can be created through a distortion of God's will and that wealth can arise from the mistreatment of the poor. Pius XI, in *Quadragesimo anno*, cites the great number of people who, "solely concerned with adding to their wealth by any means whatsoever, sought their own selfish interests above all things; they had no scruple in committing the gravest injustices against others."[21] Thus, the creation of wealth in Catholic social teachings cannot be categorically defined as something positive simply because gross domestic product (GDP) has increased. It is good when wealth, received as God's gift, serves the human community. It is bad when only the few benefit and the poor are exploited.

Catholic social teaching is quite clear on the distribution of wealth: wealth needs to be widely shared and not hoarded. Pius XI argues that

> not every kind of distribution of wealth and property among men is such that it can satisfactorily, still less adequately, attain the end intended by God. Wealth, therefore, which is constantly being augmented by social and economic progress, must be so distributed among the various individuals and

classes of society that the common good of all . . . be thereby promoted. In other words, the good of the whole community must be safeguarded. By these principles of social justice one class is forbidden to exclude the other from a share in the profits. . . . Each class, then, must receive its due share, and the distribution of created goods must be brought into conformity with the demands of the common good and social justice. For every sincere observer realizes that the vast differences between the few who hold excessive wealth and the many who live in destitution constitute a grave evil in modern society.[22]

According to Pius XII, social justice requires us to look at the relationship between wealth and the community as analogous to that of blood to the body: "Wealth is like the blood in the human body; it ought to circulate around all the members of the social body."[23] This is why the right to private property must be subordinated to the created reality of the "universal destination of material goods." It is not enough, as John XXIII argued, "to assert that man has from nature the right of privately possessing goods as his own, including those of [a] productive character, unless, at the same time, a continuing effort is made to spread the use of this right through all ranks of the citizenry."[24]

The Church also asserts that those who have control of wealth have special responsibilities in regard to their use of it.[25] In *Rerum novarum*, Leo XIII states the principle of the "right use of money," a rule that is supported by reason as well as by faith: "[I]t is one thing to have a right to the possession of money, and another to have a right to use money as one pleases."[26] The right of private property is always restricted by the social responsibility to use it toward the common good. Thus, part of the "right use of money" is the duty of charity, to give to those who are less fortunate out of one's surplus. Later social encyclicals have extended this duty of charity to a duty to change unjust social structures that create inequality (thus requiring true charity).[27]

As one would expect, the Church has also continued the biblical tradition of regarding wealth as a possible distraction to our higher calling. As John Paul II notes in *Sollicitudo rei socialis*:

A disconcerting conclusion about the most recent period should serve to enlighten us: side-by-side with the miseries of underdevelopment, themselves unacceptable, we find ourselves up against a form of superdevelopment, equally inadmissible, because like the former it is contrary to what is good and to true happiness. This superdevelopment, which consists in an excessive availability of every kind of material goods for the benefit of certain social groups, easily makes people slaves of "possession" and of immediate gratification, with no other horizon than the multiplication or continual replacement of the things already owned with others still better. This is the so-called civilization of "consumption" or "consumerism," which involves so much "throwing-away" and "waste." An object already owned but now superseded by something better is discarded, with no thought of its possible lasting value in itself, nor of some other human being who is poorer.[28]

The problems caused by consumerism are threefold. First, the pursuit of more and more goods, especially when all legitimate needs and wants are being met, becomes a false god and distracts us from the real God. This is a main point of the Old and New Testaments, as we have seen. The second problem stems from metaphysics and not religion. It is the problem of seeking to have instead of seeking to be: "[W]hat is wrong is a style of life which is presumed to be better when it is directed toward 'having' rather than 'being' and which wants to have more, not in order to be more, but in order to spend life in enjoyment as an end in itself."[29] This is, of course, the essence of the neoclassical vision of human nature and utility as the ultimate good. In fact, it is impossible to find happiness in such an existence, for one can never fulfill the unlimited wants that neoclassical economics assumes. Humans have a desire for the unlimited; however, nothing limited (such as material goods) can ever satisfy that desire. Too much of the success of large corporations can be traced back to their ability to co-opt this craving for the unlimited, which is a craving for God, into a craving for goods. Here, consumerism becomes a substitute for God, exactly the distraction that the Old and New Testaments warn us about. The third problem caused by consumerism and "superdevelopment" is that the greed of the affluent promotes scarcity for the poor, thus contributing to the problem of poverty. This inverse relationship between wealth and well-being is noted frequently in the history of economic theory, to which we now turn.

WEALTH IN ECONOMIC THEORY

Wealth has always been one of the fundamental issues in economic theory; in fact, economics has often been called the "science of wealth." Wealth is important in economic theory because it is typically seen as the primary goal of economic activity (the accumulation of capital) as well as an important determinant of economic outcomes. (A causal factor in determining economic output is the country's capital stock, an important part of the wealth of a nation.) Thus, wealth, in economic theory, is both a cause (at once final and intermediary) and an effect of economic activity. It is no wonder that all the worldly philosophers discussed the role of wealth in the economic and social life of the community.

Plato

Our discussion of the dual aspects of wealth (social/individual, abundance/ scarcity, good/bad) in economic theory starts with the first serious student of economics, Plato.[30] In the *Republic* and the *Laws,* Plato sets out a scheme of economic development that is very insightful for our purposes. He thought that history went in cycles, with beginnings, middles, and endings. These endings were typically caused by a deluge, a wiping clean of the slate that allowed for a new cycle to begin. For Plato, the first stage of economic development is the period in which people only live in the mountains. Here they face a limited existence due to the lack of abundance provided by the terrain. The people of the mountains must spend all of their time working to eke out a minimal existence, which leaves them no leisure for learning to read and write as well as for other activities. Eventually some of the mountain people move down to the lowlands where they discover that nature is more accommodating. Here they find abundance, which allows for the growth of society and of social institutions, learning, and the development of the soul. If their society is virtuous, that is, if it lives within the limits of moderate consumption and a stable population growth, the people can stay in this state of abundance indefinitely. In this "abundance state," all are provided with a comfortable existence, with emphasis placed on living the good and virtuous life. Here we have a society that defines wealth as well-being.

However, unlimited greed and all that it brings—which for Plato is population growth, crime, and, most important, poverty—break the stability of this state of affairs. The push to accumulate more wealth by those with power causes the society to quickly outstrip its natural resources, so the society can only continue its pursuit of unlimited gain by going to war and taking over the land and resources of its neighbors. We will call this the "over-abundance state." Plato thought that the Athens of his day was in this state. This unlimited greed causes an imbalance that cannot be restored and that eventually forces the cycle to start over again, either through a deluge, caused by stripping nature clean, or by the intervention of the gods. Here we see that wealth, or the unlimited desire for wealth, becomes the major problem of such a society, a barrier to its happiness and the cause of war and poverty. Plato's "over-abundance" state bears some similarity to John Paul II's analysis of "super-abundance" in that both are created by a desire for wealth over and above what is needed to support a comfortable and virtuous life.

In Plato we see a dual conception of wealth. The "abundance state" conception is based on the need for sufficient material provisions so that all can live a good and virtuous life. In such a society wealth is seen as a means to an end (supporting people) and not as an end in itself. In the "over-abundance state" wealth is clearly based on scarcity and exclusion. Speaking through the voice of Socrates in his *Republic,* Plato tells us why both wealth and poverty are bad for society: "Wealth and poverty . . . the one brings luxury, idleness, and revolution, and the other illiberality and the evil of bad workmanship in addition to revolution."[31] Socrates suggests that a guard be placed at the gates of the city to keep wealth and poverty out. Yet wealth and poverty are not seen as two evils but as different sides of the same evil, for the hoarded wealth of the rich is the cause of the poverty of the poor. For Plato, the high consumption of the rich creates shortages for the poor. He suggests that once the greed of the rich creates the "over-abundance state" (overabundance here for the rich only, and a "state of scarcity" for the poor), social harmony is destroyed and two cities are created, one rich and one poor, which are necessarily at war with each other. Plato's insight that inequality causes social disorder and conflict is also in the Old Testament, where the functional purpose of the redistribution of wealth (that is, land) in the Jubilee is to reduce the conflicts that arise from inequality, from too much concentrated economic power, and from tensions over conflicting claims of ownership.

Adam Smith

At the time when Adam Smith was writing *The Wealth of Nations*, the dominant economic ideology was Mercantilism, which held that wealth consisted of gold and silver and that governments needed to promote policies that maximized the supply of gold and silver in their countries. Smith rejected this definition of wealth as money. He defined "real wealth" as "the annual produce of the land and labour of the society,"[32] thus rebutting the traditional, Mercantile definition of wealth.[33] According to Smith, the fallacy of the Mercantilists rested in their confusion of means and ends. Though the immediate end of the merchant might well be gold and silver, for the larger society these were merely means to an end, namely, purchasing goods and services. The Mercantilists had adopted an individualistic conception of wealth, whereas Smith had a social conception.

As wealth is the annual produce of land and labor, Smith devoted most of his efforts to examining the ways in which this produce can be increased. The chief means for promoting increases in the annual produce of the community are increases in inputs of land and labor, and improvements in productivity through the division of labor, which increases the skill and dexterity of the worker, saves time in production, and, most important, leads to the improvement and development of machines (that is, technological change). In Smith's understanding, labor is the active force that creates wealth and value (see Haughey's essay for a theological argument of this point).[34] Moreover, Smith was well aware that individual initiative was the driving force behind this creation of wealth, but that initiative demanded the right social context, including competitive markets that turned self-interested actions toward the common good.

Smith stated very clearly that wealth must be widely distributed:

> No society can surely be flourishing and happy, of which the far greater part of the members are poor and miserable. It is but equity, besides, that they who feed, cloath and lodge the whole body of the people, should have a share of the produce of their own labour as to be themselves tolerably well fed, cloathed and lodged. . . . [T]he liberal reward of labour, therefore, as it is the effect of increasing wealth, so it is the cause of increasing population. To complain of it is to lament over the necessary effect and cause of the greatest publick prosperity.[35]

Smith also noted that the liberal reward of labor "increases the industry of the common people. The wages of labour are the encouragement of industry, which, like every other human quality, improves in proportion to the encouragement it receives."[36] This argument is contrary to the ideals of the Mercantilists, who promoted policies designed to reduce domestic consumption and increase concentration in wealth by imposing tariffs, monopolies, and low wages.

Smith's analysis of the accumulation of wealth emphasized its positive aspects. He asserted that the "invisible hand" of competition would, for the most part, prevent wealth from being too concentrated and would therefore protect the tendency of wealth toward uses that would best promote further production for the common good. Like Plato and the Old Testament, Smith denounced the unlimited pursuit of wealth as damaging to the well-being of the community, although such observations are scattered and are not his central concern.[37] Again like Plato, Smith revealed that there is a limit to the accumulation of wealth, through his analysis of what happens when the division of labor is carried too far. For Smith, the division of labor was the main source of economic growth; yet if this principle is carried out to its natural or logical conclusion, it results in an extreme alienation of the vast majority of the population, thereby stunting economic growth. Smith's words are quite damning here (and we should remember that he is supposed to be the great prophet of capitalism!):

> In the progress of the division of labour, the employment of the far greater part of those who live by labour, that is, of the great body of the people, comes to be confined to a few very simple operations, frequently to one or two. But the understandings of the greater part of men are necessarily formed by their

ordinary employments. The man whose whole life is spent in performing a few simple operations, of which the effects too are, perhaps, always the same, or very nearly the same, has no occasion to exert his understanding, or to exercise his invention in finding out expedients for removing difficulties which never occur. *He naturally loses, therefore, the habit of such exertion, and generally becomes as stupid and ignorant as it is possible for a human creature to become.* The torpor of his mind renders him, not only incapable of relishing or bearing a part in any rational conversation, but of conceiving any generous, noble, or tender sentiment, and consequently of forming any just judgment concerning many even of the ordinary duties of private life. . . . His dexterity at his own particular trade seems, in this manner, to be acquired at the expense of his intellectual, social and martial virtues. But in every improved and civilized society this is the state into which the labouring poor, that is, the great body of the people, must necessarily fall, unless government takes some pains to prevent it.[38]

Here, problems in the subjective dimension of labor (workers' conditions and the authentic development of the person) undercut the objective dimension of labor (their productivity). The workers' alienation as persons causes their alienation as producers. Although Smith here is emphasizing only the economic effects of this alienation, clearly his concerns are quite similar to those of John XXIII and John Paul II, as cited above.

Like Plato, Smith noted the damaging effect that the love of wealth has on public morals:

This disposition to admire, and almost worship, the rich and the powerful, and to despise, or, at least, to neglect persons of poor and mean condition, though necessary both to establish and to maintain the distinction of ranks and the order of society, is, at the same time, the great and most universal cause of the corruption of our moral sentiments. That wealth and greatness are often regarded with the respect and admiration which are due only to wisdom and virtue; and that the contempt, of which vice and folly are the only proper objects, is often most unjustly bestowed upon poverty and weakness, has been the complaint of moralists in all ages.[39]

Smith saw the pursuit of wealth as the cause of material prosperity, but not real happiness. It leads, through the intervention of the "invisible hand," to material prosperity, and it benefits the poor almost as much as the rich, yet he noted that it also generates great inequality and gives the rich more power.[40]

Wherever there is great property, there is great inequality. For one very rich man, there must be at least five hundred poor, and the affluence of the few supposes the indigence of the many. . . . The acquisition of valuable and extensive property, therefore, necessarily requires the establishment of civil government. . . . Civil government, so far as it is instituted for the security of property, is in reality instituted for the defense of the rich against the poor, or of those who have some property against those who have none at all.[41]

Smith had great faith in the "harmony of interests" and the "invisible hand" of competition to keep the creation, distribution, and use of wealth geared toward the common good, but he was aware of the dangers of allowing the pursuit of wealth to become the central focus of either the individual or society as a whole. He clearly saw that some of the negative aspects of wealth can be the natural result of markets and recognized the need for government and religious institutions to intervene and try to thwart the negative market forces. Smith's faith in the "invisible hand" stemmed from its being an instrument of Divine Providence to turn private, self-interested actions toward promoting the common good. In the economics of the late nineteenth century, however, scarcity would begin to edge over abundance. The moral sentiments, which for Smith were the basis of sociality (what makes the social bond), were replaced by market forces as the basis of sociality, and the dual Enlightenment goals of freedom and equality were replaced with the ideology of "freedom to choose."

The Neoclassical View

The switch from a well-being, material-production view of wealth to a scarcity view comes to economic theory with the transition from the "objective" to the "subjective" theory of value (not to be confused with John Paul II's subjective dimension of work). This switch coincides with an overall move in philosophy from social to individualistic explanations, from understanding reality as we find it, in its historical and social context, to emphasis on subjective evaluations and emotions best exemplified by Friedrich Nietzsche. The Marginal Utility revolution caused many changes in economic theory:[42] the basing of the value of goods, and the ultimate measure of value in the economy, on utility and scarcity, both concepts that were rejected by Adam Smith and the classical school of economics; the reduction and eventual elimination of historical and social context from our understanding of economic activity;[43] and the employment of mathematical modeling and formalism as the language of economic discourse.

The shift from the classical view of value (variations on the cost-of-production approach) to the marginal utility theory of value meant, among other things, the eventual end to making interpersonal comparisons in economic theory. This theoretical stance rejected the view that one could evaluate whether a particular distribution of income or wealth was good or bad. This prompted the elimination, at least within neoclassical economic theory, of the "complaint of moralists in all ages," mentioned above by Adam Smith, that wealth does not lead to happiness or that wealth was a reflection of merit or virtue. To support this theoretical stance, neoclassical economists developed a rigid demarcation of economics into "positive" (value neutral) and "normative" (based on value judgments) branches, with only "positive" economics having any real theoretical legitimacy.[44] One of the most important conclusions of "positive" economics was that the distribution of wealth and income was determined by natural laws and thus unalterable without damaging the economic well-being of the community—what has since become known as the equality/efficiency tradeoff (which is discussed by Stefano Zamagni in chapter 8).

The switch to "scarcity" as a fundamental concept in economic theory greatly changed the theoretical handling of wealth. It now became directly linked to issues of scarcity and transferability, qualities normally associated with financial assets. The most important neoclassical economist, Léon Walras, stated early in his *Elements of Pure Economics* that "[b]y social wealth I mean all things, material or immaterial (it does not matter which in the context), that are scarce, that is to say, on the one hand, useful to us and, on the other hand, only available to us in limited quantity."[45] This scarcity view of wealth eventually came to dominate economic thinking:

> Wealth is not such for economic purposes, unless it is scarce and transferable, and so desirable that some one is anxious to give something for it.
>
> —Walter Bagehot[46]

> [Wealth]. . . . These sources of human welfare which are material, transferable and limited in quantity.
>
> —John Bates Clark[47]

> Wealth is not wealth because of its substantial qualities. It is wealth because it is scarce.
>
> —Lord Robbins[48]

As wealth was no longer directly related to the production of goods and services, it was also no longer connected with improving the well-being of the whole population, especially the lot of the poor. "That mankind as a whole shall become richer does not, of necessity, involve an increase in human welfare."[49]

Karl Menger offers the clearest and most consistent statement on what wealth is. In his *Principles of Economics,* he tells us that "wealth" can be defined "as the entire sum of goods at an economizing individual's command, the quantities of which are smaller than the requirements for them."[50] He goes on to state: "if there were a society where all goods were available in amounts exceeding the requirements for them, there would be no economic goods nor any 'wealth.'"[51] Menger then notes that wealth for the individual is different from wealth for the community. The individual's increases in wealth demonstrate a greater ability to meet his needs and desires. For the community as a whole, by contrast, the more successfully needs and desires are met, the lower the value of wealth. "The problem," he writes, "arises from the fact that a continuous increase in the amount of economic goods available to economizing individuals would necessarily cause these goods to lose their economic character, and in the way cause the components of wealth to suffer a diminution. Hence we have a 'queer contradiction' that a continuous increase of the objects of wealth would have caused, as a necessary final consequence, a diminution of wealth."[52] Menger argues that this queer contradiction, in which an increase in the production of goods leads to a fall in wealth, stems from confusion created by terms such as "national wealth." This is a fiction. There exists only individual wealth, and the effect is only at the individual level.

We can see from Menger's analysis that the conflict between individual and social wealth, which we have seen in the Old and New Testaments and in Plato and Adam Smith, is done away with by the elimination of the category of "social" or "national." The elimination is accomplished by adopting a fully atomistic and mechanical view of society in which society becomes a mental fiction and is easily dropped from theoretical discussions. The value of economic goods in Menger's analysis exists in the heads of the economizing individuals, and the reason that their wealth falls as they consume more is the law of diminishing marginal utility. But since all the action takes place in the minds of economizing individuals, it is not valid to make comparisons among individuals; thus, questions of distribution and use do not arise. As long as individuals freely choose how to employ their wealth, it is put to the best possible use, because the best possible use is whatever the individual chooses.[53] The analysis is a mere tautology. Individuals desire and use goods because the goods have utility, and the proof that the goods have utility is the fact that individuals desire and use them. Individuals maximize utility by choosing goods, and the proof that the goods maximize their utility is that individuals choose them. One cannot argue with that logic. By eliminating the social aspects of wealth and the economy as well as interpersonal comparisons, and by reducing the analysis to a tautology, the neoclassical economists have eliminated the recognized contradictions in the term "wealth."

The irony is that the development of the scarcity view of wealth takes place just when real scarcity ceases to be the main economic problem facing capitalist economies. When Plato and Adam Smith referred to wealth as the production of goods and services that provided for the material needs of the community, meeting these needs was the central concern—that is, the central economic problem was how to produce sufficient output to supply all the necessary goods and services to the existing population. The Industrial Revolution tackled this problem so success- fully that, by the second half of the nineteenth century, the central economic prob- lem was how to consume enough, given the existing distribution of income, of all the potential output of businesses at rates of return that were acceptable to those busi- nesses. Western capitalist economies had become "supply-constrained" rather than "demand-constrained." In a "demand-constrained economy," scarcity takes on a new meaning, for the scarcity of the neoclassical economist is not real; that is, it is not based on the inability of the economy to provide the necessities of life to support the population of a society. It is instead an "artificial" scarcity created by the busi- ness system in order to maintain the rate of return on wealth and the social power that attaches itself to "scarce" wealth.

Veblen and Keynes

Thorstein Veblen and John Maynard Keynes both fully understood the shift from a supply-constrained to a demand-constrained economy and society. Veblen stated that two processes maintained the value of wealth at the expense of the com- mon good: conspicuous consumption and industrial sabotage. In *The Theory of the Leisure Class*,[54] he noted the important role of displays of wealth and economic power in social control. Veblen's analysis is, in many ways, reminiscent of Adam Smith's in *The Theory of Moral Sentiments,* in that he argued that the role of conspicu- ous consumption in social control lies in gaining the acquiescence of the lower classes to the consumption of the leisure class through the establishment of social morals and values. By setting its behavior, in this case its consumption, as the stan- dard of the good and the honorable, the leisure class wins the submission of the lower classes. This submission is solidified by the attempts of the lower classes to mimic the consumption patterns of the leisure class, whose central concern is not "Is this social order just and the best that can be?" but instead, "How can I become rich and join the leisure class?" Thus, Veblen goes beyond Smith, for he linked the control of morals and values to the social power of the leisure class. (Smith had lim- ited this power to the power over goods and the labor of the working classes.)

Admission to the leisure class, of course, is strictly limited in numbers, since this admission is based on the ability to consume at levels that are much higher than the average of the community. As the ability to produce goods and services grows in such a society, some manner must be devised so that the lower classes do not fully mimic the consumption patterns of the wealthy. If the consumption of the rich is held constant, then the success of the Industrial Revolution would eventually allow all to enjoy such a level of consumption. (This is the Enlightenment's notion of freedom and equality, to a certain extent.) Yet this would completely undermine the position of power of the leisure class and lead to a radical transformation of society (a threat to the maintenance of "the distinction of ranks and the order of society"). This potential danger to the power structure is alleviated through two means: (1) the artificial creation of unlimited wants for both the rich and the rest of society, so that the rich keep on raising the bar that the working classes are striving for (creating inequality); and (2) the artificial limiting of production to create scarcity (reducing freedom). Salesmanship is the mode by which the former is achieved (what today we would call advertising and marketing), while the latter strategy Veblen calls "industrial sabotage," the limiting of the production potential of the economy so as to keep the rate of return on capital high by keeping prices high. Industrial concentration, as well as the many forms of industrial planning used by large corporations, is the means by which production is limited to maintain the value and exclusivity of wealth, and thus its social power.[55]

John Maynard Keynes, in the last chapter of *The General Theory of Employment, Interest, and Money* (clearly the most important work in economic theory in the twentieth century), states, "The outstanding faults of the economic society in which we live are its failure to provide for full employment and its arbitrary and inequitable distribution of wealth and incomes."[56] He then goes on to argue that these two are connected, that inequality of wealth and incomes is one of the main causes of high unemployment. Inequality in wealth and incomes is maintained by keeping capital artificially scarce. This scarcity shows up in terms of macroeconomics as insufficient levels of investment, which, through standard mechanisms, lead to involuntary unemployment.

"Our problem," Keynes writes in his famous essay on "The End of Laissez Faire," "is to work out a social organization which shall be as efficient as possible without offending our notions of a satisfactory way of life."[57] Keynes notes the usefulness of acquisition as a social and individual characteristic (Smith's trick of nature) when society has a low state of economic development, but he suggests that once society has reached sufficient affluence, it should move on to higher values and morals:

> When the accumulation of wealth is no longer of high social importance, there will be great changes in the code of morals. We shall be able to rid ourselves of many of the pseudo-moral principles which have hag-ridden us for two hundred years, by which we have exalted some of the most distasteful of

human qualities into the position of the highest virtues. We shall be able to afford to dare to assess the money-motive at its true value. The love of money as a possession—as distinguished from the love of money as a means to the enjoyments and realities of life—will be recognized for what it is, a somewhat disgusting morbidity, one of those semi-criminal, semi-pathological propensities which one hands over with a shudder to the specialists in mental disease. All kinds of social customs and economic practices, affecting the distribution of wealth and the economic rewards and penalties, which we now maintain at all costs, however distasteful and unjust they may be in themselves, because they are tremendously useful in promoting the accumulation of capital, we shall then be free, at last, to discard.[58]

Keynes, like Smith, was an optimist, for he thought that once it became obvious that the grossly unequal distribution of wealth was a barrier to full employment, society would make the necessary changes in its economic organization to eliminate this barrier. Keynes writes: "Our argument leads towards the conclusion that in contemporary conditions the growth of wealth, so far from being dependent on the abstinence of the rich, as is commonly supposed, is more likely to be impeded by it. One of the chief social justifications of great inequality of wealth is, therefore, removed."[59]

In *General Theory*, Keynes makes four proposals to reduce the scarcity value of capital: (1) employing policies designed to generate a more equal distribution of income (such as a progressive income tax); (2) imposing a low rate of interest on money and therefore limiting returns on wealth (an expansionary monetary policy reduces the scarcity value of capital); (3) effecting a "euthanasia" of the rentier class by using low returns to force the eventual expenditure of large accumulations of wealth, due to rentiers' inability to live off the interest income;[60] and (4) socializing investment, which for Keynes meant that society should, acting through the state, do everything it can to promote a high level of investment in order to protect and promote society's vested interest in full employment (investment tax credits are a good example).

By increasing the quantity of capital to reduce its scarcity, Keynes argues, one can uphold the positive aspects of competitive capitalism while gradually eliminating the "cumulative oppressive power of the capitalist to exploit the scarcity-value of capital. Interest today rewards no genuine sacrifice, any more than does the rent of land. The owner of capital can obtain interest because capital is scarce just as the owner of land can obtain rent because land is scarce. But whilst there may be intrinsic reasons for the scarcity of land, there are no intrinsic reasons for the scarcity of capital."[61] The cost to society of maintaining the inequality that is a necessary aspect of maintaining a high rate of return for wealth is high unemployment and lower economic growth. Just as Plato saw it, Keynes shows how wealth, in a very real sense, can become a cause of poverty.

In both Veblen and Keynes there is a clear idea that social wealth is the result of human efforts and intelligence as well as nature's bounty. (In Veblen's analysis, nature's bounty only becomes valuable when humans discover how to use it; for him, resources are made and not discovered.) In both there is a contradiction between the processes of individual and social wealth creation, with the former necessarily causing scarcities and harming the common good. Furthermore, both affirm the economic necessity, as well as the moral imperative, of a wider distribution of wealth. The economy operates more effectively with a wider distribution, which allows for higher levels of participation and larger aggregate outputs. And finally, as do the Catholic social tradition and both Plato and Smith, Veblen and Keynes note the harmful effects of individual wealth creation, unequal wealth distribution, and the improper use of wealth by the wealthy, including dire consequences for the morals of society.

Creating Wealth

So far our analysis has been on the level of intellectual history and has skirted the issue of how wealth is created, distributed and used. In keeping with the methodology of the Catholic social tradition and St. Thomas Aquinas, it is important for us to observe how in the real world wealth is created, distributed, and used so that we can apply the analysis of the Catholic social tradition (and those of the economists considered here) to our economy and society.

Wealth is created by two processes. First, social wealth is generated by additions to either the capital stock of the nation, in terms of the means of production, or increases to and the spreading of the stock of knowledge. Increases in the supply of natural resources are not as critical as the development of the knowledge of how to use the resources. The second process is the creation and valuations of rights to social output. This is individual wealth. In a modern economy this process belongs mostly to the equity markets, though not exclusively, as government policy often determines such rights.

It is clear that today, in both the popular imagination and in economic theory (not to mention the other business disciplines), the dominant view of wealth is not the material abundance view of Adam Smith and Plato but is instead the scarcity/ exclusion view of modern neoclassical economics—what Plato called the "over-abundance state," based not on meeting the material needs of the community but on the desires of the affluent. The increase in material provision for society as a whole is often incidental to the creation of wealth. Certainly, there are numerous examples of wealth being created due to increases in production or to innovation (such as increases in quality rather than quantity), but these are not essential to the process of wealth creation. Smith thought that the "invisible hand" would ensure that this would be the case, but the very visible hand of economic power has long since replaced the invisible hand of perfect competition as the dominating force in the economy.

Today, we look at wealth as the ownership of assets that generate income (or more properly, purchasing power). These assets are many and varied, with stocks and bonds making up the bulk of them. Many assets that we would consider wealth, such as houses, have an implicit rate of return, and they only have an explicit rate of return when they are rented out. Other assets included in our accounting are any goods that can be easily transformed into purchasing power. Wealth is increased (created) when these assets rise in value, due either to their increased productivity, profitability, or scarcity. Any increase in productivity is clearly linked to the view of wealth in Adam Smith, increasing the annual produce of land and labor. However, increases in profitability, and scarcity clearly can, and often do arise from restricted output, monopolized production and distribution, manipulated markets, corporate welfare, and a long list of activities that do not promote the common good.

One of the most successful methods of creating wealth is to shift cost onto someone else. Providing a decent standard of living for workers as well as a safe work environment, and not polluting the outside environment, are part of the "real" costs of production of any good or service. Yet, wealth is often created by shifting some of these costs onto workers (paying them less than a living wage, injuring or infecting them) or onto consumers (making unsafe or damaging products) or onto those who live near production facilities (polluting the environment). The moving of plants and factories from areas where the full costs are imposed by statute to areas without such regulations is, in effect, making others pay part of the cost of production. Add to this the tactic of blackmail in order to obtain preferential tax treatment from governments (companies will not locate in a region without great tax concessions or other subsidies), and considerable wealth has been created without promoting the common good. The most common way of using the government to create wealth is to partially socialize the costs of production (let the taxpayers pick up part of the tab) and to privatize the benefits. A classical example of this is the Internet. Developed and activated with taxpayers' money, Internet commerce has generated economic benefits that are flowing mostly to private companies.

Veblen's sabotage and conspicuous consumption also greatly contribute to wealth creation. The main motivation behind mergers is not the so-called synergies or economies of scale that Wall Street experts like to mention on business news broadcasts. The fact of the matter—and it is one that almost all economic investigations into this question demonstrate—is that the motive behind mergers is to increase market power by limiting competition as well as to exploit technological economies of scale. Mergers are, for the most part, about reducing the number of competitors and limiting price competition, thus making capital scarcer.[62]

Last, we cannot escape the role of theft, fraud, and force. Richard Tawney's comment that not all property is theft, but that all theft becomes property, is equally true of wealth. The basis of Bill Gates's enormous wealth is Microsoft's monopoly and its anticompetitive business practices. Because of these practices, everyone has to transfer a part of their income to Microsoft. No guns are used, but the transfer is forced, nonetheless. Looking at the bigger picture, we see that the basis of exorbitant wealth is often theft, fraud, and force. The wealth of the United States of America was partly subsidized by defrauding the Native Americans of their land, kidnapping and enslaving black Africans to work the land (thus shifting the costs to them), and exploiting immigrants.

Even technological change, the part of wealth creation that contributes to the common good by increasing output, is monopolized and controlled to maintain scarcity. Wealth is created not by technological developments but by the controlling and limiting of such developments. Major technological developments are often heralded as bringing unlimited wealth and providing free goods (the Niagara Falls dam was supposed to make electricity so cheap that it would be inefficient to monitor it), yet this largesse is impossible given the power structure of our society, which is based on artificial scarcity and could not survive along with universal affluence.

Wealth only remains wealth if it is kept scarce and if the majority of the population is excluded from owning and controlling it. In the United States it is often stated that most of the wealth, in terms of stocks, is owned by the people, but this ownership is in the form of insurance and pension funds over which the people (that is, the workers) have no control. The notion that everyone can become wealthy, in the modern neoclassical sense, is nonsense, since wealth only exists if it is limited and if its value is directly tied to maintaining its scarcity and exclusivity. Schemes to manipulate the stock market to make everyone a millionaire can only work if the term "millionaire" loses all of its meaning. It would be like replacing one-dollar bills with thousand-dollar bills. On paper people would be richer, but their purchasing power would not improve much because the rise in income would be greater than the output of goods and services to purchase, thus causing the prices to rise.

Growth in wealth, or in wealth that is tied to scarcity and exclusion, has not had the net effect that Adam Smith had hoped for: reduction of poverty and a rise in all people's standards of living. The past decade has seen an enormous increase in wealth, but this has been accompanied by only marginal benefits for the poor and middle classes.[63] A recent economic analysis of the growth in wealth states:

> Wealth creation was one of the dominant themes of the U.S. economy in the 1990s. Between the end of 1989 and the end of 1999, the real net worth of U.S. households increased by nearly $15 trillion, or by more than 50%. Per capita net worth at the end of 1999 was slightly more than $150,000. At the top of the wealth distribution, the rise of great fortunes has led many to compare the 1990s to the Gilded Age of the late 19th century, when Carnegie, Rockefeller, Vanderbilt and others amassed their financial empires. In October 1999, the Forbes 400 included 267 billionaires, 200 more than ten years earlier. . . . More than 60% of the wealth creation during the 1990s was due to the rising value of household stock holdings.[64]

Yet increases in per capita income and productivity have risen less than 20 percent in this same time period. Real wages have risen even less. From 1988 to 1997 real average hourly and weekly earnings decreased at an annual rate of -0.2 percent. While this trend in real wages turned around from 1998 to 2000, the increase in no way matches either the growth in output or in productivity and is nowhere near the growth in wealth.[65] This suggests that much of this 50 percent increase in wealth has not been due to factors that promote the common good but instead has been due to the redistribution of costs, the creation of scarcity, and the promotion of exclusion.

CONCLUSION

There is no Wealth but Life.
—John Ruskin

One of the central economic questions that Christians need to address is the issue of the creation, distribution, and use of wealth in capitalist economies. Any investigation into these questions requires an underlying set of values and a vision of the "good" society—that is, the direction in which society should be moving. In this, Catholic social thought is no different from classical, neoclassical, Marxian, Keynesian, and other schools of economics: its two underlying premises are the intrinsic dignity of all human persons and the preeminence of promoting the common good. With these two premises of Catholic social thought in mind, it is obvious that a Christian must view wealth from the "well-being" perspectives of Plato and Adam Smith. This attitude toward wealth has the possibility of promoting the common good and should therefore protect the dignity of all humans. However, it should be equally clear that the Christian perspective must reject the idea and the promotion of scarcity-based wealth. Wealth that is created for the individual at the expense of the community is repugnant to human dignity and the common good due to its promotion of poverty. This sort of wealth requires for its existence that the economy operate at a level below its potential, that the fruits of the economy be distributed in a grossly unequal manner, and that consumers' wants be artificially encouraged to perpetuate the rat race. Furthermore, the conditions under which workers labor are an important factor in the creation of social wealth. Catholic social thought argues that the well-being of the worker, specifically her authentic development as a person, is the primary goal of work. Thus, not only is cost-shifting as a form of wealth creation a social evil, but so too are the structures of work that retard the development of workers and do not promote their personal well-being.

Consumerism is, for the Christian, probably the most offensive aspect of our current obsession with wealth, since it is the chief economic mechanism responsible for fostering the development of secular societies that increasingly efface the role of God and faith in modern culture. We are the subject of Jesus' warning: "You cannot serve God and money."[66] In the United States especially, this culture of decadence has developed to the highest degree. We see its negative effects on the morals of our society in the two-decade "war on the poor" that has been waged in our public policy. In a very public way, with the consent and support of the majority of the population, the poor have been demonized and criminalized in the United States. Their relative economic position and their absolute economic position have declined over the past twenty years. At the same time, those of the rich have increased, the latter being the cause of the former. As a society, it seems, we would not fare well when compared against the standards of the Parable of the Talents in Matthew 25:31 ff.[67]

One could argue that many social problems in the United States and in the rest of the world are at least partially, and in many ways largely, the result of keeping wealth scarce and of maintaining the exclusive position of those who own against those who do not. Few have seen this problem as clearly as Plato:

> First and foremost there is concupiscence with its domination over a soul stung to savagery by unsatisfied lusts. Now this is chiefly found concerned with . . . wealth, with the power wealth gets alike from native bias and pernicious wrong education to breed countless cravings for insatiate and unbounded possession of itself. And the source of this perverse education is the credit given to false praise of riches . . . they promote wealth to the first

place among good things, whereas in truth it holds but the third, and thus they deprive not only themselves but their posterity. It were for the truest good and glory of all societies that the truth be told of riches. They are for the service of the body, as the body itself [is] for the service of the soul. Since, then, there are goods to which wealth is but a means; it must hold a third place, after goodness of body and soul.[68]

The scarcity view of wealth perverts wealth's true purpose, which is the promotion of material well-being in service to the full development of the human person. Promoting wealth that secures well-being serves this goal. Promoting wealth that is based on scarcity and exclusion is contrary to this goal. The Christian must turn a critical eye toward the accumulation of wealth. As with the institution of private property, the underlying reality is that wealth is only justifiable when it promotes the common good and satisfies a "social mortgage" to this effect. From a Christian perspective, it is not sufficient to say that the current modes of wealth creation, distribution, and use have yielded the high standards of living in the Western capitalist economies. This is not the Christian yardstick. Indeed, such arguments are really beside the point. This economistic perspective would tell us to evaluate the Beatitudes based on their impact on productivity and consumer confidence. Or better yet, rewrite them to say: "Blessed are those who accumulate capital, for they will inherit the Kingdom of God." Jesus did not promise us SUVs and two hundred cable channels. Different evaluation criteria produce differing evaluations, and I suspect that if we applied the criteria of the Gospels to our "affluent society," we might find that we do not measure up.

Notes

1. See Robert E. Lane's *The Loss of Happiness in Market Democracies* (New Haven: Yale University Press, 2000) as well as the positive psychology literature.

2. Robert L. Heilbroner, "Wealth," in *The New Palgrave: A Dictionary of Economics*, ed. John Eatwell, Murray Milgate, and Peter Newman, vol. 4 (London: Macmillan, 1987), 882.

3. See Karl Polanyi, *The Great Transformation* (Boston: Beacon Press, 1944), chapter 14, "Markets and Man," on how the creation of markets, necessary for the generation of wealth in capitalism, by necessity must create individual economic insecurity.

4. President Harry Truman complained that whenever he asked his economic advisers a question, they always gave him "on the one hand/on the other" answers. Thus, he once quipped that all he wanted was a one-handed economist.

5. Jacques Maritain, *Natural Law: Reflections on Theory and Practice* (South Bend, Ind.: St. Augustine's Press, 2001).

6. Cicero, *On Duties*, ed. M. T. Griffin and E. M. Atkins (Cambridge: Cambridge University Press, 1991), 134.

7. Economists might be tempted to refer to these as short-term and long-term (eternity) maximization, but I will resist such a temptation.

8. See Mary E. Hobgood, *Catholic Social Teaching and Economic Theory* (Philadelphia: Temple University Press, 1991); and more recently, Charles M. A. Clark, "The Challenge of Catholic Social Thought to Economic Theory," *Journal of Peace and Justice* 12, no. 2 (2002): 163–77.

9. The economists whom Robert Heilbroner has called the "Worldly Philosophers," many of whom we will look at later in this chapter, did not take such a narrow view of human nature, and included historical and social contexts in their analyses. These factors, which play such a prominent role in Catholic social thought, are particularly missing from the dominant school of thought in economics today—neoclassical economic theory.

10. See, for example, Gen 26:12–14 and 24:35. It is a common interpretation of the New Jerusalem passages in Isaiah that God offers the Israelites the promise of material well-being if only they follow his rules. It is in this section of Isaiah that we come across the phrase "wealth of nations," which figures so prominently in later economic writings: "The riches of the sea shall be lavished upon you and you shall possess the *wealth of nations*" (Isa 60:5; emphasis added); "[Y]ou shall be called priests of the Lord, and be named ministers of our God; you shall enjoy the *wealth of other nations* and be furnished with their riches" (Isa 61:6; emphasis added); and finally, "Rejoice with Jerusalem, and exalt in her, all you who love her; share her joy with your heart, all you who mourn over her. Then you may suck and be fed from the breasts that give comfort, delighting in her plentiful milk. For thus says the Lord: I will send peace flowing over her like a river, and the wealth of nations like a stream in flood. She shall suckle you, and you shall be carried in her arms and dandled on her knees. As a mother comforts her son, so will I myself comfort you, and you shall find comfort in Jerusalem" (Isa 66:11–13). The phrase "wealth of nations" will be familiar to all students of economics because of Adam Smith's *An Inquiry into the Nature and Causes of the Wealth of Nations* (1776). This book is often called the bible of economics, and with good reason: it forms the foundation of all currently existing schools of economic thought. The central point of Smith's *Wealth of Nations* is that if countries follow the economic laws depicted in his book, they will experience material prosperity. This is one of the messages of Isaiah.

11. In Deuteronomy (8:17–18) we are told to remember the true source of wealth: "Nor must you say to yourselves, 'My own strength and energy have gained me this wealth,' but remember the Lord your God; it is he that gives you strength to become prosperous."

12. Thomas Crump, *The Phenomena of Money* (London: Routledge, 1981).

13. Eccl 5:10–13.

14. Ezek 28:4–17.

15. Thomas Cahill, *Desire of the Everlasting Hills* (New York: Doubleday, 1999).

16. Mt 6:19–24.

17. Mt 6:33.

18. John Paul II, *Laborem exercens*, 4–7. For its implications for economic theory, see my "John Paul II and the Value Theory of Labor," in *Work as Key to the Social Question*, ed. Simona

Beretta, Michael J. Naughton, and Johan Verstraeten (Vatican City: Libreria Editrice Vaticana, 2002), 147–62.

19. *Mater et magistra*, 82–83.

20. See John Paul II, *Laborem exercens*, Part V, where he writes about a spirituality of work.

21. *Quadragesimo anno*, 134.

22. Ibid., 57–58.

23. See Michael Naughton, *The Good Stewards* (New York: University Press of America, 1992), 21.

24. *Mater et magistra*, 113.

25. "Those whom fortune favors are warned that freedom from sorrow and abundance of earthly riches are no guarantee of that beatitude that shall never end, but rather the contrary; that the rich should tremble at the threatening of Jesus Christ—threatening so strange in the mouth of our Lord; and that a most strict account must be given to the Supreme Judge for all that we possess" (*Rerum novarum*, 18).

26. Ibid., 19.

27. Paul VI, *Populorum progressio*, 66–75; and U.S. Catholic Bishops, *Economic Justice for All* (1986) 357–58.

28. John Paul II, *Sollicitudo rei socialis*, 28.

29. John Paul II, *Centesimus annus*, 36.

30. This section has benefited greatly from Janina Rosicka, "*Topos*, Economy and Transition in Plato," in *Economic Transition in Historical Perspective*, ed. Charles M. A. Clark and Janina Rosicka (Aldershot, U. K.: Ashgate, 2000).

31. Plato, *Republic*, trans. G. M. A. Grube (Indianapolis: Hackett Publishing Company, 1992), IV: 422a.

32. Adam Smith, *An Inquiry into the Nature and Causes of the Wealth of Nations* (1776; reprint, Oxford: Oxford University Press, 1976), 12.

33. Many now believe that Smith's criticisms of the Mercantilists went too far, that few actually held the position that gold or silver, and not goods, was the basis of wealth.

34. David Ricardo, in his *Principles of Political Economy and Taxation* (1817), pointed out that nature also works along with human labor in the creation of wealth; but then he goes on to develop a labor theory of value that is more extreme than Smith's and excludes land and capital completely from determining the value of goods.

35. Smith, *Wealth of Nations*, 96, 99.

36. Ibid.

37. In *The Theory of Moral Sentiments*, Smith asks: "How many people ruin themselves by laying out money on trinkets of frivolous utility?" He tells us that the idea that the pursuit of wealth will make us happy is a trick of nature, which, if viewed in a philosophical light, would be seen as "in the highest degree contemptible and trifling." Adam Smith, *The Theory of Moral Sentiments* (1759; reprint, Oxford: Oxford University Press, 1976), 180, 183.

38. Smith, *Wealth of Nations*, 781–82 (emphasis added).

39. Smith, *Theory of Moral Sentiments*, 61–62.

40. Ibid., 183–85.

41. Smith, *Wealth of Nations*, 709–15.

42. The main "discoverers" or, more accurately, originators and inventors of the marginal utility theory of value were the Austrian Karl Menger (1871), the Frenchman Marie-Ésprit Léon Walras (1874–77), and the Englishman William Stanley Jevons (1871). The central claim of these economists is that value, and hence prices, were determined by utility and not labor content. Alfred Marshall attempted to combine the objective approach of Adam Smith, David Ricardo, and John Stuart Mill with this new subjective approach, mostly by looking at costs as disutility.

43. See Charles M. A. Clark, *Economic Theory and Natural Philosophy* (Aldershot, U. K.: Edward Elgar, 1992).

44. The multiple problems of the distinction between positive and normative economics are discussed in Clark, "The Challenge of Catholic Social Thought," 163–77.

45. Léon Walras, *Elements of Pure Economics* (New York: Augustus M. Kelly, 1954), 65.

46. Walter Bagehot, *Economic Studies* (London: Longman's, Green, 1880), 132.

47. J. B. Clark, *The Distribution of Wealth* (New York: Kelly & Millman, 1899), 1.

48. Lord Robbins, *The Nature and Significance of Economic Science* (London: Macmillan, 1932), 47.

49. J. B. Clark, *The Philosophy of Wealth* (Boston: Ginn & Co., 1886), 107.

50. Karl Menger, *Principles of Economics*, trans. James Dingwall and Bert F. Hoselitz (1871; reprint, New York: New York University Press, 1976), 109.

51. Ibid., 109–10.

52. Ibid., 110.

53. See James Gordley, "Virtue and the Ethics of Profit Seeking," in *Rethinking the Purpose of Business: Interdisciplinary Essays from the Catholic Social Tradition*, ed. S. A. Cortright and Michael J. Naughton (Notre Dame, Ind.: University of Notre Dame Press, 2002), 65–80.

54. Thorstein Veblen, *The Theory of the Leisure Class* (New York: Macmillan, 1899).

55. John Kenneth Galbraith, *The New Industrial State* (Boston: Houghton Mifflin, 1967).

56. John Maynard Keynes, *The General Theory of Employment, Interest, and Money* (London: Macmillan, 1936), 372.

57. John Maynard Keynes, *Essays in Persuasion* (New York: Norton, 1963), 321.

58. Ibid., 369–70.

59. Keynes, *The General Theory*, 373.

60. Keynes here is a moderate, content with the prospect of this process taking many generations. John Stuart Mill, who was much more radical, argued for a 100 percent inheritance tax.

61. Keynes, *The General Theory*, 376.

62. David J. Ravenscraft and F. M. Scherer, *Mergers, Sell-offs, and Economic Efficiency* (Washington, D.C.: Brookings Institution Press, 1987).

63. Charles M. A. Clark, "Does a Rising Tide Lift All Boats? How Poverty Has Become Immune to Economic Growth," *Vincentian Chair of Social Justice* 5 (1999): 43–53.

64. James M. Poterba, "Stock Market Wealth and Consumption," *Journal of Economic Perspectives* 14, no. 2 (Spring 2000): 99–118.

65. U.S. Department of the Census, *Statistical Abstract of the United States of America* (Washington: GPO, 2001).

66. Mt 6:24.

67. That this "revolt of the haves against the have-nots" coincides with both the legalization of killing unborn babies and convicted prisoners—what John Paul II calls the "culture of death"—shows that this is not just an economic trend but permeates all aspects of our society and culture.

68. Plato, "Laws," in *The Collected Dialogues of Plato*, ed. Edith Hamilton and Huntington Cairns (Princeton: Princeton University Press, 1987), 9:870a–b.

TWO

Wealth Creation within the Catholic Social Tradition

ROBERT G. KENNEDY

One of the distinctive characteristics of Christianity is its emphasis on community. This is especially true of Catholicism. First-century Christians considered themselves members of a community defined by faith, not by physical relationship, citizenship, language, or geography. As we know well, this conception of community modified and expanded upon the Jewish notion of a people of God formed by a covenant. Members of the Christian community become part of the people of God and heirs to a new covenant not by birth, but by faith and baptism.

In contrast with Christians of some other denominations, Catholics believe that a person is saved not only by cultivating a unique personal relationship with Jesus but also by becoming a member of this faith community. Each person is, after all, a social creature, destined by nature to live and find fulfillment in a community, and each person is shaped and formed by the communities in which he lives. It should come as no surprise, then, that Catholics have always had a keen interest in the character of communities and societies.

This tradition is rooted in scriptural categories and conceptions. In its broadest conception, it comprises two elements, one critical and one constructive. The first is a criticism of the shortcomings of the social arrangements in which Christians find themselves. Since justice is the fundamental language of human relationships, this criticism often focuses on the justice of structures and practices. But criticism is not enough. The second element is an exploration of ways in which societies might be better structured and more just policies and practices adopted.

As even the earliest Christians reflected on the world in which they lived, a world they were called to evangelize, their thoughts turned quite naturally to what we today would call political and economic issues. The Catholic social tradition germinated in the fertile soil of these reflections. It took shape in a variety of pastoral contexts over two millennia, and it continues to develop. Like a sturdy tree, it grows and spreads its branches in new directions while at the same time sending its roots more deeply into the soil from which it emerged.

Over the last two centuries, parts of the world have experienced an unprecedented growth in wealth and material well-being. Although the majority of the world's population has not yet participated in this growth, the realization of the age-old dream of abundance has posed new questions for the Catholic social tradition that go beyond former questions of the just distribution of resources. This essay attempts to take up three questions related to this new situation.

The first question has to do with the very nature of wealth. What is it that the Catholic tradition understands wealth to be? Does wealth consist of material resources, such as money, land, food, and chattel of all sorts? Is wealth an *excess* of such things, or could it be the possession of them in abundance? The second question asks whether wealth, however it is defined, can be the legitimate object of deliberate pursuit. In other words, does the tradition firmly discourage Catholics from intentionally pursuing wealth, is it neutral toward such a pursuit, or does it encourage Catholics to become wealthy if they can?

The third question concerns the quantity of wealth. As philosophers have long observed, we live in a finite world; no actual infinity can exist. Consequently, it is reasonable to suppose that the sum total of the world's wealth, on the assumption that it is something that can be quantified, must be finite. We can, however, still ask whether the quantity of wealth that we possess at any given time is bounded or potentially boundless. For example, the amount of gold in the world is actually bounded. We may not have discovered or extracted every ounce that exists on the planet, but unless future alchemists are successful, there will never be any more gold than there is now. On the other hand, some things can be created, so to speak, and therefore there is no actual boundary to the quantity that might exist over time. For instance, we can grow more wheat than exists now. In theory we could even turn every arable plot of land on the planet to the task of growing wheat and therefore hugely increase the amount we have available; and if this season's crop is not enough, we can grow more next year. A more abstract example might be the writing of poetry. Since it is composed by individual minds, and there is a finite number of individuals, the amount of poetry must also be finite. Nevertheless, there is no actual limit to the number of lines of poetry that could exist. As long as the human mind survives, another line can be written. An important question for us is whether wealth as it is conceived and discussed in the Catholic tradition is finite and bounded, like the quantity of gold, or finite but potentially boundless, like the harvests of wheat or the lines of poetry. In order to approach an answer to these questions we will look briefly at some key sources and representatives of the tradition—scriptural, patristic, medieval and early modern—and conclude with some comments about modern papal contributions.

The Old Testament on Wealth

The starting point for the Catholic social tradition is not, in fact, *Rerum novarum*, or even the New Testament, but the experience of Israel. In the Old Testament, wealth is not conceived abstractly (as perhaps a philosopher or economist might think of it). The Old Testament authors speak rather about the "rich man," or the fruitfulness of the land, or the prosperity of a people. Wealth is understood generally to be an abundance of the material things appropriate to human life. Absolutely considered, wealth is a good thing, but in a particular context or in the hands of the wicked it can be corrupting and the cause of great evil. Four key points should be emphasized.

1. *The Garden of Eden is a place of abundance:* The story of the Garden is crucial for an understanding of wealth in the Old Testament. Immediately upon creating the first man, God creates a garden, in which "various trees [grew] that were delightful to look at and good for food."[1] The ancient Greek translation of Genesis calls the garden a "paradise," and generally it was conceived as the paradigm of earthly abundance and well-being.[2] While the man was assigned to "cultivate and care for" the garden, it was a place intended by God to be pleasant and delightful.[3] Like the rest of God's creation, the garden was good, as was the abundance it provided for its inhabitants. Conceptually, the garden represents the human condition as God intended it to be—a condition of peace, abundance, and friendship with the Creator. As John Haughey argues from New Testament sources (chapter 3, this volume), wealth, understood simply as abundance (and not hoarded excess), can never be *malum in se* (evil in itself) because it is part of God's plan for creation.[4]

2. *The Covenant seeks to restore God's friendship with, and the abundance that He intended for, humanity:* The Covenant offered to and continued with the people of Israel through Moses has at its heart the promise of Yahweh to lead His people to a land of abundance, the "land flowing with milk and honey."[5] This blessing is gratuitous; the people of Israel have done nothing to deserve it, nor is Yahweh in any way obligated prior to the Covenant to provide this blessing. The structure of Genesis and Exodus, from the Fall through the call of Abraham to the Covenant on Sinai, indicates clearly that Yahweh is acting to restore humanity's relationship to Him. Part of this project entails restoring Israel to a position of prosperity, that is, restoring to the people the condition of abundance enjoyed in the garden.

The restoration, however, cannot be complete because the human condition has forever been changed by the Fall. Men and women will never again enjoy the harmony with nature and the easy abundance that was once theirs.[6] Nevertheless, they can enjoy some approximation to it. For our purposes, the important point is that wealth (understood here as an abundance of the things required for a physically comfortable life) is held to be a good thing. The most obvious manifestation of divine favor is wealth, and one of the more obvious manifestations of divine power is that Yahweh is able to guarantee that wealth for His chosen people.

There are conditions, however, attached to the ongoing possession of this wealth. The principal condition, under which a variety of others are subsumed, is fidelity to the Covenant.[7] This fidelity entails worship as well as upright personal and social conduct.[8] As long as Israel remains faithful, the people possess the land, even against overwhelmingly powerful opponents. When Israel fails in fidelity, despite fidelity's rewards, Yahweh eventually withdraws His support and protection.[9] On such occasions, Israel is exposed to the harshness of the world and lapses into poverty, famine, and slavery.[10] The message is unmistakable: fidelity to the Covenant results in prosperity; infidelity results in the withdrawal of Yahweh's favor and inevitable disaster. Neither poverty nor any other form of material scarcity is counted as a good in the Old Testament. Prosperity, however, is a good, but only relatively so.

3. *Pursuing wealth for the sake of security is a form of infidelity:* The God portrayed in the Old Testament is a jealous God.[11] He attempts to teach the people of Israel again and again that their only security, both as individuals and as a nation, is fidelity to the Covenant. He alone is capable of ensuring their prosperity and happiness. Yet time and again they turn away and seek security in something else. Often enough, they find a sort of false security in their prosperity, forget Yahweh, and turn to the worship of other gods.[12] Their wealth in such cases, and there were many, corrupts them.[13] Many who are thus corrupted turn to idolatry so as to be more like their pagan neighbors and trading partners. Others powerful in their lust for even greater wealth oppress and abuse the weak.[14] Wealth, then, is a mixed blessing. For those who remain faithful to the Covenant, it brings life and joy.[15] For those not grounded in fidelity, it is likely to corrupt and to kill, and so we see in the later Wisdom literature a certain anxiety or apprehension about the possession of wealth.[16] In such cases, wealth is not merely abundance but also an excess of material goods.[17]

4. *Diligence and industry bring prosperity to the just:* It is worth noting that, while there are certainly passages that emphasize the generosity of Yahweh to those who are faithful, there is also a recurrent theme suggesting that He does not simply give wealth or abundance to His people.[18] It would be better to say that in the Old Testament, Yahweh makes the work of His people fruitful. He assures them that the labor of the just will not be in vain.[19]

A common theme employed in Proverbs is that diligence leads to prosperity.[20] A contrast is evident, though, between the prosperity enjoyed by the honest man who works hard to cultivate his fields, tend his flocks, or manage his business, and the rich man who frets constantly about his wealth and preys upon the poor to increase it.[21] A further contrast is drawn throughout the Wisdom literature between the wise man, who fears the Lord and obeys His Commandments (that is, the just man), and the fool, who denies the reality of God and disdains wisdom.[22] The result is that the just and diligent man is the mean between two wicked extremes. The fool rejects God, loses control of himself, ridicules study and hard work, wastes his time and energy in frivolity, and ends in poverty and disaster. The rich man, unless he is very careful, becomes perverted by his wealth. He replaces the worship of God with the worship of gold, becomes inured to whatever injustice is required for him to increase the number of his possessions, worries constantly about the loss of his property, and also ends in disaster. Only the just man can find contentment, for he alone is wise enough to realize the dangers of the extremes.

The concept of wealth in the Old Testament is a complicated one, and it undergoes some development from the earlier, historical books, through the prophets, to the Wisdom literature. In the historical books the wealth of the patriarchs and the kings is presented as a sign of divine favor and reward. Their fidelity, and the fidelity of the nation, is tested, found solid and strong, and rewarded with abundance and stable prosperity. The prophets still see Yahweh as the ultimate source of wealth, but they call attention with great bitterness to the abuses of the strong, who accumulate the abundance of the nation in their hands. Rather than lead their people to general prosperity, they create poverty and misery in the midst of Yahweh's abundance. The luxury they enjoy is an affront to Yahweh's justice, an affront that will certainly be remedied in time. In contrast, the Wisdom literature focuses less on the condition of the nation and more on the situation of individuals. The oscillation of Israel between fidelity and infidelity is played out in microcosm between the just and faithful man and his rich but wicked neighbor.

As to the creation of wealth—distinct from its possession or consumption—it seems clear that the Old Testament commends those whose labor is fruitful. The earth and the Garden of Eden are given to human persons "to cultivate and care for it," and the land promised in the Covenant will bear fruit under Israel's care.[23] The wealth of the nation is rooted in the labor required to make the land fruitful, a labor shaped and protected by Yahweh's fidelity to the Covenant. Later the just man is celebrated, not because he has redistributed wealth but because his work is fair and fruitful. In contemporary terms, we might say that he creates value and profits fairly from it. The rich man, by contrast, is consistently portrayed as one who transfers wealth unjustly from others (for example, by means of unfair prices or wages), not as one who creates wealth by his own labor.

THE NEW TESTAMENT ON WEALTH

The concept of wealth is addressed less comprehensively in the New Testament and is placed within the context of the general concern for the supernatural end of human persons. The themes present in the Old Testament are not repudiated, but they are given a different emphasis. The land promised in the Covenant becomes the kingdom of heaven, but this kingdom is not the foundation of material wealth and abundance (as was the land in the Old Testament). It is itself the (immaterial) wealth we long to possess. The natural and legitimate concern for material welfare that runs throughout the Old Testament is largely set aside in the New Testament in favor of an intense focus on the orientation and behaviors that suit the Christian for the kingdom. Yet consideration is still paid to issues surrounding wealth, and four themes deserve our attention.

1. *Christians must seek their security above all in God's providential care:* The central text in an analysis of the morality of the New Testament is certainly the Sermon on the Mount.[24] A key element of the Sermon is an exhortation to Christians not to be distracted by concerns for material security. We are advised not to "lay up . . . an earthly treasure" but instead to concentrate on a "heavenly treasure."[25] "No man," Jesus says, "can serve two masters. . . . You cannot give yourself to God and money [*mamona*]."[26] Immediately following these comments, He addresses at some length the anxiety that must have been in the minds of His listeners by telling them not to worry about their livelihoods.[27] Christ says that we must seek first the kingship of the Father over us and never turn aside because of anxiety over our day-to-day problems. The same theme is addressed in the Parable of the Rich Farmer,[28] where the folly of the rich man who sought security in his wealth is exposed. This parable is followed by the Lucan parallel to the Sermon that exhorts the listeners to trust in Providence.[29] This note is sounded once again in the story of Lazarus and the Rich Man.[30]

2. *Christians must not permit possessions to become a distraction:* The anxiety about wealth that is evident in parts of the Old Testament is even more strongly emphasized in the New Testament. Jesus offers something more valuable than all the wealth in the world, something a person would be a fool to exchange for that wealth.[31] Each of the first three Gospels tells the story of the rich man who is told to sell all his possessions.[32] His distress at this command prompts Jesus to say that "only with difficulty will a rich man enter into the kingdom of heaven."[33] Even more emphatically, Jesus tells a crowd that they cannot be His disciples unless they set aside all of their possessions.[34] We see in Acts that the early Christian community followed this advice and for a time held their property in common.[35] St. Paul even boasts of his poverty.[36] Jesus' admonitions, and early Christian example, are sometimes interpreted to mean that Christians ought not to own property, but this interpretation ultimately conflicts with other elements of New Testament teaching.

On reflection, wariness against property ownership may seem to be a curious doctrine for the New Testament to teach. Most scholars believe that first-century Christians were overwhelmingly drawn from the poorer classes of society. That those with almost nothing are exhorted to avoid an attachment to possessions may seem ironic, to say the least, until we reflect further that riches can possess the heart by their absence as well as by their presence. Dissension and hostility, writes St. James, are rooted "in the desires fighting within you . . . [Y]ou want something, and you haven't got it."[37] There is, then, some reason to think that the message of these passages is not that Christians should not own property, but that they must not be preoccupied with it;[38] that is, Christians must be prepared to abandon anything that serves to distract them, as individuals, from their wholehearted devotion to the kingdom.[39]

3. *Wealth and property must be used well:* The word "talent," originally a Greek word naming a unit of weight and later a valuable coin, entered the English language through the Parable of the Talents.[40] Christians interpreted the parable as referring primarily to a person's raw abilities, but it is at root a story about the wise use of money. The parable does not criticize the master for his possession of wealth, nor does it condemn the servants for failing to use the money to help the poor. Instead, it commends those who make fruitful use of the resources at their disposal. The following chapter in Matthew describes the anointing at Bethany and Jesus' insistence that the expensive perfume was well used, even though its value might have helped the poor.[41] Other passages discourage a sort of false asceticism that would demand extraordinary sacrifices.[42] From passages such as these we may legitimately conclude that the goods of the earth may be properly owned and enjoyed by followers of Christ, provided that such ownership and use is consistent with pursuit of the kingdom. "Everything God created is good," and everything is available for human use—if received in the proper spirit and used for good ends.[43]

St. Paul's discussion of the Gifts of the Spirit echoes the Parable of the Talents.[44] The Spirit distributes gifts to individuals according to His will and for the common good. These gifts are not the private possessions of certain individuals, who may use them for their own aggrandizement. They are well used only when they are put to work creating benefits for the community. By extension, we may understand the possessions of an individual to be legitimately owned when they are used for the purposes intended by God; that is, to promote that individual's genuine vocation. Wealth can be one of these gifts, and there is no reason to believe that the authors of the New Testament thought that creating prosperity in the community would be a bad thing. On the contrary, we have reason to believe that the creation of value and prosperity was good for the community and to be commended among Christians, as long as it was properly used (to which end proper use might include relieving the suffering of the poor).[45]

4. *Christians ought to earn their living:* St. Paul is proud to remind the Thessalonians that, while among them, he worked to earn a living rather than depend upon their meager resources for his livelihood.[46] He further advises them to tend to their own affairs and to do their own work.[47] This diligence is to make them a good example for others and to encourage their independence. In his second letter to this community, Paul strongly criticizes members of the community who lazily depended upon the work of others for their sustenance. He reminds them that he had always worked while among them and that "anyone who would not work should not eat."[48]

The teaching of the New Testament authors on wealth and its creation may seem to be inconsistent. On the one hand, Christians are encouraged to avoid wealth and property, and on the other they are encouraged to enjoy every good thing in creation and to work for their living. These conflicts, however, are more superficial than real. In the Old Testament, the ideal of a good human life is essentially one of material prosperity lived by a person of justice and wisdom. This is, in fact, quite similar to the sort of ideal commended by such pagan thinkers as Plato and Aristotle. In the New Testament, this life of natural happiness is superseded by an ideal of supernatural happiness, which Jesus calls time and again the kingdom of heaven or the kingdom of God. Achievement of this happiness so far exceeds natural happiness in value that any reasonable person should be quite willing to sacrifice every aspect of natural happiness (that is, health, honor, prosperity, etc.) for its sake. But such sacrifices are not always required, even though the Christian must be ready to make them. Where they are not required, and where the enjoyment of natural goods does not distract the individual from the pursuit of his supernatural destiny, the creation, possession, and enjoyment of natural goods is legitimate.

Indeed, it is noble to use one's property to relieve the burden of poverty borne by other Christians.[49] The obligation to do so, however, does not entail the duty to impoverish oneself.[50] By a modest extension, we can also conclude that Christians ought to use their Spirit-given gifts to manage material goods well and even to create and accumulate such goods and to justly distribute them. What the New Testament does not commend, and emphatically so, is the pursuit and accumulation of property as an end in itself. The Scriptures are forceful in saying that this is a deadly ambition that must be aggressively resisted. The occasional rhetorical emphases employed to drive this point home should, however, not be misunderstood as an exhortation to poverty for its own sake. St. Paul's dictum on the necessity of work for everyone suggests that there is a right "use" of poverty as well as of riches. These themes will be further developed by patristic authors struggling with the social realities of the ancient world.

PATRISTIC THINKING ON WEALTH

The thought of the Church on many social matters has matured and changed over the centuries. There are, however, three convictions about wealth and its creation that were held by many prominent leaders of the early Church and are still commonly held today. The extant patristic literature is enormous and spans several centuries as well as a variety of political, cultural, and economic settings. Virtually all of it arose as a pastoral response to contemporary needs and problems, as opposed to systematic academic reflection. As a consequence one often searches in vain for a discussion of fundamental principles, so apparent conflicts about basic issues seem frequent. Still, there are three broad common themes that can be described.

1. *All good things are gifts from God:* At the foundation of the common Christian view of economic matters was, and is, the conviction that all good things—all talents and all possessions—are gifts from God.[51] Several ideas follow from this conviction. One is the proposition that individuals are not truly the owners of their possessions in the fullest sense. Only God Himself is an owner in the sense that He alone may dispose of property as He wishes. Human persons are owners only in the sense that they may possess property, but they possess it contingently and temporarily. They have a duty to dispose of it not as they wish personally, but as God wishes.

Related to this conviction is the idea that gifts demand a response from the recipient. The concept underlying the practice of idolatry is that service and gifts rendered to the idol, the physical representation of a god, create a duty on the god's part to serve the worshipper. Judaeo-Christian theology opposes and abolishes this practice because it insists that there is nothing that human persons can do that would genuinely constitute the sort of service to God that would obligate Him to respond. Instead, God's free gift of creation to humankind calls for men and women to respond by disposing of these gifts according to His will.

This brings us to a final point. Since God loves and desires the salvation of all men, and since the goods that He has given to mankind are unevenly distributed, it follows that His will is that His gifts should be shared by individuals so that no one lacks the basic material requirements for a decent human life.[52] As a consequence, anyone who possesses goods in abundance while his neighbors suffer for lack of these goods is objectively sinful. The great economic disparity of the ancient world, where the wealthy often enjoyed staggering luxuries at the expense of the poor, was a scandal. Early Christian bishops frequently exhorted their congregations in the strongest terms to remedy that situation by sharing what they had.[53]

These views were in conflict with the very roots of Roman private law, which provided strong protections for property rights, not limited by the needs of others. However, even Christian thinking was (and is) ambivalent about the extent to which a person ought to share his property with others. Paul's famous rule that "anyone who would not work should not eat"[54] suggests that, just as ownership has limits, so also do claims upon ownership. On balance, the Fathers did not deny the legitimacy of private ownership, but they did insist upon significant limitations of that right.

2. *The pursuit of wealth may be a danger to salvation:* The parables about the dangers and distractions of wealth were a fertile source for preaching on economic matters.[55] A second fundamental conviction among Christians has long been that those who pursue wealth endanger their salvation, so that those who find themselves in possession of wealth (perhaps those among the wealthy who became Christians) must distance themselves from it by prudently using it to relieve the needs of others. The wealthy man should rejoice in his possessions, to paraphrase Clement of Alexandria, because he ought to realize that what he owns he owns for the sake of his brothers in need.[56] Clement contrasts the rich man who is not enslaved to his wealth, but is able to use it well according to God's will, with the man who is so focused upon wealth that he cannot think of salvation.

Clement also realized that material possessions are necessary for a decent human life. As God has created them, goods are indeed good, provided that we recognize their place. Common ownership of all property, he thought, was not likely to liberate people from concern about the material dimension of life but rather to make them unnecessarily anxious and focused upon physical security. Furthermore, only when one possesses goods can one share, and this sharing is itself an important and worthwhile aspect of Christian life. Consequently, we might expand upon Clement's teaching and say that a Christian may fulfill his vocation by acquiring material goods and making them available to others. He falls short either by refusing to share what he has acquired or by neglecting to acquire what is needed. While Clement does not specifically address this issue, we might note that making goods available (whether by farming, craft, or trade) for sale at a fair price is consistent with his notion of the role of property. That is to say, the goods of the earth do not exist so that they may merely be given away by those who labor to acquire them, but neither do they exist solely for the benefit of those who come into possession of them, even as the result of hard work.

Moreover, the accumulation of wealth can be an obstacle to salvation for another reason. As Jesus reminds us in Luke, wealth can create in us a false sense of security, such that we forget about God and place our faith in our possessions.[57] The danger of this focus on the illusory power of wealth did not escape the Fathers.[58] Nor did they overlook another danger inherent in the aggressive pursuit of wealth, the temptation to injustice. In commenting on the Parable of Lazarus and the Rich Man, John Chrysostom insisted that the possession of great wealth was not only founded upon robbery but also consisted in robbery if the wealthy did not share their abundance with the poor.[59] His position was that, since the goods of the earth were given to humankind as a common possession, any significant inequality in actual possessions must be the result of a sort of theft. At the foundation of this view, however, is the belief that the goods of the earth were at one time possessed by all in common. Any inequality, then, must be the result of deliberate efforts to gain an unfair portion of these common goods. This theme is also found in Ambrose, who recommends that the wealthy return whatever abundance they have to the needy as the repayment of a debt, not as an act of charity.[60] Similar convictions may be found in other patristic writings.

The early Christians, of course, were not the last ones to think that wealth is usually the result of deceit, treachery, and theft. No doubt it was often true in the ancient world, just as it may be true in the modern world. Nevertheless, the confidence with which this view was asserted by many (though not all) of the Fathers suggests a limited conception of economics. They appear to have conceived of the goods of the earth as limited in quantity. While it is certainly true that there is a finite supply of some goods (say, gold or silver), it is not the case that all goods are similarly limited. The Fathers' attitude may well reflect their preoccupation with the question of arable land. Given the political economy and technology of late antiquity, land was a strictly limited good; its concentration in estates led to severe conflicts between the immediate interests of owners and the needs of whole communities. Still, the Fathers' views seem suited to a subsistence economy, or one in which the self-sufficiency (autarky) of an individual, a family or a community is the goal of economic activity. They did not, it appears, give adequate attention to the real human importance of trade or to the possibility that human effort could create wealth and not merely transfer it from one hand to another.

The Fathers were right to insist on limitations to property rights for the sake of human need. They were, however, mistaken in assuming that the distribution of wealth is like a zero-sum game, where an increase in benefits to one party can only come at the expense of another party. To the extent that they did so, they were also mistaken in assuming that communities ought to be self-sufficient. In fact, since the goods of the earth are unevenly distributed throughout the world, it is in keeping with the Christian celebration of sharing that extensive trading be developed between communities.

3. *Human work ought to serve the common good:* A third conviction, firmly grounded in the Letters of St. Paul, but less explicitly developed than the first two, is the idea that human talents and human work ought to serve the common good.[61] It is a strongly held Christian conviction that human beings are essentially social and that the fullness of life cannot be had outside of a community. Each community has a common good. In modern terms, the most general definition of this common good

is a set of conditions that enables each person within the community to flourish, to live the best life possible. Since whatever gifts given to a person, whether talents or resources, are given by God for the sake of the individual *and* others, it follows that the employment of those gifts must support the common good; that is, one is not faithful to the generosity of God unless one uses His gifts in the service of others.

In contrast, business is often understood as being conducted in pursuit of a private good, certainly benefiting the merchant but not necessarily promoting the common good. Indeed, at times the merchant serves his private good in ways that undermine some aspect or aspects of the common good. This conflict has created a tension in Christian thinking from at least the time of Clement of Alexandria, and it shows no signs of disappearing. The resolution of this tension depends upon a common recognition of the ways in which the talents and energies of the businessperson genuinely and directly benefit the community, and upon the conformity of business practices to this goal.

Christian thinkers have been suspicious of commerce and merchants from the early days of the Church. Their suspicion has been rooted in the conflict that they have perceived, rightly or wrongly, between the ordinary and necessary practices of business and several fundamental Christian convictions about life in society. They have questioned the social utility of trade for money, though they can appreciate that this sometimes results in the availability of useful products from distant cities. They have been deeply concerned about the distractions and injustices associated with business, and further distressed at the way that commerce regularly emphasizes the individual over and against the community as a whole. Nevertheless, without abandoning the essence of these principles, the Church has come to modify the harsh judgments that they initially implied. This modification has been the result of a number of historical processes, which have resulted in a much more mature vision of what business is and what it could be if it were to realize its full potential.

MEDIEVAL AND EARLY MODERN VIEWS ON WEALTH AND WEALTH CREATION

The reign of Charlemagne was a sort of high point for the early Middle Ages. Schools were established, a code of laws combining elements of Roman law and Frankish law was systematized, much of mainland Europe was pacified, and new technologies were introduced, including agricultural technologies, which would significantly increase production. However, after his death in 814, dynastic conflicts destabilized much of Europe for generations. Although an empire in name, Europe was not united politically. This political disunity stood in contrast to a heightened degree of cultural unity, stimulated in large measure by the activities of the Church. Latin, though no longer the language of most people, was still the language of the educated classes and permitted them to move rather freely. The growing regularization of liturgy and preaching encouraged by Charlemagne contributed to this cultural unity.

The Church, of course, also provided a degree of governance through its geographic divisions into archdioceses and dioceses, and in so doing it gained a new appreciation for the importance of material resources and the activities of wealth creation and management. Increasingly during this period, the Church stimulated and organized economic activities. Monastic communities also provided a measure of organization and stability, eventually providing leadership in commercial affairs for some regions and even acting as bankers.[62] There is also some record of "merchant churches" in more remote areas that apparently ministered to traveling merchants and often also served as warehouses for trade goods.[63] Not least in importance, though, was the growing need in the Church, on both the local and papal levels, for cash revenues. Where once the activities of the bishop of Rome might have been funded by local donations, the growing international responsibilities of the pope required a larger income. This income was supplied by a growing variety of taxes on dioceses, monasteries, and other institutions as well as on persons.[64] Similarly, bishops came steadily to depend upon income (first in goods and later in cash) generated as rents from property in their dioceses and from taxes upon parishes.

During these early centuries, as the Church came to rely more and more upon revenues from agricultural operations (its own and others), a number of towns began to grow as centers of trade. At first they probably served the local rural populations (much like the small towns of the American Midwest over the past century or so), with goods produced locally or transported over relatively short distances. Soon, however, trade goods from exotic places became available, and by the tenth century, regularly scheduled fairs for merchants were important in Germany and France. Travel, though never entirely safe, became more ordinary, stimulated in part by the imposition of pilgrimages to holy sites as penitential practices. Recognizing the value of this increased trade and travel, the Church made formal provisions to protect merchants and pilgrims.[65]

The increase in travel had the effect of encouraging trade, but not nearly so dramatically as did the Crusades. However unsuccessful they were in securing the Holy Land for Christendom, they did enormously and irrevocably expand opportunities for trade.[66] As an unintended side effect, the Crusaders reestablished contacts with Byzantium and opened the way for wider contact with Islam. Europe's horizons were so expanded by the experience—intellectually, scientifically, commercially, and otherwise—that self-sufficiency was never broadly desired again.

It is probably not a mere coincidence that the twelfth century, the century of the Crusades, was also one of revolutionary commercial activity.[67] Commerce became, especially throughout Italy, the key to a new prosperity in Europe and to the growth of major cities. At this same time, as canon law coalesced into a systematic form, legal scholars devoted considerable attention to recovering the Roman law of sale and contract for a Christian context.[68] We can also see that theologians in the twelfth and thirteenth centuries took a rising, though still modest, interest in business activities.[69] St. Thomas Aquinas is exemplary. In his best-known work, the *Summa theologiae*, he briefly discussed the ethics of trade and argued that it is indeed legitimate for merchants to make a profit by selling their wares for more than they paid.[70] (Subsequent theologians pursued this point and recognized a variety of justifications for the profitability of commerce beyond the mere labor of the merchant.) In contrast with Leo I, Aquinas insisted that merchants can conduct their business honestly and that they can provide a genuine service to the community if they do their work well.[71] Still, he had reservations about the genuine value of commerce. He regarded it as necessary to repair defects in community rather than as a primary means to improve life and create wealth.[72]

Aquinas's lifetime (1224–1274) represents a period of great change for Europe. The seeds planted in the twelfth century came to full blossom in the thirteenth. Cathedrals were built, the first universities were founded, cities grew enormously in population and importance, and in every way Christendom matured into a vibrant civilization. But it was also a civilization that could not be sustained simply by agriculture and crafts. Commerce was critically necessary not only to supply goods lacking in certain areas but also to produce the wealth that a mature civilization requires. This point was not lost on the institutional Church, whose increased activities were made possible to a significant degree by the wealth-creating work of the merchants.

Furthermore, the economic presuppositions that were held in late antiquity and even in the Dark Ages were no longer true by the late Middle Ages. The importance of land as the economic foundation of society was diminishing and commerce was taking its place. Self-sufficiency was no longer regarded as a goal for a community, but production for trade was. Furthermore, the Church had become a major institution in the new society and could never again be content to encourage change from the margins. By the fifteenth century, prominent theologians such as St. Antonino, archbishop of Florence (1389–1459), and St. Bernardino of Siena (1380–1444), convinced that commerce could be a redeemed and noble vocation, explored in detail how the Christian businessman ought to conduct his affairs.[73] There is no small irony in the fact that the modern discipline of economics has its origins in the investigations of late medieval theologians.[74]

In responding to the challenges of the Middle Ages, the Church was magnificently successful, but, as is so often the case, the very success of an organization provides a seedbed for its eventual failure. For a variety of reasons, not least its own mishandling of wealth and revenue, the Church of the late Middle Ages provoked the Reformation. The spectacular economic progress of the next centuries has deep roots in medieval Europe and in some ways is merely a successful extension of the foundations laid down in the thirteenth and fourteenth centuries. However, the splintering and eventual collapse of Christendom greatly diminished the influence that the Church would have had on the development of business during this time.

Some twenty-five years after Columbus came ashore in the Caribbean, Martin Luther issued his formal challenge to the Church. These two events are illustrations of the two great challenges facing the Church in the period following the Middle Ages. The external challenge was to evangelize a brand-new world, which included both the newly discovered Americas and Asia, which, though known to medieval travelers and scholars, was largely inaccessible before sea travel. The internal challenge was to preserve the integrity of Christendom. Sadly, in contrast with its success in the Middle Ages, in this period the Church failed dramatically. The Reformation permanently divided Christianity in the West and destroyed it as a Christian society. Furthermore, the close association of missionary activity with colonialism severely limited the success of evangelism, especially in North America, Africa, and Asia.

Despite its diminished influence in society, however, the Church did develop another role. Both the Protestant Reformation and the discovery of the New World provoked Catholic bishops and theologians to reflect deeply on the character of the world of the time. In response, the bishops instituted far-reaching reforms, while the theologians developed an extensive body of analysis and doctrine in moral theology, much of it concerning the practice of business and political economy.

The starting point for the theologians' analysis was probably pastoral. As trade became a larger part of life, bishops and pastors were more frequently confronting issues in the confessional and in public life involving moral questions about business affairs.[75] The theologians, especially the Spanish scholastics of the sixteenth and seventeenth centuries, framed elaborate and insightful responses. In doing so, they sincerely assumed that Christian businessmen genuinely wished to be guided by their analysis (just as, perhaps, Catholic physicians looked to theologians for moral guidance earlier in the twentieth century).

They recognized that the world of commerce was not exclusively a Catholic, or even a Christian, one, and so they situated their discussions in the context of treatises on justice. By and large, then, the requirements of morality for business were understood to be the requirements of the virtue of justice and not the principles of the Gospel (though these requirements were hardly in conflict with the Gospel). These theologians also acknowledged the legitimacy of commerce and its vital role in providing goods for the community and in increasing the nation's wealth. The honest merchant, in their view, carried on God's work by distributing fairly the resources that the Creator had scattered unevenly about the earth. Commerce, as a result, was an instrument of justice and a vehicle for promoting the fellowship of the human race.

Moreover, they built upon, and considerably expanded, medieval discussions of profit by recognizing the value of the contributions of merchants and businessmen in making goods and services available even if they do not alter what they sell. Their careful and detailed analysis of the legitimate grounds for profits would be quite familiar to a modern economist. However, in contrast with modern economic theory, they also reaffirmed the traditional opposition to seeking profit for its own sake. Their justification of profit always, in one way or another, depended upon showing that it was fair compensation. They made no attempt to justify the activity of the merchant who sought gain without limit, nor could they do so within the framework of Christian theology.

Until the eighteenth century, business and trade, and the businessman and the merchant, were virtually synonymous. The latter half of the eighteenth century saw the development of a new form of business, namely, large-scale manufacturing. As this and other forms of industrialization developed in the nineteenth century, they posed yet another challenge to moral theology. In a sense, though, the issues were similar to the ones addressed so forcefully by Ambrose and Chrysostom many centuries earlier. The emergence of large-scale enterprises, whether in manufacturing, transportation, communications, retailing, or any other field, concentrated the control (if not the actual ownership) of productive resources in the hands of a small number of businessmen. These men not only possessed great wealth, but they also controlled jobs, goods, and services for many other people. Like the wealthy of the ancient world, these men, in the view of moral theologians, had serious responsibilities not only toward the poor, but also toward all those who depended upon them (for example, employees and customers). The inadequate discharge of these responsibilities may be said to have provoked socialism as a political force as well as the emergence of Christian social thought as a distinct body of doctrine. The development and augmentation of this body of doctrine have been a major occupation of the magisterium in the twentieth century.[76]

Modern Papal Views on Wealth and Wealth Creation

There are, no doubt, many factors that account for the attention given by the modern papacy to the economic problems of the contemporary world, but not least among these is the emergence of dramatic new forms of economic organization, with their unparalleled potential to create new wealth. Most of the popes from Leo XIII to John Paul II have taken a serious interest in the challenges to, and opportunities for, human welfare presented by modern economies, though none has focused systematically on the question of the legitimacy and duty of wealth creation (see Francis Hannafey's essay, chapter 4, this volume, for more details on the papacy and wealth). They have, however, developed other concepts at length that permit us to extract a contemporary posture on the question. Three such concepts are critical: the nature and purpose of human work, the role and legitimacy of private property, and the nature of true human development.

1. *The nature and purpose of human work:* As Leo XIII states bluntly near the beginning of *Rerum novarum,* "when a man engages in remunerative labor, the very reason and motive of his work is to obtain property, and to hold it as his private possession."[77] This urge to possess property is both a natural inclination and a natural right, which the popes consistently and emphatically defend.[78] But work is more than simply a means to acquire property. Work is as natural to humankind as breathing and is an integral element of human dignity. As an image of the Creator, the human person collaborates with Him in developing the created order through his work.[79] To deny someone meaningful work is not only to deny him the means of providing for his own livelihood and that of his family, but it is also to prevent him from fully realizing his humanity.

Though it is rarely discussed explicitly, there is an idea of progress inherent in the popes' discussions of work (and later, of development). This idea is relatively new; it is not evident in patristic or medieval discussions about wealth and property. The idea is that progress can be made through human labor to increase the general level of prosperity in the community and to unfold the rich resources for addressing human needs that are embedded in the created order. Human work, then, is not merely directed to manipulating static and finite resources, but rather to expanding the potential of the material world to sustain human life more fully by "wrest[ing] nature's secrets from her and find[ing] a better application for her riches."[80] Where human work was once thought to be largely a matter of "harvesting" resources from the earth, by the twentieth century the popes clearly see (as others had seen before them) that human intelligence, when properly applied, can greatly expand the possibilities for natural human fulfillment.[81] These possibilities for creating something new—possibilities both created by and constituted in technology and industrialization—bring new horizons to human work. They also create new roles and responsibilities, such as those of managers and entrepreneurs.[82] The work of these people makes a positive contribution to the common good by increasing the prosperity of the community.

2. *The role and legitimacy of private property:* As is well known, Leo XIII was a determined defender of the individual's right to possess private property, including capital resources and productive equipment, yet he was just as determined to insist that this right is not an absolute one. Instead, he taught that persons who found themselves in possession of a significant amount of property could not legitimately use or consume this property solely for their private benefit. All property (including the individual talents that enable some people to acquire more than others) is a gift from God, intended both for the benefit of the possessor and the benefit of others.[83]

Leo's successors have strongly affirmed this position, though the concerns that prompt them have sometimes varied. Leo was especially intent on articulating a counterpoint to the socialist movements that were roiling Europe at the end of the nineteenth century, while Pius XI was at pains to show that property ownership (even of the means of production) was legitimate in principle in order to oppose powerful statist systems such as Fascism and Communism. Later, John XXIII and Paul VI discussed the right to property (as well as a broad array of other human and civil rights) in the context of human development. For his part, John Paul II, while affirming Leo's expression of Catholic thinking, has been quick to add comments about the spiritual dangers of "superdevelopment" and "consumerism."[84]

Nevertheless, however legitimate private ownership may be, each of these popes has insisted that material poverty is not a condition to be admired or idealized; rather, it is a great human evil, which calls for an energetic and even sacrificial response on the part of those who possess the available resources. The popes are less clear about what the limits might be to the duty to share one's property with others, but we might take a clue from the concept of vocation.

The ancients and the medievals tended to think that a person was entitled to the income or amount of property that suited his class and position in society.[85] They were accustomed to a sharply stratified society in which persons ordinarily were born into a class and remained in that class throughout their lives. Greater possessions as a sign of one's higher class helped to engender the respect that was due. Such wealth also served as both a resource for those in higher classes (who commonly had governance and defense responsibilities toward the community) and as a personal reward. In return, they had a responsibility, or *noblesse oblige*, to attend to the needs of those less fortunate. Their persistent failure to do so ultimately led to the demise of these classes. Catholic social thought, however, has never formally repudiated the concept that there may legitimately be a disparity of income and wealth in the community, though such disparities are no longer defended on grounds of class.[86]

A more modern, and better, way to think about the just limits to ownership is to consider the vocation of the person as well as the context of the society in which he lives. Parents, for example, have a presumptive vocation and a duty to care for their children, and so they have a right to accumulate sufficient property to enable them to do so according to the reasonable standards of their society. This includes sufficient income to meet their children's basic physical needs as well as to provide for their education, their participation in the culture, and their entry into the world of work and adult responsibilities. The parents also have a right to assets sufficient to enable them to provide for their own retirement and for other reasonable contingencies.[87]

In principle, anyone may reasonably accumulate (or seek to accumulate) the resources required to live out a properly discerned vocation. The activities necessary to acquire such resources, in fact, may be part of what is required to live out one's real vocation. This could include not only financial resources but also education, experience, associations, and whatever else is legitimately needed. When all of these vocational needs are satisfied, Christians have a duty in charity (at least) to use their excess means to help relieve the unmet needs of others.[88] This responsibility extends beyond individuals to nations as well. Paul VI and John Paul II have been particularly forceful in urging wealthy nations to forgo unnecessary consumption in favor of helping the poor.[89] On a personal level, the virtue of solidarity can be understood to entail a determination to resist accumulating resources beyond what is needed to fulfill one's vocational commitments and to use any excess to meet the real needs of others, near or far.

3. *The nature of true human development:* The relationship of wealth and human development is a fundamental issue for Christians since Christian anthropology, unlike modern economics, does not see ultimate human fulfillment to be rooted in possessions and experiences. In the memorable words of the Second Vatican Council, "A man is more precious for what he is than for what he has."[90] Being is more important than having, but is having still important to a good human life, to a good Christian life? The answer is that *having* is indeed important but that its subordination to *being* must be properly understood.

The Christian understanding of human development and fulfillment, as it has been discussed in papal documents over the past forty years or so, steers a path between two extremes.[91] At one extreme is modern materialism, which sees human development as consisting in economic progress, that is, in an increase in the productive capacity and the economic assets of a community. This is the ordinary way, for example, in which we think of the difference between developed and developing countries, yet this can easily lead (and has often led) to an overemphasis on material welfare to the detriment of the spiritual and cultural dimensions of human well-being.

At the other extreme is a kind of asceticism that does not have its roots in a spiritual life. The Church's teaching about social and economic realities is not only a counterbalance to the materialism and injustices of the external, secular world, but it is also a corrective to a sort of clericalism within the Church itself. Catholic social doctrine, from the very fact of its existence as a body of thought and doctrine, affirms the importance, the relevance, and even the holiness of ordinary life.[92] One need not aspire to the priesthood or to a consecrated life in order to be an exemplary Christian. The point of the Gospel is not necessarily to draw men and women out of the home and marketplace and into the monastery, but to sanctify every aspect of human existence—even commerce—and to bring it into harmony with the Creator's plan.[93]

Genuine human development, then, can only be understood by reference to its endpoint: holiness. Development, whether personal or civil, is not merely an accumulation of resources. Nations are not authentically developed when they have become wealthy, nor are materially poor peoples necessarily underdeveloped. In the most fully human sense, development has taken place when persons have become more truly human, which is to say more saintly. In the Christian tradition, development that increases material prosperity without enhancing personal holiness is false and destructive.

God wills that all men be saved and brought to share in the abundance of His love.[94] This abundance is not only spiritual but bodily as well. The whole of Catholic social doctrine is directed toward encouraging the policies and behaviors that can ensure as complete a sharing of bodily goods among the human family as possible.[95] This is a challenge of enormous proportions. Nevertheless, however noble and important this goal is, it must still be subordinated to the salvation of souls.[96] The relationship between earthly welfare and salvation is easily misunderstood, and the Church is often criticized for either placing too much or too little emphasis on our supernatural destiny.

A particular focus of papal reflections since the early 1960s has been on this issue of the relationship between the bodily goods we rightly seek to have and to enjoy now and the complete goodness we hope to possess in the future. Papal thought on this subject might be summarized as follows: The whole of creation is good and intended by the Creator to serve the needs (as distinct from wants) of the entire human family.[97] This creation has an abundant capacity to satisfy these needs.[98] Human persons quite properly and nobly seek to care for themselves and their families by applying their labor and ingenuity to the task of making use of the created order for this purpose, in collaboration with God and His plan.[99] This activity may often go awry when men and women lose their confidence in God's Providence and keep more of the world's goods for themselves than they truly need, when they selfishly satisfy wants in the face of others' unmet needs, and when human sinfulness intrudes in countless other ways.[100] Still, those with greater gifts and greater resources, far from legitimately claiming these gifts and resources for their own consumption, have a strict duty to put their gifts to work to serve all of humankind.[101] Not least among these obligations is the duty to apply their intelligence and ingenuity to devise new ways of making use of creation, and so to expand the quantity of good things available to satisfy human needs.[102]

CONCLUSION

We may now return to the three questions with which we began this essay and propose some answers. In doing so, we need to recall that the Catholic social tradition, rooted as it is in Scripture and developed in many contexts over two millennia, is not a tradition of preserving *applications*, but rather a tradition of adapting *principles* to concrete situations. Some applications of Christian convictions, no matter how passionate and sincere, may not be appropriate to modern times and circumstances.[103] Nevertheless, there are perennial principles that must be respected.

1. *What is wealth?* The term "wealth" is probably an unfortunate one for our discussion. In contrast to both the discipline of economics and colloquial usage, the tradition tends not to treat wealth as an abstract concept.[104] Instead, there are countless references either to the wealthy as a group or to the rich man. Seen in this way, wealth is generally understood to be an excess of resources—typically money, but perhaps also land, food, and anything else of common value. Such material wealth is contrasted with spiritual wealth, and the tradition sometimes recognizes that those who possess much material wealth may be spiritually poor, and vice versa.

There is a related concept that plays a more important role in the tradition. If wealth is understood to imply excess, then "abundance" and "prosperity" suggest something slightly different. The person who possesses wealth is ordinarily portrayed as unjust and impious in the tradition. The common assumption is that his wealth is obtained and held in opposition to the needs of the poor, and perhaps directly at their expense. Abundance and prosperity, however, are more commonly seen as gifts of God and as characteristic of God's unlimited love for His creatures. The man who possesses wealth is not usually regarded as blessed, but the person or community who enjoys abundance or prosperity does so as a blessing from the Lord. Abundance and prosperity, then, are good conditions just as surely as poverty is a condition that requires a remedy.

2. *Can wealth be deliberately pursued?* The concept of wealth developed in the previous paragraphs suggests an answer to this question. If wealth is understood as an excess of material goods, then it is not a legitimate ambition for a Christian, or for anyone else, for that matter. Even Plato and Aristotle discouraged its pursuit as a life's ambition on the grounds that wealth is merely a tool, not an end. To pursue

the possession of a tool without regard for its purpose is foolish and futile. On the other hand, some of the reasons for seeking wealth are themselves empty. One might seek wealth for the sake of security, for protection against the vagaries of life. For the Christian, as observed before, this comes too quickly to replace confidence in Providence and to distract one from the unique vocation that God intends. Or one might seek wealth as a means to pleasure and comfort, or as a tool to obtain honor or power. None of these reasons, however, is consistent with the supernatural destiny of the person; and, as the early Christians saw so clearly, each of these goals is ultimately distracting and deadly. The contemporary experience of the developed world is striking evidence of people's limitless appetite for each of these goals and of their capacity to crowd out and extinguish spiritual goods.

Wealth, then, when understood as an excessive or perhaps unlimited quantity of money or material goods, can never be a legitimate objective for a Christian. The accumulation of wealth for the explicit purpose of concentrating resources to support the common good in major ways might be a noble ambition, though a very dangerous one.[105] Far better is the goal of achieving abundance for oneself and one's family as well as prosperity for one's community.[106] Implied in this goal is a level of possessions adequate for one's own genuine needs and security, but no more. This abundance, bounded as it is by a clear focus on authentic human development and fulfillment, is certainly an ambition to be pursued by Christians. It is a blessing and an integral element of the common good of a political community. The Christian virtue of solidarity aims precisely at establishing such abundance and prosperity in every human community.

3. *Is wealth bounded or boundless?* Abundance and prosperity are genuinely good conditions and worthy of pursuit, but how are they to be achieved? For much of Christian history the very strong tendency was to regard material goods, and the wealth they represented, as bounded in a strict sense. In other words, the quantity of wealth in the world was more or less fixed; if some people were quite wealthy (in the excessive sense), they could only be so at the expense of the poor. Thus, the problem of how to create prosperity in the community was essentially viewed as a problem of distribution. Prosperity meant devising means to distribute more evenly the limited resources available rather than finding ways to expand the quantity of resources.

More recently, it has become clear that the capacity of creation to serve genuine human needs, though perhaps finite in some sense, is practically unbounded (see John Haughey on this point). This is not to say naively that the quantity of natural resources is so great that we cannot imagine exhausting it, but rather that human persons, in collaboration with the Creator, possess a capacity to create wealth, not merely to consume it. Creating wealth means bringing greater order to the world and employing human intelligence and ingenuity to unlock nature's secrets and devise new ways to satisfy human needs. It means using new tools to make the earth productive, from growing more and better crops, to employing new forms of energy, to squeezing greater efficiencies from all sorts of activities. It means sharing technologies and techniques—among individuals and among nations—so that more and more people can participate in bringing about their own prosperity and that of their communities. It means, above all, using intelligence and knowledge to address real human needs, as understood within the context of an authentic anthropology and vision of human development. The possibilities for this activity, released as it is from simple bondage to land or any other finite resource, are truly boundless.[107] It is a solemn Christian obligation, where possible, to seek not merely to distribute abundance but also to create it.

We are poised at the beginning of a new millennium, but perhaps also at a set of other new beginnings as well. Catholics were strenuously encouraged by popes and bishops in the later half of the twentieth century to pay serious attention to the problems of poverty and inequity that characterize the human community. These problems persist and still deserve our attention, whether we are members of developed communities or of those yet to develop fully. As business educators, one of our specific vocational responsibilities is to teach students how to be just in the exercise of their technical skills in the workplace, but surely another responsibility is to encourage these students to understand why they create wealth and for whom. The world little needs more wealthy men and women; it desperately needs more men and women who can create abundance and prosperity and distribute it justly. We need to help them see their abilities to do so as charisms—gifts from God— that are given by a loving Father for the benefit of the entire human family.

Notes

1. Gen 2:9.
2. See Isa 51:3; Ezek 28:13, 31:8 f., 36:35; Joel 2:3.
3. Gen 2:15.
4. See Wis 1:13–14.
5. Ex 3:8, and passim.
6. Gen 3:17–19.
7. See, for example, Lev 26:3–12; Deut 6:3, 7:12–15, 28:1–14, and passim.
8. See Deut 30:1–20.
9. See Amos 8:4–12.
10. See Jer 34:12–22.
11. Ex 20:5; Deut 4:24, and passim.

12. See Prov 18:11; Sir 5:1–10; Hos 10:1–4, among many other passages.

13. Solomon is perhaps the most famous example. See 1 Kings 10 for an extended description of his wealth, followed by an account of his infidelity in the next chapter.

14. See Amos 2:6–8 for a typical catalog of such sins.

15. See Job 42:10–17.

16. See Prov 30:7–9, where the author expresses his anxiety about the very real dangers of wealth.

17. See Sir 31:1–11 for a description of the rare rich man who has been "tested by gold" and not found unequal to the test. Here, as commonly elsewhere in the Wisdom literature, the rich man is one who has far more than he really needs to live comfortably. The glory of the rich man in this passage in Sirach is that he is generous with his wealth and does not turn from the path of justice to pursue further riches.

18. Notable contrary examples are Ps 127:2 and Prov 10:22. Here, however, the meaning is probably less that idleness is favored by Yahweh, but rather that even the most strenuous efforts to amass wealth are likely to end in failure unless the person is just and faithful. Compare these passages with Ps 112. Other passages that emphasize Yahweh's generosity, especially to the poor, should be understood as reminders of His fidelity to the Covenant and as promises to compensate those who have suffered injustices. See, for example, Ps 18:21–31.

19. See Sir 33:1–3.

20. See Prov 10:4, 14:23, 20:13, 21:5, 28:19 for examples.

21. See Prov 19:1, 22:7, 28:6, 28:20; Eccl 5:11; Sir 13:4, 18 f. for examples.

22. See Ps 14:1; Prov 11:29, 12:11, 18:2; Eccl 2:14, 10:3; Sir 6:21, 21:18 f. among others.

23. Gen 1:28–30, 2:15.

24. Mt 5:1–7, 29.

25. Mt 6:19–20.

26. Mt 6:24.

27. Mt 6:25–34.

28. Lk 12:13–21.

29. Lk 12:22–31.

30. Lk 16:19–31.

31. Mt 16:26.

32. Mt 19:16–24; Mk 10:17–25; Lk 18:18–25.

33. Mt 19:23, and parallels.

34. Lk 14:33.

35. Acts 2:44–45, 4:32–37.

36. 2 Cor 6:10.

37. Jas 4:1–2.

38. The common Christian understanding of the story of the rich young man is that wealth, insofar as it is a created good that cannot be evil in itself, may nevertheless be a danger to salvation. Patristic and medieval commentators explain that this is so either because the pursuit and preservation of wealth is a distraction from the pursuit of holiness or because one foolishly looks to wealth for that security that only God can provide. Most modern

commentaries take up a similar theme. See, for example, Rudolf Schnackenburg, *The Moral Teaching of the New Testament* (New York: Seabury/Crossroad, 1965), 121–32; and C. E. B. Cranfield, "Riches and the Kingdom of God: St. Mark 10.17–31," *Scottish Journal of Theology* 4 (1951): 302–14. Similar interpretations can be found in "classic" as well as contemporary commentaries. See W. F. Albright and C. S. Mann, *Matthew,* Anchor Bible, vol. 26 (New York: Doubleday, 1971), 230 ff.; W. D. Davies and Dale C. Allison, Jr., *The Gospel according to Saint Matthew,* International Critical Commentary, n.s., vol. 3 (Edinburgh: T. & T. Clark, 1988), 38–65; Ezra P. Gould, *The Gospel according to St. Mark,* International Critical Commentary, o.s. (Edinburgh: T. & T. Clark, 1896), 189 ff.; Vincent Taylor, *The Gospel according to St. Mark,* 2d ed. (New York: St. Martin's Press, 1966), 424 ff.; D. E. Nineham, *The Gospel of St. Mark,* Pelican Gospel Commentaries, rev. ed. (London: Adam & Chas. Black, 1968), 269 ff.; C. S. Mann, *Mark,* Anchor Bible, vol. 27 (New York: Doubleday, 1986), 397 ff.; with some ambivalence, R. T. France, *The Gospel of Mark* (Grand Rapids, Mich.: Eerdmans, 2002), 398 ff.; John R. Donahue, S.J., and Daniel J. Harrington, S.J., *The Gospel of Mark,* Sacra Pagina, vol. 2 (Collegeville, Minn.: Michael Glazier, 2002), 302 ff.; Alfred Plummer, *The Gospel according to St. Luke,* International Critical Commentary, o.s., 5th ed. (Edinburgh: T. & T. Clark, 1922), 424 ff.; Joseph Fitzmyer, S.J., *The Gospel according to Luke,* Anchor Bible, vol. 28A (New York: Doubleday, 1985), 1201 ff.; and Luke Timothy Johnson, *The Gospel of Luke,* Sacra Pagina, vol. 3 (Collegeville, Minn.: Michael Glazier: The Liturgical Press, 2002), 275 ff.

In the twentieth century, another rather different interpretation that does not have its roots in the traditional understanding of the text has gained currency. This interpretation is situated within a broad conviction that Jesus was an advocate of revolutionary social change, perhaps that He was even a sort of proto-socialist. In this context, warnings about the dangers of wealth are subtly transformed into condemnations of wealth and disparities in property ownership. See, for example, Dan O. Via, Jr., *The Ethics of Mark's Gospel—In the Middle of Time* (Philadelphia: Fortress Press, 1985), 136–55; Herman Hendrickx, *The Third Gospel for the Third World,* vol. 3 (Collegeville, Minn.: Michael Glazier, 2001), 105–16; and, with some ambivalence, Ulrich Luz, *Matthew 8–20,* Hermeneia (Minneapolis: Fortress Press, 2001), 508–23. This line of interpretation is also strongly reflected in Martin Hengel, *Property and Riches in the Early Church* (Philadelphia: Fortress Press, 1974). An earlier writer of impeccable activist credentials who did not share this radical view is John A. Ryan. See his carefully argued little volume, *The Alleged Socialism of the Church Fathers* (St. Louis: Herder, 1913). While it is true that Jesus insisted His disciples recognize that material wealth was neither a sign of divine favor nor the proper objective of a life well-lived, it is a novelty—not solidly grounded in text or tradition—to assert that the renunciation of wealth (or, more strongly, the radical reconstruction of a society in which it was impossible to accumulate wealth) is a requirement of authentic Christian discipleship.

39. See Mt 16:24–28; Lk 14:25–27.

40. Mt 25:14–30; Lk 19:11–27.

41. Mt 26:6–13.

42. See Rom 14:3 f.; Col 2:3; 1 Tim 4:3.

43. See 1 Tim 4:4 f.

44. See 1 Cor 12:4–11.

45. See 2 Cor 8:1–15. Note here that while Paul praises the generosity of the Corinthians, he does not want their gifts to impoverish them. Instead, they should give out of their surplus, and those whom they help now should be prepared later to help the Corinthians if the situation should change. Generous giving is only possible when some amount of wealth is possessed.

46. 1 Thess 2:8 f.

47. 1 Thess 4:11–12.

48. 2 Thess 3:6–12.

49. See 2 Cor 9:6–12.

50. See 2 Cor 8:10–14.

51. Notable representatives of this view in the early Church include Clement of Alexandria (late second century), Basil (330–379), Ambrose (339–397), John Chrysostom (347–407), Jerome (342–420), and Augustine (354–430).

52. 1 Tim 2:4.

53. Chrysostom is prominent and forceful on this theme, as in his *Homilies on the Gospel of Matthew*, especially Homily 66, where he suggests that all poverty in the city could be eradicated if only the rich and the middle class would share their surplus with the poor. On the larger theme of intercity trade, see the comments in Justo L. González, *Faith and Wealth: A History of Early Christian Ideas on the Origin, Significance, and Use of Money* (San Francisco: Harper, 1990), 202 ff.

54. 2 Thess 3:10.

55. Mt 19:16–24; Lk 16:19–31.

56. Clement of Alexandria, *The Salvation of the Rich Man*, 16.

57. Lk 12:16–21.

58. See, for example, Augustine, *Sermon IX* (12, 20), where he asks parents why they prefer to trust their children to an inheritance rather than to the Creator who made both parent and child.

59. John Chrysostom, *Homiliae in Lazarum*, 2, 4. Cited in Charles Avila, *Ownership: Early Christian Teaching* (Maryknoll, N.Y.: Orbis Books, 1983), 132.

60. See Avila, *Ownership*, 66.

61. Note the famous passage on the Gifts of the Spirit in 1 Cor 12.

62. Sr. James Eugene Madden, C.S.J., tells the fascinating story of the fate of a community of Cistercian monks in England whose business activities and subsequent overextension resulted in bankruptcy. See "Business Monks, Banker Monks: The English Cistercians in the Thirteenth Century," *Catholic Historical Review* 49 (1963): 341–64.

63. Canon 19 of the Fourth Lateran Council (1215) strictly prohibits this practice except in times of emergency.

64. The classic study by W. E. Lunt, *Papal Revenues in the Middle Ages* (New York: Columbia University Press, 1934), gives extensive evidence of just how sophisticated the finances of the papacy were in this period.

65. Two canons of the First Lateran Council (1123) are aimed at the protection of commerce. Canon 15 makes the counterfeiting of money an excommunicable offense. Canon 16

imposes the same penalty on those who attack pilgrims *and* anyone who attempts to impede merchants by imposing new taxes or tolls.

66. The first four Crusades bear principal responsibility for this, though this was hardly the intention of the organizers and leaders. Subsequent Crusades floundered through poor organization and lack of support and had little impact on the European economy.

67. One of the best treatments of medieval thinking on this subject is Odd Langholm, *Economics in the Medieval Schools* (Leiden: Brill, 1992).

68. See John W. Baldwin, *The Medieval Theories of the Just Price: Romanists, Canonists, and Theologians in the Twelfth and Thirteenth Centuries,* Transactions of the American Philosophical Society, n.s., 49, pt. 4 (Philadelphia: American Philosophical Society, 1959), 21–57, for an outline of the work of the canonists.

69. See ibid., 63–67, for a discussion of thirteenth-century treatments of the moral status of merchants.

70. The more prominent theologians of the thirteenth century, such as Alexander of Hales, St. Albert, and St. Bonaventure, all recognized the right of the merchant to make a profit on the sale of goods that he did not alter or improve, that is, to be paid for his efforts and his risks. However, while granting the principle, they still had a narrow conception of what the merchant really contributes and thought to limit sharply the level of profit he could honestly receive.

71. St. Thomas Aquinas, *Summa theologiae,* IIa-IIae, q. 77. It is ironic that his discussion of business is in the context of an essay on the vice of cheating. Furthermore, while he admits that some kinds of commerce are commendable, he is quick to add that trade in the pursuit of wealth is justly scorned. Nevertheless, his authority for later theologians was enormous, and this sort of partial approval opened the door for a much more insightful and positive review in later centuries.

72. See Aquinas's *On Kingship,* chapter 7. He and his contemporaries acknowledged that in a community characterized by specialization and division of responsibilities, trade is necessary. Aquinas, however, tended to regard trade between nations, which ought to be as self-sufficient as communities, as a sign of deficiency.

73. Two prominent studies of these men and their work in English are Bede Jarrett, *S. Antonino and Medieval Economics* (St. Louis: Herder, 1914), and Raymond de Roover, *San Bernardino of Siena and Sant'Antonino of Florence* (Boston: Harvard Business School, 1967).

74. There is a large and competent bibliography on this subject, a neglected area of study, not least in Catholic intellectual circles. For a summary introduction, with an extensive bibliography, see Domènec Melé, "Early Business Ethics in Spain: The Salamanca School (1526–1614)," *Journal of Business Ethics* 22 (1999): 175–89. See also Alejandro A. Chafuen, *Christians for Freedom* (San Francisco: Ignatius Press, 1986), and Juan Antonio Widow, "The Economic Teachings of Spanish Scholastics," in Kevin White, ed., *Hispanic Philosophy in the Age of Discovery,* Studies in Philosophy and the History of Philosophy 29 (Washington, D.C.: Catholic University of America Press, 1997), 130–44.

75. The issue of usury has been investigated at great length by a number of authors. It played a prominent role in early economic analysis by the theologians because they confronted the need to reconcile the traditional conception of the nature of money with a wide

variety of novel business practices. They soon realized that the conception of money that underlay the prohibition of usury was inadequate to describe the real uses of money in a sophisticated economy. This problem led them to analyze more deeply other aspects of commerce to determine their moral character.

76. The commonly accepted view is that this work began in the Catholic Church with the encyclical *Rerum novarum,* issued in 1891 by Pope Leo XIII. This work has continued to the present day in a number of other papal encyclicals as well as in documents prepared by national conferences of bishops, such as the American bishops' *Program for Social Reconstruction* (1919) and later, *Economic Justice for All* (1986).

77. *Rerum novarum,* 4.

78. Ibid., 5–10; *Quadragesimo anno,* 45; *Mater et magistra,* 43, 109 ff.; *Pacem in terris,* 21; *Gaudium et spes,* 71; *Laborem exercens,* 13; *Centesimus annus,* 30.

79. *Laborem exercens,* 25.

80. *Populorum progressio,* 25.

81. "Harvesting" is meant here as not simply agricultural work but as all work that aims to be productive by taking something of value from the natural world (for example, mining or fishing). Leo XIII seems still committed to this view (see *Rerum novarum,* 7), but Paul VI and John Paul II see new possibilities (see *Populorum progressio,* 25; *Laborem exercens,* 25; and *Centesimus annus,* 32).

82. "The degree of well-being that society enjoys today would be unthinkable without the dynamic figure of the business man, whose function consists of organizing human labor and the means of production so as to give rise to the goods and services necessary for the prosperity and progress of the community" (John Paul II, Address to Business Leaders and Managers in Milan, May 22, 1983, quoted from Robert G. Kennedy, Gary Atkinson, and Michael Naughton, eds., *The Dignity of Work: John Paul II Speaks to Managers and Workers* (Lanham, Md.: University Press of America, 1994), 12.

83. See *Rerum novarum,* 19: "Whoever has received from the divine bounty a large share of blessings, whether they be external and corporal, or gifts of the mind, has received them for the purpose of using them for perfecting his own nature, and, at the same time, that he may employ them, as the minister of God's Providence, for the benefit of others."

84. See *Sollicitudo rei socialis,* 28; *Centesimus annus,* 36.

85. A *locus classicus* is Thomas Aquinas, *Summa theologiae,* IIa-IIae, q. 32, a. 6.

86. Note, however, that this idea persists even as late as *Quadragesimo anno* in 1931 (see par. 50).

87. See *Gaudium et spes,* 69.

88. See *Rerum novarum,* 19: "When necessity has been supplied, and one's position fairly considered, it is a duty to give to the indigent out of that which is left over. . . . It is a duty, not of justice (except in extreme cases), but of Christian charity—a duty which is not enforced by human laws."

89. See *Populorum progressio,* 49; *Sollicitudo rei socialis,* 7; *Centesimus annus,* 34 and passim.

90. *Gaudium et spes,* 35; *Sollicitudo rei socialis,* 28.

91. See *Sollicitudo rei socialis,* 28–31.

92. See *Gaudium et spes,* 1; *Sollicitudo rei socialis,* 6.

93. See *Gaudium et spes*, 57; *Populorum progressio*, 1, 13.

94. See *Gaudium et spes*, 24.

95. See ibid., 29; *Populorum progressio*, 43.

96. See *Populorum progressio*, 14 ff.

97. See *Gaudium et spes*, 69; *Populorum progressio*, 22; *Sollicitudo rei socialis*, 7.

98. See *Laborem exercens*, 4, 25; *Centesimus annus*, 31.

99. See *Gaudium et spes*, 64; *Populorum progressio*, 25, 27; *Laborem exercens*, 4.

100. See *Populorum progressio*, 19; *Sollicitudo rei socialis*, 36; *Centesimus annus*, 33.

101. See *Populorum progressio*, 48; *Sollicitudo rei socialis*, 38–40; *Centesimus annus*, 34.

102. See *Centesimus annus*, 32, 43.

103. For example, Pope Leo XIII is sometimes cited, by critics and defenders alike, as an opponent of jobs and careers for women (see *Rerum novarum*, 33). A more appropriate reading of this text finds a defense of the value of motherhood and the family within the context of a more comprehensive defense of the worker. Leo was concerned that the new modes of employment in industry were likely to undermine the unity of the family and to expose children and women to demands of the workplace in ways that would attack their human dignity. He expresses analogous concerns about men in the same place. The application of the principle of protecting the dignity of workers that he recommends may seem unsuitable to us today (that is, we are now more willing to see women in the workplace and less willing to see children), but we can still embrace the principle that lies behind this older application.

104. Charles Clark presents an excellent précis of the modern history of economic theory regarding wealth, in which a concept of wealth understood in terms of the well-being of persons was displaced by one conceived in terms of scarcity (see chapter 1, this volume). Clark shows how the suppression of the earlier concept, which is more congenial to the notion of wealth endorsed here (see also Haughey), resulted in an association of wealth with sin and evil. The wheel has turned again and yet again. Where the Old Testament regarded wealth as a blessing and the early Church viewed it with suspicion (because of its tainted sources and misuse), early modern thinkers such as Adam Smith recovered an appreciation for the real benefits of wealth and prosperity in a community only to have this appreciation rejected by the Marginalists. Defining wealth in terms of scarcity, as Clark shows, leads to an excessive concern with the problems of distribution (as distinct from creation) and to a disdain for the efforts necessary to create wealth.

105. It is easy to be reminded of Andrew Carnegie's famous essay, "The Gospel of Wealth" (*North American Review* 148, no. 391 [June 1889]: 653, 657–62), in which he offers a sort of apologia for his life and the lives of others who have amassed great fortunes. He exhorts these men to use their wealth and power for the sake of the common good and urges the community to permit them to dispose of their wealth as they see fit. The very abilities that allowed them to acquire this wealth, he argues, make them the best suited to put it to use. Furthermore, the concentration of wealth in the hands of a few makes possible magnificent efforts that would be impossible if it were widely distributed (and so diluted). However, one can hardly fail to observe that such wealth is rarely, if ever, accumulated by just men and this is rarely employed for the common good by men unaffected by injustice, vanity, power, and so forth.

106. There is a reasonable question to be raised here about motivation as well. The creation of abundance in the community, as a real element of the common good, is a worthy goal for Christian individuals, provided that this is their vocation. Someone called to be a teacher, for instance, who seeks instead to build a fortune, may be just and successful, but he is also unfaithful. While the creation of wealth can be understood as a goal open to Christians, individuals must seriously discern whether it is the goal to which they are called. For some the answer will be affirmative, but for others the pursuit of wealth becomes a distraction from their real vocation. And a culture that honors the wealthy while diminishing the value of other achievements will inevitably discourage many people from faithfully responding to their true vocations.

107. See *Centesimus annus,* 32. Pope John Paul II clearly sees that human knowledge and skill is a resource distinct in kind from land and capital, and so he presents possibilities for human prosperity and fulfillment that also differ in kind.

THREE

A Pauline Catechesis of Abundance

John C. Haughey, S.J.

When theologians or Church leaders address the question of wealth, they usually begin with the elements of stewardship: supporting the Church, avoiding the love of money, meeting prevalent needs. In this chapter I would like to go in the opposite direction by addressing the subject of wealth and its generation as something that God intends. I believe that evidence for this contention can be found in both the New Testament and the Old. Further, I would like to claim that in some people the Holy Spirit is the source of the gift that enables them to be generators of wealth. In order to do this, I want to show how the moral criteria for evaluating wealth, its generation, and its distribution need to be complemented by criteria that derive from an understanding of the Spirit's action in the world. One of the roles that the Spirit plays in the world is to imbue individuals with gifts for others. I want to explain the generation of some wealth that at times is linked to the scriptural category of gifts for others, or charism.

CHARISM IN THE LOGICS OF ABUNDANCE AND OF SCARCITY

A number of texts in the New Testament testify that Jesus understands God to operate with what one might call a "logic of abundance." Think of the Parable of the Sower: the sower's work is expected to yield increases of 30-, 60-, and 100-fold.[1] Think of the Parable of the Talents: their expected increment is a source of blessing from the owner and a further conferral of largesse.[2] Think of the five barley loaves and two fish: blessed by Jesus and distributed to the multitude, they feed five thousand.[3] Whether the inspired New Testament authors attribute this abundance to God apart from human involvement, or (more usually) to human cooperation with God, increase marks God's action in time. In the least grain of faith, Jesus foresaw a full growth that would provide for the needs of many.[4] In brief, He read the present in terms of the future, so His picture of the kingdom was of a condition of fullness, abundance, and plenty that had its beginning in time. But between now and the fullness of the kingdom there was to be industry—an industriousness in those to whom a little was given so that a plentiful harvest could come about because they took the little they had and multiplied it.

The logic of scarcity is contrary to this logic of abundance (see Charles Clark's "Wealth as Abundance and Scarcity," chapter 1, this volume). By holding on tightly to the little that one has and by not investing it or not acting to increase its potential or not imagining what Jesus envisioned, namely, fields ripe for the harvest, one is mired in the logic of scarcity. Judas was one of Jesus' followers whose logic was held in this tight calculus. He could not smell the perfume anointing Jesus' feet because he was too intent on calculating its sale price (300 denarii, he guessed).[5] But he was not alone. "What good is that [paltry amount] among so many?" the disciples wondered before Jesus fed the five thousand from such meager portions. The widow who donated her last "mite" is a ready example of someone who lived in the same logic of abundance as Jesus.[6] He cited her action at the temple treasury because they were both investing "all (they) had to live on," in the belief that God was the source of all abundance.

We miss the point of this logic if we discard its material aspect by spiritualizing it. A spiritualization of abundance does not do justice to the Scriptures' insistence on tangible abundance. From Israel's story of origin, for example, in the Adam and Eve myth, we find humans called to be agents of productivity by cultivating the Garden. They were also to act as overseers of the bringing to abundance and flourishing of all that God had made.[7] While human flourishing is spiritual and moral, it is no less social, material, and economic. Abundance, too, has all these dimensions. It is not achieved by persons who are meeting their own needs independently of one another, but by those who are producing, with others' help, what is possible from the resources available to them.

While the Creator made everything good and made it in abundance, much of the world knows scarcity, deprivation, and want—the diametrical opposite of God's intention. What happened? There was an affront to God's plan, which a long tradition has called original sin. With sin, the logic of scarcity takes hold in human imagination and intention and results in endless ersatz justifications of reckless consumption and reckless accumulation alike. Forgetful of God's logic, humans enthrone self-providence over an economic world in which the logic of scarcity is worked out as "dog eat dog" and "every man for himself." Nevertheless, humankind's call to co-produce abundance for each and all, in concert with God, was not revoked by human sin. God was still the ultimate author and source of all abundance. To achieve abundant well-being, however, a new level of God's favor had to be conferred on humans. The favor of God—God's *charis*—was needed now to elevate minds and wills made dull by sin. One genre of this grace or divine favor was the *charismata*, or *charisms of the Spirit*, which are given for the community's well-being.

Since I will be placing much weight on the charism of wealth generation in this chapter, more needs to be said about charisms in general, and first of all about what they are not. There are two ways in which we can be misled by the language of charism. One of these is to confuse it with Max Weber's *charisma*, which is a forceful quality of leadership, able to command attention. Weber saw charisms in sociological terms and as rare; we see them in scriptural terms and as widely dispersed. Their ubiquity is hinted at by St. Paul: "To *each* a manifestation of the Spirit is given for the common good."[8]

The second way of being misled is by identifying charisms with a prayer style called "charismatic." Paul's treatment of the charisms is different, as we will see. Suffice it to say here that for him their purpose was the well-being or the upbuilding of the community. So wherever a community in its smallest form, such as a family, or in its larger forms, such as a congregation or a neighborhood or a state, knows some degree of abundance, there the favor of God through charisms, helping to cause that effect, might be found to be in play.

Catholic theology has traditionally distinguished the forms in which God's favor is poured out. Graces, both actual and sanctifying (with all their subdistinctions), are generally understood to be given for the sake of making their receiver more pleasing to God. The Latin for these is *gratia gratum faciens*. But the charisms are God's favor that is given, not for the sake of those who receive them but for the sake of those who will benefit from their exercise by those who have received them. The Latin for these is *gratia gratis data*. Furthermore, charisms have usually been construed in terms of their ecclesial benefit and therefore have not usually been associated with social, civic, political, and economic benefits. But that does not do justice to them, as the Second Vatican Council saw. A narrowly ecclesial understanding was superseded at the Council by the realization that "from these charisms there arise for each believer the right and duty to use them in the church and in the world for the good of mankind."[9] Here I simply want to advance the idea that where an abundance—wealth generation, in particular—proves beneficial to a community, there the favor of God, or more specifically, a charism of the Spirit, may be at work.

Although I have distinguished God's favor in the above two ways, it should immediately be noted that God's favor is ceaseless and manifold. While it is important to resurrect and differentiate charisms from the more usual ways of looking at God's favor in order to reexamine what has been neglected and even, for the most part, lost, once charisms are distinguished from all their surrogates, they should probably be returned to the more general category of divine gifts, as long as their destiny for others is kept in mind. So, I will use the less arcane term "gifts" interchangeably with "charisms" in the rest of this chapter.

The evidence of God's abundance can be glimpsed if one thinks of it exploding in the still-expanding galaxies and on planet earth in its teeming, still uncounted species. If abundance does not strike one immediately as a tangible intention of God, I must think such a one to be spiritually deaf, dumb, and blind. Once this aspect of God impresses itself on us, we would expect abundance to be experienced by the conscious members of creation, by humans in particular. But, as has already been mentioned, their experience is largely the opposite—poverty, deprivation, want, and scarcity, all of which are antithetical to God's clear intentions. At the root, to repeat, stands sin, the genus of human failure; the specific causes are many and complex. I want to name two of these causes of scarcity here: (1) capability deprivation; and (2) unnecessary accumulation in the service of "neighbor-numb" consumption.[10]

The analysis of poverty undertaken by the Indian economist, Amartya Sen, illumines the thesis I am trying to develop. Sen received the Nobel Prize for advancing the idea that the major cause of poverty in the world is what he called capability deprivation. And its major solution is individual agency, the creating of the conditions in which individuals may develop and act on their own capabilities. The poor have assets, but these have to be teased out. Development in the economic sense can best be achieved in and through free, social and individual interaction; thus, personal flourishing and social flourishing are interlinked economically. If there is no freedom for the individual's giftedness to develop, then there will be commensurate poverty in the society of which the individual is a part.

Sen's most famous work, *Development as Freedom,*[11] has moved economic thinking beyond the ideology of economism that immediately connected poverty to low income and expanded it into issues such as freedom and human rights. What must be stressed here is the importance that Sen places on the mistake of the worldwide community of economists who have missed the connection between wealth and what can generate it—namely, the opportunity for individuals to know and exercise their peculiar capabilities with a view to their own and others' flourishing. His work forces the reader to be open to the economic implications of personal giftedness without, at the same time, being economically reductionist about them. The tragedy of poverty, he would say, is the undeveloped personal resources that lie unsuspected, unattended to, and unused in the impoverished populations of the world.

A picture that illumines the opposite pole of Sen's capability deprivation is framed for us in Jesus' parable of the man with the gain in grain.[12] Jesus describes a man whose gifts for successful farming were notable. He was so gifted at reading all the contingencies agriculture is exposed to, that he produced a bumper crop. So far, so good. But then, paradoxically, he begins to apply the logic of scarcity to his unexpected overabundance. By this logic, wealth means having things and is in itself life-giving, so that the more things one has the more life one will have. His neighbors and their needs do not even enter his mind. Apparently, his relationships with them are not of value to him, since "me," "mine," "my," and "myself" tumble from this farmer's lips as he anticipates what he will do with the his increase. The fruits of his gift mesmerize him; mistaking them for an expression of his own worth, he congratulates himself on being the author of his felicity: "you have blessings in reserve for years to come. Relax! Eat heartily, drink well. Enjoy yourself."[13]

For what is the abundance that came from the utilization of his gifts? To whom will all this "piled-up wealth" go?"[14] The answer given in the parable is not abstract. Provoked by the farmer's numbness toward others, God counters, "You fool! This very night your life shall be required of you." And Jesus comments offstage, "That is the way it works with the man who grows rich for himself instead of growing rich in the eyes of God."[15] The gifted man should grow rich in the sight of God by being generous with, and attentive to, his neighbor. The new grain silo, to be built to contain the overabundance, symbolizes a man who rejects both his gifts *as* gifts and their Giver *as* Giver. This parable was introduced by Jesus with the moral: "Avoid greed (*pleonexia*) in all its forms. A man may be wealthy, but his possessions do not guarantee him life."[16] *Pleonexia* is a Greek word indicating a passion for more of what one has. It connotes goods moving to the extreme of excess and thus needing to be curbed to the mean of industrious self-provision but with a view to others' needs. The tragedy here is confusion: having more of what the wealth-generating gift can produce is confounded with the deeper meaning of one's wealth.[17]

This might be a good place to pause and remind ourselves of the frequency with which self-deception has attached itself, in the American experience, to many people who have accumulated great wealth. Their self-deception frequently became almost impenetrable when it was clothed in religious language. All the way back to Puritan times, righteousness and fortune came to be linked as effect to cause. This was doubly unfortunate not only because it was a self-conferred righteousness (which was no righteousness at all), but also because it judged misfortune or poverty as evidence of one's being outside the pale of divine favor. "Self-deception is a *policy* of avoiding the real story . . . [t]he biblical story[, which] continually calls us beyond self-serving exploitation of the land or of other people and into covenantal existence."[18] The real story is the favor of God, manifested in the Covenant. Covenantal existence is life in the embrace of God. The Covenant is a commitment made by God that is meant to comfort deeply those who are "embraced." But covenantal existence demands the conviction that everything that those who are embraced have comes from the God of gifts and is meant to benefit others as well as themselves. Covenantal existence, then, must be lived in the awareness of complete dependence on the God who gives. Therefore, those embraced by the Covenant were to understand that their "piled-up wealth" was meant for others.

The embodiment of this awareness can be read in the idealized picture of material abundance enjoyed by the first community of Jesus' followers, which follows hard on the heels of the outpouring of the Spirit on the day of Pentecost. Acts 2:42–47 and 4:32–35 portray the considerable well-being enjoyed by these first Christians because they shared with one another, even to the point of selling their property and donating the proceeds to the Apostles, with the result that "there was no one needy among them."[19] Even if one doubts that Luke's portrait is historically accurate, still, the Spirit inspired Luke to paint it so that readers and hearers of this Word might connect material abundance with the designs of the Spirit.

CHARISM IN THE GENERATION OF WEALTH

How is wealth generated? It can be invested so that returns can accrue by way of interest and stock dividends, that is, by making money on money. But besides investing, there are three other ways of producing monetary abundance: through invention, entrepreneurship, and management. Let someone invent something that others need or want. The inventor is an innovator, usually with the creativity and technological know-how for making the imagined something or for developing a new process for improving what is already being done. Another way to create wealth, not usually the skill of the same person, is that of the entrepreneur, who assumes the risk of moving the invention or innovation from its conception to a commercial enterprise. The entrepreneur can be an individual or a corporate entity or a venture capitalist who funds the enterprise. (There are also financial entrepreneurs who seek to create wealth when equity shares or stocks or debt claims or bonds are issued to fund new ventures.) Finally, there is the manager, whose oversight and coordination of the commercial process are essential for the product to be profitably produced and sold.

These four usual ways of wealth generation are necessary for the creation of jobs and for the productivity that generates wealth. Without any one of them, the other three would not suffice. I am not blind to the fact that although these are the key agents of a process, I am looking at it in its simplest, most stripped down, interpersonal rudiments. While admitting the enormous complexity that corporate life brings to it, I would still say that wealth comes to three kinds of gifted people: inventors, entrepreneurs, and managers.

Where and when is God allegedly present in this process of wealth generation? And when is He not? The usual way of answering these questions is to appeal to solely moral criteria. Thus, if the common good is advanced in the sense that a greater abundance is available to the community, then this is a good sign that God has some degree of presence in the consciences and skills of those who are responsible for generating the abundance. The moral criteria in part depend on such questions as: (1) whether a just wage is paid to those employed in producing the goods that generate the wealth; (2) whether the producers and the wider community are being served by those who determine the distribution of the wealth, so that a few individuals are not gaining disproportionately; (3) whether working conditions enhance or diminish the health and dignity of those who produce the goods; (4) whether the wealth-generating enterprise responds to, or ignores, genuine human needs; and (5) whether natural resources and the environment are taken into account in the making of profitable products. (These issues are pursued in this volume by Dennis McCann, Carlo Dell'Aringa and Claudio Lucifora, Michael Naughton and Robert Wahlstedt, and Lee Tavis in chapters 7, 10–12).

If it can be verified that moral criteria are not being violated, then the road is clear for seeing God more directly involved in the process of wealth generation. Moral criteria are, then, necessary but not sufficient for ascertaining the presence of the Spirit in a given person or activity. If my thesis is correct, if some people are functioning from charisms in their notable productivity, then further criteria are needed to judge whether what they are doing is consonant with the new creation that is the work of the Spirit. So, assuming the morality of the generation of wealth, we want to go a step further to criteria implicating the Spirit. Are there such? Where good is being done and evil avoided, there God's Spirit is already at work in the moral agent. But in the new creation, which has been brought about by Christ's incarnation and redemption, a further degree of the presence of the Spirit can become operational. And with it comes a new horizon, a new world of metaphor, and a new vision of one's purpose in life. In view of this promised, experienced newness, we can look for Spirit-led criteria.

At this point in our study, one of the important distinctions that surfaces is the *finis operis* in contrast to the *finis operantis*. Briefly, the *finis operis* refers to the finality intrinsic to the action or project or work undertaken by the acting subject(s). And, conversely, the *finis operantis* is the finality intended by the acting subject(s). It should be obvious that wealth, neither for its own sake nor for oneself, can be the sole purpose of Christian moral agents, who have been called to "the things that are above." By the same token, if "to each has been given a manifestation of the Spirit for the common good,"[20] then the exercise of this charism or gift is meant for the well-being of that community, or those communities, to which each agent belongs.

How can we conjoin these two seemingly opposite directions? I believe the *operis/operantis* distinction does this succinctly. If one's gift has the effect of generating wealth, then the economic common good is benignly attained. But the intention of the giftbearer would be not the wealth as such, but fidelity to the gift. To be in the "new creation" is not tantamount to being in a condition in which manna comes from the sky. Rather, it entails taking the particular seeds available to us and planting them, not in order to be wealthy ourselves but to be faithful stewards of the abundance that God intends for us.

It would surely be a crude understanding of Spirit were it to involve a disdain for the material world or for the productivity that can turn mere matter into a balm for meeting human needs. Does not every human being have a right to material conditions worthy of those who are made in the image and likeness of God? Indeed every person does; hence, the economic and material well-being of the human community is one of God's major interests! This being the case, who is to vindicate God's interest and sustain these conditions, if not primarily those who can generate the abundance that God's interest and these conditions demand? The Gospels present a divine Sower strewing seed almost profligately and humans planting it, nurturing it, and enjoying its yield.

Since, presumably, the horizon and therefore the intentionality of the charism-bearer have been deepened by the collectively conferred charisms of faith, hope, and love, it can be expected that the meaning of wealth will be transformed so as to conform to the divine interest. But this assertion prompts further questions. Once we take this pneumatological or "new creation" route, it is only reasonable to examine the source of the skills that operate in the generation of wealth. Are these gifts of God, that is, charisms of the Spirit? Or are they simply natural talents mobilized by love toward divine ends? I am not sure that it matters, since what is "natural" can, by God's elevation of it, become part of the "supernatural existential," to use Karl Rahner's terminology. So, whether the gifts or talents that generate wealth originate in the gene pool or develop over time, the *finis operantis* must be brought to see the peculiar abundance that characterizes the "new creation." Furthermore, although materially the wealth yield might be the same whether we are talking natural talent or charism of the Spirit, formally the difference is *toto caelo*.

In light of the previous remark, matters of intentionality need to be complemented by the matter of meaning, specifically, the question of where meanings come from. Our nurturing at its most significant level was a nurturing in meaning and meanings. Among other things, we were socialized into giving meaning to wealth. From the world of meanings—those that were attached to human activity by our nurturers—we learned by encouragement, affirmation, education, and training to go from small steps to occasional acts to more frequent undertakings, each a fuller expression of the meanings we eventually live out in life. If the process of nurture and meaning-making has been one of faith, with its metaphors and models and embodiments, then one gains a broader horizon about life and career and purpose. As it pertains to wealth, meaning, whether wrong or right, is contagious. Right and wrong meaning—hence, right and wrong intentionality—about wealth is passed from generation to generation.

CHARISM AS TOUCHSTONE: 1 CORINTHIANS REVISITED

One way to build a firebreak between the right and wrong meanings of wealth, and the right and wrong ideas about the ends toward which to use wealth, is to go back to the beginning—to St. Paul—and to inquire anew about his understanding of charism. Perhaps the major reason that charisms have received so little attention in Christian history is that Paul's treatment of them in 1 Corinthians 12–14 has been erroneously taken to be a theological treatise rather than an ad hoc correction of abuses in the Corinthian prayer assemblies. Taking Paul's writing as a treatise, all subsequent probes confined themselves to phenomena such as speaking in tongues, prophecy, and discernment of spirits. But 1 Corinthians records a course correction exercised by the pastoral Paul, not a theology of charism. The latter would have to begin with the phenomenon of abundance and trace it to its source in God. Nevertheless, we can still gain considerable insight into charisms by going back to Paul's primary text.

The *locus classicus* for understanding charism remains, then, 1 Corinthians. In its twelfth chapter there are several insights that are germane to our inquiry. The first is differentiation. Each gift is seen not only as distinct but also as a part of the upbuilding of a whole. Both the whole and the part are authored by the Spirit: "There are different gifts but the same Spirit; different ministries but the same Lord; different works but the same God who accomplishes all of them in everyone. . . . It is one and the same Spirit who produces all these gifts [ministries, works], distributing them to each as he wills."[21] Paul's understanding of gifts in this letter is considerably more ecclesial and parochial than it is in the later Letter to the Ephesians, where Christ, having ascended on high, is now seen as a much more cosmic sovereign, His gifts distributed more universally.[22] In both letters, the whole is seen as a single organism, with each of its parts grasping itself as a contributor to the whole.

The second insight is connected to this first one: there is a conscious interdependence among gifts. The foot knows itself both through its contribution to the body's wholeness and through its dependence on the leg, the ear, the eye, and so forth. "The eye cannot say to the hand, 'I do not need you.'"[23] So, too, in the human community that answers to Paul's metaphor even those lowly members of the body who do not seem so important—for example, the unskilled laborer—"are in fact indispensable."[24] All the interdependent parts are to be "concerned for one another. If one member suffers, all the members suffer with it; if one member is honored, all the members share its joy."[25]

Where the Spirit is, there abundance begins to develop, because all sustain, and are members of, one another. A "member identity" is an identity of interdependence, and interdependence proves to be the source of the resulting abundance (which, in Paul's immediate context, is an abundance of worship). Were one's performance to be measured independently of others', or were agendas developed without reference to others, by a privatized sense of self, then the whole would be impoverished. (Recall that the words "deprived" and "private" are from the same root.) The picture conveyed in the text is of members, not of individuals—members whose agendas, as also their gifts, are of a piece with a whole organism.

But, wait! Isn't Paul referring to spiritual gifts such as prophecy and speaking in tongues and healing? He is, and on this point the doctrine of charisms has stalled for these many centuries. We are being witless if we cannot extend Paul's understanding beyond this specific correction and grasp the import of the very idea of charisms that are given severally so that there might be "a manifestation of the Spirit for the common good."[26] The abundance that God intends was never meant to be confined to a spiritual abundance or, for that matter, to merely spiritual concerns. We are not angels, nor have we been created spirits. We must extend the import of some of the Spirit's gifts to include material and economic effects, because God's will for abundance and human flourishing is meant to touch all aspects of our material and spiritual humanity. As long as Pauline texts are left confined to the moment and place in time that their author first addressed, our literalism will leave his inspired insights underutilized and unexplored, almost criminally so. We do a serious disservice to the text and to Paul when we impose on it a dualism (the spiritual versus the material) and a dichotomy (the ecclesial versus the secular) that was far from his mind and vision of God at work in this world, for Paul taught that there was nothing that was not to come under Christ's feet.[27]

In Paul's next chapter, 1 Corinthians 13, his vision becomes even more germane to our topic. It is introduced by the exhortation, "set your hearts on the greater gifts." What are these? The foundation-establishing charisms of faith, hope, and love. These three differ from the other charisms because they are received by all who are in Christ, and because they not only equip persons for the common good but also make them pleasing to God, as sanctifying grace does. These three foundational charisms, if exercised, will have a major effect on how wealth is understood. They situate financial wealth within a horizon that relativizes its worth by the worship in faith of the One who is of absolute worth. Again, unless the charism of hope actively affects one's horizon, wealth will easily assume an importance that it does not deserve. But catching a vision of the great hope to which we are called presumes the active exercise of the charism of faith, which prepares the heart and mind to seek out true, lasting abundance and its source. Financial abundance is subjected to a severe critique by faith, and is relativized by hope so as to be lightly possessed and, therefore, distributed according to a radically different measure by those whose love of God is their wealth.

Finally, love, like faith and hope, is a charism of and for the body of Christ, and as such, being greater than all the rest of the personal charisms, it is to be sought after eagerly. Without love, the exercise of the lesser gifts can easily divide people and create factions and classes, even competition. The exercise of any charism entails a certain self-transcendence, precisely because charisms are meant for others' benefit. As for Paul, he sees love plus the personal charisms as moving one in the direction of self-emptying. As the quality that shapes and informs personal charisms, love is the best evidence that the Spirit is their origin. Love is also the best criterion that the Spirit is at work in the area of intersubjectivity. "Love is patient . . . kind . . . not envious or boastful . . . does not insist on its own way."[28] An absence of love would leave a person, otherwise blessed, still radically deprived. For example, Paul claimed that, "if I give everything I have to feed the poor and hand over my body to be burned, but have not love, I gain nothing."[29] Finally, Paul observes that all other charisms have their moment in time but then they cease. But not love! "And now faith, hope, and love abide, these three; and the greatest of these is love."[30]

The fourteenth chapter of 1 Corinthians seems at first to have less relevance than the previous two for our subject, since it is more clearly focused on the conduct of the assemblies of prayer in the Corinthian house churches. Paul's main concern is that a congregation's order of worship be harmonious and edifying. The Corinthians were evidently not in harmony, so Paul is anxious to elaborate an order for the exercise of the gifts of the assembled. The criterion he uses is this: What will build up the good of the community by the exercise of the gift? Priority is to be given to those gifts that edify or upbuild. There is no room for self-promotion or for a self-referential use of one's gifts. The criterion of this chapter of Paul is a variation on the one mentioned in 1 Corinthians 12, namely, that the common good trumps any one individual's particular good; and it recalls his earlier instruction in 1 Corinthians 10: a Christian seeks not his own advantage but that of the many. In brief, all charisms are to be exercised with a view to the well-being and upbuilding of the community.

But there are two organisms to be built up: the body of Christ and the body of the human family. The criteria that Paul applies explicitly to the former need to be applied to the latter, because the charisms are meant to upbuild both. By confining

Paul's theology of charism to ecclesial communities, we miss an opportunity to imbue the world of finances with a causality that it seldom, if ever, imagines. We must extend Paul's nonsystematic treatment of charisms to extraecclesial forms of civic communities in order to gain insight into the manner in which God's abundance might be assured in these latter. Not to do so results in the myopia of economism, which denies to economic activity—to a realm of human action—elements of its human, that is, its moral and spiritual, character.

The reader may now ask, How do these criteria that derive from the pneumatology of 1 Corinthians 12–14 relate to the traditional, natural law, moral reasoning and criteria about wealth? These two sources of morality complement one another. One can be faithful to right reasoning as the natural law guides it; one can be faithful to the horizon of the Gospel as the Spirit inspires one. Neither should contradict the other. The value of citing the Gospel (and Paul, in particular) to understand the meaning, sources and uses of wealth is that those who are its generators and identify themselves as Christian can see their lives' meaning in a whole new light, by which wealth cannot appear autonomous, cordoned off from the practices of faith. The specific form that the call to follow Christ takes is the call of one's charism.

Understanding oneself as called to be a source of wealth generation for the common good or of abundance for others, if that is being faithful to one's charism, is the value of going the Spirit route rather than the natural law route. Certainly, if the Gospel is one's source of meaning it would be disorienting to find oneself gifted to produce material abundance but unable to subsume that gift, and one's work in the world, under one's vocation in the Spirit.

John Paul II has enlarged the Pauline vista on charisms. He commented on them and did so creatively. Here I will touch on only one aspect of how he has enlarged the world's understanding of charism. In the Catholic sacramental tradition, the charism of love is accompanied by hope and faith at the time of the conferral of the sacrament of baptism. They are referred to in this tradition as virtues—infused theological virtues, to be precise. But John Paul's understanding is that the virtue/charism of love is meant to get legs, so to speak. It is to develop into the moral virtue of solidarity, which he defined as "a firm and persevering determination to commit oneself to the common good; that is to say, to the good of all and of each individual, because we are all really responsible for all."[31]

This is a significant development for those who would be formed in a catechesis or logic of abundance. It conveys an ideal to be striven for in the understanding and exercise of one's personal charism, which we can describe in terms of a calling. As love matures, it commits itself more and more effectively to others. Insofar as it commits itself, in John Paul's words, to "the good of all and of each individual," it builds up some aspect of the common good—which may include the common weal—of the communities of which one is a part. "Solidarity helps us to see the 'other'—whether a person, a people or a nation—not just as some kind of instrument . . . but as our 'neighbor,' a 'helper' (Genesis 2:18–20), to be made a sharer, on a par with ourselves in the banquet of life to which all are equally invited by God."[32]

This pope's vision of solidarity does not stall at the level of the interpersonal but moves out beyond the love and resultant solidarity among individuals to a breathtaking vista that includes whole nations, in particular those of abundance vis-à-vis those of indigence. John Paul's meditations on these situations of disparity invariably led him to the parable of the rich man, "Dives," who, on becoming apprised of Lazarus in his misery, chooses to ignore him.[33] John Paul II shows the paradox of abundance as the fuller meaning of abundance is transmogrified. It is now Dives who needs and Lazarus who can meet his needs. The parable moves from charity to justice to justification in only a few lines. The abjectly miserable Lazarus, carried up into the bosom of Abraham, comes into an abundance he never knew in time. Dives, on the other hand, who was mired in his own overabundance on earth, turns out to be the one in dire need on the other side of time.

The poor nations, like poor persons, have an abundance to give if the rich nations can be touched by their needs and initiate a solidarity with them. Otherwise, a chasm builds and the condition of eternity cannot bridge it, as Dives, to his great sorrow, found out. Solidarity enacted ensures a common good and a common weal; solidarity refused eventually results in woe for those who had the wherewithal to effect it and did not. John Paul did not tire of citing this parable as an incentive for those who can build solidarities to do so. The paradoxical nature of abundance is made tangible by the parable: an abundance hoarded creates an eventual deprivation and corruption in the hoarders. In terms of the Parable of the Talents: those who fail to use their gifts and talents for others will eventually lose everything they have.

Solidarity grows where our interdependence on each other and on the goods of the earth is perceived and acted upon. According to John Paul, "Interdependence must be transformed into solidarity, based on the principle that the goods of creation are meant for all. That which human industry produces . . . must serve equally for the good of all."[34] The economy, whether in its simplest or its most complex objectifications, was made for man, not man for the economy.

By their fruits you shall know them. The fruits of the gifts that the Spirit gives, and the logic of abundance, are of a piece. But the fruits of a life lived in the flesh, in the Pauline view, is the opposite. Paul cites some of the fruits of such a life: "idolatry, hostilities, bickering, jealousy, outbursts of rage, selfish rivalries, dissensions, factions, envy."[35] Each of these produces its own kind of scarcity. The fruits of the Spirit, on the other hand, produce lives led with an eye to both the future abundance of eternal life and to others' present well-being. "The expectation of a new earth must not weaken but rather stimulate our concern for cultivating this one," the Second Vatican Council asserts. The Fathers continue: "For here grows the body of a new human family, a body which even now is able to give some kind of foreshadowing of the new age."[36] Only our failure in imagination would have us disconnect present sources of abundance from the gifting Spirit, or would confine the interests of God's Spirit to ecclesial well-being.

Conclusion

I have sought in this essay to suggest that Christian spirituality must be much more worldly than it is. It must move economic and financial matters beyond merely moral considerations to considerations that are specific to those who would have Christ as their wealth (Phil 3:8). The pursuit of monetary wealth must be judged on that distinct plane of meaning. A charism is like a seed deep in one's being, which calls for attention and nurture. It is the particular way that one is to minister to the concrete needs of others. Through one's gifted activities, God intends to favor and minister to the world. One's charism is the very particular way one is called to fulfill Christ's commandment to love one another. The wealth generated or not generated is neither the point of this chapter nor the purpose of the charism's exercise. The point, rather, is the discernment of charism as wealth-generating: where wealth is, there the abundance-intending God may be at work.

Notes

1. Mk 4:1–9.
2. Mt 25:14–30.
3. Lk 9:12–17.
4. Mk 4:30–32.
5. Jn 12:4–6.
6. Mk 12:42–44.
7. Gen 1:28–30.
8. 1 Cor 12:7; emphasis added.
9. "The Decree on the Apostolate of the Laity," *Vatican Council II: The Conciliar and Post Conciliar Documents*, ed. Austin Flannery, O.P. (New York: Costello Publishing Co., 1992), 3. Subsequent citations of the conciliar documents are from this source.
10. See Charles Clark's "Wealth as Abundance and Scarcity" and Dennis McCann's "Inequality in Income and Wealth" (chapters 1 and 7, this volume) for further connections between Sen and the thinking of the U.S. bishops in *Economic Justice for All*.

11. Amartya Sen, *Development as Freedom* (New York: Anchor Books, 1999), 86–110. The concept of poverty as capability deprivation shapes Sen's arguments throughout the book.

12. Lk 12:15–21.

13. Lk 12:19.

14. Lk 12:20.

15. Lk 12:21.

16. Lk 12:15.

17. For more development on this point, see John C. Haughey, *Virtue and Affluence: The Challenge of Wealth* (Kansas City, Mo.: Sheed & Ward, 1997).

18. Roger G. Betsworth, *Social Ethics: An Examination of American Moral Traditions* (Louisville, Ky.: Westminster/John Knox Press, 1990), 50–51.

19. Acts 4:34.

20. 1 Cor 12:7.

21. 1 Cor 12:11.

22. Eph 4:10.

23. 1 Cor 12:21.

24. 1 Cor 12:22.

25. 1 Cor 12:26.

26. 1 Cor 12:7.

27. 1 Cor 15:27.

28. 1 Cor 13:4–5.

29. 1 Cor 13:3.

30. Ibid.

31. John Paul II, *Sollicitudo rei socialis*, 38.

32. Ibid.

33. Lk 16:19–31.

34. John Paul II, *Sollicitudo rei socialis*, 39.

35. Gal 5:19–21.

36. Vatican Council II, *Gaudium et spes*, 39.

FOUR

Entrepreneurship in Papal Thought

Creation of Wealth and the Distribution of Justice

FRANCIS T. HANNAFEY, S.J.

Entrepreneurs are key actors in any understanding of wealth creation. It has long been recognized that they bring creativity, vision, and change to economic and business life. As innovators, talented organizers, risk-takers, and dynamic leaders who start businesses that generate new products and services, they bring together people, ideas, capital, and other resources to pursue market opportunities. Entrepreneurs mediate between, and creatively combine, diverse factors of production after making a reasoned assessment of consumer needs. Entrepreneurial activity is a leading source of new business development, job creation, and economic growth in many regions of the world.

In recent years, Roman Catholic social teaching has directed renewed attention to the subject of entrepreneurship and the role of the entrepreneur in creating wealth. John Paul II's 1991 encyclical, *Centesimus annus*, praises "initiative and entrepreneurial ability" and examines its moral importance for society.[1] Official papal pronouncements prior to *Centesimus annus* have been thought to pay relatively little attention to entrepreneurs and their role in business enterprise, but this judgment is not accurate. Earlier studies of papal teaching on the subject are not comprehensive, nor do they consider recent papal literature.[2] This study considers all the relevant papal sources—encyclicals, addresses, speeches, letters, and allocutions—from Leo XIII's *Rerum novarum* (1891) to John Paul II's *Centesimus annus*. Since Leo XIII, there have been significant papal efforts to understand entrepreneurs and their activities. While John Paul II's teachings on the subject break new ground in the tradition, they remain in close continuity with those of earlier popes. Achieving a more complete understanding of what the popes have officially taught on entrepreneurship provides us with important insights into overall patterns of Catholic social teaching on wealth creation as well as on wealth distribution.

Papal teachings present an important message on business entrepreneurship. This essay examines these teachings and studies their coherence and consistency. I trace the development of these teachings, explore moral concerns at their basis, and offer a theory of coherence to aid in their interpretation.[3] Papal teachings on entrepreneurship have developed gradually: the interests and concerns of individual popes, secular business theories of entrepreneurship as well as entrepreneurs themselves, and general economic conditions in society have influenced them.

The modern popes consistently describe entrepreneurship, and its wealth-creating ability, as an important kind of human work whose moral value is derived from its orientation to global economic justice. In many places, papal teaching directly links formal discussion of the wealth-creating capacity of entrepreneurship with the wealth-distributive concerns for global economic development. The popes see entrepreneurship in light of its capacity to develop the resources of the earth and serve human needs—especially those of the world's poor. After illustrating this point in the papal documents, I will discuss future directions for its development, drawing on contemporary business understandings of entrepreneurship. Finally, I will discuss the importance of wealth creation and distribution in the entrepreneurial process.

LEO XIII (1878–1903)

The pontificate of Leo XIII spanned twenty-five years and produced a sizeable literature, including the landmark encyclical *Rerum novarum* (1891). Leo's teachings do not directly refer to entrepreneurs, but he occasionally acknowledges their activities. Discussing political and economic liberty in the encyclical *Immortale dei* (1885), Leo shows openness to creative business innovation by stating that the Catholic Church "willingly and most gladly welcomes whatever improvements the age brings forth, if these really secure the prosperity of life."[4] He praises human "intellect and industry" and observes that Catholic teaching "earnestly wishes that the talents of men may bear more and more abundant fruit by cultivation and exercise."[5] Leo welcomes creative business activity, sound management, research, and productive innovations that serve human well-being.

Leo XIII often reflects on human labor and its importance to society. Defending a natural right to private property, *Quod apostolici muneris* (1878) praises the "labor of brain and hands" and recognizes "the different powers of body and mind" that exist among persons.[6] This encyclical sees the great value of such human powers in society's "distribution of the goods which are necessary for life and use."[7] *Rerum novarum* shows nuanced openness to work that may be associated with a broad understanding of entrepreneurship. The encyclical states:

> That which is required for the preservation of life, and for life's well being, is produced in great abundance from the soil, but not until man has brought it into cultivation and expended upon it his solicitude and skill . . . when man thus turns the activity of his mind and the strength of his body toward procuring the fruits of nature, by such an act he makes his own that portion of nature's field which he cultivates—that portion on which he leaves, as it were, the impress of his personality.[8]

Leo grasps that physical and intellectual work cultivates the earth's material resources and improves economic conditions for persons.

In places, *Rerum novarum* uses the term "industry" rather than "enterprise," yet entrepreneurship appears to be the implied meaning. For example, in defending private property rights, Leo notes that "the limits of private possession have been left to be fixed by man's own industry."[9] Criticizing socialist calls for abolition of private property and unjustified interference by civil government in family life, he predicts that "the sources of wealth themselves would run dry, for no one would have any interest in exerting his talents or his industry."[10] Further, *Rerum novarum* proposes that "social and public life can only be maintained by means of various kinds of capacity for business."[11] Here, Leo teaches that those who have received a large share of temporal blessings, including the gifts of mind and business ability, are to "employ them, as the steward of God's providence, for the benefit of others."[12] The pope understands human "industry" to include intellectual ability, strength of mind and body, and business talent.

Notably, Leo recognizes that the individual human capacity for business has great potential to improve material conditions in society for others. Leo does not specifically name entrepreneurs in contemporary terms, yet he was in conversation with several entrepreneurs as *Rerum novarum* was being drafted. The pope was particularly fond of the French entrepreneur Léon Harmel, whose worker pilgrimages to Rome impressed him greatly.[13] Leo saw in Harmel as well as in other entrepreneurs and employers a creative intellectual capacity to recognize productive opportunity and an ability to pursue more effective ways of cultivating this opportunity for the service of others. Of Harmel, Leo said, "It is necessary that Harmels be multiplied."[14]

Leo XIII's teachings do not reveal a comprehensive understanding of entrepreneurship, but they demonstrate recognition of some business activities that are associated with it. Leo's successors build on his insight into the intellectual and creative dimensions of human work—a view that later becomes important to papal understandings of entrepreneurship. With Leo XIII, official papal teaching begins to associate creative work with improved material well-being.

Pius XI (1922–1939)

Beginning his papacy in the years after World War I, Pius XI faced turbulent economic times. Conditions of unemployment and economic uncertainty led him to address business life often in his teachings. Pius, too, does not refer to "entrepreneurs" directly, but he shows a remarkable grasp of the entrepreneurial process. Oswald von Nell-Breuning, the acknowledged lead author of *Quadragesimo anno* (1931), later observed that Pius XI carefully recognizes the entrepreneur in his famous encyclical.[15] Using varied terms, *Quadragesimo anno* advances papal understanding of entrepreneurship and its wealth-creating capacity.[16]

Quadragesimo anno describes the creative business process as the application of human intelligence to productive activity. Discussing Church teaching authority in social and economic matters, Pius XI states that "the capacities of the human body and mind determine the limits of what productive human effort cannot and of what it can attain in the economic field."[17] Like Leo XIII, Pius sees that human creative capacities of body and mind make possible material production. *Quadragesimo anno* points to the contributions of "those who manage work and those who carry out directions" and "exercise the energies of mind and body."[18] Considering issues of distributive justice and human work, the pope urges the diligent use of "time and energies of body and mind."[19] Pius is critical of managers and others in established corporations who participate in financial speculation, while he often expresses appreciation for entrepreneurs and persons in small businesses. *Quadragesimo anno* underscores the importance of human intelligence in work and business activity— an insight frequently emphasized by later popes.

The encyclical's most direct acknowledgment of entrepreneurship appears in a discussion of human work. Paragraph 69 proposes that wealth cannot be created "unless mind, material things, and work combine and form as it were a single whole."[20] Nell-Breuning has observed that this part of *Quadragesimo anno* points favorably to the role that entrepreneurs play in economic life and understands entrepreneurship to be a three-part process.[21] Entrepreneurs exercise their intelligence (*intellectus*) to combine varied factors of capital (*res*) and labor (*opera*).[22] Pius brings papal teaching to a new stage of internal theoretical development by recognizing that entrepreneurs are persons who use their intelligence to transform matter through labor.

With Pius XI, official papal teaching begins to reflect on entrepreneurial ethics in a more direct way. *Quadragesimo anno* outlines in initial form a virtue ethic for the entrepreneur. Drawing on Thomas Aquinas, the pope writes:

> Expending larger incomes so that opportunity for gainful work may be abundant, provided, however, that this work is applied to producing really useful goods, ought to be considered, as we deduce from the principles of the Angelic Doctor, an outstanding exemplification of the *virtue of munificence* and one particularly suited to the needs of the times.[23]

The English translation of the "virtue of munificence" may not entirely convey the meaning of the official text. In the Latin text, Pius refers to the virtue of the entrepreneur as *"opus virtutis magnificentiae"* in a direct reference to the Thomistic (and Aristotelian) virtue of magnificence.[24] In this paragraph of the encyclical the pope directly references the *Summa theologiae,* which describes the special virtue of "magnificence" as "doing some great work."[25] Nell-Breuning has named this section of the encyclical "The Virtue of the Entrepreneur: Its Conditions." According to Nell-Breuning, Pius modernizes the medieval understanding of magnificence and transforms it into a modern virtue of producing something great for others. He observes that "the *magnificentia* of Pius XI is a genuinely capitalist virtue; indeed, the pope makes it the virtue of the entrepreneur."[26] For this pope, a primary virtue of entrepreneurship is service to others. By facilitating the production of useful goods and services and by creating and maintaining conditions that make possible gainful employment, the entrepreneur addresses the needs of others in society.

Later in the encyclical, Pius XI emphasizes the virtue of justice and its importance in wealth creation and distribution. *Quadragesimo anno* 69, which describes the wealth-creating capacity of the entrepreneur as *intellectus, res,* and *opera,* proposes that human work be evaluated "justly" and be compensated "according to justice."[27] Pius connects his three-part understanding of entrepreneurship with the virtue of justice. Magnificence (which Thomas Aquinas describes as a form of courage) requires alongside it the virtues of justice and prudence. Acknowledging the importance of economic enterprise, Pius deliberates about fairness and justice in wages and teaches that the lack of entrepreneurial initiative must not lead employers and entrepreneurs to "deprive workers of their just wage."[28] Wealth creation causes great harm to the common good when it promotes inequities. Similarly, discussing "initiative and industry" in the course of the encyclical's famous essay on the principle of subsidiarity, the pope uses the term "injustice" to characterize improper functioning of social organizations.[29] Further, citing "the free struggle of competitors," the encyclical again draws on a broad notion of justice and argues that entrepreneurial competition is "justified . . . provided it is kept within certain limits,"[30] in particular, the limits of the common good. For Pius, entrepreneurship and its wealth-creating function in society must not be seen apart from the virtue of distributive justice.

With Pius XI, papal teaching begins to consider entrepreneurship in a serious way. He introduces the idea that entrepreneurial ethics involve moral virtue—particularly the special Thomistic virtue of magnificence. Entrepreneurs do great things for society by performing highly complex and necessary tasks that most others are unable to accomplish. For this pope, the moral life of the entrepreneur involves dedicated service to the human community. At this stage in the development of papal teaching, entrepreneurship is associated with moral virtue, and especially with promotion of the common good through creating useful products and services, providing employment, and fostering a community of work. The responsibility of entrepreneurs to their firms and to society founds this newly emerging social ethic.

PIUS XII (1939–1958)

Pius XII never issued an encyclical on economic life, but he did make significant contributions to Catholic social thought in his 1,350 addresses and allocutions. His speeches and radio addresses draw on teachings of *Rerum novarum* and *Quadragesimo anno* and show an enduring interest in business. In many of these addresses he considers entrepreneurship.

Pius XII uses a number of terms to name entrepreneurs and their activities. He refers to them as business leaders, persons who take economic initiative, risk-takers, organizers, inventors, and persons with significant intellectual ability, and he sees that entrepreneurs use the capital of others. He is also the first pope to acknowledge the "entrepreneur" directly by this specific name. In a 1956 address to small-business managers, he praises the important and indispensable role of the contemporary entrepreneur in fostering "remarkable progress" in economic development (see Robert Kennedy, chapter 2, this volume, on this point).[31] Here the pope links entrepreneurship with economic progress—an association he makes often in his speeches and addresses.

Pius XII fleshes out his sense of entrepreneurship descriptively. In a 1956 address to economists, he uses the original French word *entrepreneur* and praises the leadership of "the enterprising man" and "men of initiative."[32] Elsewhere, he adopts the descriptions: men of initiative, the enterprising man, the businessman, and undertakers.[33] For him, entrepreneurs are managers, leaders, risk-takers, persons with technical skills, and businesspersons with extraordinary intelligence. As the first pope to adopt more consistently descriptive language in discussions of entrepreneurship, Pius XII inaugurates an important new stage in the development in the tradition.

In entrepreneurs, Pius recognizes persons who perform a number of important functions in the economy. They must make precise judgments about potential market opportunities and respond to changing consumer demand. Speaking to small business leaders, he observes that the

> marks of technical qualification and of adaptability to the demands of the consumer impress their requirements on the structure and the development of your enterprises. We should like to stress at this point the necessity for management to possess the qualities of true leadership . . . this calls for a man in whom the most varied intellectual gifts are united to a strong and versatile character.[34]

For this pope, entrepreneurship involves the creative human intellect—an idea previously advanced by Pius XI. In a 1955 address, Pius XII encourages savings banks to provide necessary assistance to "the enterprises which need considerable capital to fulfill their economic functions."[35] Further, he exhorts bankers to sustain "the institutions which are destined to promote individual initiative or small enterprises."[36] Pius XII teaches that banks are to "support progress" and the "path of development" as they make capital available to enterprises in different sectors of the economy.[37]

Pius XII often relates entrepreneurship to society's need for material progress and economic development. Speaking in 1956 to economists, he states that economic science has revealed

> the true meaning of the role of the enterprising man and his constructive action in determining economic progress . . . these leaders, the men of initiative, who imprint upon passing events the stamp of their individuality, discover new ways of doing things, communicate a decisive driving force, transform methods, and multiply to an astonishing degree the efficiency of men and machines.[38]

During the closing years of his pontificate, Pius praises entrepreneurship as necessary for worldwide economic development that improves the lives of the poor. Speaking to employers in 1955, when severe poverty existed in the south of Italy, he urges them to "become interested in new enterprises."[39] Two years later, he again observes that "private initiative will evidently have its important role in the struggle against destitution."[40] A recurring theme for Pius is that entrepreneurship can improve the lives of those who live in poverty.

Building upon Pius XI's focus on virtue, Pius XII points regularly to the moral responsibilities of entrepreneurs.[41] In an address that considers private "undertakings" and entrepreneurial initiative, he praises "the right to private property in stimulating initiative and fixing responsibility in economic matters."[42] Business leaders are to be attentive to "the serious moral consideration of the role and responsibilities of commerce."[43] He often discusses entrepreneurial responsibility alongside formal consideration of economic development issues. Citing "initiative" and "enterprise," he entreats business leaders: accept "your responsibility to see to it that the treasures of this life are henceforth increased."[44] Further, he states that moral responsibility in business involves sensitivity to "all human beings, even the poorest, the most helpless."[45] Speaking to business professionals about the importance of "private initiatives," Pius reminds them of their "grave responsibility, in regard to those, and especially those of a lower station, who call upon you to promote progress."[46]

Pius XII often refers enterprise to "common responsibility" and the "common good." He urges Catholic employers to accept their "full recognition of this common responsibility" and exhorts them to embrace the "common responsibility of all those who take part in production."[47] Further, when discussing business enterprise, he points to "the joint responsibility of all."[48] Like his predecessor, Pius understood well that entrepreneurs perform an important service to the wider community. Following his 1956 statement praising "the indispensable functions of the private entrepreneur," he proposes that firms be responsible for "services rendered to the national community."[49] He teaches that "private enterprise and small businesses must be thought of in terms of the nation as a whole."[50] In short, Pius does not accept an entrepreneurial ethic based on "private interests."[51] Rather, in his view, entrepreneurship is comparable "to a scientific invention or to an artistic work" that is "directed to the whole human community, which it enriches with new knowledge and with more powerful means of action."[52] The responsibility of businesspersons to the common good is at the center of Pius XII's moral evaluation of entrepreneurship. For him, private entrepreneurial initiative is inseparable from responsible attention to the economic needs of human communities.

JOHN XXIII (1958–1963)

Two of John XXIII's major encyclicals, *Mater et magistra* (1961) and *Pacem in terris* (1963), offer insight into his views on entrepreneurship. *Mater et magistra* recognizes entrepreneurial initiative as it provides for material human needs. The terms "initiative" and "enterprise" appear frequently throughout the encyclical, and the pope also adopts Pius XII's "undertakings" terminology.[53]

John XXIII emphasizes in *Mater et magistra* the importance of personal economic initiative within the context of the principle of subsidiarity. Drawing upon *Quadragesimo anno,* John states that it is an injustice for larger associations to claim responsibility for activities that can be performed by smaller associations or individuals.[54] In light of this principle of action, he maintains that "in the economic order first place must be given to the personal initiative of private citizens working either as individuals or in association with each other in various ways for the furtherance of common interests."[55] Discussing theories of industrialization, John urges that economic systems not lessen "opportunity for exercising personal initiative,"[56] since to deny "freedom of action" to individuals deters them from taking the only avenue toward perfecting their personality.[57] He explains that "there is an innate demand in human nature that when men engage in production they should have the opportunity of exercising responsibility and of perfecting their personalities."[58] Restating Catholic teaching on the right to private ownership, he suggests that "it would be quite useless to insist on free and personal initiative in the economic field, while at the same time withdrawing man's right to dispose freely of the means indispensable to the achievement of such initiative."[59] *Mater et magistra* describes personal initiative exercised through human work as an important part of economic enterprise. For John, the freedom to take initiative enables individuals to actualize themselves more fully as persons created and loved by God.

Mater et magistra and *Pacem in terris* closely link the right of enterprise and initiative with the responsibility of global economic development. In *Mater et magistra* the pope expresses concern that "less developed areas" receive necessary services and that conditions in such areas be considered in economic policy making.[60] John maintains that economic policy should be "designed to promote useful employment, [and] enterprising initiative," while "private enterprise too must contribute to an economic and social balance" in the political community.[61] Further, he states that "public authority must encourage and assist private enterprise, entrusting to it, wherever possible, the continuation of economic development."[62]

Pacem in terris also directly connects enterprise, or economic initiative, with economic development. The encyclical urges nations to assist each other in developing "an adventurous and enterprising spirit, and the resolution to take the initiative for their own advancement in every field of endeavor."[63] The pope supports progress in industry and in other human activities and observes that "every day provides a more important, a more fitting enterprise to which they must turn their hands."[64] In *Pacem in terris,* a well-ordered society that yields "abundant resources" requires "the involvement and collaboration of all men in the many enterprises which our present civilization makes possible."[65] John XXIII's encyclical teachings also describe entrepreneurial initiative in light of its potential contributions to economic development in regions of the world where economic deprivation is severe.

Like his predecessors, John's vision of entrepreneurship is consistently linked to moral reflection about responsibility to the common good. *Mater et magistra* and *Pacem in terris* display this pattern. *Mater et magistra* sees "personal initiative" in the economic order as morally directed to "the furtherance of common interests."[66] The pope explains that "personal initiative" in economic systems is part of a properly human "sense of responsibility."[67] Discussing the need for economic advancement in "less developed areas," *Mater et magistra* urges that economic productive activity enable persons to act and to be treated as "responsible human beings."[68] John insists that entrepreneurial initiative must not be seen apart from moral responsibility, yet he does not specify the precise moral implications of this responsibility.

John also advances a human rights argument in his considerations of entrepreneurial initiative. *Mater et magistra* defends the right to the private ownership of property, "including productive goods," and argues that such a right extends to "free and personal initiative in the economic field."[69] *Pacem in terris* again connects economic initiative with responsibility: human dignity requires that each person has the "right to engage in economic activities suited to his degree of responsibility."[70] Further, all have "the right to exercise their own initiative and act on their own responsibility."[71] *Pacem in terris* proposes that human dignity demands scope for a man to "act on his own initiative, conviction, and sense of responsibility."[72]

John XXIII relates economic initiative to the need for economic development in the world's poorest regions. Entrepreneurship's promise as an engine of development accounts for its appearing to John—albeit indirectly—in a favorable light. Like Pius XII, John XXIII argues for a close association between economic initiative and moral responsibility. Human rights, based on the dignity of the person in community, ground this pope's ethic of responsibility.

PAUL VI (1963–1978)

Although his pontificate was preoccupied with implementing decisions of the Second Vatican Council, Paul VI brought fresh ideas to Catholic social teaching on business life. In his encyclical *Populorum progressio* (1967), global economic development emerges as a central concern. This encyclical closely connects economic initiative with global economic development.

Populorum progressio praises economic initiative in individuals and organizations. Expressing deep moral concern for the "impoverished and disunited," Paul states that these persons are "deprived of almost all possibility of acting on their own initiative."[73] Further, he observes that "lacking the bare necessities of life, whole nations are under the thumb of others; they cannot act on their own initiative."[74] But individual economic initiative alone is not enough to meet pressing needs for development. *Populorum progressio* praises the economic initiatives of "intermediary organizations" since "individual initiative and the interplay of competition will not insure satisfactory development."[75] Discussing efforts to promote economic development, the pope urges public authorities to "see to it that private initiative and intermediary organizations are involved."[76] For him, both individual and organizational initiatives are necessary to facilitate economic development where severe poverty exists.

Paul VI uses the term "entrepreneur" less frequently than earlier popes. Nevertheless *Populorum progressio* describes with precision a variety of entrepreneurial activities in a section of the encyclical entitled "Man's Complete Development."[77] When considering the industrialization necessary for "economic growth and human progress," Paul proposes that through "intelligent thought and hard work, man gradually uncovers the hidden laws of nature and learns to make better use of natural resources. As he takes control over his way of life, he is stimulated to undertake new investigations and fresh discoveries, to take prudent risks and launch new ventures."[78] Here, Pope Paul describes what entrepreneurs typically contribute to economic development.

At times, Paul directly acknowledges entrepreneurship and refers to entrepreneurs by this name. Speaking to the Christian Union of Employers and Executives in 1964, he states:

> We have a true respect for what you are: leaders of industry, as you are called today, entrepreneurs, executives, producers of wealth, organizers of modern businesses . . . it is you who create opportunities for work . . . you are in the forefront of those who transform society, who have the greatest influence on living conditions, and who open the way to new, undreamt-of developments.[79]

The pope's broad definition of entrepreneurs succeeds in highlighting their transformative and developmental functions. Later in this address, the pope offers a more concise description: "you are men of dynamic ideas and brilliant initiatives; you are used to taking healthy risks, to making beneficial sacrifices and resolute forecasts."[80] For Paul, entrepreneurs are moved by a kind of practical idealism to take initiative and to accept business risks.[81]

Paul VI's understanding of entrepreneurship develops during his pontificate. By the 1970s, he sees that entrepreneurship brings together business initiative or market insight with capital and that the creation and survival of business enterprises require both. During a 1972 address to French executives, he distinguishes between economic and technical power. Economic power is "connected with all the conditions that are outside the work of the enterprise properly speaking; not just the original initiative and capital without which the enterprise could not have come into being or survived."[82] Further, Paul discusses the need for sound direction and management and urges that these questions receive "deep reflection among Catholic entrepreneurs."[83] He praises the "initiative" entrepreneurs bring to enterprises, exhorts them to "create working conditions which make possible the exercise of initiative,"[84] and concludes that the world needs "bold and creative innovations."[85] Paul's vision of entrepreneurship emphasizes the human mind, intelligent work, and creativity. He looks favorably on scientific and technological advances that foster economic development.

Paul VI also strengthens the relationship in papal teaching between entrepreneurial initiative and moral responsibility. This is apparent in *Populorum progressio.* The encyclical juxtaposes worldwide economic inequalities by which many persons "are deprived of almost all possibility of acting on their own initiative and responsibility,"[86] with the condition for economic growth, which requires persons to "take prudent risks and launch new ventures, to act responsibly."[87] Paul VI's many messages to businesspersons are striking calls for entrepreneurs to embrace their moral obligations to make the world a better place.

John Paul II (1978–2005)

John Paul II makes important contributions to Catholic social teaching on entrepreneurship. He singles out entrepreneurs and their activities by name more often than do his predecessors. Many of John Paul's teachings suppose the moral importance of wealth creation and distribution.

In *Laborem exercens* (1981), his first major encyclical on economic life, John Paul makes four direct references to entrepreneurs, all of which appear in the context of the conflict between labor and capital and the problem of ownership and wealth distribution.[88] Entrepreneurs are seen to be influential persons on the side of capital, who exercise power over labor through the pursuit of maximum profit.[89] In a section entitled "Importance of Unions," where he defends the Catholic social principle of the right to association, he examines the historical development of labor unions and the importance of human work. He observes that "the modern unions grew up from the struggle of the workers . . . to protect their just rights vis-à-vis the entrepreneurs and the owners of the means of production."[90]

Laborem exercens relates the often difficult conflict between entrepreneurs, employers, and labor to questions concerning ownership of the means of production. In a section entitled "Work and Ownership," John Paul argues that economic production does not involve abstract concepts or "impersonal forces," but that rather "behind both concepts there are people, living, actual people."[91] Hence, "the issue of ownership or property enters from the beginning into the whole of this difficult historical process [of the dissociation of labor from capital]."[92] John Paul proposes that one way to mediate the conflict is to examine how wealth is distributed. While the pope refuses to endorse particular ownership programs or proposals, he states that "it is clear that recognition of the proper position of labor and the worker in the production process demands various adaptations in the sphere of the right to ownership of the means of production."[93] When entrepreneurs share with their employees the ownership of the firm, the likelihood of creating an authentic community of work increases.

In *Sollicitudo rei socialis* (1987), John Paul does not directly name entrepreneurs, but following *Populorum progressio* he closely connects the encyclical's discussion of business initiative with global economic development.[94] Discussing worldwide poverty, he affirms that persons have "the right to share in the building of society, the freedom to organize and to form unions or to take initiatives in economic matters."[95] Further, considering Church teachings on economic underdevelopment, he concludes that "development demands above all a spirit of initiative on the part of countries which need it. . . . Each must discover and use to the best advantage its own area of freedom. Each must make itself capable of initiatives responding to its own needs as a society."[96] John Paul urges nations to encourage conditions that foster the business initiative necessary for improved economic development. In *Sollicitudo rei socialis,* he praises creative initiative and teaches that the freedom to take economic initiative is a human right, respect for which is necessary to ensure global economic development. While not directly naming entrepreneurs, *Sollicitudo rei socialis* accurately depicts many of the business initiatives that they often carry out.

In *Centesimus annus* (1991), John Paul brings Roman Catholic teaching on entrepreneurship to a new stage. Reflecting on this encyclical, Rocco Buttiglione has observed that "very seldom has the role of entrepreneurship as the creative side of human work been so clearly set forth and so highly evaluated."[97] Further, Buttiglione notes "the encyclical's extraordinarily positive evaluation of human freedom in the economic field and the function of the entrepreneur."[98]

Centesimus annus describes entrepreneurship as intelligent work that enables business to meet human needs. Entrepreneurs possess the uniquely important ability to assess consumer needs and then make realistic judgments about production. Paragraph 32 describes entrepreneurship as "know-how, technology, and skill" essential to the creation of material and nonmaterial wealth.[99] *Centesimus annus* sees in entrepreneurship constructive human work that involves creative intelligence and insight into both "productive possibilities" and "the needs of those for whom their work is done."[100] Entrepreneurs are persons who excel at this special kind of work.

An important description of entrepreneurship follows the encyclical's discussion of human work. John Paul writes:

> It is precisely the ability to foresee both the needs of others and the combinations of productive factors most adapted to satisfying those needs that constitutes another important source of wealth in modern society. . . . Organizing such a productive effort, planning its duration in time, making sure that it corresponds in a positive way to the demands which it must satisfy, and taking the necessary risks—all this too is a source of wealth in today's society. In this way, the *role* of disciplined and creative *human work* and, as an essential part of that work, *initiative and entrepreneurial ability,* become increasingly evident and decisive. This process . . . should be viewed carefully and favorably.[101]

John Paul expresses high appreciation for entrepreneurs,[102] for their creative ability to foresee market needs and to organize the right combinations of productive resources to meet those needs.[103] Following a pattern in earlier papal teachings, *Centesimus annus* stresses "initiative."[104] More than his predecessors, John Paul emphasizes that entrepreneurs are persons who carry out the work of fructifying others' work, a task that requires special talent and ability.

It is noteworthy that John Paul grasps the centrality of risk-taking to entrepreneurial initiative.[105] He acknowledges the risks entrepreneurs accept in starting new businesses and advocates "prudence in undertaking reasonable risks."[106] The encyclical observes that entrepreneurial risk requires knowledge often unavailable to persons who are economically marginalized, and it specifically cites citizens of "the Third World."[107] When such necessary knowledge is unavailable to marginalized persons, "economic development takes place over their heads."[108] Accordingly, immediately following the encyclical's celebrated description of entrepreneurship, John Paul carefully considers global economic development issues. In this way, *Centesimus annus* closely connects its teachings on entrepreneurship with urgent moral concern for global economic development. This pattern is also discernable in John Paul's many addresses to various groups.

In his speeches to business groups, John Paul frequently singled out entrepreneurs when discussing global economic development. Meeting with workers, technicians, managers, and entrepreneurs in Fiorano, Italy, he exhorted them to "use those areas of freedom that are today in the hands of workers and entrepreneurs above all to promote and create new activities that provide employment."[109] A 1985 address to entrepreneurs on production and economic development notes:

the task of entrepreneurs and executives in this regard will have to include the study of ways of illuminating, explaining and inventing the strategies of action that may serve man, orient his choices and find remedies for the possible negative aspects, in order to ensure that human beings always be the privileged users and conscious architects of development.[110]

Meeting with Bolivian businesspersons three years later, John Paul directly connected entrepreneurship with economic development and urges that attention be devoted to:

the person, his nature, his relationship with other creatures and with his Creator, in order to achieve the necessary balance of development for the benefit of all. Only by taking the person as the starting point will you succeed in making enterprise an agent of this development, taking risks and raising the creative potential to its highest level in the production of goods and the creation of jobs at the service of all.[111]

John Paul's encyclical teachings devote considerable attention to entrepreneurial morality. *Laborem exercens* relates entrepreneurship to questions of ownership and wealth distribution.[112] *Sollicitudo rei socialis* recognizes a human right to take "economic initiative,"[113] a right that is "important not only for the individual, but also for the common good."[114] Hence, *Sollicitudo rei socialis* juxtaposes economic initiative to its consideration of world poverty and development issues; immediately prior to "the right of economic initiative" proposal in paragraph 15, the encyclical examines poverty and global development in detail.[115] Here the pope refers repeatedly to "economic development" and notes "the widening gap between the areas of the so-called developed North and the developing South."[116] *Sollicitudo rei socialis* also locates its discussion of economic initiative in the context of "poverty" and "concern for the poor."[117] John Paul sees an urgent, worldwide demand for productive entrepreneurship that will serve the needs of human beings.

Among John Paul's encyclicals, *Centesimus annus* brings new depth to considerations of entrepreneurship. Prior to the encyclical's description of "initiative and entrepreneurial ability," John Paul uses theological language to describe how through work—that is, through the exercise of intelligence, freedom, and business creativity—persons respond to God's gift of the earth for the sustenance of all (see Simona Beretta, chapter 5, this volume). Moreover, the encyclical affirms a "responsibility not to hinder others from having their own part of God's gift."[118] Paragraph 32, which contains the well-known statement on "entrepreneurial ability," cites "the right to freedom, as well as the duty of making responsible use of freedom."[119] Morally responsible entrepreneurship must preserve the rights of all people to share in the fruitfulness of the earth. As in many of John Paul's teachings, the good of the human person in community is a fundamental moral category.

Unsurprisingly, therefore, *Centesimus annus* brings entrepreneurship within the scope of the traditional moral virtues: "Important virtues are involved in this process, such as diligence, industriousness, prudence in undertaking reasonable risks, reliability and fidelity in interpersonal relationships, as well as courage in carrying out decisions which are difficult and painful but necessary, both for the overall working of a business and in meeting possible setbacks."[120] While John Paul cites the virtues, he does not offer a precise explanation of their bearing on entrepreneurial activity. This much may be immediately gathered: the pope wishes to resist any notion that entrepreneurship could be reduced to technical know-how or could be exercised except as a fully human—morally significant—activity. Thus, he cites the virtue of prudence, which, for Thomas Aquinas, founds the other moral virtues.

Centesimus annus clarifies earlier papal pronouncements, which have centered on moral evaluations of entrepreneurship on practical rationality, shaped by virtue. Prudence is acknowledged as fundamental: entrepreneurs must proceed on the basis of reasoned judgments about market realities. Courage is also necessary in making difficult decisions that entail risk. John Paul's "diligence" recalls Aquinas's virtue of perseverance, which involves acceptance of "a special kind of difficulty" and "enduring delays . . . so far as necessity requires."[121] Difficulties are the normal course for entrepreneurs—challenges that require "special" virtue and commitment. *Laborem exercens* argues that industriousness is the personal virtue by which a person orders her toil to the achievement of common prosperity. Reliability and fidelity seem to be specifications of justice proper to business relationships. We may conclude that John Paul brings greater specificity to papal teaching by advancing the outline of an ethic of entrepreneurial virtue drawing on the traditional moral thought of Thomas Aquinas, although he does not take up *Quadragesimo anno*'s consideration of the virtue of magnificence.

Like earlier popes, John Paul stresses the responsibilities of entrepreneurs. In a 1990 speech at an Olivetti plant, he urged the responsible use of computer technologies, suggesting that "this presupposes, on the part of *entrepreneurs,* a breadth of vision and an alert awareness of their own responsibility which extends beyond the purely managerial and financial field."[122] In the following year he reaffirmed that entrepreneurs are responsible to the common good: dignity and responsibility "become evident in a special way in enterprise and in the entrepreneur who, under the impulse and according to the dispositions of the State, are called to play an irreplaceable social role in the order of the common good."[123]

At times, John Paul adopts communitarian language to describe the responsibilities of entrepreneurs. In a 1985 address, he stated that "the ethical commitment which would impose itself upon the Christian conscience of entrepreneurs and executives [is to be so] . . . understood that with regard to these questions it was necessary to reflect and search not in an isolated but in a communitarian way."[124] Further, he urged them to discover "a renewed sense of personal and communitarian responsibility . . . working in . . . [a] spirit of service."[125] John Paul's entrepreneurial ethic takes shape within a vision of business organizations as communities of persons,[126] signed with the mark of community, a common good.

John Paul reaffirms and extends the teachings of his predecessors. Entrepreneurs have responsibilities to, and for, the common good, and especially for promoting the common good of ready opportunities for dignified, sufficiently remunerative employment. These responsibilities extend to persons within organizations as well as to the wider sociopolitical community. The cultivation of virtues specific to entrepreneurial activity is required if entrepreneurs are to meet their responsibilities. Yet, like his predecessors, John Paul does not carry this analysis down to the particulars of work-a-day business practice. His teaching stops short of a full normative theory of entrepreneurship and of a theory of welfare economics.

Summary and Future Directions

While their teachings are varied and have undergone gradual development, the documentary evidence reveals that the modern popes present a coherent moral message on business entrepreneurship. The papal teachings show internal coherence in two key areas.

Dignity of Entrepreneurial Work

The popes have sought to reaffirm in modern economic life the great dignity of human work. They have positively affirmed the entrepreneur's important role in initiating economic processes by integrating "mind, material things, and work" in "a single whole,"[127] in the words of Pius XI. As doctors, teachers, laborers, craftsmen, farmers, lawyers, and others have their unique roles to play in a healthy society, so also do entrepreneurs. In particular, entrepreneurs are to be guaranteed the rights to economic initiative and private property in order to carry out freely their vocation to provide goods and services and thereby to create wealth. They must also personally develop the virtues of diligence, industriousness, courage, and prudence so as to exercise these rights. The rights articulated by the popes look to secure entrepreneurs' freedom of action, and the virtues look to guide that freedom's use to certain ends: providing abundant, accessible goods and services, and promoting human flourishing.

As John Paul insists, the dignity of entrepreneurial work is in part predicated on its "subjective dimension."[128] When entrepreneurs work, they are not only achieving material, economic objectives or goals, since the activity of work does not terminate only in objects. Entrepreneurs change the world and themselves; they transform nature and the conditions for others' development. Enterprise is, like all human action, reflexive. Entrepreneurs not only shape the objective dimensions of work but also, and simultaneously, shape its subjective dimension. That is, they open for themselves and for their collaborators opportunities to work, in John Paul II's phrase, "for themselves": for their development in skill, in virtue, and in solidarity; as colleagues, parents, and citizens, and in all ways, as participants in common goods.

John Paul II's teachings on the dignity of entrepreneurial work affirm the role of the individual entrepreneur, yet his teachings are not new in the papal tradition. Contrary to views expressed by commentators such as Michael Novak and George Weigel, there have been significant efforts by earlier popes to understand the unique role of entrepreneurs and their activities.[129] This study has shown that John Paul's own teachings are closely linked to these earlier pronouncements. The suggestion that *Centesimus annus* marks a dramatic shift in papal thought on the subject does not survive examination of the entire documentary tradition. John Paul does consider entrepreneurs more often and, at times, in greater depth than do his predecessors, but his teachings are remarkably consistent with those of earlier popes.

Goal of Entrepreneurial Work

A consistent element of papal teaching is that the wealth created by the entrepreneur in providing goods and services needs to be justly distributed. (For a concrete discussion of how this can be done, see Michael Naughton and Robert Wahlstedt, chapter 11, this volume.) While the right to economic initiative is crucial to the entrepreneur, the corresponding responsibility to promote economic development, especially in regard to the poor and marginalized, is no less central. Indeed, this responsibility represents the central point of coherence in papal teachings on entrepreneurship in the modern period. While the right to private property must be guaranteed, this right is subordinated to the universal destination of material goods and to the moral demand to alleviate poverty. When these corresponding responsibilities are neglected, the dignity of entrepreneurial work suffers.

The virtues are at the center of papal teachings on entrepreneurship because they are the nexus between effective business activity, including wealth creation, and effective and just forms of wealth distribution. The list of entrepreneurial virtues includes not only perseverance, ingenuity, persistence, and prudence but also magnificence, justice, and solidarity. Pius XI's emphasis on magnificence, for example, contrasts significantly with business models that make autonomy the entrepreneur's signal "virtue." The popes exhort entrepreneurs to do great things because they redound to others' benefit and give birth to common goods. Further, the popes highly value entrepreneurs as persons called to a life of special virtue, that is, to power in the community. Entrepreneurs bring new vitality to economic structures that profoundly shape social relationships. Papal teaching sees new ventures as complex social networks, vibrant organizations of persons, pregnant with opportunities for both material and human benefit.

Papal teaching on entrepreneurial virtue represents a rich resource for continuing reflection on entrepreneurship. Both papal teaching and business scholarship devote significant attention to the dynamic persons who are entrepreneurs. Since these individuals often exercise decisive personal influence on the business cultures that emerge from their ventures, their personal ethics are of continuing theoretical interest. The papal focus on the virtues is well suited to contribute to further developments in thinking on entrepreneurship.

We may hope that future papal documents will explore in greater detail how entrepreneurial virtue emerges from—that is, captures—and refines excellence in entrepreneurial practice. Likewise, we may hope for a correspondingly detailed account of entrepreneurial responsibility. In particular, since financial profits are fundamental to contemporary business theories of entrepreneurship, a normative teaching on profit is to be desired. Catholic reflection on wealth creation should also devote more attention to entrepreneurs inside corporations and other organizations, the so-called intrapreneurs. They are bound to become increasingly important to global entrepreneurial activity. And since entrepreneurship varies with differences among societies and cultures around the world, the long-standing papal concern with comparative conditions for development might naturally be extended to comparative entrepreneurship. In any case, future papal teaching on wealth creation will look to develop Catholic social doctrine as "a category of its own" out of "careful reflection on the complex realities" presented by the times and in light of the Gospel and tradition.[130] The times may dictate new emphases, but we can expect overall certainty with the development detailed in this essay.

Notes

A version of this essay first appeared in *Louvain Studies* 26 (2001): 217–44, entitled "Entrepreneurship in Papal Thought." I am grateful to Terrence Merrigan, managing editor of *Louvain Studies,* for granting permission to publish a revised version in the present volume. I am also grateful to Helen Alford, Charles Clark, Elizabeth A. Dreyer, Stephen M. Fields, S.J.,

Paul F. Lakeland, Thomas J. Massaro, S.J., Michael J. Naughton, William R. O'Neill, S.J., and John E. Thiel for their helpful recommendations to improve this essay. I also wish to acknowledge Fairfield University for granting a sabbatical that facilitated the completion of this study as well as the Jesuit School of Theology at Berkeley for generous academic and research support.

1. *Centesimus annus*, 32.

2. See Raymond J. Miller, "Papal Pronouncements on the Entrepreneur," *Review of Social Economy* 8 (March 1950): 35–44; and Bernard W. Dempsey, *The Functional Economy: The Bases of Economic Organization* (Englewood Cliffs, N.J.: Prentice-Hall, 1958), esp. 353–65.

3. For a useful study of theories of coherence in papal teaching, see Michael J. Schuck, *That They Be One: The Social Teaching of the Papal Encyclicals, 1740–1989* (Washington, D.C.: Georgetown University Press, 1991), esp. 173–88.

4. Leo XIII, *Immortale dei*, 38.

5. Ibid., 39. The term "cultivation" and the importance of creative human talent are repeating themes in Leo XIII's teachings. See also *Rerum novarum*, 9, 34.

6. Leo XIII, *Quod apostolici muneris*, 1, 9.

7. Ibid., 9.

8. *Rerum novarum*, 9. The original text reads *"ex se sine hominum cultu et curatione non posset,"* where persons cultivate through the use of mind and body the goods of nature. The Latin term *cultus* can mean "physical" or "mental" cultivation. See *Rerum novarum*, 9, in *American Ecclesiastical Review* 5 (August–September 1891): 145.

9. Ibid., 8. The original text uses the term *industriae hominum*, which appears to refer in a general way to "human industry," but implied in this phrase is the idea of human "initiative." See *Rerum novarum*, 8, in *American Ecclesiastical Review* 5 (August–September 1891): 145.

10. Ibid., 15.

11. Ibid., 17.

12. Ibid., 22.

13. Joan Coffey, *Léon Harmel: Entrepreneur as Catholic Social Reformer* (Notre Dame, Ind.: University of Notre Dame Press, 2003), see chapter 4, "Pilgrimage to Rome."

14. Joseph Gremillion, *Catholic Movement of Employers and Managers* (Rome: Gregorian University Press, 1961), 26.

15. See Oswald von Nell-Breuning, *Reorganization of Social Economy: The Social Encyclical Developed and Explained,* English edition prepared by Bernard W. Dempsey (New York and Chicago: Bruce Publishing Company, 1936), 115. This section of Nell-Breuning's commentary refers specifically to *Quadragesimo anno*, 69.

16. In *Quadragesimo anno*, business activities are cited by different terms. Among the more frequently used phrases to describe creative business endeavors are "technique" (41), "industry" (49, 63, 79), and "initiative" (72, 79).

17. Pius XI, *Quadragesimo anno*, 42.

18. Ibid., 53.

19. Ibid., 57.

20. Ibid., 69. The original text reads "*quod maius est, consocientur ac quasi in unum conveniant intellectus, res, opera, nequit fructus suos gignere efficientia hominum.*" See *Quadragesimo anno,* 69, in *Two Basic Social Encyclicals* (Washington, D.C.: Catholic University of America Press, 1943), 132.

21. See Nell-Breuning, *Reorganization of Social Economy,* 167–68. See also Michael Novak, "Enterprise," in *The New Dictionary of Catholic Social Thought,* ed. Judith A. Dwyer (Collegeville, Minn.: Liturgical Press/Michael Glazier, 1994), 338–41.

22. Nell-Breuning, *Reorganization of Social Economy,* 167–68.

23. Pius XI, *Quadragesimo anno,* 51, emphasis added.

24. See *Quadragesimo anno,* in *Acta Apostolicae Sedis,* 23 (1931): 194.

25. See Thomas Aquinas, *Summa theologiae* IIa-IIae, q. 134.2.

26. Nell-Breuning, *Reorganization of Social Economy,* 115.

27. *Quadragesimo anno,* 69. The official Latin text uses the terms *intellectus, res, opera.* See *Quadragesimo anno,* in *Acta Apostolicae Sedis* 23 (1931): 200.

28. Ibid., 72.

29. Ibid., 79.

30. Ibid., 88. See also Schuck, *That They Be One,* 83.

31. Pius XII, "Address to the First National Congress of Small Industry, January 20, 1956," in *The Pope Speaks* 3 (1956–57): 50.

32. See Pius XII, "Address to the First Congress of the International Association of Economists, September 9, 1956," in *The Pope Speaks* 3 (1956–57): 244. Here, Pius uses the term *entrepreneur* in the French text of this address. He praises "*la signification vraie du rôle de l'entrepreneur, son action constructive et déterminante dans le progrès économique*" and also acknowledges "*les chefs, les hommes d'initiative.*" See "Address to '*le premier congrès de l'association internationale des economistes,*' September 9, 1956," in *Acta Apostolicae Sedis* 48 (1956): 672. Here the pope associates the entrepreneur with economic progress.

33. References to "undertakers" and "undertaking," terms once used by economists to describe entrepreneurs and their activities, appear regularly in Pius XII's documents. Concerned about poverty, Pius observes that "private undertakings . . . with a lively impulse and laudable determination, now strive to put an end to such conditions." See "Address to the Seventh National Congress of the Christian Employers' Association of Italy, June 5, 1955," in *The Pope Speaks* 2 (1955): 154. See also "Address to the Delegates to the Catholic International Congresses for Social Study and Social Action, June 3, 1950," in *Catholic Mind* 48 (August 1950): 508; and "Address to the International Federation of National Associations of Technicians, October 9, 1953," in *Catholic Documents* 16 (December 1954): 5.

34. "Address to the First National Congress of Small Industry, January 20, 1956," 50–51. Speaking to a group of business leaders the following month, Pius XII suggested that those who lead entrepreneurial businesses "must have a mind always quick to understand and follow up economic trends as they develop." See Pius XII, "Address to the Italian Federation of Commerce, February 17, 1956," in *The Pope Speaks* 3 (1956–57): 46.

35. "Address to the Administrative Council of the International Savings Institute, May 16, 1955," in *The Pope Speaks* 2 (1955): 143–44.

36. Ibid., 144.

37. "Address to the Directors and Staff of the Bank of Naples, May 29, 1955," in *The Pope Speaks* 2 (1955): 145.

38. "Address to the First Congress of the International Association of Economists, September 9, 1956," 244. Immediately following this description, Pius XII states that enterprise does not coincide with "private interests," but rather, such activity is "directed to the whole human community." In the French text of this address the pope uses the terms *l'entrepreneur* and *les hommes d'initiative.* See *Acta Apostolicae Sedis* 48 (1956): 672.

39. "Address to the Seventh National Congress of the Christian Employers' Association of Italy, June 5, 1955," 156. Here, Pius uses the term "undertaking" in discussing the need for enterprise to combat widespread poverty, and he urges that "private undertakings . . . strive to put an end to such conditions."

40. "Address to the 'Stations de Plein Air' Movement, May 3, 1957," in *The Pope Speaks* 4 (1957–58): 208. In this text, given in French, Pius speaks of *"initiative privée."* See *Acta Apostolicae Sedis* 49 (1957): 354.

41. Pius XII does not focus on the virtues in his moral evaluations of entrepreneurship, but on one occasion he refers to magnanimity. Speaking to small-business managers and detailing the moral significance of entrepreneurial leadership, he states: "[t]his calls for a man . . . in whom, above all, there is a sense of morality that is sincere and magnanimous." See Pius XII, "Address to the First National Congress of Small Industry, January 20, 1956," 51.

42. "Address to the Delegates to the Catholic International Congresses for Social Study and Social Action, June 3, 1950," 508. Immediately prior to this statement the pope discusses the "personal responsibility" of persons engaged in business.

43. "Address to the World Congress of Chambers of Commerce, April 27, 1950," in *Catholic Mind* 48 (August 1950): 510.

44. "Address to Catholic Associations of Small- and Medium-sized Businesses, October 8, 1956," in *The Pope Speaks* 3 (1956–57): 409. When addressing technicians he also praises "the good and beautiful created by men's initiative" and teaches that professionals in enterprises are "entrusted with responsibility, to be left to take initiative." See Pius XII, "Address to the International Federation of National Associations of Technicians, October 9, 1953," 4.

45. "Address to Catholic Associations of Small- and Medium-sized Businesses, October 8, 1956," 409.

46. "Address to the University Graduates' Division of Italian Catholic Action, May 24, 1953," in *Catholic Mind* 51 (August 1953): 502. Speaking to Christian executives in 1957, he repeatedly points to their "personal responsibility." See Pius XII, "Address to the Christian Union of Executives and Businessmen, March 7, 1957," in *The Pope Speaks* 4 (1957–58): 88–89.

47. "Address to the International Association of Catholic Employers, May 7, 1949," in *Catholic Documents* 2 (August 1950): 15.

48. Ibid., 16.

49. "Address to the First National Congress of Small Industry, January 20, 1956," 50. In a speech to small-business leaders, immediately following a discussion of entrepreneurs, Pius describes "the transcendent vocation of the human being, and his personal responsibility before God."

50. Ibid.

51. "Address to the First Congress of the International Association of Economists, September 9, 1956," 244.

52. Ibid. In an address that acknowledges the spirit of initiative and activities of the private business person, Pius XII argues that productive activity is "for the greater good of the community." See "Address to Catholic Associations of Small- and Medium-sized Businesses, October 8, 1956," 406.

53. For example, see *Mater et magistra*, 51, 83, 84, 87.

54. Ibid., 53.

55. Ibid., 51. In the Latin text, the pope describes "personal initiative" as "*singularium hominum industriae.*" See John XXIII, *Mater et magistra* (Rome: UCID, 1962), 37. Here, John notes the importance of both individual and organizational initiative in economic life. He also mentions the importance of an active state of fostering human initiative as well as regulating and limiting its abuses.

56. *Mater et magistra*, 83.

57. Ibid., 55.

58. Ibid., 82.

59. Ibid., 109. In the Latin text when discussing "free and personal initiative," the pope uses the phrase "*facultas permittitur libere deligendi.*" See John XXIII, *Mater et magistra* (Rome: UCID, 1962), 57.

60. Ibid., 150.

61. Ibid., 150, 152.

62. Ibid., 152. The Latin text is consistent with much of the tradition in using the term *inceptis* in reference to enterprise activity. Here the pope uses the phrase "*privatorum hominum inceptus.*" See John XXIII, *Mater et magistra* (Rome: UCID, 1962), 77.

63. *Pacem in terris*, 120.

64. Ibid., 156. Here the encyclical refers directly to business enterprise, using the Latin phrase "*incepta suscipienda.*" See John XXIII, *Pacem in terris*, 156, in *Acta Apostolicae Sedis* 55 (1963): 298.

65. Ibid., 33. Here, when referring to "many enterprises," John uses the phrase "*plurimis inceptis*" to mean undertaking many business enterprises. See John XXIII, *Pacem in terris*, 33, in *Acta Apostolicae Sedis* 55 (1963): 265.

66. *Mater et magistra*, 51.

67. Ibid., 83.

68. Ibid., 151.

69. Ibid., 109.

70. *Pacem in terris*, 20.

71. Ibid., 23.

72. Ibid., 34.

73. *Populorum progressio*, 9.

74. Ibid., 30. Paul VI has "enterprise" in mind here as he writes in the official text "*inceptum sua sponte inire,*" which may be translated "to enter upon an enterprise freely" or "on

their own initiative." The term *inceptum* may be associated with business enterprise and is translated as "beginning" or "undertaking." See *Populorum progressio*, 30, in *Acta Apostolicae Sedis* 59 (1967): 272.

75. Ibid., 33. In the official text, Paul uses the Latin term *incepta* in two direct references to enterprise initiative. See *Populorum progressio*, 33, in *Acta Apostolicae Sedis* 59 (1967): 273.

76. Ibid. Paul again uses the term *incepta* in the encyclical when discussing obstacles to development. See *Populorum progressio*, 33, in *Acta Apostolicae Sedis* 59 (1967): 273.

77. See *Populorum progressio*, 6–42.

78. Ibid., 25. Later in the encyclical, the pope links new-enterprise expertise with the urgent need for economic progress and development. For example, see ibid., 72.

79. "Address to the Christian Union of Employers and Executives, June 8, 1964," in *The Pope Speaks* 10 (1965): 46. In the Italian text of this address, Paul uses the term *imprenditori* in two places when referring to entrepreneurs. This term is related to the verb *imprendere*, meaning "to undertake" or "to begin." See Paul VI, "Address to *Unione Christiana Imprenditori e Dirigenti*," in *Acta Apostolicae Sedis* 56 (1964): 574–75. The pope discusses entrepreneurs and economic development in this section.

80. "Address to the Christian Union of Employers and Executives, June 8, 1964," 50.

81. Paul VI shows awareness of "risks of the marketplace." See "Address to the Board of the Christian Center for Owners and Managers of French Businesses, March 31, 1976," in *The Pope Speaks* 21 (1976): 184.

82. "Address to the '*Centre chrétienne des patrons et dirigeants*,' March 22, 1972," in *L'Osservatore Romano* [English edition], April 6, 1972, 4.

83. Ibid. In the French text of this address, Paul repeatedly uses the terms *entreprise* and *chefs d'entreprise catholiques*—phrases he often adopts when discussing entrepreneurs. See *Acta Apostolicae Sedis* 64 (1972): 301.

84. "Address to the Board of the Christian Center for Owners and Managers of French Businesses, March 31, 1976," 184. Here the pope uses the phrase "[v]*otre fonction de chefs d'entreprise.*" See *Acta Apostolicae Sedis* 68 (1976): 271.

85. Ibid., 183.

86. *Populorum progressio*, 9.

87. Ibid., 25. Paul makes this point again when speaking to business persons in 1976. He suggests that the innovative process involves "burdensome responsibility," and at times "these responsibilities can be so great that you are perhaps unable to see how you can accept further risks." See "Address to the Board of the Christian Center for Owners and Managers of French Businesses, March 31, 1976," 182.

88. See *Laborem exercens*, 11, 14, 20.

89. Ibid., 11. In the official text of the encyclical, John Paul uses the Latin word *conductores* to name entrepreneurs. In this paragraph's second reference he also uses the term *capiendi* to identify entrepreneurs. See *Acta Apostolicae Sedis* 73 (1981): 603–4. Here the pope is not precisely clear about the relationship between owners and entrepreneurs, as he initially appears to associate entrepreneurs with those who own and control capital.

90. Ibid., 20.

91. Ibid., 14. The official Latin text here uses the genitive plural *conductorum* to describe entrepreneurs, which may be literally translated as "leaders of the works." See *Acta Apostolicae Sedis* 73 (1981): 612.

92. Ibid.

93. Ibid.

94. John Paul associates business leadership with economic development in many places throughout his teachings. In Naples, for example, he addresses "the city's business leaders, who play such an important role in the city's development." See "Address to Entrepreneurs and Neapolitan Business Leaders, November 11, 1990," in *L'Osservatore Romano* [English edition], December 3, 1990, 9. Addressing business leaders and managers in Milan, he states that "the degree of well-being which society enjoys today would be unthinkable without the dynamic figure of the businessman, whose function consists of organizing human labor and the means of production so as to give rise to the goods and services necessary for the prosperity and progress of the community." See "Address to Businessmen and Economic Managers at Milan's Champion's Fair, May 22, 1983," in *The Pope Speaks* 28 (1983): 264.

95. *Sollicitudo rei socialis*, 15. In the Latin text, the pope proposes that persons have "*propia ineundi coepta rebus oeconomicis*" ("the right to take initiative [or to begin one's own enterprises] in economic matters"). In the very next sentence the pope refers twice to economic development by using the term *progressio*. See John Paul II, *Sollicitudo rei socialis* (Vatican City: Libreria Editrice Vaticana, 1987), 20.

96. Ibid., 44. Here, John Paul also recognizes the economic initiatives of entire nations using the phrase "*incepta valeat inire.*" See John Paul II, *Sollicitudo rei socialis* (Vatican City: Libreria Editrice Vaticana, 1987), 65.

97. Rocco Buttiglione is reported to have worked closely with John Paul in drafting *Centesimus annus*. See Rocco Buttiglione, "The Free Economy and the Free Man," in *A New Worldly Order: John Paul II and Human Freedom, A "Centesimus Annus" Reader*, ed. George Weigel (Washington, D.C.: Ethics and Public Policy Center, 1992), 69.

98. Ibid.

99. *Centesimus annus*, 31–32.

100. Ibid., 31.

101. Ibid., 32, emphasis in original. The official Latin text describes "initiative and entrepreneurial ability" as "*facultatis consilia capiendi et opera conducendi*" and "the necessary risks" as "*pericula suscipere.*" See John Paul II, *Centesimus annus*, 32. In this part of *Centesimus annus*, John Paul II references *Sollicitudo rei socialis*, 15, which defends the "right to economic initiative."

102. John Paul expresses interest in entrepreneurs in other pronouncements. Speaking to Italian Catholic business leaders, he praises their "managerial and entrepreneurial ability." See "Address to Italian Catholic Business Leaders, April 12, 1991," in *L'Osservatore Romano* [English edition], April 22, 1991, 5. Addressing workers at an Olivetti plant in Italy, he praises the accomplishments of "Adriano Olivetti, the courageous entrepreneur." See "Speech to Workers at the Olivetti Complex in Scarmagno, Italy, March 19, 1990," in *The Pope Speaks* 35 (1990): 291.

103. John Paul recognizes that entrepreneurs carry out necessary economic tasks. Introducing *Centesimus annus,* he acknowledges the "value of the free market and of entrepreneurial activity within it, of the ability to 'arrange the meeting' between consumer needs and adequate resources to meet them by free bargaining." See "Address to a General Audience Introducing the Encyclical Letter *Centesimus annus,* May 1, 1991," in *The Pope Speaks* 36 (1991): 270. Speaking to business executives and entrepreneurs, he observes: "without you, entrepreneurs and executives, a modern organization of the business firm is unthinkable, nor is it possible to realize that constant adjustment between market needs, worker expectations and the demands of correct business management." See "Address to Participants in the National Convention of the Union of Christian Executive Entrepreneurs, December 14, 1985," in *The Pope Speaks* 31 (1986): 65–66.

104. This pattern is evident in other places in John Paul's teachings. Speaking to workers and business people citing the loss of jobs, he expresses concern that "entrepreneurial initiative has developed very little." See "Address to Workers and Businessmen of Sicily, May 10, 1993," in *L'Osservatore Romano* [English edition], June 2, 1993, 8. Addressing business leaders about unemployment, he declares that "it is urgent . . . to promote a 'culture of initiative.'" See "Address to Business Leaders of Sicily, May 9, 1993," in ibid., May 26, 1993, 5.

105. Addressing business groups, John Paul discusses entrepreneurial risk and its importance to economic progress. To entrepreneurs he states that "ever greater segments of the population are rediscovering the indispensable contribution that enterprising risk and executive professionalism are called to make to social progress." See "Address to Participants in the National Convention of the Union of Christian Executive Entrepreneurs, December 14, 1985," 65. To employees of Proctor and Gamble he states that "with his enterprise and insight, [man] manages to create work opportunities for his peers. This implies managerial ability and calculated business risks." See "Address to Executives and Employees of Proctor and Gamble, March 28, 1994," in *L'Osservatore Romano* [English edition], April 20, 1994, 3. To artisans he observes about business initiative that "the great work of organizing and coordinating [requires] the many factors of production, as well as the fact of risk." See "Address to the National Congress of Artisans, April 15, 1991," in *L'Osservatore Romano* [English edition], April 22, 1991, 8.

106. *Centesimus annus,* 32. The official text reads "*sedulitas prudentia in aequis periculis suscipiendis,*" where John Paul recognizes *periculis* (risk) in the context of *suscipio,* meaning "to undertake a business," "to take up," or "to begin." Here, John Paul associates entrepreneurship with the virtue of prudence.

107. Ibid., 33.

108. Ibid.

109. "Address to Industrialists and Workers at Ferrari Motor Works in Fiorano, June 4, 1988," in *L'Osservatore Romano* [English edition], August 1, 1988, 9. See Robert Kennedy et al., eds., *Dignity of Work: John Paul II Speaks to Managers and Workers* (Lanham, Md.: University Press of America, 1994).

110. "Address to Participants in the National Convention of the Union of Christian Executive Entrepreneurs, December 14, 1985," 67–68. This reference appears in a section entitled "Task of Entrepreneurs."

111. "Address to Business Persons at La Salle College, Santa Cruz, Bolivia, May 12, 1988," in *L'Osservatore Romano* [English edition], June 13, 1988, 16.

112. See *Laborem exercens*, 11, 14. The first two references to entrepreneurs in this encyclical appear in a discussion of wage justice.

113. See *Sollicitudo rei socialis*, 15.

114. Ibid.

115. See ibid., 12–14.

116. Ibid., 14.

117. Ibid., 42–44.

118. *Centesimus annus*, 31.

119. Ibid., 32.

120. Ibid.

121. See Thomas Aquinas, *Summa theologiae* IIa-IIae, q. 137.1. See also q. 137.2–137.4.

122. "Address at the Olivetti Plant in the Lancia Region, March 18, 1990," in *L'Osservatore Romano* [English edition], March 26, 1990, 7.

123. "Angelus Reflection, March 3, 1991," in *L'Osservatore Romano* [English edition], March 4, 1991, 1.

124. "Address during Papal Audience with Members of the Union of Christian Executive Entrepreneurs, December 14, 1985," in *The Pope Speaks* 31 (1986): 64–65.

125. Ibid., 66.

126. See Robert G. Kennedy, "The Virtue of Solidarity and the Purpose of the Firm," in *Rethinking the Purpose of Business: Interdisciplinary Essays from the Catholic Social Tradition*, ed. S. A. Cortright and Michael J. Naughton (Notre Dame, Ind.: University of Notre Dame Press, 2002).

127. Pius XI, *Quadragesimo anno*, 69.

128. *Laborem exercens*, 6.

129. See, for example, Michael Novak, *Free Persons and the Common Good* (New York: Madison Books, 1989), 133; "The Pope of Enterprise," Forbes 143 (June 26, 1989): 70–71; and "The Virtue of Enterprise," *Crisis* (May 1989): 19–25. See also *A New Worldly Order*, 14–15.

130. *Sollicitudo rei socialis*, 41.7.

FIVE   # Wealth Creation in the Global Economy

Human Labor and Development

Simona Beretta

The aim of this essay is to rethink the basic source of wealth creation—human labor—and its ultimate goal—development of each person and of the whole person—against the backdrop of our present time of rapid change and "global" integration. Such an inquiry into the nature, or "ontological dimension," of human labor and development is needed in order to adequately ground an ethical perspective on work and development as well as to provide economists with a more solid basis for policy prescriptions on these questions. An effort will be made to point out the distinctiveness of the Catholic social tradition on these matters.

WEALTH CREATION IN THE CATHOLIC SOCIAL TRADITION

While it is very common to concentrate on distributive issues when discussing the ethical dimension of labor and of development, the Catholic social tradition provides a very stimulating environment for firsthand inquiry into the nature of wealth creation, both in positive and normative terms. As my comparative advantage lies in economics, and not in philosophy or moral theology, I will elaborate only briefly on the tradition's perspective on wealth creation in order to single out the points that I have found most inspiring for economic theory and policy research and for direct personal involvement in social and political life. The four complementary essays in Part I, this volume, offer a more thorough philosophical and theological analysis.

The Goods of the Earth as a Gift

At the very beginning of all that exists, we find a gift. The earth is given to the human family, so that humankind might have dominion over it by their work and enjoy its fruits. This aspect of the Genesis story is translated into the Catholic social tradition as the principle of the "universal destination of the earth's goods," leading us to see human dominion over all things in terms of "care-taking" or stewardship, for the good of oneself and of one's relations.[1] The original dynamic generated by the act of giving has very interesting ontological and ethical implications, which are also relevant to economic issues.

As we know from everyday experience, a gift entails a free action by which the giver means to initiate or to consolidate a relationship; furthermore, accepting a gift constitutes a free action that signals the willingness of the recipient to enter into a relationship with the giver. Most important, the initial gift generates a dynamic process of reciprocal gift-giving that expresses and substantiates personal or social relations. This process generates a story in which things and meanings circulate, a story that can either be freely nurtured (so that, at the end, we can say, "We owe each other so much!"), or truncated ("I owe him nothing anymore.")[2] As these expressions make clear, "giving" and "owing" represent two faces of the same substantive relation, which is curious, considering the contrasting meaning of these same words in everyday language, which reflects the prevalence of market transactions (see Michael Naughton and Robert Wahlstedt, chapter 11, this volume, on Native Americans and gift exchange).

The Human Being as a Co-Creator

While the universe is a gift to us, God the Creator also made us to be like Him, thus making us co-creators of sorts in the unending act of creation.[3] The capacity for wealth creation as a distinct human ability goes beyond the material aspect of wealth accumulation that is necessary for life; what is distinctively human in wealth (or welfare or well-being) creation is the original, unpredictable, and surprising aspect that human work gives to the existing material world.[4] As the original creation is a gift, by analogy we become collaborators when we give in our turn. As collaborators, we can only transform and give what we have been given; still, by the exercise of our freedom, we can contribute to creation by giving a fuller and richer sense to the earth's goods, by "giving a story to matter" (even material creation has a destination, which will be revealed in due time). As Helen Alford explains (see chapter 9, this volume), foundational goods such as capital can be "ennobled" when they are incorporated into the pursuit of excellent ends such as human development. This "ennobling" occurs when we understand capital as a "gift."

Because creation is an ever-unfinished story, one in which space and time really matter and freedom "in action" is of the essence, human participation in the effort is by no means automatic. To collaborate with the Creator, we need to be grateful recipients of a gift that we recognize as such; we participate in creation by freely giving in order to consolidate relationships with the One-Who-Has-First-Given and with others, against a horizon that includes all present, past and future generations.

Universal Destination of the Earth's Goods

In the Catholic social tradition, the universal destination of the earth's goods indicates and specifies the human vocation in wealth creation: wealth creation is to be for the benefit of all. We are free to listen to this vocation and to respond, or else to distance ourselves from the logic of gift (gratefully to receive and gratuitously to circulate) in order to follow a different logic of accumulation, exploitation, and depletion. In *Gaudium et spes* we are told that "God intended the earth and all that it contains for the use of every human being and people."[5] This is a call for economic equity. The logic of gift supports this call and leads us toward this goal, whereas the logic of accumulation, exploitation, and depletion causes us to exclude large portions of humanity from the benefits of economic progress. This exclusion comes about when we allow too much wealth to be concentrated in too few hands; when we allow economic power to exploit the poor and transfer wealth from the poor to the affluent; and when we allow current generations to abuse the environment, either by depleting the earth's natural resources or by making an environmental mess that later generations will have to pay for. In all three cases there is a disorder—a disorder in the relationship between persons and their true nature, between persons and the community in which they live, and between persons and the creation. The disorder is caused by the rejection of the logic of gift; it generates alienated positions. These consist in refusing the logic of gift by rejecting the gift itself or by denying its inner dynamism, which bids us to conceive of ourselves in relation to the Giver and those to whom we give. Curiously enough, by reflecting on ourselves "in action," we can see how unreasonable it is to abstract ourselves from the logic of gift. Our own life is given to us, and reason should not discard as irrelevant what is primary evidence.

Labor as Response to a Gift

"But the earth does not yield its fruits without a particular human response to God's gift, that is to say, without work."[6] In the Catholic social tradition, human labor, a basic source of wealth creation, is not merely regarded as a factor of production (that is, as a means to an end) but as a free action that is at one and the same time both means and end—possibly instrumental to other ends but also significant in itself. Seen in the context of creation as a gift, labor, in fact, is sharing in the activity of the Creator and participating in the dynamic circle of reciprocal giving in a never-ending, meaningful exchange.[7] While labor is a basic source of wealth creation, the origin of true wealth is God, who shares this wealth with us in the form of gift (see Robert Kennedy and John Haughey, chapters 2 and 3, this volume). I would like to underline how suggestive it is to interpret human work and wealth creation by analogy to God's work: human beings, made in His image, create new wealth not in isolation but in a reciprocal dialogue, in a network of stable connections that can only happen because someone first has the courage to take the risk of action—the courage to give something to others (material as well as immaterial goods, such as trust and knowledge) in the reasonable hope of establishing new wealth-enhancing relations.

Alienation

Interestingly enough, John Paul II defines alienation (a topical theme in social analysis and political praxis) as the refusal to take part in the dynamic of gift. Alienation occurs when means and ends are reversed. He argues:

> When man does not recognize in himself and in others the value and grandeur of the human person, he effectively deprives himself of benefiting from his humanity and of entering into that relationship of solidarity and communion with others for which God created him. Indeed, it is through the free gift of self that man truly finds himself. . . . [He] is alienated if he refuses to transcend himself and to live the experience . . . of an authentic human community. . . . A society is alienated if its form of social organization, production and consumption make it more difficult to offer this gift of self and to establish this solidarity between people."[8]

What John Paul II makes clear, and what I as an economist want to assert, is that the gift of creation by the Creator is not some quaint theological assertion that sits on the sidelines of economic analysis, but that it is, rather, a central concept in understanding wealth creation. Denying it leaves us in an alienated condition.

DEVELOPMENT AS A "STORY" OF WEALTH CREATION

Within the Catholic social tradition, development is conceived as a dynamic process in which each step is fully valuable in itself, since *how* you get a result is as essential as *what* result you get.[9] This is why I would like to point out the meaning of development as a real "story" of wealth creation, one that takes place in space and time because of real people taking the risk of entering a gift relation in the reasonable hope of consolidating these relationships as wealth enhancing for the future. Development, then, refers to the story itself, not just to the possible happy ending.

To see the implications of the above distinction, compare the development policies that follow from two distinct perspectives. On the one hand, if you care about reaching a predefined set of development indicators, you will rationally look for viable technical solutions and possibly apply them in an efficient way; over time, you will be able to measure your performance in terms of degree of achievement of the desired outcomes. The more seriously you care about performance, the more you will be inclined to apply efficient, top-down decisions and initiatives in order to produce the desired effects.

On the other hand, if you care about the process, that is, if you deem important *how* you get to a more desirable situation, you will concentrate on the conditions that favor decentralized action; there will be an inclination toward a bottom-up approach. Take the objective of eradicating poverty as an example. In the "development as an outcome" perspective, poor people would mostly play a passive role, as aid recipients; in the "development as a process" perspective, poor people would be actively involved as the crucial decision makers.

Unfortunately, top-down, technocratic approaches to development are all too common in thinking and in practice: caring for *what* you will eventually get as a result of deliberate policies tends to dominate caring about the process, about *how* you proceed. While I obviously cannot enter detailed discussion on these topics, I would suggest revisiting the terms of the debate within recent United Nations conferences on development.[10] Rightly, the need for development policies to be "owned" and "participated in" by the people is often raised, but even these goals tend to be pursued technocratically. While techniques can obviously be very useful and should be fully taken advantage of, caring for the *how* means really caring for each and every person right now—in a true proximity, which starts with a gift and becomes a durable relation. This stands as the key characteristic of the past and present practice for development promotion within the Christian tradition. While this tradition typically does not fix deadlines and quantitative objectives, it nonetheless proves to be very effective in promoting development in a truly sustainable way. While a systematic study of the development approach and impact of Christian presence on development is still much needed, let me single out some reflections and teachings on development as a story of wealth creation that we can find in Catholic social teaching.

Development as a Truly Dynamic Process

The Catholic social tradition exhibits a prophetic attention to what we now call, in economic terms, structural change; that is, the tradition acknowledges that development indicates the appearance of something new, something possible, but not automatically implied by reproduction of what already exists. As a consequence, the Catholic social tradition, lived in practice and written in documents, pays remarkable attention to the adjustment costs that go along with structural change. Notably, structural change as a field of economic enquiry, which represents a reappraisal of long-overlooked classical issues, has only recently been explicitly examined within mainstream economic theory and policy design. Development as a truly dynamic process is, in fact, a matter of structural change: knowledge is widened, new goods appear, new techniques are adopted, and the structure of production and of labor markets changes, along with the spatial distribution of economic activities, both within and among countries. Such changes entail "strong" uncertainty and real costs to real people. No wonder the Church's social documents speak of these issues in real time. Practically involved in caring for each person and for all humanity, the Church can be better equipped than outside observers for recognizing these costs in real time.[11]

Institutions Matter

The Catholic social tradition pays particular attention to qualitative dimensions in development, and especially to formal and informal institutions, while these factors have only recently come to the forefront of systematic attention by development policymakers. Compare the timing of Catholic social initiatives and documents with, for example, the timing of the appearance of qualitative dimensions of development in the titles and indexes, year after year, of one of the most authoritative annual documents on development, the World Bank's *World Development Report*. The qualitative elements necessary for development were strongly emphasized, back in the 1960s, in the papal documents *Mater et magistra* (1961) and *Populorum progressio* (1967), with special attention to the importance of "institutions" and what today we call "governance." At that time, theoretical economics and development policy design almost exclusively focused on industrialization, income growth, and infrastructure in general, with a strong bias toward quantitative dimensions. Nowadays, intrinsically "relational" words such as "institutions" and "governance" have entered the common vocabulary of those same international economic organizations that largely overlooked them in the 1960s and 1970s. The significance of institutions such as property rights and entitlements to wealth creation has also been recognized in recent debate.[12]

Interdependence

We observe in the Catholic social tradition an early recognition of another crucial category: interdependence. It is no less crucial an analytical tool than a moral category. In a sense, observed interdependence (that today nobody would deny) may be interpreted as empirical evidence of the intimate relational nature of human life: relations with God, with other people, and with the earth's riches.[13] Interdependence is the objective frame in which human work can create wealth, since wealth creation is an essentially relational process. Particularly in Catholic social teaching, interdependence is clearly recognized as the call to practice the virtue of solidarity; conceiving interdependence only as a form of dependence—as an outside constraint to personal, social, or national autonomy—implies a distorted (alienated) perspective that has abandoned the fundamental logic of the gift. In fact, as John Paul II explains, "[t]he advancement of the poor constitutes a great opportunity for the moral, cultural and even economic growth of all humanity."[14]

Implications of Catholic Social Thought for Policy Design and Research

As a consequence of the above features, the Catholic social tradition delineates a complex and interesting approach to development policies that deserves a great deal of attention from scholars, social actors, and institutions alike:

There is urgent need to *reconsider the models which inspire development policies*. In this regard, the legitimate requirements of economic efficiency must be better aligned with the requirements of political participation and social justice. . . . [I]n practice, this means making solidarity an integral part of the network of economic, political and social interdependence which the current process of globalization is tending to consolidate. These processes call for rethinking international cooperation in terms of a new culture of solidarity.... [C]ooperation cannot be reduced to aid or assistance ... [R]ather, it must express a concrete and tangible commitment to solidarity which makes the poor the agents of their own development and enables the greatest number of people ... to exercise the creativity which is characteristic of the human person and on which the wealth of nations too is dependent."[15]

John Paul II here states that the wealth of nations depends on the exercise of creativity, and we have seen that creativity in its essence can be described as entering a gift relationship, upstream and downstream. In terms of policy, solidarity for development (and solidarity in general) is not a one-way, top-down material transfer of some kind. It is a "tangible commitment" implying the fostering and care of a durable relationship, by means of an initial gift that begins a story in which, over time, each partner will end up better off, will end up "owing so much" to the others. But the Catholic social message, conceiving development as a dynamic process directly involving the poor, also represents a formidable theoretical challenge for innovation in economic analysis and policy design. Time and uncertainty are central to it;[16] they tend to complicate the "neat" analysis that economists are accustomed to, but they remain the unavoidable dimensions in which human labor shares in the work of the Creator, that is, the dimensions in which real wealth is really created.[17]

DEVELOPMENT, WEALTH CREATION, AND SOCIAL JUSTICE

The concept of social justice is usually applied to wealth distribution, but I would like to stress that social justice is at the heart of wealth creation. Social justice is relational in its essence and hence nourished by the gift.

Social Justice in Human Relations

Distributive justice is obviously important on its own,[18] but here I would like to point out that the Catholic social tradition's concept of social justice is not circumscribed by the domain of material goods. It includes justice in the realm of formal institutions that frame where interpersonal relations happen.[19] The domain of social justice also includes the specific relations among people that allow material wealth to be created. One important application concerns relationships between the employer and workers within the firm. Social justice requires not only paying a just wage to the workers, but much more: justice also requires sharing freedom of action, initiative, and responsibility within the firm, as is movingly documented by the following papal quotation (dating back to 1956):

> The economic and social function to which every man aspires requires that control over the way in which he acts be not completely subjected to the will of others. The head of the undertaking values above all else his power to make his own decisions. He anticipates, arranges, directs, and takes responsibility for the consequences of his decisions. . . . Can he deny to his subordinates that which he values so much for himself?[20]

Freedom of initiative and responsibility for each person in the firm (we could say subsidiarity within the firm) are then a matter of social justice. Recent management studies would probably suggest that they are also a matter of effectiveness in wealth creation.

Gift and Social Justice

Social justice exceeds commutative justice as well; in a sense, it implies some "unequal exchange" going beyond narrowly defined market transactions. It implies some gift: "Even prior to the logic of fair exchange of goods and the forms of justice appropriate to it, there exists *something which is due to man because he is a man,* by reason of his lofty dignity. Inseparable from the required 'something' is the possibility to survive and, at the same time, to make an active contribution to the common good of humanity."[21] As I said before, an act of gift is originally needed to generate relations, to create a society. Hence, social justice is based on the priority of the logic of gift—a gift that is due to any human being, because each of us has received gifts of all kinds and, above all, the gift of life. Social justice, as based on the logic of the gift, is needed for a society to exist. Without it, chaos would prevail: the dominance of the powerful would become overwhelming; the weak would be marginalized; formidable struggles would likely be normal in social life. Unfortunately, we have clear empirical evidence that injustice and violence and disorder go hand in hand.

Social Justice as Participation

When people lack a way to contribute to the life of the human community, they are bound to passivity and marginalization. Hence, social justice is essentially social participation—not only access to the distribution of material goods but also to the very process of wealth creation. Dennis McCann (chapter 7 in this volume) elaborates on this when he connects reflections within Catholic social thought to the capabilities approach pioneered by Amartya Sen. In the language of 1937, Pius XI explained:

> It is of the very essence of social justice to demand for each individual all that is necessary for the common good. But just as in the living organism it is impossible to provide for the good of the whole unless each single part and each individual member is given what it needs for the exercise of its proper function, so it is impossible to care for the social organism and the good of society as a unit unless each single part and each individual member . . . is supplied with all that is necessary for the exercise of his social function.[22]

Using today's language, John Paul II maintains that "[t]he challenge, in short, is to ensure a globalization in solidarity, a globalization without marginalization."[23] In the speech here referred to, the pope interestingly mentions two particularly offensive forms of injustice in globalization: (1) the exploitation of women and children; and (2) not having fair access to credit, which excludes people from the possibility of participation in wealth creation.[24]

Globalization and Social Justice

Globalization paradoxically allows a drastic simplification, since the "global" economy is, after all, merely a (very large) closed economy where unresolved problems cannot be wiped away by discharging their consequences somewhere else. Let us also notice that the original vocation of the Church is to be "global," since she pertains to all nations "by divine right."[25] But "much remains to be done,"[26] even within the Church, in developing and practicing the lines traced by Catholic social thought and summarized by the expression "globalization without marginalization":

> There is a collective responsibility for promoting development. . . . [A] *great effort must be made to enhance mutual understanding and knowledge, and to increase the sensitivity of consciences.* This is the culture which is hoped for, one which fosters trust in the human potential of the poor, and consequently in their ability to improve their condition through work. . . . But to accomplish this, the poor—be they individuals or nations—need to be provided with realistic opportunities. Creating such conditions calls for a *concerted worldwide effort to promote development,* an effort which also involves sacrificing the positions of income and of power enjoyed by the more developed economies.[27]

Gift and subsidiarity, though not explicitly mentioned, represent the inner dynamic forces noted in the quotation. I will try to substantiate the reasonableness of this approach.

REFLECTING ON ELEMENTARY ECONOMIC EXPERIENCE

Economic analysis should be grounded on a solid anthropological foundation, and the easiest test of its adequacy is to reflect on oneself "in action" as well as on one's elementary economic experience. This seems to me a reasonable, realistic, and exquisitely "lay" perspective that deserves to be pursued.

A closer look at wealth creation, as seen from the "lay" perspective, reveals that the essential source of wealth (human labor) and its possible outcome (development) almost inevitably entail personalized relationships, as opposed to anonymous participation in impersonal markets. All relevant economic decisions in everyday life tend to take shape within personalized relationships; who one's partner is in the transaction usually is very relevant, even when considering "market" transactions. This is especially so when current decisions produce their effects over time or entail strong uncertainty. Each of us can roughly estimate the share of total transactions that are strictly impersonal ones. It is very likely to be a small share, concerning spot transactions about goods whose quality is very easy to ascertain—newspapers, brands of food—but even for haircuts we might prefer a personalized relationship.

If we look at the economic system as a whole, all relevant economic decisions that permanently shape its characteristics—creating an enterprise, innovating, investing in human and in physical capital, lending and borrowing, and so on—are typically taken and realized within personalized and potentially durable relationships. Almost by definition, economic relationships among "large" agents such as firms, banks, governments, and international institutions are obviously "personalized," albeit in a possibly different sense. As a matter of fact, good economic theory teaches that, when it is costly or virtually impossible to gather all relevant information, when information is asymmetrically distributed, when economies of scale and concentration of market power are relevant, and when "strong" uncertainty is present, then it is crucial to be able to create personalized relationships in order to trade and more generally to pursue one's objectives. In many cases, it is also important that personalized relationships be potentially durable. Of course, whether they will be or not depends upon the substantive thickness of the relationship; in other words, trust has a peculiar "economic" value.

In order to avoid confusion, it is useful to make it clear at this point that there is nothing intrinsically good about personalized and potentially durable relations. For the perspective I am interested in, it is pointless to categorize impersonal market transactions or bureaucratic, top-down allocation of resources as "bad" and personalized relations as good. Personalized relations are merely a fact of life; they can be a powerful force for the good, but they can also be the worst trap imaginable. Just think about the word "trust" and consider its two quite different meanings! In particular, personalized relations as they are analyzed in this essay should not be confused with "relational goods," an expression that is gaining attention among economists. The term "relational goods" signifies a peculiar kind of immaterial good hidden in relationships such as friendship,[28] but human relations as such are deeply ambivalent.

Even gift relations, with all their importance, mirror the profound ambivalence of any human relation, either with the earth's riches or with other human beings.[29] The same ambivalence turns interdependence into vulnerability on the one side and dependence on the other. Besides transferring an existing good, a gift from one person to another conveys a precise intention, a meaning the giver intends; and accepting or refusing a gift also expresses a meaning. These meanings are constitutive of the relations—hence, constitutive of the self at the micro level and constitutive of social, economic, and political life at the macro level. But they can be various: offering true friendship or also manipulating the other person and possibly tying him or her into submission; creating new opportunities for participation or closing them. We know from fairy tales as well as from personal experience that a gift can be "poisoned" so that the receiver ends up being bound into dependence.[30] Dependence is a purely vertical relation, an obligation with no exercise of freedom, and it represents the end of participation, which is a dynamism of reciprocal giving. As an example, think about "tied" international aid: though formally a gift, it nevertheless includes specific obligations for the receiver, who becomes dependent on the giver.[31]

We know very well from elementary experience that the gift is needed for nurturing relations: even market contracts, diplomatic initiatives, and business relations may depend on some gratuitous act in order to be preserved.[32] Furthermore, a gift has to be perceived as "spontaneous" and "sincere" in order for it to help us win a friend or even a client; there is indeed an "interest" in giving, but not in that term's narrow sense. The gift can only be imagined in an intertemporal horizon, being a story of "open," unbalanced relations, which are kept going because each partner is tied to the other in a permanent, ever-changing indebtedness. Giving is an intriguing game in which much is said, and still more has to be guessed, hoped, or signaled but not openly spoken. An unbalanced circulation of goods is needed to keep the game going, though not any level of unbalance will do.

Only the truly "gratuitous" gift, the one that preserves the freedom of the other partner, is generative and sustains relations over time, while the "poisoned" gift transforms the gift relation into something completely different. Notice that the word "gratuitous" is itself an ambivalent word. It can indicate that someone received a useful good without paying any money (positive use value, zero exchange value), but it can also mean "unmotivated," "unjustified," and possibly "irrational." Here I would like to preserve the "gracious" aspect of gratuity, related to the surprise (the marvel) of unexpectedly being given for free something beautiful and valuable, of participating in an unexpected but desirable relation.

Only our Creator and Redeemer, as we know, gives in a perfectly gratuitous way, intensely desiring to establish a relation with each of us, yet leaving us totally free to accept or to refuse the gift and not binding us into dependence. An icon of gratuitous giving may be the image of mothers and fathers nurturing their children. They are so pleased to give because they are overwhelmed by the marvel of a new life, a life given *to* them and given *by* them at the same time. For human beings, giving is always, in a sense, giving back.[33] We have been granted gifts to start with. Furthermore, it is not difficult to find in daily life situations in which one's well-being, even one's material well-being, has been so much improved by a hint of gratuity perceived in a market transaction or in a public office, that is, by something received neither as the impersonal counterpart of one's money nor as the result of strict adherence to the formal rules of a hierarchical organization.

RETHINKING ECONOMICS: A CRITIQUE

While mainstream economists are very good at analyzing the economic behavior of agents in isolation or within impersonal markets, they rightly suspect they are on shaky ground when modeling personalized economic relations or decisions under "strong" uncertainty. In fact, textbook representations of "economic" behavior end up being analytically indistinguishable from "mechanical" behavior, as in solving a profit-maximizing (or a cost-minimizing) problem in light of full information. A "mechanistic" approach can be easily detected even in game theory, which studies complicated strategic interactions; however, game theory at least has the advantage of stating clearly that interdependence is constitutive of most economic relations.

Notice two important aspects of what remains the best analytical tool that we have at our disposal for describing interactions. First, and very interestingly, the analytical results of game theory are typically indeterminacy and the existence of multiple equilibria. For example, a one-shot game and the same game repeated over time have very different solutions, and no mechanistic story can explain how one equilibrium is selected out of the many possible. Second, while the strategic approach to economic decisions may explain in some cases why an option is chosen among a finite number of alternatives, a plausible story about how to identify all relevant alternatives is utterly missing. In other words, taking interdependence as seriously as we can, we end up realizing that "closed" models of economic relations—such as game theory—cannot possibly tell the whole story. We need to "open" them.[34]

"Opening" models makes perfect sense. Real economic decisions and transactions take shape as personal actions in a substantially unpredictable environment, where the alternative forms of behavior that are "rationally" anticipated can be seen as merely a small subset of all possible actions and reactions. Surprise is a key element in deterministic games such as chess—imagine how important surprise is in real economic "games"! The relational nature of economic transactions, especially under strong uncertainty, largely exceeds strategic interaction. Even serious advances in formal economic theory point in the same direction, evidencing that economics has to do with substantive human freedom to accept or to refuse relationships, to take or not to take the risk of action.[35] Only in highly hypothetical situations can economic rationality be thought of as a "complete" and coherent system, but it is very dangerous for any scientist to take the part as the whole, applying what is possibly a useful partial explanation—economic rationality as a "closed" system—to situations that obviously go beyond a closed one.

Coming to the topic of wealth creation, we see that the need for something better than a closed system of thought becomes even more urgent. This is especially the case at a time of rapid structural change, where wealth creation has obviously more to do with innovation (seizing new opportunities, detecting feeble and possibly ambiguous signs of change, making an economic resource out of something previously dismissed as useless) than with optimization (solving a maximizing problem starting from given data). Living in a time of rapid change makes it clear that behaving mechanically, according to calculation and optimization, as common sense would define "economic behavior," is the quick and ready recipe for personal and social implosion. As a matter of fact, no deterministic story about wealth creation sounds reasonable.

RETHINKING ECONOMICS: SOME HINTS BASED ON ELEMENTARY EXPERIENCE

Having addressed the destructive part of the critique, I will now attempt an exploration of the constructive side by sketching a nonmechanistic paradigm for economic analysis, powerful enough to explain how innovative actions come about, how economic relations are generated and sustained over time, and how uncertainty is handled; that is, how wealth is created and not merely accumulated, and ultimately how economic and social systems develop together.

Opening the Model—Action versus Behavior

The most relevant economic questions—human labor, wealth creation, and development—can be properly addressed and understood only within an adequate anthropological setting, that is, one "open" and nonmechanical in character. This is why it seems very useful for economists—and not just for moral philosophers—to use the category of free and purposive *action*, as opposed to mechanical and instrumental *behavior*, as the analytical basis for addressing issues concerning wealth. I take the word "action" to express a dynamic concept: action is a synthetic response, given here and now, to a complex situation that the actor never fully knows; ultimately, action is an unpredictable answer, to which freedom and responsibility are co-essential. Interaction, as a consequence, is something more than purely strategic interdetermination. From an analytical point of view, it requires an "open" system of thought.

"Closed" mechanistic systems of thought are bound to be weak. In particular, the logical approach of the kind commonly found in economic analysis needs to specify in advance all relevant exogenous dimensions, which is obviously impossible when unpredictable events occur—and we know from experience that they do occur. From a mechanistic perspective, we could be able to "explain" afterward what has changed in the economic system; that is the relatively easy part. But "closed" models usually fail to signal future changes. Why? Because such models imply a closed logical loop. The typical economic perspective is based on the idea that a given "interest" (not necessarily self-interest) is pursued according to a "rational" process that determines economic decisions.[36] Decisions, in this framework, consist in an affirmation of one's own sphere of autonomy with respect to the system, and they come from a calculating rationality. Freedom is reduced to deciding between alternative means for pursuing given ends.

Reflecting on ourselves "in action," we perceive that freedom has more to do with possibility than with necessity—that freedom is being open to the unpredictable, to the unfinished, to the indefinite. An interest does move our action, but an "open" definition of interest is relevant in this case.[37] In a "closed" model, the meaning of interest is reduced to some finite and measurable aspects assumed to be relevant. In assessing whether the model works, we observe actual behavior and test for the relevance of the specific definition of interest we assumed to start with. Were we to reduce the "open" definition of interest to a relevant subset, we might be lucky enough to perceive that our "closed" model is indeed a "good" model—that it works to explain economic behavior. The logical loop would be closed. Obviously, explaining the past is one thing and exploring the future is a completely different thing: it is very unlikely that the same "closed" system that was good for the past will be any good in predicting future behavior. We are likely to run into this logical weakness of the "closed" loop model even when considering micro problems.[38] It would be hopeless to try to penetrate the unpredictable dynamics of economic change using "closed" models.

When Adam Smith was discussing the wealth of nations (significantly, after a reflection on the theory of moral sentiments), he had before his eyes the visible evidence of an economic system largely based on agricultural production. Still, he pointed to the importance of the division of labor and the extension of the market as the driving forces for understanding the wealth of nations by referring to phenomena that could indeed be observed in his times—but only as feeble signals of change, not as the obvious, macroscopic foundation of the actual wealth creation of nations in his day. This was his genius. He would have gone nowhere with a "closed" system of thought. (See Charles Clark, chapter 1, this volume, for more on Smith.) We need something similar today for understanding what drives change, and possibly even for shaping change. Moreover, we need to give up "closed" rationality for something better, founded on a more realistic and inclusive conception of human reason. For "good" economic theory and practice, we need good anthropology— strong enough to stand comparisons with one's elementary experience and not merely with the arbitrary subset that we are accustomed to understand as narrow "economic rationality."

Opening the Model—Reproduction versus Generation

As I have been opposing behavior and action at the micro level, I would like to contrast *reproduction* and *generation* at the macro level. The two words suggest two quite different perspectives: on the one hand, a mechanical, "closed" dynamic story; and, on the other, a rather mysterious process by which something new appears.[39]

It is not easy to explain why economic thinking is mostly centered on production and overlooks the issues of wealth creation, as if nowadays the answers to the question about the wealth of nations were obvious. The preeminence of the sphere of production of goods and services in modern society may be an explanation. As Charles Clark points out, wealth is commonly understood to be whatever produces an income stream. Creativity is seen as a peculiarity of artists, not as a typical feature of human action; it is respected, but it is considered apart from economic production. If production, as distinct from creation, becomes the central value, we tend to concentrate on understanding how the existing system enlarges itself and to neglect the problem of understanding the discontinuities by which new things enter the system.

The idea of generation, as distinct from reproduction, seems to me very evocative when applied to economics. Think about human reproduction versus human generation. It is clear that by concentrating on material output, we cannot distinguish between the two situations: in both cases, we observe a new baby. But in the one case, this new baby is at the beginning of a thick story of relations in which everyone will give and receive; in the other case, there is no story. Generation, in the family as well as in the economy, implies not only "producing" an output but also taking care of the underlying relationship (circulating the "gift").

The distinction between wealth creation versus mere economic growth can be understood by analogy with generation. Think about how important it is for one's well-being, for example, that private or public health care should provide not only a technically effective service but also "care" in a truly human sense. Or think about one firm employing ten people. How different must the firm and its production process be if these ten people count, in the mind of the entrepreneur, as partners in the same creative adventure, or count as merely ten anonymous, interchangeable workers! (See the Naughton and Wahlstedt essay for a concrete example of the former.) In other words, the quality of the relation that goes with the material access to any given good is important. Material circulation of produced goods is obviously necessary for economic growth, but human wealth creation typically occurs when such circulation is meant to foster relationships, when it is a generative circulation. Human work as a story of economic generation, not as mere material reproduction, multiplies wealth in a very real sense, which is even measurable in material terms.

Opening the Model—Ethical Implications

An interesting corollary of the above reflections concerns the debate over ethics and economics. If we keep thinking about economics as optimizing behavior in pursuing a "closed" definition of interest (scarce resources, many competing needs; what's the best we can do?), ethical considerations may only be expressed as if they came from outside the economic sphere. If optimization counts as *the* economic behavior, then pursuing ethical goals entails a cost almost by definition; it implies sacrificing optimization. Obviously, such a sacrifice may be regarded as desirable by ethically minded people, but that is understood as another story with respect to economic behavior. Within this framework, we get the usual ideas on the presumed trade-off between efficiency and equity in economics. While the trade-off may indeed be there, I maintain that it is not the full story (see Stefano Zamagni, chapter 8, this volume).

If the part is not wrongly taken for the whole; if optimization is not taken to be *the* economic behavior, the story changes. The ethical dimension is to be recognized as constitutive of any human action, including those with a relevant economic dimension. In the actions of working, trading, investing, and so on, freedom is exercised in a relational situation to which we respond, that is, for which we bear responsibility. If we consider interactions in an "open" framework and do not confine our attention to "closed" strategic games, we recognize that the ethical dimension constitutes the "thickness" of the relation itself. We observe, for example, that interdependence can easily transform itself into dependence, on the one side, and the exploitation of vulnerability, on the other; this is why the virtue of solidarity is never optional for true interdependence.

As a second example, we know from experience that intentions are relevant ethical dimensions of a "thick" situation of interdependence. We often deem important what we perceive to be the intentions of others, and the importance of those intentions for our well-being may very well exceed the importance of others' material actions. Hence, intentions themselves are far from irrelevant in creating wealth, that is, in creating well-being. Words such as "responsibility," "solidarity," and "intentionality" (which could appear external to formal economic discourse) make perfect sense within the discourse of experience. Hence, seemingly paradoxical economic actions make perfect sense in the perspective of generation. A "true" gratuitous gift can indeed be very effective in establishing a long-lasting economic relation. So, too, we are told, "losing ourselves" is the condition for "gaining our life."

Our efforts at rethinking economics from elementary experience bring us back to the same ideas with which we started: the Church's suggestion that we can better understand our being "human" by analogy with God, who made us in His image. We promote development and exercise proper dominion over the earth if we remember the fundamental relational dynamics that constitute the deep fabric of all that exists, since the dynamism of all creation is supported by the gift.

ECONOMIC RELEVANCE OF GIFT RELATIONS

While economic systems based on gift may appear to belong to past history or to rather exotic or marginal situations, a deeper look at the connections among gift relations, market transactions, and state intervention in modern times and modern societies reveals quite a few surprises.[40]

Markets and Hierarchies

Markets and hierarchies, in their extremely stylized form, represent two—the only two, in most representations—distinct organizational structures for circulating goods and services. In its essence, market circulation consists in exchange of equivalents that occur in a network of horizontal relationships: no one can be forced by another to trade; no obligation arises for the parties beyond contractual obligation. State intervention, the typical example of hierarchical organization, provides for the circulation of goods and services through a vertical structure within which power is exercised, as in taxation and redistribution, for example.[41] In this oversimplified representation, hierarchies and markets are taken respectively to represent the loci of a purely vertical versus a purely horizontal circulation of goods, but notice that both circuits have in common the logical preeminence of production. When entering a market transaction, you must be able to sell something in order to satisfy your needs—either a good you produce or your time as a worker in a productive process. In any case, some form of production has to take place for a horizontal circulation of goods to happen. Since production constitutes the logical starting point for market circulation of goods, producers must "know better" what consumers need and then turn out exactly that, or at least persuade people that indeed they need what is produced.

A vertical circulation of goods occurring within a hierarchical structure logically requires a prominent position for the productive dimension, more or less in the same way as in markets. For example, if the state collects taxes in order to produce goods and services, it must presume to "know better" the needs of its citizens and to be able to organize an effective bureaucratic response to those needs.[42] In some cases (not too far-fetched), even "good citizens" can be thought of as one "product" of state intervention—for example, in the case of compulsory state-provided education, where families play no role; or again, in the case of mass events aimed at creating consensus in totalitarian regimes.

There is no reason to deny that state and markets are useful structures for the vertical and horizontal circulation of goods. Markets can allow liberation from suffocating ties of personal dependence and make it possible to exchange market equivalents instead of being forced into an asymmetric economic relationship that gives the powerful side an exorbitant advantage over the other side. But market systems are no panacea for dependence. When big actors (for example, very big enterprises[43]) dominate markets, we return to situations of dependence, albeit not in regard to a physical person.[44] Similarly, state intervention can liberate needy persons, who have no access to markets, from dependence on others' charity; or a widely held consensus that each individual is equal before the law also can counteract asymmetric power relationships. We know that both systems can be very effective at promoting enlarged reproduction, although decentralized markets seem to be better at this than top-down, centralized state bureaucracies. We understand from textbooks that in many cases the two should complement each other, as when state intervention is required because of "market failures" and vice versa.

Development Policies and Subsidiarity

We know from historical experience that both the horizontal circulation of goods in markets and the vertical bureaucratic circuits are weak generators of development, exactly because they both suffer from the preeminence of the logic of production, which is by its nature a "closed" logic. Development as generation requires instead an "open" circulation of goods that intersects, connects, transcends, and vitalizes both markets and hierarchies; it requires, that is, a "gift" circulation, with its inherently unbalanced structure (recall the state of reciprocal indebtedness/ gratitude indicates that the relationship is working) and also its profundity in time. These features of gift sharply contrast not only with vertical power relations but also with horizontal, impersonal market transactions, where an exchange of equivalents occurs at a given point in time. As a matter of fact, impersonal transactions are not even suited for market circulation of goods where duration in time and uncertainty matter.[45] A gift relationship does indeed involve a horizontal circulation of goods, but according to "strange rings" that do not require immediate equivalence and that consolidate connections by reinforcing mutual bonds over time and space. Still, they call for a free, noncompulsory new round of circulation in a potentially never-ending chain. These are orderly connections. The circulation of goods in a gift relationship is not chaotic but follows an orderly "strange hierarchy," by which the receiver feels obliged toward the giver, thus reinforcing reciprocal obligations within a freely chosen relation according to a noncoercive hierarchy.

Development, seen from the perspective of wealth generation as an "open" process and not merely one of "enlarged reproduction" marked by income growth and accumulation of riches, is a story of real people, acting in real time and space to give answers to their desires, to provide for their needs. Human needs are "open" and never finished, and they can seldom find an appropriate answer in material goods disconnected from human relations.[46] Taking care of relationships is taking care of actual needs as such, that is, creating wealth.[47] Hence, development can be seen as building and consolidating useful relationships that effectively answer needs and give meaning to interactions. Especially when we consider structural change— investment in physical capital, education, and innovation—personalized and durable relations are required, and they can be "thickened" by gift relationships.

At least as a reasonable working hypothesis, I would maintain that the strength of "gift" relationships within societies is crucial for development. By intersecting and connecting markets and hierarchies, "thick" gift relations can vitalize substantive relations and can make it much easier for societies to adapt to changing circumstances and to generate new initiatives in an uncertain environment. Conventional discussions about the respective role of "state" and "market" in development may prove to be the reverse of illuminating, unless we make an effort to put them into an appropriate, open, and nonmechanical setting that recognizes the gift relation as essential. Such an "open" model can help us to understand how structural and institutional change comes about; that is, it can illuminate the inner dynamism of manmade, historically, and socially determined institutions such as markets and hierarchies.

Understanding the development of poor countries represents no exception. Some initial gift from the advanced countries to less-developed ones is required to generate a process in which the poor will contribute, in due time, to global well-being. By the way, this policy implication is not surprising, since it is confirmed by the results of the theoretical literature on economic growth: by nonlinear models of growth, in which a "critical mass" of initial investment is needed for "taking off;" and by the "poverty trap" literature as well. But the "gift" perspective is somewhat richer. The point is not "aid," which we know can be a poisoned gift. A true gift for development is a meaningful act of durable commitment aimed at fostering relations over time.[48] The initial receiver is not bound into passivity.

We may call a "subsidiary approach" to development one in which active participation of the poor is fostered. Development can be best understood as a bottom-up dynamic process of wealth creation and institutional change realized by human action, that is, by the exercise of personal freedom and responsibility in shaping and taking care of social relations. Many observers, including international institutions, would recognize nowadays that top-down development policies do not work and that effective policies must be sustainable, participated, and "owned" by the people. Subsidiarity as a principle is indeed taking hold, possibly more on the basis of enhanced efficiency than on the basis of a sense of social responsibility.[49] Behind subsidiarity you may find the common-sense idea that local culture is best equipped to understand, interpret, and give answers to local needs and that, if decisions about the uses of resources are taken "close" to where the actual needs are, it is more likely that those needs can find an effective (and possibly an efficient and equitable) use.

The principle of subsidiarity, however, is not merely an organizational device for more effective intervention, a new development technique to be discreetly applied. A subsidiary approach to development goes well beyond the devolution of decision-making power to regional or local levels of government (where decision making remains a top-down, vertical process) and also goes well beyond the practice of co-financing nongovernmental organizations' (NGOs') development projects. The inner force of the principle of subsidiarity is not operational in the first place but, ontological: each and every person is an image of God, and each is inserted into the generative, relational dynamic of the gift.[50] Applying this principle to the design of development policies begins by taking seriously the "strange rings" of gifts within personalized, durable, gratuitous relations that already exist, effectively fostering development as the concrete path to be traced and trekked in time and space by the very people who should be protagonists—and not passive beneficiaries—of development policies.

CONCLUSION

"Strange rings" of gift relations are central to wealth creation and development. At this point, I would like to underline two points: (1) "strange rings" are not a mirage; and (2) we cannot do without them.

As to the first, we should look at the facts. Only facts can tell us whether gift relations are wishful thinking or can indeed create wealth, shape structural change, and promote development. If we look at history, we see that "new" things in wealth creation and development—even grand things from a strictly economic point of view—have typically come from creative gift relations. New technologies, impressive for their times, were developed within the connected network of monasteries spread all over Europe. We still can see how much gratuity there was in monks' labor by looking at the beauty of their buildings, where amazing details are practically invisible to visitors, but are there because beauty and perfection in buildings are gifts given for the glory of God. Economic and social history confirms that monasteries have been a remarkable innovation in economic organization, revitalizing the economic life of wide territories and promoting "multinational" relations in ways that exalted and connected local cultures. Relations within and around a monastery were obviously a "strange ring" of "participative hierarchies" and also very efficient in constituting and promoting *do ut des* horizontal market transactions.

In later centuries, fraternities of arts and crafts—essentially structured as "strange rings" of reciprocal obligations cutting across markets and political hierarchies—were also essential to European social and economic development, favoring the accumulation and intergenerational transmission of technological knowledge.[51] Again, charitable initiatives aimed at answering the needs of newly urban populations produced striking institutional innovations. Hospitals, for example, and other agencies of social assistance gathered and managed huge economic resources within gift relationships. Interestingly, some of these charitable institutions and their riches, meant to serve the poor, survived all sorts of political turmoil, foreign invasions included. Gift relations are indeed resilient. We could also recall other concrete accomplishments of gift relationships: not only schools and universities but also innovations in the financial system.[52] Even if we look at the present time, we observe that nonmarketable new needs tend to find an answer within networks of pre-existing, durable "gift" relations (families, churches, clubs, and so on) that create valuable goods and services, or wealth.

Before commenting on the second point, it will be well to recall that relations cannot merely be assumed to exist or to persist;[53] they have to be reinforced (or regenerated) at each moment. Any society is permanently undetermined, incomplete, "open" to human action. Each generation inherits from the previous one a wealth of relations to be transmitted to the next one, but while intergenerational transmission is an important dimension of gift circulation, it does not happen automatically. *Foedus*, that is, making alliances and trusting each other, is the founding principle of any society; for a society to be generated and to be generative, its members must prove to each other that their mutual trust is deserved. This happens through the complex "game" of exchanging gifts. Without this generative game, the thickness of society—the basic trust relationships that make it possible to circulate goods through markets and hierarchies—would disappear. Refusing the strange logic of gift, we might find ourselves in a society so "thin" that it would be extremely difficult, almost impossible, to sustain wealth creation within the wide network of market and state transactions that we are accustomed to and that we (wrongly) take for granted as a sort of "state of nature."

A last remark concerns the specific role of researchers and teachers in economics and politics. They have a calling, which can be negatively expressed in terms of resisting "closed" thinking. The centerpiece of their analyses is naturally "open": they deal with persons, both historical and real, and with the personalized relations that each real person generates or regenerates. The openness of their object strongly contrasts with the closedness of the consolidated paradigm to which we are accustomed. That paradigm presents society as an aggregation of substantially interchangeable individuals who play their roles in markets and hierarchies according to a "closed" rationality (whether as consumers, producers, or voters). Their well-being can be taken care of by a (horizontal) exchange of equivalents in anonymous markets, or by vertical (and possibly egalitarian) policies, or by a mix of the two. Unfortunately, in practice this "anonymous markets, interchangeable citizens" paradigm predominates in policy making and institutional design, both in markets and in bureaucracies.

To reaffirm the centrality of personalized relations is not to deny a role for markets and for state policies. Markets can be an effective avenue for wealth-creating interactions, but it should be made clear that they can also degenerate into a crystallized structure of asymmetrically distributed economic power, generating dependence and precluding interdependence. Public policies, on their side, can facilitate social creativity, freedom, and responsibility, or else they can deny (even with violence) space for social creativity or make creativity hard to exercise. The difference between these opposing outcomes is what I consider the generative balance point in wealth creation. People either acknowledge the gift relationship, which is constitutive of each person and of society, and nurture it; or they behave as if the "closed" logic of self-interest indeed exhausts the horizon of possibilities.

Researchers and teachers are called to challenge "closed" thinking systematically, by serious confrontation with experience as well as with scientific advances that tend to underline the inadequacy of the "anonymous markets, interchangeable citizens" paradigm in the many circumstances that cry out for personalized and durable relationships. This intellectual and operational resistance is the first step in our response to John Paul II's call for "*a new and deeper reflection on the nature of the economy and its purposes.*"[54]

NOTES

I am deeply grateful to the organizers of the Puebla Fourth International Symposium on Catholic Social Thought and Management Education and of the Rome Seminar, "Rethinking the Wealth of Nations," for the intense and stimulating occasions of debate. I am especially grateful to the Rome discussant of my paper, Lee Tavis, for his constructive comments. Among the many friends with whom I discussed these ideas, Marco Martini, Carlo Beretta, don Ferdinando Citterio, Mario Maggioni, Mike Naughton, and Genia Scabini deserve special mention. I take full responsibility for the positions expressed in this essay and its shortcomings.

1. Bishop Diarmuid Martin made this point at the conference on "New Wealth, New Poverty: Towards a New Humanism," Catholic University, Milan, September 6–7, 2000, in Lorenzo Ornaghi, "Globalizzazione: Nuove ricchezze e nuove povertà," *Vita e Pensiero*, Milan, 2001. See also John Paul II, *Laborem exercens*, 14.

2. Jacques T. Godbout, *L'esprit du don* (Paris: Editions La Découverte, 1992), p. 226 of the Italian translation, *Lo spirito del dono* (Turin: Bollati Boringhieri, 1993).

3. In a paper submitted to the follow-up seminar held in Rome at St. John's University Campus, November 29–December 2, 2001, T. Whitmore uses a particularly suggestive image referring to the person as "performer of the divine symphony."

4. Many animal species accumulate wealth in the form of food; furthermore, some species exhibit an impressive ability to build durable forms of wealth (shelter, and also productive capital, in some sense), as is the case with beavers and bees. Animals are also impressively predictable as builders, their ability consisting in adapting the same, perfect constructive archetype to a variety of circumstances. But nobody would label their work as "creative" in the same sense as human work.

5. *Gaudium et spes*, 69.

6. John Paul II, *Centesimus annus,* 31.

7. *Laborem exercens,* 25.

8. *Centesimus annus,* 41.

9. See for example, John XXIII, *Mater et magistra,* 60, 179; Paul VI, *Populorum progressio,* 14, 20.

10. Especially the 2001 Monterrey Conference on "Finance for Development" and the 2002 Johannesburg "World Summit on Sustainable Development," which followed the 2000 United Nations Millennium Declaration explicitly stating the Millennium Development Goals (www.un.org).

11. Think of the centuries-long involvement of the Church in the field of education. In recent decades, education—especially basic education—has gained a crucial position in international development policies. Notice that the Pontifical Society of the Holy Childhood, which is more than 150 years old, has led the way in educating children without discrimination against race, culture, or religion and, interestingly enough, in explicitly involving children themselves as donors. Many references in Catholic social teaching point to the need to invest in people (Paul VI, *Populorum progressio,* 35; John Paul II, *Sollicitudo rei socialis,* 44) and to the role of education and knowledge in wealth creation and development, respectively (John Paul II, *Laborem exercens,* 12.3; *Centesimus annus,* 33.1).

12. Take, as an example, the recent debate around Hernando de Soto, *The Mystery of Capital: Why Capitalism Triumphs in the West and Fails Everywhere Else* (New York: Basic Books, 2000).

13. *Sollicitudo rei socialis,* 14.

14. *Centesimus annus,* 28.

15. John Paul II, "Address to the Fiftieth General Assembly of the United Nations Organization," October 5, 1995, as summarized by John Paul II in "Message for the Celebration of the World Day of Peace," January 1, 2000 (emphasis in original).

16. Uncertainty about the future is a recurrent definition that poor people give to poverty, as it emerges from an innovative research project realized within the World Bank's *Voices of the Poor* initiative, concerning how poor people experience poverty. See World Bank, *World Development Report, 2000–2001* (Washington, D.C.: September 2000), ch. 8, "Helping Poor People Manage Risk."

17. Simona Beretta, "Facing Strong Uncertainty in the 21st Century: The Generative Nature of Human Labor," given at a conference at the University of Notre Dame, April 4–7, 2002.

18. Leo XIII, *Rerum novarum,* 27.

19. Pius XI, *Quadragesimo anno,* 88.

20. Pius XII, "Address to the International Congress of Catholic Associations of Small- and Medium-sized Businesses," 1956. Jean-Yves Calvez drew my attention to this point in his entry on "Social Justice," prepared for a forthcoming publication on keywords in Catholic social teaching, sponsored by Centro di Ricerche per lo Studio della Dottrina Sociale della Chiesa, Università Cattolica del Sacro Cuore, Milan. See also Jean-Yves Calvez and Michael J. Naughton, "Catholic Social Teaching and the Purpose of the Business Organization: A Developing Tradition," in *Rethinking the Purpose of Business: Interdisciplinary Essays from the*

Catholic Social Tradition, ed. S. A. Cortright and Michael J. Naughton (Notre Dame, Ind.: University of Notre Dame Press, 2002).

21. *Centesimus annus*, 34 (emphasis in original).

22. Pius XI, *Divini redemptoris*, 51.

23. John Paul II, "From the justice of each comes peace for all," from the "Message for the Celebration of the World Day of Peace," January 1, 1998.

24. Notice that credit is an economic good where time and uncertainty matter most, and where personalized relationships of some kind are crucially needed.

25. *Mater et magistra*, 178.

26. *Centesimus annus*, 58.

27. Ibid. (emphasis in original).

28. Relational goods are "good" by definition; they do not exhibit any ambivalence.

29. Walther Zimmerli, *La mondanità dell'Antico Testamento* (Milan: Jaca Book, 1973).

30. Godbout, *L'esprit du don*, 14–15.

31. If this is the situation, in the end it might have been better for the receiver to choose the "exit" option, if such an option existed, that is, refusing the gift and going to the market.

32. George Akerlof, "Labor Contracts as Partial Gift Exchange," in George Akerlof, *An Economic Theorist's Book of Tales: Essays that Entertain the Consequences of New Assumptions in Economic Theory* (Cambridge: Cambridge University Press, 1984), 145–74.

33. Maternity is a clear example: giving birth to a baby, a woman revives with gratitude her experience of being a mother.

34. Ferruccio Marzano has discussed this idea of an "open" economic theory as opposed to a "closed" one. See, for instance, his *Economia ed etica: Due mondi a confronto. Saggi di economia ed etica dei sistemi sociali* (Rome: AVE, 1998).

35. Carlo Beretta, *Is Economic Theory Up to the Needs of Ethics?* ISEIS Paper no. 9401 (Milan: Università Cattolica del Sacro Cuore, 1994); Carlo Beretta, *Having Alternatives, Being Free and Being Responsible*, ISEIS Paper no. 9501 (Milan: Università Cattolica del Sacro Cuore, 1995).

36. The revealed preferences approach fits into this description exactly as the more traditional utility function approach.

37. We may use the word "convenience" in the sense in which St. Thomas uses it, that is, where it includes what is good, beautiful, and just.

38. Say, exchange-rate forecasting.

39. Which may be a very interesting story in itself, by the way. For example, as a matter of personal taste, I find Piero Sraffa's *Production of Commodities by Means of Commodities* (Cambridge: Cambridge University Press, 1963) one of the most elegant models in economics. In a reappraisal of classical issues concerning labor and development, it provides fascinating results that allow us to explore the inner logic of economic reproduction. Still, the qualitative change we observe in reality largely exceeds what can be analyzed within Sraffa's model.

40. Godbout, *L'esprit du don*, second part.

41. Notice that hierarchies are used in order to realize economic transactions not only in the public administration but also within firms with bureaucratic, vertical structures. In

the wide literature on transaction costs, see O. E. Williamson, *Market and Hierarchies: Analysis and Antitrust Implications: A Study in the Economics of Internal Organization* (New York: The Free Press; London: Collier, MacMillan, 1983).

42. This description of vertical circulation assumes that state decisions are taken and implemented according to a well-defined, hierarchical, top-down organization. Quite a different picture would emerge if we considered a "subsidiary" state that valued the initiative of citizens and groups of citizens according to a bottom-up approach.

43. This point was especially raised in the presentation by P. Dembinski and J. L. Dherse at the follow-up seminar held in Rome, St. John's University Campus, November 29–December 2, 2001.

44. In a sense, we do not have a real "market" anymore. A true market should be an institution granting the possibility of participation on the basis of principles of justice; that is, an institution in which unequal partners can deal with each other on the basis of rules designed to make their interaction occur "as if" they were equal.

45. Finance is a relevant example of an economic transaction where time matters and uncertainty is the rule. Impersonal transactions are indeed an exception in finance, and they tend to be very unsafe and unstable. Simona Beretta, "Ordering Global Finance: Back to Basics," in J. S. Boswell, F. P. McHugh, and J. Verstraeten, eds., *Catholic Social Thought: Twilight or Renaissance?* Bibliotheca Ephemeridum Theologicarum Lovaniensium, vol. 157 (Leuven: Leuven University Press: Uitgeverij Peeters, 2000).

46. See the Message of the Holy Father in the Pontifical Council for Justice and Peace's *Work as Key to the Social Question* (Vatican City: Libreria Editrice Vaticana, 2002), 9–11.

47. This should not come as a surprise in advanced economies, where services account for the largest share of production and consumption.

48. For an application to debt relief, Simona Beretta, "Con-dono e dono sociale: Il problema del debito dei paesi in via di sviluppo," in G. Rossi and E. Scabini, eds., *Dono e perdono nelle relazioni familiari e sociali,* Studi interdisciplinari sulla famiglia, no. 18 (Milan: Vita e Pensiero, Università Cattolica, 2000), 103–34.

49. Lee Tavis made this interesting point in his comment on a preliminary version of this essay.

50. For a theological analysis of subsidiarity see Dennis P. McCann, "Business Corporations and the Principle of Subsidiarity," in *Rethinking the Purpose of Business: Interdisciplinary Essays from the Catholic Social Tradition,* ed. S. A. Cortright and Michael J. Naughton (Notre Dame, Ind.: University of Notre Dame Press, 2002), 169–89.

51. D. Zardin (a cura di), *Corpi, "fraternità," mestieri nella storia della società europea* (Rome: Bulzoni, 1998).

52. We already noticed that finance is a peculiar good, where personalized relations of some kind are required to face the challenge of time and uncertainty. While the families of banker-merchants experienced the typical ups and downs of financial market instability, long-lasting financial institutions—many of them still active today—developed within charitable initiatives providing finance for the poor, such as the *Monti di pietà* created in many medieval cities. In more recent times, financial innovation has been again spurred by gift

relations: for example, in the second half of the nineteenth century, the Catholic Movement created in northern Italy a tight network of micro-finance institutions, cooperatives of credit, and nonprofit banks still active today. It is widely held that these institutions played a crucial role in widening development in these regions.

53. For an application of the above, see Luigi Curini, "Capitale sociale e microfinanza: 'Sentieri' di sviluppo. Un caso di studio—l'Arsi e Bale, Etiopia" (Ph.D. diss., Università Cattolica, Milan, 2001).

54. John Paul II, "Message for the Celebration of the World Day of Peace," January 1, 2000 (emphasis in original).

PART TWO

Wealth Distribution

Introduction

The Christian social and moral tradition cannot be criticized for the lack of a body of thought on wealth distribution. This is not surprising, since it is a theme well addressed in the foundational texts of the Christian faith that form the Bible, and it has therefore been a central theme in the development of Christian social thought.

The focus of the biblical texts concerning wealth distribution is on sharing the good things of the earth with those in need. This concern follows from the biblical idea that all good things come from God and ultimately belong to Him. In Genesis, God creates the world teeming with life and beautiful things, which He sees to be good, and gives dominion over His creation to humankind. In making a covenant with His people, God again makes a gift to them of His never-ending fidelity and promises them a land that will be abundant as a sign of His blessing. The Old Testament, in particular, emphasises the fundamental point that all the bounty of the earth is a gift from God to human beings. It follows that the rich have a duty to share with the poor because all human beings are children of God and all have, therefore, a right to share in the abundance that comes from God. This is especially the case where the poor are in some way disadvantaged—orphans, widows, aged, sick, handicapped, strangers—but it is not limited to them. The overall thrust of the biblical texts on wealth distribution is to ensure that the poor and needy have enough to live on and can therefore share in God's abundance. The prophets are especially clear in their condemnation of the wealthy when the latter do not share with the poor and even make a god out of their gold. Jesus' Parable of the Rich man and Lazarus, the former ending up in the fiery torments of hell because of his total lack of concern for the poor man outside his door, is a frightening reminder of our duty to share with the poor (Luke 16:19–31).

At the same time, there are many biblical texts that emphasize the importance of work, both in the Old and New Testaments, and chide the loafer and shirker—the most famous one being from St. Paul's Second Letter to the Thessalonians: "If anyone will not work, let him not eat" (3:10). Nevertheless, while the biblical texts are not naïve about the human capacity for laziness, in the light of the first set of texts, they do not amount to a condemnation of the poor for not having worked hard enough. Indeed, most of the texts found in the Bible on wealth and poverty are focused on the oppression of the poor by the rich. Many of the poor mentioned by the biblical authors are unable to work, and others are sometimes excluded because of oppression on the part of the rich and powerful. The poor in these situations are not shirkers (often they are working very hard but simply do not earn enough for their labor) and are considered deserving of support by the rich as a result.

Beyond the biblical texts, one could demonstrate a deep concern for the importance of a just distribution of wealth in the Church Fathers, the medieval scholastics, the Renaissance theologians—such as the Dominican Saint Antoninus of Florence—the nineteenth-century Christian social reformers, the twentieth-century social teaching, and the work of the liberation theologians. For instance, *Rerum novarum*, the first of the series of modern social encyclicals, was published in 1891 by Leo XIII to deal with the problems of the poor working classes, and it insists on their right to own property and to a living wage. In *Quadragesimo anno*, Pius XI—writing in a period when the totalitarian systems of Soviet Communism and Italian Fascism were well established, and Nazism was soon to gain power in Germany—outlines some of the problems of liberal capitalism that were partly to blame for the rise of these regimes, and he argues that social justice and charity are needed to control the operation of free competition in the market so as to move toward a more just distribution of wealth. In particular, he argues further that the principle of "subsidiarity" must be followed in the operation of the economy, whereby no higher organization takes away local decision making and initiative from smaller or lower groups (thus defending the rightful autonomy of local councils, small businesses, voluntary organizations, and so on). This is also a form of distribution, in this case, of power and decision-making capability, which is relevant to our discussion, since the pattern of the distribution of power is often closely connected to that of the distribution of wealth. At the end, one begins to wonder what more could be added by the contributors to this volume on a theme that, one might say, has already been worked practically to death—an "old warhorse" of the Christian tradition.

The contributions in Part II show that there *are* new things to say about the question of wealth distribution from within the Christian social tradition. This becomes less surprising when we recognize that the distribution question now has new dimensions or, to continue our metaphor, the old warhorse now has "new teeth." In other words, there are new problems that require new thinking in order to be resolved. One of the most glaring of these is the hugely increased, and increasing, wealth gap between rich and poor countries as well as between a few hundred extremely wealthy individuals or families and the vast mass of the poor who have access to few financial or other resources (see Stefano Zamagni's and Helen Alford's essays). On this basis alone, the insights of the Christian tradition take on new relevance and bear repeating.

The contributions here, however, go beyond merely repeating and reminding us of what the tradition has said so far on these issues. In at least three ways, new insights have been proposed in this section to enrich and further this tradition of thought.

First, Charles Clark's contribution challenges the commonly assumed relationship between wealth and poverty and the conclusion that more wealth creation will lead to less poverty. In Zamagni's chapter, there is *a re-examination of the anthropological basis of both Catholic social thought and economic theory*. Zamagni maintains that the limits of the *homo oeconomicus* are well known to economists, who would be willing to consider a different anthropological basis if such a consideration would prove fruitful: "It is obvious that recapturing the relational or personalistic dimension from within the economic discourse will be well received, or at least not opposed, by the profession if we succeed in proving that while complying with the canons of scientific praxis, it can amend quite a few of the discipline's *aporiai* and shortcomings, thus making possible a closer grip on reality." He considers how the straitjacket of methodological individualism prevents economists from dealing with the problems of global inequality in an effective way, and indicates why a personalist approach— taking the human person, rather than the individual, as the starting point of the analysis—is more productive. Zamagni, therefore, takes some new steps forward in showing how basic underlying economic concepts can have a large influence on the way one deals with the wealth distribution problem.

Second, there is a consideration of the importance of effective means to achieve proper wealth distribution in our present economic situation, without undermining other important social goals, not least of which is the creation of wealth. The means discussed here include effective institutions and practical techniques— at the levels of the individual business and international trade relations—for bringing about more equitable wealth distribution in the concrete situation of the world in which we find ourselves. Carlo Dell'Aringa and Claudio Lucifora analyze the impact of different institutions on wage differentials in various Organization for Economic Cooperation and Development (OECD) countries. They are particularly interested in knowing whether the institutions referred to by name in the encyclical *Laborem exercens* under the title "indirect employer" really do have an impact on wage rates, as John Paul II suggests. Their meticulous statistical analysis indicates that indeed, the two institutions mentioned (unions and the state) do have a significant role in preventing excessive income inequality, even if the mechanisms through which they have such impact are not always the same.

Third, as in Part I, the authors of this section *examine links between new developments in economic theory and the Catholic social tradition.* Dennis McCann brings out the strong resemblance between the idea of the U.S. bishops in *Economic Justice for All* that unacceptable economic inequality involves the exclusion of people from participating effectively in society, and Amartya Sen's economic analyses of "capabilities" and "functionings." McCann proposes that the bishops could present their case much more forcefully to economists and politicians if they were to use Sen's language and analysis. Meanwhile, Helen Alford's essay attempts to use the idea of public goods to help examine a more equitable global wealth distribution. "Public" goods cannot be generated effectively by market mechanisms, or solely by market mechanisms, and this category covers such wide-ranging and important benefits as traffic control systems, systems of standards, common land, and states of peace and justice. This thinking on public goods offers an opportunity for the Christian tradition to extend its analysis of distribution questions with a further set of analytical tools. It also offers a way of bringing the language of the common good into economic and business discourses on distribution, which, given the provenance of this idea in political theory, is not always easy to do, despite the fact that the economy and business institutions are vital components in the creation of the common good.

We started off this introduction by considering the foundational texts of the Christian faith and what they say about the importance of distribution and redistribution, and so it is appropriate to conclude this short introduction to our essays on wealth distribution by returning to these texts. An acute reader of the Bible might remind us of another of Jesus' sayings recorded in the Gospels: "The poor you will always have with you" (Jn 12:8). Viewed on its own, out of context, such a phrase could have led Christians toward a kind of "quietism" or fatalism in the face of poverty and glaring wealth inequality. Dorothy Day supposedly responded, "the good Lord never thought there would be this many poor." However, Christians have not interpreted Jesus' saying fatalistically; rather, in the light of the general teaching we have discussed here, it has impressed Christians as a call to emphasize continuously the importance of generosity, of solidarity, and, in our modern, institutionally organized societies, of policies and mechanisms for favoring wider wealth distribution. The question of the poor and the excluded will always be with us, whatever economic advances we make, and therefore Christians will need to keep on riding this old warhorse into the battle over what makes for a good society. The essays in this section do so by building on the Christian social tradition while extending it in new directions. Their authors are perhaps unwittingly following another saying of Jesus', that the good scribe or scholar brings out of his storehouse of knowledge "things both old and new."

SIX   # Wealth and Poverty

The Preferential Option for the Poor
in an Age of Affluence

CHARLES M. A. CLARK

Wealth and poverty are relational terms, both with each other and in reference to some other factor. Wealth is typically understood as an abundance of some factor, while its opposite, poverty, is viewed as a shortage or scarcity of that same factor. In economic and business analysis, the factor by which we define wealth and poverty is money or, more properly, that which money commands (goods and services, security, power over the economic process). Our understanding of wealth and poverty is framed in materialistic terms, mostly because of the adoption of a neoclassical economic theory and a utilitarian view of human nature, that is, that man finds happiness through consumption of goods in the marketplace. In contrast, Catholic social thought is based upon an anthropology that emphasizes the dignity of the person (and all persons) and the promotion of the common good, and thus it frames the purpose of human activity in nonmaterialistic terms.

This broader and deeper understanding of the nature of the person allows for a fuller understanding of the meaning of wealth and its relation to poverty, bringing us (often kicking and scratching) to the conclusion that the Christian value of taking an "option for the poor" is fundamental to any discussion of wealth, from its role in the macro economy to its function in the individual business enterprise. Our argument in this chapter is based on the contention that by formulating our understanding of wealth and poverty solely according to materialistic terms, we greatly limit our ability to see the real connections between the economy, business, wealth, poverty, and human happiness. These interconnections are multifaceted and are not

easily reduced to simple formulas or economic trade-offs. Furthermore, these interconnections are fundamental to how Catholic social thought understands and evaluates the creation and distribution of wealth.

The relationship between wealth and poverty is always complex. In some ways,
Catholic social thought multiplies this complexity, for it forces an interdisciplinary
investigation of this interrelationship that looks at all the social, political, cultural,
and economic interconnections. But Catholic social thought also forces us into a
much deeper level of analysis that probes the soul of the human person, at which
level the interconnections obtain a clarity that escapes the solely materialistic investigations. Here we see that wealth only becomes real wealth—that is, the wealth
promised in Isaiah, wealth that is a gift from God, wealth that promotes well-being
and human happiness—when it is put to the service of the poor in its creation, distribution, and use. A Christian understanding of wealth therefore sees it through
the eyes of the poor and evaluates it based on *their* criteria.

No sound explication of Catholic social thought could fail to place the interests
of the poor front and center. Indeed, any putatively Christian treatment of economic
and social issues that does not adopt an option for the poor forfeits, in a very real
sense, its claim to be Christian.[1] This is why the preferential option for the poor is a
central theme in Catholic social thought. Furthermore, Catholic social thought understands wealth and poverty in terms of meeting human needs and promoting ultimate human ends. That is to say, Catholic social thought brings the philosophical
and theological anthropology that grounds the Christian understanding of poverty
to bear on the analysis of wealth and its uses. Business shapes a major part of life in
modern society. To the extent that business is centered on issues of wealth, and given
that participation in business is a legitimate form of participation in the economic
life of the community, any discussion of wealth from a Catholic perspective must address the issue of exclusion, or failure to promote economic (and consequently social
or political) participation (which we will see is the cause of poverty).

Catholic social teaching argues that this understanding of wealth and poverty
should ground both the evaluation and the redirection of our economic efforts,
for the sake of protecting the human dignity of all, and of promoting the common
good. Efforts to create "real" economic wealth (using material goods that promote
well-being) and to fight "real" poverty (denying to persons the human right to economic, social, and political participation) will be futile unless they are based on a
"real" appreciation of persons and their happiness. Christian anthropology tells us
that human beings flourish by serving God through others.[2]

In this chapter we will first explicate wealth and poverty from two relevant
principles of Catholic social thought: participation and solidarity. Second, we will
show that Catholic social thought's preferential option for the poor is the concrete

application of the principles of participation and solidarity. The remainder of the chapter will examine how the creation, distribution, and use of wealth impact the poor, with the aim of developing criteria for judging whether the actual patterns of wealth creation, distribution, and use promote the well-being of all persons, beginning with the poor.

THE MEANING OF WEALTH AND POVERTY IN CATHOLIC SOCIAL THOUGHT

In "The Nature of Wealth" and several essays in Part I of this book, we saw that the term "wealth" is often linked to the idea of an abundance of well-being, usually of material well-being. This abundance, we saw, could be treated at the level of the political community (Adam Smith's "wealth of nations") or at the level of the individual ("Mr. Smith is wealthy"). Furthermore, we noted that modern economic theory, as well as common opinion generally, link wealth to the "individual," while Catholic social teaching, in common with many nonneoclassical economists, has traditionally viewed wealth in a social light, and treated its creation, distribution, and use in terms of the whole community. For the purposes of this chapter, we will stress the "personalism" implicit in the social view of wealth. The sense in which Catholic analysis of social phenomena, economic and otherwise, entails personalism is best conveyed by comparing the Catholic approach to the "methodological individualism" of neoclassical economics and neoliberalism, on the one hand, and the "collectivism" of Karl Marx and much socialist analysis, on the other.

The individualistic perspective abstracts economic actors from their social and historical situations and views them as mere individuals lacking any antecedent communion with family, class, nation, or any other group. Since to be human is to be profoundly social, this individualistic perspective leads to a reduced notion of persons as individual, calculating "animals" unsuited to explain their own actions. Human persons are distinguished above all by moral imagination and intelligence and are thus capable of communion with others, of comprehending the social whole, and of acting in view of both, that is, of acting toward the common good.

The collectivist perspective takes the contrary path to the same destination. It considers economic actors to be no more than functors in their social relations, thus emptying subjects of their personhood by reducing them to mere parts of the social whole. The collectivist forgets that moral imagination and intelligence make of each single person, though a part of the social whole, an integrated, autonomous part who can comprehend his social relations and act in light of that comprehension, namely, for the common good.

The individualist and collectivist, respectively, reduce economic actors from persons to mere individuals, or even further to the social trappings of their individuality. As we will argue below, their reductionism entails materialism. Real human agents act neither as mere isolated seekers of their individual advantage nor as mere social functionaries. Real human agents understand even their material well-being and frame their economic purposes in more than simply material terms. We must break with the individualists' and collectivists' anthropologies if we are to theorize human action adequately. Moreover, only in doing so can we address the worst failing of both modern economic theory and practice: the failure to treat economic actions as a species of moral action.[3]

Christian Anthropology

Catholic social thought, like the wider tradition of Catholic moral theology, has always flown (in John Paul II's metaphor) on the two wings of faith and reason. The understanding of the nature of the human person is no exception to this rule. Christian anthropology rests on revelation and reason, on inspired Scripture and the natural law.

Catholic social thought begins with the assertion of the dignity of every human person. That dignity consists in this: each person is created by God in His image and likeness; that is to say, each exercises intelligence (reason) and free will, and each is capable of knowing and loving the good in creation and the Creator. This assertion not only identifies the essential characteristics of human nature (intelligence and free will) but also the goal or ultimate purpose of human actions: union with God. As John Paul II has stated,

> The dignity of the human person is a transcendent value, always recognized as such by those who sincerely search for the truth. Indeed, the whole of human history should be interpreted in the light of this certainty. Every person, created in the image and likeness of God (cf. Gn 1:26–28), is therefore radically oriented towards the Creator, and is constantly in relationship with those possessed of the same dignity. To promote the good of the individual is thus to serve the common good, which is the point where rights and duties converge and reinforce one another.[4]

Christian doctrine asserts that humans' dignity, the personhood conferred on each by the God who is One in Three Persons, images divine personhood. The dignity of each person supposes communion with other persons; since ours is a social nature that is fulfilled only by living fruitfully and peaceably with others. Our personal good is interconnected with the common good, such that what affects the person's good affects the good of the whole, and vice versa. The human dignity of each person and the finality of the common good among the purposes of human action are inseparable complements. Pursuit of the common good entails the protection of human dignity, and the protection of human dignity, in turn, requires the promotion of the common good.

The twentieth-century philosophical argument for human dignity through life in community is perhaps most closely associated with the writings of Jacques Maritain and Karol Wojtyla (John Paul II), but both are respondents to a very long tradition. Maritain has illuminated the distinction between the human individual and the human person in the following way:

> [T]he human being is caught between two poles; a material pole, which, in reality, does not concern the true person but rather the shadow of personality or what, in the strict sense, is called individuality, and a spiritual pole, which does concern true personality. . . . As an Individual, each of us is a fragment of a species, a part of the universe, a unique point in the immense web of cosmic, ethnical, historical forces and influences—and bound by their laws. Each of us is subject to the determinism of the physical world. Nonetheless, each of us is also a person and, as such, is not controlled by the stars. Our whole being subsists in virtue of the substance of the spiritual soul which is in us a principle of creative unity, independence and liberty.[5]

Maritain also notes that the "person requires membership in a society in virtue both of its dignity and its needs."[6] These include not only basic physical needs (food, clothing, shelter) but also social ones (companionship) and above all our need of "others," those necessary partners and respondents in our work of intellectual and moral development.

In an independent parallel, John Paul II (as Karol Wojtyla) argues that solidarity—unqualified dedication to promoting the common good—is founded on the processes by which a person seeks self-actualization. We become most authentically ourselves when, "working jointly with others," we give gifts of our persons: our unique talents and insights, to be sure, but also those deficiencies that call forth others' gifts. Because participation with others in the work of society is thus fundamental to self-development, John Paul II has criticized "individualistic" systems, that is, theories that take human beings to exist, atom-like, in mutual opposition to one another. As he says,

> Individualism accomplishes this by isolating the self . . . to itself and to its own good, that is, a good that exists in isolation from the good of the others and

from the common good. In this system, the good of the individual has the quality of being opposed to every other individual and his good. This kind of individualism is based on self-preservation and is always on the defensive, and is also defective. Acting and existing jointly with others is, according to this individualism, an imposed necessity to which an individual has to submit. But there is no positive aspect in this necessity. It does not serve the development of his individuality. "The others" are for the individual only a source of limitations and may even be opponents and create polarizations.[7]

Christian anthropology proposes that because persons transcend their material destiny, every material circumstance is an object of use to the person. Thus, wealth and poverty are means to the achievement of ultimate human ends: temporal happiness and union with God. Whether abundant or scarce, riches are to be accounted as a means to an end, and never an end in themselves. In the Catholic tradition, the classic statement of this principle belongs to St. Thomas Aquinas:

> As a matter of fact, external riches are necessary for the good of virtue; since by them we support our body and give assistance to other people. Now, things that are means to an end must derive their goodness from the end. So, external riches must be a good for man; not, of course, the principal one, but as a secondary good. For the end is the principal good, while other things are good because they are ordered to the end. This is why it has seemed to some people that the virtues are the greatest goods for man, while external riches are his least important goods. Now, things that are means to an end must be measured in accord with the requirements of the end. Therefore, riches are good, to the extent that they advance the practice of virtue, but if this measure is departed from, so that the practice of virtue is hindered by them, then they are not to be numbered among goods, but among evils. Hence, it happens to be a good thing for some people to possess riches, for they use them for the sake of virtue, but for others it is a bad thing to have them, for these people are taken away from virtue by them, either through too much solicitude or affection for them, or also because of mental pride resulting from them.
>
> So, poverty is praiseworthy according as it frees man from the vices in which some are involved through riches. Moreover, in so far as it removes the solicitude which arises from riches, it is useful to some, namely, those disposed to busy themselves with better things. . . . However, in so far as poverty takes away the food which results from riches, namely, the assisting of others and the support of oneself, it is purely an evil; except in the case where the temporal help that is offered to neighbors can be compensated for

by a greater good, that is, by the fact that a man who lacks riches can more freely devote himself to divine and spiritual matters.[8]

Poverty as mere deprivation of the means or the opportunity to pursue human goods is an unmixed evil; poverty as a deliberate foregoing of the means to some goods for the sake of a greater good (freedom for spiritual devotion is the example that Aquinas gives) is an instrumental good, just as is wealth. Used to promote the common good or to relieve a particular human need, wealth, like poverty, takes goodness from the ends that it is made to serve; pursued for its own sake, denied to just uses, or made a matter of boast, wealth is an evil, for it separates its owners from virtue and obscures or usurps God as the ultimate human good and the object of worship.

Participation and Solidarity

Because Catholic social thought takes economic agents to be persons, it has many fundamental disagreements with the reigning neoclassical economic theory. Neoclassical theory supposes an economic actor, "rational economic man," who is guided solely by self-interest; the promotion of the common interest is left to the "invisible hand" of the market. Catholic social thought takes "economic man" for an abstraction; actual human agents are persons guided signally by religious or moral commitments as well as by cultural affinities, political allegiances, and self-interest. Only by reducing persons to mere individuals can neoclassical economic theory abstract from these other factors.[9]

Some argue that "economic man" and economic theory are like Siamese twins, born together in Adam Smith's analysis and somehow inseparable. Dispense with "economic man," and you have dispensed with economic theory. For if, in Smith's famous phrase, it is not from the baker's benevolence—but from his self-interest—that we expect our daily bread, then it is "economic man" alone whose actions count for economic theorizing. We have to say that "economic man" is more at home in the world of Bernard Mandeville, where private vice leads to public "virtue" (that is, power for economic growth) than in the world of Adam Smith and classical economics.[10]

In Adam Smith's universe of discourse, human beings cannot be circumscribed by their self-interested passions:

> How selfish soever man may be supposed, there are evidently some principles in his nature, which interest him in the fortune of others, and render their happiness necessary to him, though he derives nothing from it except the

pleasure of seeing it. Of this kind is pity or compassion, the emotion which we feel for the misery of others, when we either see it, or are made to conceive it in a very lively manner. That we often derive sorrow from the sorrow of others, is a matter of fact too obvious to require any instances to prove it; for this sentiment, like all the other original passions of human nature, is by no means confined to the virtuous and humane, though they perhaps may feel it with the most exquisite sensibility. The greatest ruffian, the most hardened violator of the laws of society, is not altogether without it.[11]

Thus *The Theory of Moral Sentiments*: social life evokes and develops an original human capacity for other-regarding, moral sensibility. Without it, the only social order imaginable would be the equable tyranny of Thomas Hobbes's "sovereign." Adam Smith knew perfectly well that self-interest is insufficient to generate sociability or market order. A minimum of "solidarity," or what Smith called "fellow feeling"—individual agents regulating their actions in view of their foreseeable effects on others—is necessary in order to have an economy of free agents. He did not attribute to the market a mystical power to create the moral conditions of the markets' existence. He knew that if "markets" are to promote the common welfare through orderly exchange, then morality and religion must work up moral sentiment into moral character, providing virtuous agents—persons of their word, for instance—as the indispensable check against the lust for gain.

Contemporary Catholic social teaching on solidarity supposes the interdependence of all persons, and it incorporates those precepts that interdependence ultimately implies.[12] This understanding of solidarity is so far opposed to the individualism supposed by neoclassical economic theory that it not only denies that any person *may* use others for strictly economic ends, but it also denies that any person *can* achieve any *genuine* human end—any *real* good, economic or otherwise—except by assisting others to achieve it. In John Paul II's now classic formulation,

> [Solidarity] is not a feeling of vague compassion or shallow distress at the misfortunes of so many people, both near and far. On the contrary, it is *a firm and persevering determination* to commit oneself to the *common good;* that is to say, to the good of all and of each individual, because we are *all* really responsible *for all*. This determination is based on the solid conviction that what is hindering full development [namely, of all, not merely the poor or the oppressed] is that desire for profit and that thirst for power already mentioned. These attitudes and "structures of sin" are only conquered—presupposing the help of divine grace—by a *diametrically opposed attitude:* a commitment to the good of one's neighbor with the readiness, in the gospel

sense, to "lose oneself" for the sake of the other instead of exploiting him, and to "serve him" instead of oppressing him for one's own advantage.[13]

We can perhaps suggest the importance of solidarity as an *unqualified* commitment to the good common and to humanity *tout court* by following Adam Smith in a consideration of solidarity as a *qualified* commitment, that is, a commitment to a good common to certain human activities and certain human agents. Thus, a certain solidarity among traders—that is, a commitment by each to promote by preference ends common to all—is necessary to reduce the transaction costs of trading, and a much higher level of solidarity is necessary to establish the social context of economic activity.

Unqualified Christian solidarity calls on us to extend the social bond to all, especially to the poor and marginalized. The Gospel roots this call for solidarity in Jesus' command that we love one another as we love ourselves. The fullness of His command appears in Luke 6:32–33: "If you love only those who love you, what credit is that to you? Even sinners love those who love them. Again, if you do good only to those who do good to you, what credit is that to you? Even sinners do as much." Here, Jesus indicates the fullness of human solidarity: showing love to all, not simply to those who love us in kind. John Paul II suggests the economic implications of this kind of solidarity: "*Solidarity* helps us to see the 'other'—whether a *person, people or nation*—not just as some kind of instrument, with a work capacity and physical strength to be exploited at low cost and then discarded when no longer useful, but as our 'neighbor,' a 'helper' to be made a sharer, on a par with ourselves, in the banquet of life to which all are equally invited by God."[14] It should not surprise us that natural reason has led most of the world's major religions and perennial philosophies toward this conclusion.[15] The call to solidarity comes not only from the Gospels, but it is also an expression of natural law affirmed by natural reason, a precept discoverable by reflection on what it is to be a human person and to treat humanly with other persons.

Preferential Option for the Poor

Christian solidarity, an unqualified commitment to promote the unqualified human good, entails what has already been referred to as the preferential option for the poor:

> The exercise of solidarity *within* each society is valid when its members recognize one another as persons. Those who are more influential, because they

have a greater share of goods and command services, should feel *responsible* for the weaker and be ready to share with them all they possess. Those who are weaker, for their part, in the same spirit of *solidarity*, should not adopt a purely *passive* attitude or one that is *destructive* of the social fabric, but, while claiming their legitimate rights, should do what they can for the good of all. The intermediate groups, in their turn, should not selfishly insist on their particular interests, but respect the interests of others.[16]

From a Christian perspective, involuntary poverty is exclusion—the abridgement or denial of every person's right to participate in the fullness of the human enterprise, a right as unqualified as the divine image is ineradicable from the children of Adam.

The strongest economic message in the New Testament calls those with means to care for the poor, the marginalized, and the excluded. This message is delivered most clearly in Matthew 25:31 ff., where Jesus declares that "anything you did for one of my brothers here, however humble, you did for me ... and anything you did not do for one of these, however humble, you did not do for me." The humble, the least of our brothers, include the hungry, the thirsty, the stranger, the naked, and those in prison: in other words, the impoverished and the excluded. If we are to be accounted friends of Jesus at the Last Judgment, we must be active friends to these, the impoverished and the excluded.

It is sometimes suggested that the option for the poor entails a different kind of exclusion: it seems to "exclude" the rich. As the U.S. bishops have noted in *Economic Justice for All* (1986),

> The primary purpose of this special commitment to the poor is to enable them to become active participants in the life of society. It is to enable *all* persons to share in and contribute to the common good. "Option for the poor," therefore, is not an adversarial slogan that pits one group or class against another. Rather it states that the deprivation and powerlessness of the poor wounds the whole community. The extent of their suffering is a measure of how far we are from being a true community of persons.[17]

Ultimately, the involuntarily poor are excluded—that is, denied a role in the cultivation and enjoyment of the common good—by others' sinful decisions and actions, whether direct or consolidated in social institutions (which are thus structures of sin).[18] (By contrast, as we have seen St. Thomas argue above, voluntary poverty in the service of God and neighbor is—as voluntary—a mode of participation, a way of cultivating and enjoying the common good.)[19] As such, the refusal of the wealthy either to treat the involuntarily poor as a gift of God for the perfection of the human community, or to treat their wealth as a good (like all goods) to be diffused, amounts to self-exclusion from the cultivation and enjoyment of the common good.

In proclaiming the preferential option for the poor, the Church (as the U.S. bishops stress above) calls everyone, rich or poor, to promote the common good according to their gifts. By the same token, the Church warns everyone, rich or poor, that to neglect the commonality of the human good, which is achieved by universal participation, is to fail in an essential: it is to fail as a community; it is to deny one's neighbor. Hence, John Paul II insists that the Church's commitment to the poor is "proof of her fidelity to Christ."[20] For every faithful Christian, therefore, the option for the poor is not optional at all. Donal Dorr has noted that this principle must be realized on two levels, individual and societal:

> An option for the poor is a commitment by individual Christians and the Christian community at every level to engage actively in a struggle to overcome the social injustices which mar our world. To be genuine it must come from a real experience of solidarity with the victims of our society. This means that one aspect of an option for the poor has to do with sharing in some degree in the lives, sorrows, joys, hopes, and fears of those who are on the margins of society. Without this, the attempt to serve the interests of "the poor" will be patronizing—and it will make them feel more powerless and dependent than ever. But an option for the poor is not primarily the choice of a less affluent life-style by individuals or groups. It is a commitment to resist the structural injustice which marks our world. The person who makes such an option is undertaking to work to change the unjust economic, social and political structures which determine how power and resources are shared out in the world.[21]

Poverty is always caused by exclusion, which comes in many forms and is institutionalized in many ways. Therefore, our first obligation—and it is a strict obligation in justice—is to stop generating wealth by creating poverty.

Who Are the Poor?

For our purposes, the poor will be defined in the terms used by market economics. Neoclassical economic theory argues that incomes are "earned" based on how much one contributes to the profit-making process. The poor, therefore, are those who, for whatever reason, contribute little. In reality, however, incomes are not apportioned according to "contributions" but according to what one has the "right" to claim. Such "rights" may or may not be based on contributions. Winning the lottery, inheriting millions, being born white, male, and American: all these factors may contribute to raising one's income, yet none contributes significantly to the economy. Bill Gates has contributed to the economy, but his income owes more to the monopoly position of his company than to his marginal revenue product, which, according to neoclassical economic theory, is the determinant of incomes.

Moreover, all of us at least once (and usually at many points) in our lives are economically nonproductive: we neither contribute to the production of goods and services nor have property to sell or rent out for the production process. That is to say, all of us were once children, and many of us have been (or will be) sick or disabled, old and retired, or engaged at home in nonmarket caregiving. All of these are natural occurrences, part of the human experience, yet the market makes no allowance for them. Luckily, we do not have a pure market economy; in fact, a pure market economy is not possible. Elements of tradition and command influence economic arrangements and outcomes. The economic well-being of those who are not market participants is determined by their relatives—that is, by traditional familial support—or by charitable or governmental agencies devoted to assisting the economically disabled.

Economically, the preferential option for the poor makes sense because it recognizes that all of us are individually vulnerable and in need of support and protection, at least at some point in our lives. The condition is universal: as individuals we are poor. Our social relations and connections give us the possibility of rising above our natural poverty, and only by acting with others can anyone hope to rise above the most abject poverty. Nevertheless, "acting with others" can take a mutually beneficial form (cooperation aimed at greater productivity) or a zero-sum game form (use of power to establish preferential "rights" for "me and mine" at the expense of "them and theirs"). It is a matter of economic and social efficiency that social relations include everybody, both as benefactors and as contributors. We are all made poor by poverty—economically, socially, politically, culturally, and, most important, spiritually.

Among other things, therefore, adopting an *economic* option for the poor means that our first criterion of progress is how those at the bottom of the ladder fare. It also means that those at the bottom must be encouraged, morally and materially, to become more active social, political, and economic agents. Thus, "income support"— the dole, or public housing, or the comprehensive state support that used to characterize formerly Communist countries—is not the aim. Rather, promoting full social participation, or full citizenship, is the aim.

WEALTH AND THE POOR I: WEALTH CREATION

Wealth can be created in two ways: by expanding the productive capabilities of the community (social wealth), or by owners acquiring and employing assets to generate an income stream (private wealth).[22] The two methods are not mutually exclusive; the creation of individual wealth often adds to the community's productive capabilities. An example might be the purchase of capital goods (machines, factories, etc.) by a business enterprise. These become part of the owner's private store of wealth and, at the same time, increase the output of the community.

The creation of private wealth can also involve no more than a legal transfer of ownership rights. Such transfers do not necessarily increase the productive capabilities of the community and may change the productive mix in favor of one group at the expense of another. The transfer of factories from state to private ownership in the former Communist economies of Eastern Europe is instructive. When private owners use these assets more productively than did the state, they increase output generally; the community as a whole sees benefits and, provided that these benefits are widely shared, local poverty is reduced. All too frequently, the initial phases of the transition from communism to capitalism in Eastern Europe, and especially in the former Soviet Union, saw productive assets "privatized" at below-market valuations, thus allowing the new owners to resell for a one-time profit. Privatization thus generated no efficiency gains that could lead to increased social wealth or reductions in poverty. An institutional redistribution of power—historically, the rise of democracy and the welfare state—seems to be the channel down which the benefits of such changes trickle to the poor.

There is no doubt that economic growth makes possible, and in many cases achieves, the reduction of poverty. Too often, however, economists and policymakers emphasize changes in the statistical measures of economic growth or poverty and forget that these are rather imperfect indicators of either. Gross Domestic Product (GDP), the main statistical indicator of economic growth, merely measures the level of market transactions, not well-being. Crime, pollution, national disasters, and the breakup of the family all increase the volume of market transactions and so promote increases in GDP; they hardly promote well-being. Similarly, the way poverty is measured is often disconnected from the phenomena of marginalization and deprivation.[23] When we examine the relationship between the creation of wealth and the incidence of poverty, we should look to causal connections—How can wealth creation increase poverty? How can it reduce poverty?—and not merely to the statistical relationship between wealth creation and poverty rates.[24]

Harmful Wealth Creation

Wealth can create poverty in at least two ways: through the monopolization of property—that is, by excluding some people from benefiting from property (or what is the same thing, by not using property for the common good)—and through shifting costs away from those who benefit by something's use to those who do not.

When property (whether land, industrial equipment, or knowledge) is monopolized—that is, brought under the control of one agency for its exclusive benefit without regard to the common good—those who are excluded may also be impoverished. In history's paradigmatic case, the common lands attached to feudal manors (lands on which anyone might graze livestock) were brought under the lords' exclusive control by enclosure, thereby effecting a large transfer of wealth from the peasantry to the landlords. Even if, as is often argued, the resulting regularization of the former commons' use raised their yield and increased economic output in both the short and long run, these gains were achieved at the expense of peasant-producers, whose access to the benefits of a productive asset was permanently foreclosed. Wealth measured as general welfare was not increased. As a matter of political economy, the concept of ownership rights hedged with formal social responsibilities (such as the lords' obligation to keep commons), gave way to the concept of ownership as the exclusive, unqualified right to possess, use, and benefit from productive assets.[25]

Harmful wealth creation often involves shifting the legitimate costs of specific economic activities onto groups such as the poor, who are too powerless to resist. Much of the cost savings or profits realized by moving production to low-income countries depends on the fact that the local poor lack the economic or political power to demand living wages, safer working conditions, or environmental protections, factors that would bring production costs closer to those prevailing in developed economies. Companies that move production to these countries can thus shift much of the legitimate cost onto local workers and communities, who end up subsidizing the wealth of the companies' owners and the well-being of the consumers who buy the goods at reduced costs.

The economic logic of cost shifting was best stated by Lawrence Summers, former chief economist to the World Bank, now president of Harvard University, in his now infamous memorandum from 1991. Summers followed the logic of neoclassical economics to the conclusion that rich countries should move "dirty industries" to less developed countries. He reasoned that since the economic value of a life ("foregone earnings from increased morbidity and mortality") is lower in the poor versus rich countries, the costs of pollution would be lower in the poor countries.[26] Closer to home, much of the wealth created in the "new economy" is, in fact, a shift of costs away from capital and onto labor. The labor market flexibilities called for by businessmen entail the reduction of protections for workers, while these very protections have historically obstructed the shifting of costs onto the workers.[27]

Cost shifting often depends on government policy. Here we see how the political power of wealth shapes the "common good," that is, the aims of public policy, according to the interests of the wealthy and powerful. Consider the establishment of limited liability laws. Limited liability is a device to protect the property of the wealthy by capping the liability of a business (or its owners) at what has been invested in the business itself. Under the law of limited liability, if a total of one million dollars is invested in a corporation whose operations have caused three million dollars in damages, the owners are responsible for one-third of the damages, the total of their investment. Society must cover the other two-thirds in one way or another. In addition, limited liability entails a rather substantial subsidy of big businesses that would otherwise have to buy insurance to cover the costs actually hazarded by their operations.

One would have difficulty finding any large corporation or established industry unsupported by numerous laws and regulations that subsidize or protect it. All such laws and regulations involve shifting costs away from the rich. Some will be found to promote the common good, that is, to improve the well-being of the population generally; and no doubt most are justified in language that suggests that they are promoting the common good, but sadly this is not always (or usually) the case. We should remember that none other than Adam Smith stated that governments exist for the purpose of defending the property of the rich against the poor, and his call for "laissez-faire" economic policies was to limit the role that government plays in protecting the rich and powerful.[28]

Wealth Creation that Is Beneficial to the Poor

As we argued earlier, participation is essential to the development of the human person, while involuntary poverty is caused by exclusion, the denial of the human right to social, economic, and political participation. Participation, then, is a criterion for judging both whether wealth serves the purpose for which it is generated and whether wealth is justly produced and accumulated; it touches both the ends and the means of wealth creation (on this point, see Dennis McCann, chapter 7, this volume).

That economic development is friendly to increased social participation has been the experience of the advanced capitalist economies over the past three hundred years. At the dawn of the capitalist era, the thinkers of the Scottish Enlightenment introduced the notion that commercial activities and exchange can (and ought to) create ligatures of community. When the greatest of these men, Adam Smith, set out to explain economic growth, he stated that its basis is the division of labor, that is to say, increased interdependence and intelligent coordination among producers. Increased and increasingly elaborate cooperation lead to wider participation and, Smith argued, to increase in the wealth of nations. Nevertheless, he was keenly aware that the division of labor into "a few simple operations" tends to produce laborers "as stupid and ignorant"—and thus as far from human flourishing—"as it is possible for a human creature to become."[29]

Again, students of the factors that have historically promoted economic growth often cite education and technological change as the two most important catalysts. Certainly, no public policy has done more to promote economic growth than universal access to education, itself a prime catalyst of technological change. Nevertheless, on the criterion of participation, technological progress is ambivalent: while it can empower workers, it can also, as the history of industrialization abundantly shows, de-skill them and thus reduce them to dependent functionaries of production processes that are doomed to fade away. Similarly, education may be liberal, aimed at developing persons who transcend their material destinies; or it may be servile, aimed at training individuals who are no more than equal to prescribed economic or social tasks.

These deep ambivalences should remind us of something easily forgotten in this age of affluence: arts, technologies, and organizations, however spectacular their achievements, solve no problem of human use. Lacking either a right and clear view of what ultimate human purpose is at stake, or a rooted ethic of what is owed the human subjects of human action, these instrumentalities are as apt to shackle as to free, to injure as to benefit.

Hence, Catholic social teaching on the economy argues that rational wealth creation is directed, first, to the ends of human development; and second, by the criteria of particular justice. These criteria have little to do with the letter of the positive law and are rarely noted even in Catholic quarters. Therefore, they bear some remarks here. Traditionally, their exposition follows on St. Thomas Aquinas's analysis of justice as what constitutes *ius*, "right (or right order)" in human relationships. This traditional sense of justice as "right (or rightly ordered) relationships" does not yield a checklist of points that might be used piecemeal to score the status quo: right relationships are not right "on balance" or "for the most part."

Aquinas, following Aristotle, distinguished general (or legal) justice, which pertains to the common good, and particular justice, which pertains to individual persons, and he then divided particular justice further by commutative and distributive relationships. Commutative justice concerns "the order of one private individual to another . . . the mutual dealings between two persons."[30] In Aquinas's language, "commutations" amount to private exchanges, so commutative justice (rightly ordered private exchange) is of importance for any economic analysis. Commutative justice prescribes equable exchange: if I pay you five dollars for something, it should be worth five dollars, so that neither of us is the loser by the transaction. (The concept of an exchange value that preserves the quantity of each party's share of goods through a transaction is the concept of "just price."[31]) Commutative justice, then, aims at preventing one party to an exchange from taking advantage of the other.

The poor are often on the losing end of commutatively unjust transactions. Their heightened need (they cannot wait for a better deal); their relative ignorance of market values or legal conventions; their subjection to various forms of price discrimination and fraud, which are common in poor neighborhoods—these factors and more often leave the poor prey to unjust dealing.[32] And, in fact, much wealth and much poverty are the residue of past commutative injustices—the persistent effects that continue to obstruct the formation of right relationships.

Distributive justice concerns right relations between individual persons and the various communities to which they belong. It prescribes that individuals should share in goods achieved by common effort in proportion to their stature in the community. Commutative justice aims to preserve individuals' shares of goods; distributive justice aims to put the wherewithal to pursue their purposes at individuals' disposal. Aquinas, like Aristotle, discerned two opposed principles that might be invoked to realize the aim of distributive justice: one might aim ideally for equality (this aim would correspond to the democratic institutions of freemen), or one might aim for proportionality to grades of excellence (this aim would correspond to the hierarchical institutions of aristocracies).[33]

The aim of distributive justice, which concerns honors, offices, and positions as well as material rewards, might seem to demand that we compromise by insisting on neither principle alone, while invoking each in a different connection. This approach is, in fact, traditional. Indeed, traditional Catholic social thought accepts that, owing to diversity in merit, the distribution of allocated goods among the members of a community will be unequal de facto. At the same time it proposes that since every community aims to make well-being and well-doing possible to all its members, distributive justice entails that all members share in the community's material benefits, that is, the goods that the economy allocates, to a measure that meets their individual needs.

In addition, and most important, the very nature of the goods intrinsic to life in community, the properly common goods, must be shared fully by each member according to his capacity, if they are to be shared at all. For these goods are shared by participation, as a conversation or a civil right is shared; each is shared as a whole by everyone who participates. The properly common goods are "participated goods"— the benefits of civic peace, of the security of the law, of access to the riches of culture (including those that make for "human capital"), and of sound morals—that promote specifically human flourishing. Thus, patterns of wealth creation that cause exclusion are no less repugnant to distributive justice than personal favoritism or unfair discrimination (classically, the distributive vice militating directly against distributive virtue).

WEALTH AND THE POOR II: DISTRIBUTION

Distribution of income is often treated as a case of the "equity-efficiency trade-off," or the proposition, usually identified with Arthur Okun's *Equality and Efficiency: The Big Trade-off,* that economic equity is purchased at the cost of lost efficiency.[34] Okun begins with a classic argument: if market economies are to operate efficiently, they must generate a certain level of income inequality, since markets must offer higher incomes to secure rare skills, elaborate education, or high-risk investors or entrepreneurs, and so on. In order to equalize incomes, we must tamper with this market mechanism, thus weakening the role of price signals and then lowering the efficiency of markets to everyone's detriment.

Moreover (and here Okun extends the argument), any deliberate public policy aimed at redistributing income in the interests of equality must result in further inefficiency, that is, every dollar transferred from someone richer to someone poorer will increase the recipient's income by less than a dollar. Okun's famous metaphor suggests that transferring income from the rich to the poor is like transferring water from one reservoir to another in leaky buckets. Spillage, that is, inefficiency, is inevitable and results in reduced levels of total income as well as in inefficient use of resources.[35]

The argument that inequality in wealth redounds to the general welfare has a long history. It rests on the premise that wealth inequality is necessary to promote large accumulations of capital. Only those who need not consume all their economic resources here and now are able to devote some portion to future production. The rich are, of course, those who have resources for discretionary use: the richer they are, the greater their resources and the wider their discretion. Thus, large-scale inequality supplies a fund of capital wealth, concentrated in the hands of a few, and so available for capital-intensive or large-scale uses. Relatively evenly divided wealth, realized as many small surpluses, will typically support only small-scale production, not the large production units characteristic of industrial capitalism.

The central weakness of these arguments appears when we ask Okun, "How far should we prefer efficiency to equality?" or wonder, "Why shouldn't the joint capital of many small investors, or the product of many small concerns, answer to the purposes of a rational economy?" Okun's analysis implies no answer to the first question; it simply admonishes us that we must pay for increased equality with lost efficiency and vice versa. Our willingness to "pay" will depend upon whether we see equality as an economic or social end in itself or as a necessary means to other ends.

Catholic social teaching is unequivocal: one cannot prefer efficiency to equality where prevailing inequalities are a barrier to participation—economic, social, political—on the part of anyone, and especially the poor. (For a detailed discussion of *Economic Justice for All* [1986] in connection with this notion, see again, McCann's essay.) In particular (as each of the modern popes, beginning with Leo XIII, has insisted), economies must be regulated by distributive justice—that is, they must make the means of human sustenance and development (the material bases of participation) available to all. Where the right to participation is in question, appeal to efficiency cannot trump the imperative to pursue equality to the point of distributive equity, for preferring efficiency would amount to inverting means and ends. *Gaudium et spes* states: "To satisfy the demands of justice and equity, strenuous efforts must be made, without disregarding the rights of persons or the natural qualities of each country, to remove as quickly as possible the immense economic inequalities, which now exist and in many cases are growing and which are connected with individual and social discrimination."[36]

In any case, the argument that promoting greater equity in the distribution of wealth will lead to a reduction in economic activity or to a fall in output lacks empirical evidence. As we move into the postindustrial economy, the periods of highest economic growth have also been periods of decreasing inequality, not the reverse. John Maynard Keynes long ago demonstrated that promotion of capital accumulation no longer applies as the justification for large inequalities of wealth (see my "Wealth as Abundance and Scarcity," chapter 1, this volume). Hence, as to the second question: no doubt a more equable diffusion of wealth will lead to significant changes in the economy, in the types of goods produced, and in the size and scope of business enterprises. But we should not assume that a world with thousands of small hamburger restaurants is somehow worse than one with two or three large chains of such restaurants. Any industrial economist will tell you that the level of capital concentration in advanced economies far exceeds what is necessary to secure economies of scale. Moreover, if our ultimate economic goal is the well-being of persons, and neither production nor profit for their own sake, then such a change is to be desired.

According to Pius XI, "Wealth, . . . which is constantly being augmented by social and economic progress, must be distributed among the various individuals and classes of society [so] that the common good of all ... be thereby promoted."[37] The poor are members of the community who are excluded from certain aspects of its economic and social life. This exclusion is at once the cause and a consequence of their poverty, since it restricts their participation in the benefits of community and, more important, in the cultivation of community, that is, of the common good. Moreover, the latter restriction is a loss to all. The common good is not only the material security of life but also the moral richness by which unique, unrepeatable persons develop in communion with one another.

We say too little if we note that slavery—the deliberate, systematic exclusion of persons from participation in the common good—kept the South economically retrograde. The economic cost was by no means the greatest cost that the "peculiar institution" exacted from the South or from the whole nation. Similarly, we say too little when we note that exclusion weakens the moral fabric of the community or strikes at the moral integrity of those who benefit from it or countenance it.

Wealth and the Poor III: Use of Wealth

Catholic social teaching echoes the Gospels' two main economic messages: the preferential option for the poor (the expression of solidarity); and the barrier that wealth erects to individual salvation (the practice of stewardship). Catholic social teaching on the use of wealth unites them: wealth is first for the relief of human need among one's own (family, friends) and among one's neighbors (who are first the poor), and then for the direct promotion of the common good. Emphasis on relieving the poor and on the direct promotion of the common good, that is, good works, will suggest that how wealth is used pertains more to charity than to justice. (Although, following Aquinas, we note that the virtues of justice and charity are closely related; distinguishing them is often more an intellectual than a practical exercise.)

Judeo-Christian moral philosophy and theology traditionally emphasize the harmful effects that the use of wealth can have on the wealthy. The *locus classicus* in Christian Scripture, Christ's Parable of Lazarus and "Dives" or the (generic) "Rich One," expresses the universal precept with dramatic clarity: spending one's surplus on oneself when others are in manifest need is a deadly sin. The Church Fathers often noted that the surplus of the rich (regardless of how it is acquired) is, if not spent to benefit the poor, stolen from the poor.[38] Nevertheless, from a purely economic perspective, the use of wealth can have significant harmful as well as helpful impacts on the extent of poverty in a society. We will first consider the economic effects of the use of wealth on poverty and then return to the importance of the virtue of charity.

Harmful Use

Thomas Robert Malthus pioneered a still-persistent course of argument when he contended that the lavish lifestyles of the rich provide jobs and incomes for the poor and suggested that lavishness be encouraged as a way to reduce unemployment. He was extending Bernard Mandeville's argument that private vices promote public virtue (economic growth), but he was breaking with the economic analysis of Adam Smith, his predecessor.[39] Smith divided employments into productive (contributive to the output of goods and services) and unproductive (noncontributive to social output) categories: the first a source of economic growth and progress, and the second a drag on the economy.[40] While some unproductive employments are necessary (for example, police, national defense), Smith noted, many, such as the numerous servants of the rich, do not contribute to social output and, in fact, limit economic growth. His analysis is as sound in principle today as it was in 1776.

One reason that greater equality of wealth and incomes promotes economic progress is that it leads to a more productive use of labor. By giving everyone, especially the poor, greater buying power, economic equality attracts productive resources, especially labor, to uses that satisfy the needs of the many instead of the whims of the few. By contrast, we see how concentrated purchasing power can command productive resources in defiance of reason when we observe how workers in the Third World (often children themselves) labor to produce disposable toys or trinkets for American fast-food distributors instead of goods or services that would promote the economic well-being of their own communities.[41]

Contrary to the Malthusian view, conspicuous consumption exacerbates poverty through both economic and social mechanisms. Economically, it drives up prices, making necessary goods scarcer for the poor. Consider housing. The demand for large landholdings by the affluent forces the poor to live on ever smaller plots while, in nearly every city in the United States, increasing demand for real estate bids up the prices of housing and forces the poor out into the streets.[42] Again, the increased demand for gasoline generated by the boom in SUV sales means that all drivers have to pay higher prices at the pump, but for the poor increased spending on gasoline means a reduction in their consumption of other basics. On the global scale, the United States, the world's most copious food producer, is a net importer of certain foodstuffs and bids up their price even as other net importers' populations face severe malnutrition. Thus, conspicuous consumption, in raising the demand for goods and services, keeps them permanently scarce and high-priced.

Socially considered, conspicuous consumption is an essential aspect of a power system that excludes the poor. As Thorstein Veblen noted in *The Theory of the Leisure*

Class (1899), all consumption involves an element of social communication, and conspicuous consumption communicates the attainment of preeminent—as one might now say, "elite"—status, setting therewith the standard for those who would attain it by imitation. The lower classes' emulation of the elite's consumption patterns ensures their acquiescence, for it is their buying into (pun intended) the legitimacy of the social order. When the lower classes approach the consumption patterns of the elite, the elite then vary the pattern or raise the bar. The resulting intensification of consumption ensures at once the stable position of the elite and the continuing fascination of the aspiring classes with everything about the status system except its justice. Economically, it must be noted that the status derived from conspicuous consumption requires that the elite be a distinct minority and that therefore the tokens of status be scarce. If the same number of BMWs were driven as Toyotas or Nissans, their status value would depreciate to zero.

Helpful Use

Wealth, the ownership and control of productive assets, involves use in the sense of directing how productive assets will be employed as well as in the sense of spending (distributing) the income generated by productive assets. Both sorts of use will have a great impact on the extent of poverty in a country. Because we have touched on the distribution of wealth and income above, we will concentrate here on use in the sense of directing the employment of productive assets.

Just as the richest countries still number many poor people among their populations, so too do the poorest countries number many rich people. In the poorest nations, one of the biggest barriers to overcoming poverty is that productive assets are not used to promote the common good: indigenously owned assets are often employed at the whims of the rich and powerful or are diverted toward maintaining the economic, social, and political status of the wealthy in ways much less civilized than conspicuous consumption. Foreign-owned and -controlled assets are used according to the dictates of international trade and the free flow of capital, and thus in the interests of rich and powerful countries. Directing these assets in ways calculated to enhance the economic well-being of the local populations would greatly benefit the poor in these countries.

The research of Andre Gunder Frank has shown that during the Second World War, while the rich countries were busy fighting among themselves, many Latin American economies experienced substantial development.[43] He has argued that one of the factors promoting this economic development (increased small business activity and rising living standards) was that these countries were, for the first time in centuries, being ignored by the rich nations to the north and northwest and thus were directing their economic efforts toward their own needs. Sadly, when the war ended, foreign money returned and turned back the clock to the prewar situation. Frank called the process by which poor countries were encouraged to serve the needs of the rich countries the "Development of Under-development," and there is a great deal of validity in his thesis. The first step in the economic development of any country is control of the direction that it takes, which means the use of its productive assets to promote the well-being of its population.

What is true among national economies at the international level is also true among local ones at the intranational level. Owing to banks' practice of red-lining (privately identifying local communities and neighborhoods as "no-lending zones"), for example, the U.S. Congress found it necessary to pass the Community Reinvestment Act, which requires banks to lend in areas where they accept deposits.[44] Essentially, the Act looks to ensure that the wealth of these areas (what little there is) be used to promote their economic well-being.

Historically, both within and between countries, capital has flowed from poorer to richer areas. A recent UN report showed that in 2002 the net transfer of financial resources from the developing and transitional countries to the developed countries was just under $200 billion.[45] Thus, the world's poor continue to subsidize the development of the West, as they have done for some three hundred years.

Use and Catholic Social Thought

It is no exaggeration to suggest that the Christian view of the use of wealth rests on "the primacy of charity in moral theology," to invoke the title of Fr. Gérard Gilleman's classic study.[46] Unfortunately, the word "charity," often limited to its secular usage, is taken to be a synonym for "altruism" or "philanthropy." By contrast, Christian charity "is fundamentally the grace-inspired friendship of the human person for God."[47] In charity the two great Commandments are merged into one, for in charity we return God's love in the only way directly open to us, by loving our fellow creatures. This meaning of charity animates Catholic social teaching on solidarity. Apart from charity the proposition that "we are *all* really responsible *for all*" could not carry conviction, and it is this conviction of human interdependence that is required, according to John Paul II, to evoke solidarity as a personal, Christian virtue.[48]

Much contemporary discussion of social justice, even within the Catholic tradition, seems to divorce justice from charity, as if the charitable course of action must exclude the just, or the just course preclude the charitable. Somehow, it seems,

the secular meaning of charity has prevailed, and charity has declined into justice's weaker alternative. At the same time, the extent of poverty in the rich countries (to say nothing of the poor) far exceeds the "charitable" resources devoted to
alleviating it. The view of many political conservatives seems to be that helping
the least of our brothers is the proper function of private charity alone. At least,
public policy has bent to that opinion in the United States over the past two decades. Still, no one seriously believes that private charitable organizations alone
can adequately address the needs of the poor. To spend two minutes talking to
someone at Catholic Charities is to learn that it and its peer organizations are
stretched to their limits. Even so, one could argue that such charitable activities
would be sufficient to provide for the poor if only the norms of justice were also
generally observed.

Conclusion

In traditional Catholic teaching, justice and charity are paired. Justice is the
natural virtue or power of right conduct toward others; charity is the supernatural
virtue that elevates and completes justice. For charity does not seek merely to deliver what is due another person on this or that consideration; rather, charity dis-
cerns, seeks, and secures another's good without qualification, as if it were one's
own. Charity, then, is not an alternative to justice or still less a weak substitute for
the demands of justice. When Catholic social teaching calls us to the charitable relief of the poor, we are called to meet and exceed the demands of justice alone; or,
if you will, we are called to fulfill justice by allowing it to turn us toward what is yet
more excellent.

Again, when Catholic social teaching prescribes, for example, the "right use of
money," it does not merely invoke the personal responsibility of the rich to use
their wealth for the benefit of the poor and for the promotion of the common
good.[49] That is to say, Catholic social teaching does not address individual persons
as if there were no social responsibility to establish justice and protect the rights of
the poor institutionally. The call to the right personal use of money supposes a socially just context for that use. No more does Catholic social teaching enjoin works of
social charity, except on the supposition that they are to be grounded in works of social justice. The central message of Catholic social thought toward the creation, distribution, and use of wealth is that if the material goods we call wealth are to serve
the higher ends toward which we are called in the Gospels to strive, then they must
be created, distributed, and used in such a manner as to serve God and to serve others, especially the poor.

Notes

1. A Christian analysis of any issue must start and end with Christ, and not merely use Christian concepts or terms in order to produce a "Christianesque" justification for antecedent "left" or "right" agendas.

2. It should be noted that by "wealth" we mean material wealth. For a Christian, Jesus is the "real wealth," that is, the ultimate source of well-being. Here we are concerned with the bread by which man does not alone live, keeping in mind the higher value of "every word that comes from God."

3. In fact, the modern economist would argue that there is no moral aspect to our economic actions as long as we have followed the letter of the law. Here, as in many other ways, economic theory contradicts Christianity.

4. John Paul II, *World Day of Peace Message*, 1999, cited in *The Social Agenda: A Collection of Magisterial Texts*, ed. Robert A. Sirico and Maciej Zieba, O.P. (Vatican City: Libreria Editrice Vaticana, 2000), 24.

5. Jacques Maritain, *The Person and the Common Good* (Notre Dame, Ind.: University of Notre Dame Press, 1966), 33, 38.

6. Ibid., 47.

7. Karol Wojtyla, *Toward a Philosophy of Praxis*, ed. Alfred Bloch and George T. Czuczka (New York: Crossroads Publishing Company, 1981), 40–41.

8. St. Thomas Aquinas, *Summa Contra Gentiles*, trans. Vernon Bourke, vol. 3 (Garden City, N.Y.: Image Books, 1956), chapter 133.

9. See James Gordley, "Virtue and the Ethics of Profit Seeking," in *Rethinking the Purpose of Business: Interdisciplinary Essays from the Catholic Social Tradition*, ed. S. A. Cortright and Michael J. Naughton (Notre Dame, Ind.: University of Notre Dame Press, 2002), 67–75, for an account of the theoretical distortions that result from economists' unwillingness to treat economic agents as practically rational, that is, moral, agents.

10. Bernard Mandeville's infamous poem, *The Fable of the Bees* (1705), argued that economic prosperity is promoted by private vices such as greed, lust, vanity, etc. In the poem, when the bees begin to act virtuously, the hive suffers severe economic and social decline. The poem was very controversial; it was, though its author wasn't, even put on trial.

11. Adam Smith, *The Theory of Moral Sentiments* (1759; reprint, Oxford: Oxford University Press, 1976), 7.

12. "Catholic solidarity," writes Matthew Lamb, "aimed at transposing pre-modern understandings of natural law, of human beings as essentially social, and of society itself as organic and cooperative, into the modern contexts of industrialized societies with complex exchange economies" (Matthew Lamb, *The New Dictionary of Catholic Social Thought*, ed. Judith Dwyer and Elizabeth Montgomery [Collegeville, Minn.: Michael Glazer/The Liturgical Press, 1994], 908).

13. John Paul II, *Sollicitudo rei socialis*, 38 (emphasis in original).

14. Ibid., 39 (emphasis in original).

15. Thus the *Koran*: "Not one of you truly believes until you wish for others what you wish for yourself" (thirteenth of the forty Hadiths of Nawawi); Buddhism: "Treat not others

in ways that you yourself would find hurtful" (The Buddha, *Udana-Varga* 5.1); Judaism: "What is hateful to you, do not do to your neighbor. This is the whole Torah; all the rest is commentary" (*Talmud, Shabbath* 31a); Confucianism: "Do not do to others what you do not want done to yourself" (Confucius, *Analects* 15.23); and Hinduism: "This is the sum of Duty: do not do to others what would cause pain if done to you" (*Mahabharata* 5:1517).

16. *Sollicitudo rei socialis*, 39 (emphasis in original).

17. U.S. Catholic Bishops, *Economic Justice for All: Catholic Social Teaching and the U.S. Economy* (1986), par. 88.

18. See *Solicitudo rei socialis*, 36–37.

19. As St. John Chrysostom noted, "You can continue fasting, sleep on the ground, eat cinders, weep without cease. But if you are not useful to others, you are doing nothing worthwhile" (St. John Chrysostom, *Daily Readings from the Writings of St. John Chrysostom*, ed. Anthony M. Coniaris [Minneapolis: Light & Life Publishing Company, 1988], 123).

20. John Paul II, *Laborem exercens*, 8.

21. Donal Dorr, *The Option for the Poor* (Dublin: Gill & Macmillan, 1992), 3.

22. We will set aside for the moment the issue of whether these assets contribute to social output or well-being, or whether the ownership of such assets is itself a productive activity. Neoclassical economics assumes that only productive assets will yield a return in the marketplace, but this ignores the fact that many assets have their yield determined outside of the market, and that the market is a very poor evaluator of value, at least in the short run. Furthermore, even if assets are productive, this does not mean that their owners are contributing to social output, only that they can induce the community to pay them for the use of assets to which they have title.

23. These issues are discussed in my "Does a Rising Tide Lift All Boats? How Poverty Has Become Immune to Economic Growth," *Vincentian Chair of Social Justice* 5 (1999): 43–53.

24. See ibid.

25. See Amintore Fanfani's *Catholicism, Protestantism, and Capitalism* (Norfolk, Va.: IHS Press, 2003) for the classic analysis of the rise of the "capitalist spirit."

26. Lawrence Summers wrote, "I think the economic logic behind dumping a load of toxic waste in the lowest wage country is impeccable and we should face up to that." Summers is merely applying the logic of neoclassical economic analysis consistently; that alone is enough to expose its moral bankruptcy. For a copy of the memorandum text, see "Let Them Eat Pollution," *The Economist (U.S.)* 322, no. 7745 (February 8, 1992): 66.

27. The best analysis of this to date is Guy Standing's *Global Labour Flexibility: Seeking Distributive Justice* (New York: St. Martin's Press, 1999).

28. In *An Enquiry into the Nature and Causes of the Wealth of Nations* ([1776; reprint, Oxford: Oxford University Press, 1976], 715), Smith writes: "Civil government, so far as it is instituted for the security of property, is in reality instituted for the defense of the rich against the poor, or of those who have some property against those who have none at all." In the *Lectures on Jurisprudence* ([Oxford: Oxford University Press, 1978], 208), Smith is even more forceful: "Laws and government may be considered in this and indeed in every case as a combination of the rich to oppress the poor, and preserve to themselves the inequality of goods which would otherwise be soon destroyed by the attacks of the poor."

29. Smith, *Wealth of Nations*, Book V, Chapter 1.

30. St. Thomas Aquinas, *Summa theologiae*, IIa-IIae, q. 61, a. 2. See also Josef Pieper, *The Four Cardinal Virtues* (Notre Dame, Ind.: University of Notre Dame Press, 1966), for a celebrated explication of Aristotle and Aquinas on justice as right relationships.

31. Neoclassical economic theory denies the possibility, in a free-market, of a violation of commutative justice, since all exchanges are voluntary. Yet the free-market model assumes effect knowledge on the part of contracting parties, and no other market imperfections. These conditions are, in the real world, quite uncommon.

32. On the factors that expose the laboring poor to commutative injustice, see James Gordley, "Labor and Commutative Justice," in *Labor, Solidarity, and the Common Good*, ed. S. A. Cortright (Durham, N.C.: Carolina Academic Press, 2000); on the role of distributive justice in the market activity, see Gordley, "Virtue and the Ethics of Profit Seeking," in *Rethinking the Purpose of Business*, 71–75.

33. See Aristotle, *Nicomachean Ethics*, Book V, Chapters 2–4; Aquinas, *Summa theologiae*, IIa-IIae, q. 61, a. 2, c.

34. This section is based on my "Promoting Economic Equity in a 21st Century Economy: The Basic Income Solution," in *Institutional Analysis of Economic Policy*, ed. Paul Dale Bush and Marc Tool (Norwell, Mass.: Kluwer Academic Publishers, 2003), 133–56.

35. Okun is unequivocal: "the conflict between equality and economic efficiency is inescapable" (Arthur Okun, *Equality and Efficiency: The Big Trade-off* [Washington, D.C.: Brookings Institution, 1975], 120). Why, according to Okun, must the buckets leak? Redistributive programs incur administrative costs; redistribution is a disincentive to work more productively, both for those who supply the transfer and for those who receive it; savings and investment behavior is similarly chilled; and over time, attitudes (for example, motivation to increase human capital through education) are affected in the direction of passivity.

36. *Gaudium et spes*, 66.

37. Pius XI, *Quadragesimo anno*, 57.

38. See Charles Avila, *Ownership: Early Christian Teaching* (Maryknoll, N.Y.: Orbis Books; London: Sheed & Ward, 1983).

39. Much of the emphasis on Malthusian explanations of poverty is based on the desire to avoid the obvious, that poverty is often (but not uniformly) caused by wealth creation. No one, for example, could seriously argue that malnutrition and hunger are caused by an inability of the world's economies to produce enough food, especially when all the advanced economies pay their farmers to restrict output.

40. See Smith, *Wealth of Nations*, Book II, Chapter 3.

41. Supporters of globalization will argue that the income earned by producing trinkets can be used to modernize Third World economies, and this is certainly a possibility. But history teaches us that it is not a likely possibility. In most cases, the surplus generated by this process goes toward the unproductive activities of the elite in the Third World or is transferred to the rich countries as repatriated profits and royalties. The examples of technology spillovers from international trade are surprisingly rare.

42. The trend in America is toward shrinking average family size and growing average housing size.

43. Andre Gunder Frank, *Capitalism and Underdevelopment in Latin America: Historical Studies of Chile and Brazil* (New York: Monthly Review Press, 1969).

44. Interestingly enough, the default rate on these loans is the same as the default rate on loans made to affluent areas.

45. UNCTAD, *Trade and Development Report 2003* (New York: United Nations Publications, 2003).

46. Gérard Gilleman, S.J., *The Primacy of Charity in Moral Theology*, trans. William F. Ryan, S.J., and André Vachon, S.J. (Westminster, Md.: The Newman Press, 1959).

47. Stephen Pope, "Overview of the Ethics of Thomas Aquinas," in *The Ethics of Aquinas*, ed. Stephen Pope (Washington, D.C.: Georgetown University Press, 2002), 38.

48. *Sollicitudo rei socialis*, 38; see ibid., 40 (emphasis in original).

49. See Leo XIII, *Rerum novarum*, 19.

SEVEN

Inequality in Income and Wealth

When Does It Become Immoral, and Why?

Dennis P. McCann

In modernized societies that supposedly value "equality" above all other social ideals, nothing is more likely to arouse latent passions for social justice more effectively than statistics that document unequal income and wealth distribution (henceforth known, in shorthand, as "economic inequality"). That women, on average, make so many cents or dollars per hour less than men, for example, is usually regarded as at least prima facie evidence of social injustice. Similar reactions are evinced by statistics reporting income and wealth differentials among various ethnic minority groups or among workers in various countries or regions of the world. The fact that such statistics almost invariably provoke moral indignation among us, however, suggests that there may be significant tension, if not downright incompatibility, between our ethical ideals and the realities of modern economic life, particularly in market-oriented economies.

Granted, not all market economies necessarily generate income inequalities in precisely the same way, as Carlo Dell'Aringa's and Claudio Lucifora's essay demonstrates (chapter 10, this volume). Comparative studies of the "Gini coefficient" statistics that measure inequality suggest that different societies generate different levels of economic inequality. Furthermore, it has long been noted that levels of inequality typically change as a society's market institutions develop: an initial increase in economic inequality tends to be reversed, usually after the effects of universal education are felt.[1] The discretionary aspect of income inequality was noted by John Stuart Mill, who suggested in his *Principles of Political Economy* that income differentials are due more to power and custom than to market forces.[2] While the eighteenth-century ideology that had legitimized capitalism asserted that markets will produce equality and liberty, the reality of the Industrial Revolution proved otherwise. Increased economic liberty led to increases in inequality, driven by the concentrations of capital required to finance the industrialization process. Only in the twentieth century do we see inequality declining, mostly due to the changes brought about by the welfare state.

Despite some apparent exceptions in the Asia Pacific region, the trends in the Americas as well as in sub-Saharan Africa suggest that, in our own day, increasing economic inequality frequently goes hand in hand with market-oriented economic development. While this phenomenon is to be expected in newly developing countries, it is especially perplexing in the United States, which has clearly passed the level of development that feeds on inequality. Moreover, if rising inequality in the United States is not simply a result of the influence of Reaganomics over U.S. social policy, but is rather a structural consequence of the highly touted "knowledge-based society," then the widening gap in incomes may yet be globalized as the world economy becomes increasingly knowledge based. Of course, the knowledge-based economy is only one factor of income inequality, and not all economists think it is the dominant one. But the trend toward increasing income inequality must be a cause for concern unless powerful ethical, religious, cultural, and political constraints emerge to counter it.

That Catholic social teaching has been a major source of consciousness raising regarding economic injustice worldwide is now generally recognized. Nevertheless, the witness of this tradition has often been misunderstood by its advocates as well as by its critics. Those who seek to promote Catholic social teaching as a resource in business ethics and management education know only too well that the tradition's consistent protest against economic injustice has, for many, become a pretext for dismissing Catholic social teaching as "unrealistic" and "counterproductive," particularly in business school curricula. On the other hand, we all know zealous defenders of Catholic social teaching who seem determined to identify economic justice with uncompromisingly utopian visions of "equality" that, in their impracticability, provide justification for the "realists'" disdain. This essay is meant to break the impasse between "realist" and "utopian" readings of Catholic social teaching by suggesting that both have misunderstood the tradition and, ironically enough, that both have done so by falling into the trap of economistic thinking about equality and its relationship to justice and injustice.[3]

In order to address this economistic misunderstanding, I intend to focus on a question that is implicit in Catholic social teaching but which is not often openly addressed: When does inequality of income and wealth become unacceptable morally; or, when does it become immoral? My hope in posing the question in this way is that dealing with it will contribute not only to our understanding of distributive justice but also to our understanding of the ethics of wealth creation. To ask "when" economic inequality becomes immoral is to recognize that economic inequality is not *in itself* unjust. That recognition is consistent with mainline Catholic social teaching, particularly as seen in the vigorous defense of private property rights that marks the official Church from Leo XIII through to his most formidable successor, John Paul II. Neither the Greco-Roman nor the Hebrew moral and religious traditions, upon which Catholic social teaching is founded, will support the idea that economic inequality as such is unfair or immoral. If so, then we must ask, At what point does economic inequality become immoral? For as surely as Catholic social teaching's defense of private property does not hold economic inequality to be intrinsically unjust, Catholic social teaching's witness against economic injustice judges economic inequality in some degree, at some point, to be immoral.[4]

The task that I have set before myself is to clarify Catholic social teaching's assumed distinction between moral and immoral forms of economic inequality, together with the reasoning behind it. The most promising discussion on this point, in my view, is still the U.S. Catholic Bishops' 1986 pastoral letter, *Economic Justice for All: Catholic Social Teaching and the U.S. Economy*. As I hope to show here, the bishops' remarks on economic inequality are directly linked with their positive understanding of justice as "participation." I will try to make explicit that link and to suggest ways in which it can become a criterion for evaluative discussions of economic inequality.

"Justice as participation" may seem like a hopelessly nebulous concept, a qualitative notion at best, liable to divert our thinking from the rigor demanded by standard economic analysis. I will try to overcome this impression, and to defend the relevance of the U.S. bishops' perspective, by linking the pastoral letter's observations with the seminal thinking of Amartya Sen, a major contemporary economist. Sen's "capabilities approach" to defining economic inequality seems not only compatible with the bishops' perspective but also well suited to developing Catholic social teaching on this point in ways that even "realists" must take seriously. I will conclude by suggesting why and how such an approach can and should make an indispensable contribution to our discussion of the ethics of wealth creation.

U.S. Bishops on Inequality and Participative Justice

Elsewhere I have written extensively on *Economic Justice for All*, particularly on its implications for business ethics and on the way it embodies a new process of forming moral consensus—new, at least in Catholic circles—that facilitates lay participation in the development of Catholic social teaching.[5] Here, however, I wish to focus specifically on the letter's ethical perspective and economic doctrine. In particular, I aim to clarify what precisely the document means by "inequality" and how it evaluates the morality of "inequality."

The term "inequality" appears six times in the body of the text and twice in footnotes. Paragraph 21 cites "extreme inequality" as one of the "symptoms of more fundamental currents shaping U.S. economic life today." Paragraph 74 evaluates "extreme inequality" as not only incompatible with "basic justice" but also contrary to Catholic social teaching inasmuch as it is "a threat to the solidarity of the human community, for great disparities lead to deep social divisions and conflict." In paragraph 116, as part of their exhortation to "Owners and Managers" of businesses, the bishops acknowledge "that the desire to maximize profits and reduce the costs of natural resources and labor has often tempted . . . transnational enterprises to behavior that increases inequality and decreases the stability of the international order." Further on, in a section addressing the concerns of developing nations, paragraph 252 highlights "the scandal of the shocking inequality between the rich and the poor" and calls for its elimination so that "the 'quality' of interdependence [can] be improved." Paragraph 362 proposes a number of areas for future research, including "the effects of increased inequality of incomes in society," so that the problems of poverty both in the United States and in developing nations can be addressed more effectively. Footnotes 27 and 45 also specifically refer to economic literature on inequality and suggest that the bishops are aware of and interested in debates on how economists measure poverty and economic inequality.

These initial observations suggest the complexity of *Economic Justice for All*'s perspective. Economic inequality, in the bishops' descriptions, covers far more than what is available in statistics on the distribution of wealth and income, however central these may remain as measurable indices. Furthermore, in their view, Catholic social teaching's ethical framework "does not maintain that a flat, arithmetical equality of income and wealth is a demand of justice, but it does challenge economic arrangements that leave large numbers of people impoverished."[6] When an evaluation of "inequality" is offered in Catholic social teaching, the term is usually teamed with a morally loaded modifier such as "extreme" or "shocking."

The bishops provide some clues as to when, in their view, such modifiers are appropriate in their more focused remarks on "Economic Inequality."[7] They begin by citing the usual statistics on inequalities of wealth (where the "gap" between the top and bottom quintile is most severe) and income, and they note that the trend is toward increasing inequality. Nothing is unusual here. But when they begin to clarify the basis of their moral concern, a new term is introduced: "These inequities are of particular concern because they reflect the uneven distribution of power in our society. They suggest that the level of *participation* in the political and social spheres is also very uneven."[8] Economic inequalities become morally problematic not only because they may reflect "the uneven distribution of power" in society but also because, as such, they adversely affect our capacity to participate in the political and social spheres. In the bishops' view, as we shall see, participation is both a normative and a descriptive concept. Since "some degree of inequality not only is acceptable, but also may be considered desirable for economic and social reasons," the moral distinction between "acceptable" and "unacceptable" levels rests on "participation" as one of two "norms" or ethical criteria: "the priority of meeting *the basic needs of the poor* and the importance of increasing the level of *participation* by all members of society in the economic life of the nation."[9] The bishops point out that these two norms, taken together, "establish a strong presumption against extreme inequality of income and wealth as long as there are poor, hungry, and homeless people in our midst. They also suggest that extreme inequalities are detrimental to the development of social solidarity and community." Judged in light of these norms, the description of the U.S. economy that the bishops have accepted warrants their conclusion that, in fact, "the disparities of income and wealth in the United States [are] unacceptable."[10]

This conclusion is not guaranteed by the charism of episcopal ordination. Nor is it the only conclusion, as *Economic Justice for All* carefully points out, that could be argued on the basis of Catholic social thought. Were one to give reasoned assent or dissent to this conclusion, one would have to investigate further either the bishops' factual description of the U.S. economy, or their twofold ethical criteria, or both. For our purposes, nearly twenty years after *Economic Justice for All*, the bishops' ethical criteria, particularly their perspective on justice as "participation," remain worthy of note. For it is here that we can begin to appreciate the fruitfulness of their teaching in order to understand the ethics of economic inequality even today.

"Participation," it turns out, is just as rich a term in the bishops' usage as is "inequality." Taking their cue from the 1971 declaration of the universal Synod of Bishops in Rome,[11] the U.S. bishops assert that participation is a basic human right:

> All people have a *right to participate* in the economic life of society. Basic justice demands that people be assured a *minimum level of participation* in the economy. It is wrong for a person or a group to be excluded unfairly or to be *unable to participate* or contribute to the economy. For example, people who are both able and willing, but cannot get a job are *deprived of the participation* that is so vital to human development. . . . *Such participation* has a special significance in our tradition because we believe that it is a means by which we join in carrying forward God's creative activity.[12]

Thus, the right to participate is both grounded in the Christian theological vision and entailed by the requirements of "basic justice." It is both comprehensive, opposed to "exclusion" in general—to what the bishops will later define as societal "marginalization"—and specific, referring to the need for decent jobs.[13] Much of what the U.S. bishops have to say about the relationship of justice and participation is simply an expansion of these remarks.

Because participation is linked most closely to basic justice and human rights, it is important to note that *Economic Justice for All*'s perspective on both of the latter is grounded in a comprehensive understanding of "biblical justice," which the bishops discuss in the context of "Love and Solidarity."[14] Social participation must be understood, ultimately, by analogy to God's own Trinitarian identity. Theologically speaking, the concept "participation" is used to try to explain the unity between the persons of the Trinity—Father, Son, and Holy Spirit—under one Godhead. We can go on to say, by analogy, that as each of the three Persons participates equally in the Being of God, so each human being is called to participate in the Divine Life through the gift of God's love.[15] Such participation does not confer on us equality with God, but it defines the ultimate equality or equal dignity of all human persons among themselves as "children of God." As children adopted into the household or "Kingdom" of God, all persons are now empowered to share equally in God's offer of fellowship or "solidarity."[16]

The social nature of the human person, on which the virtue of "solidarity" is based, is thus theologically grounded and is not simply a brute fact about our human nature, that is, a "fact" that can be clearly separated from "values" and so considered apart from them. For the bishops, solidarity is "another name for this social friendship and civic commitment that make[s] human moral and economic life possible."[17] This correlation is neither arbitrary nor opportunistic. It is not an easy accommodation to modern Leftist ideology but is based on the central axis of Catholic social teaching and the Church's theological appropriation of the ancient wisdom of Hellenic philosophy: "What the Bible and Christian tradition teach, human wisdom confirms. Centuries before Christ, the Greeks and Romans spoke of the human person as a 'social animal' made for friendship, community, and public life. These insights show that human beings achieve self-realization not in isolation, but in interaction with others."[18]

Just as the notion that the human person as a social animal is both descriptive and normative in the tradition of Hellenic moral philosophy, so "participation" is both descriptive and normative.[19] For the U.S. bishops, if it is a fact that the human person is a social animal, then empowering others for social participation is a matter of basic justice. If it is also a fact, as Catholic social teaching always assumes and sometimes clearly asserts, that the social nature of the human person is ultimately realized only in fellowship with the Triune God, then empowering others for social participation is clearly a religious imperative as well.

According to the logic of *Economic Justice for All*, basic justice must be understood within the context of these facts. Basic justice stipulates "the 'minimum' levels of mutual care and respect that all persons owe to each other in an imperfect world." In order to clarify what is entailed in these minimum levels, *Economic Justice for All* follows Catholic moral theology in the Thomistic tradition advanced by Leo XIII and Pius XI, distinguishing "three dimensions of basic justice: commutative justice, distributive justice, and social justice." Participation is the object of "social justice," which is more comprehensive than the other two dimensions. Commutative justice governs fairness in private transactions (justice in exchange relations) while distributive justice governs fairness in public allocations (justice in public welfare arrangements): "Social justice implies that persons have an obligation to be active and productive participants in the life of society and that society has a duty to enable them to participate in this way."[20]

Participation is thus a moral obligation as well as an individual right. Because it is both, we all have a moral duty to empower others for more effective social participation. Social justice thus refers comprehensively to the set of conditions, both personal and social, that make it possible for persons to fulfill their social obligations and exercise their individual rights:

> [Social justice] stresses the duty of all who are able to help create the goods, services, and other nonmaterial or spiritual values necessary for the welfare of the whole community. In the words of Pius XI, "It is of the very essence of social justice to demand from each individual all that is necessary for the common good." . . . The meaning of social justice also includes a duty to organize economic and social institutions so that people can contribute to society in ways that respect their freedom and the dignity of their labor. Work should enable the working person to become "more a human being," more capable of acting intelligently, freely, and in ways that lead to self-realization.[21]

Participation, indeed, is the norm governing Catholic social teaching's distinctive interpretation of human rights, which are defined within the bishops' complex perspective on basic justice and not vice versa. Prior to the discussion of human rights, *Economic Justice for All* defines the "common good," following Vatican II, as "the sum of those conditions of social life which allow social groups and their individual members relatively thorough and ready access to their own fulfillment."[22] Human rights, therefore, are among the conditions comprehended in the common good and are instrumental in preserving and enhancing it. They are means to an end.

And lest anyone be confused about that end, the bishops explicitly link human rights to participation: "These conditions include the right to fulfillment of material needs, a guarantee of fundamental freedoms, and the protection of relationships that are *essential to participation* in the life of society."[23]

Much more could be said about the implications, both theoretical and practical, of the U.S. bishops' perspective on human rights. The point, here, however, is relatively narrow: to recognize how *Economic Justice for All* reorients virtually all aspects of social justice, including discourse on the common good and human rights, to their theologically grounded ideal of participation.

Just how serious the bishops are about participation can be inferred from their description and moral evaluation of its opposite, marginalization:

> These fundamental duties can be summarized this way: basic justice demands the establishment of minimum levels of participation in the life of the human community for all persons. The ultimate injustice is for a person or group to be treated actively or abandoned passively as if they were nonmembers of the human race. To treat people this way is effectively to say they simply do not count as human beings. This can take many forms, all of which can be described as varieties of marginalization, or exclusion from social life. This exclusion can occur in the political sphere: restriction of free speech, concentration of power in the hands of a few, or outright repression by the state. It can also take economic forms that are equally harmful. Within the United States, individuals, families, and local communities fall victim to a downward cycle of poverty generated by economic forces they are powerless to influence. The poor, the disabled, and the unemployed too often are simply left behind. This pattern is even more severe beyond our borders in the least-developed countries. Whole nations are prevented from fully participating in the international economic order because they lack the power to change their disadvantaged position. Many people within the less developed countries are excluded from sharing in the meager resources available in their homelands by unjust elites and unjust governments. These patterns of exclusion are created by free human beings. In this sense they can be called forms of social sin. Acquiescence in them or the failure to correct them when it is possible to do so is a sinful dereliction of Christian duty.[24]

Marginalization, as "exclusion from social life," can take many forms, economic as well as political. Its forms are also relative to specific social and cultural contexts, and thus may be analyzed and must be addressed in local, regional, national, and international settings. What the bishops say implies that, while overcoming marginalization and empowering people for participation is always and everywhere a priority under basic justice, there may be tensions, conflicts, and even fierce trade-offs involved in empowering people in one area for participation at the inadvertent expense of people elsewhere.

Enough has been said, however, to illuminate the theoretical link between the U.S. bishops' normative view of basic justice as empowering people for social participation and their view of the ethics of economic inequality. While there is no simple algorithm that will allow one to determine precisely when economic inequality becomes unjust, the principle consistently represented by the bishops seems now clear: economic inequality becomes unjust if, and only if, it has the effect of marginalizing persons and communities, that is, of excluding them from or denying them access to appropriate levels of social participation. If it can reasonably be shown that certain persons and communities experience marginalization specifically because of existing patterns of economic inequality, then those patterns must be condemned as unjust. If marginalization exists, but it can reasonably be shown not to be caused by existing patterns of economic inequality, then there is no reason to condemn those patterns as unjust.[25]

The U.S. bishops' ethical perspective in *Economic Justice for All* is hardly exhausted by appeals to justice and participation. Love and solidarity, as we have already seen, are of paramount concern theologically. Existing patterns of economic inequality, if not immoral when viewed in terms of basic justice, may yet be questionable as violations of love and solidarity. But once the moral argument shifts from considerations of justice to love, its consequences tend to become less and less imperative, at least as matters for public policy or Christian social action. Because any significant social intervention to change existing patterns of economic inequality is likely to involve the exercise of coercive authority in the form of government regulation, and because acts of love or solidarity are understood to be possible only apart from coercion, appeals to love and solidarity are not likely to be seen as sufficient to justify government intervention or even such "coercive" private intervention as boycotts or public protests. Since appeals to love and solidarity normally invoke a free response, strategies for challenging patterns of economic inequality that are just but unloving may be limited to voluntary and private initiatives.

Love may suggest to an employer certain initiatives—for example, that she voluntarily reduce the disparities among her employees' wages in order to promote a greater sense of solidarity among them—that may actually yield certain gains in productivity. But if such enlightened policies are suggested by love but not mandated by basic justice, they must be freely embraced and not coercively imposed, even though they also tend to enhance social participation. Because empowering others for social participation is an open-ended process, it will necessarily reflect a continuum of ethical concerns including both love and justice. The following diagram may help to clarify this continuum:

CST Correlations	Love and Solidarity	Justice and Participation
Theoretical categories	Common good (ultimate/maximal) Social friendship Citizenship virtues	Common good (minimal) Basic justice Human rights
Practical implementation focused on	Voluntary PVO/NGOs Civil society	Coercive government regulation political processes

Note: CST = Catholic social teaching; PVOs = private voluntary organizations; NGOs = nongovernmental organizations.

Because our concern here is to determine when existing patterns of economic inequality become immoral, the ethical argument has concentrated primarily on the right-hand column. When one moves from the theoretical aspects of moral argument—our focus in this essay—to a consideration of practical strategies for overcoming unjust forms of economic inequality, the focus tends to widen to include both columns and thus a broad range of collaborative strategies involving both government regulation and private sector initiatives in civil society. Indeed, part of the enduring contribution of *Economic Justice for All* is to call attention to the possibilities for voluntary, collaborative approaches to economic empowerment, understood as overcoming marginalization and enhancing social participation.[26]

IMPLICATIONS OF PARTICIPATIVE JUSTICE

If this interpretation of Catholic social teaching's ethical perspective on economic inequality is accepted, certain theoretical and practical conclusions can be drawn. Clarifying the distinction between what is an unjust pattern of economic inequality and one that meets the minimal test of "basic justice" is required by *Economic Justice for All*'s own insistence that not all forms of economic inequality are unjust. That the bishops find the current pattern of economic inequality in the United States morally "unacceptable" is not because they are opposed in principle to all forms of economic inequality, but because in this instance the social analysis that they find credible warrants the conclusion that some groups and individuals are, in fact, excluded from social participation as a consequence of these existing patterns. This is the logic of their moral judgment, and, as reconstructed, it involves both a principle and a factual premise, both of which can reasonably be challenged for any number of reasons.

Why is it useful to make this theoretical point? Is this anything more than technical hairsplitting? The practical problem with which we started is that our untutored passion for social justice may seem increasingly silly, if not self-serving, in a world where the benefits of economic development are likely to be realized only at the cost of disturbing increases in economic inequality. If justice demands that we oppose all increases in economic inequality, then logically we should oppose economic development as such.

We must keep in mind a principle that is fundamental to any social ethic: "To will the end is to will the means to it also." If economic development inevitably exacerbates the injustice of economic inequality, then we cannot resist economic inequality without also resisting economic development.[27] That *Economic Justice for All* in particular, and Catholic social teaching generally, refuse to endorse principled resistance to economic development as such, is not the result of some failure of nerve. The bishops cannot endorse such indiscriminate resistance because their principles, as we have seen, simply do not warrant it. If some patterns of economic inequality are not unjust but may actually be required in order to enhance the common good, then not only does Catholic social teaching not mandate principled resistance to market-oriented economic development, but it also can, and perhaps ought to, point out the moral irresponsibility of such principled resistance!

The struggle over this issue among scholars committed to Catholic social thought as well as over the controversies generated by *Economic Justice for All* in both Catholic and non-Catholic circles suggests that this point of clarification is worth making. On the principles laid down by the bishops, as I have argued, economic inequality becomes unjust if, and only if, it has the effect of marginalizing persons and communities, that is, of excluding them from or denying them access to appropriate levels of social participation. I am focusing, obviously, on economic inequality as an outcome of normal economic activity. Of course, in cases where inequality is caused by outright injustice, there is no justification for it whatsoever, regardless of its alleged positive benefit to the rest of society (see Charles Clark, chapter 1, this volume, on the ethics of artificially creating scarcities). My point is simply that, assuming normal economic activity, Catholics may in good conscience examine the ethics of wealth creation with an open mind and with more to contribute than a warning that, however wealth is produced, it must be distributed so as not to exacerbate existing patterns of economic inequality.[28] But this is largely an internal concern among serious students of Catholic social thought. What is the public relevance of this clarification?

At the time that *Economic Justice for All* was drafted, public moral argument in the United States about economic justice was still dominated by the debates between and about the opposed philosophical perspectives of Robert Nozick and John Rawls. Nozick's *Anarchy, State, and Utopia* (1977) vigorously defended property rights within a libertarian perspective that supports the conclusion: economic inequalities are unjust if, and only if, income and wealth are a result of illegal activities. Distributive justice in this perspective is reduced to procedural considerations. As long as the laws governing the marketplace are observed, there is no basis for claiming that the outcomes of economic activity are unjust. Rawls's *Theory of Justice* (1971), by contrast, argued for a concept of justice as "fairness" that did encourage ethicists to evaluate the justice of economic outcomes. Within a larger commitment to maximizing individual rights and liberties for all, Rawls argued for a "Difference Principle" that stipulates the following: "Social and economic inequalities are to meet two conditions: they must be (a) to the greatest expected benefit of the least advantaged; and (b) attached to offices and positions open to all under conditions of fair equality of opportunity."[29] Economic inequalities are not unjust, so long as they meet these two conditions.

At first glance, comparing *Economic Justice for All*'s perspective with either Rawls's or Nozick's may seem like comparing apples and oranges. The bishops' correlation of justice and participation is theologically grounded, and, as we have seen, its theological presuppositions do make a substantive difference. Their perspective, however, may seem lacking in precision compared to either philosopher's. It may seem easier to make an ethical evaluation of any concrete pattern of economic inequality from either philosophical perspective than from the pastoral letter's rich and complex understanding of what does and does not enhance social participation. Either Nozick or Rawls could be cited to argue the irrelevance of the bishops' perspective, since each seems more clearly to warrant specific approaches to public policy than does the correlation of justice with participation. On the other hand, the lack of a clear-cut ideological orientation may be one of the latent strengths of *Economic Justice for All*, since the very richness of the concept of participation may enable us to respond to or help develop new approaches to economic justice.

This hope seems especially reasonable when one moves beyond the ideologically polarizing debates between Nozick and Rawls to a comparison between Amartya Sen's new approach to economic development and the perspective of *Economic Justice for All*. For years, Sen has been a leader among economists seeking to make a critical correlation between ethics and economics.[30] While Sen acknowledges some sympathy with Rawls's attempt to go beyond utilitarianism as it is practiced in conventional welfare economics, he also challenges the adequacy of Rawls's expectation that "primary goods" should be the main object of moral concern in evaluating the ethics of economic inequality.[31] The gist of Sen's approach is to shift ethical as well as economic analysis from the distribution of "commodities" to the exercise of human "capabilities." Rawls, in Sen's view, still treats "primary goods" as commodities, and thus as subject to public policy planning motivated to enhance an equitable distribution of commodities. Thus, Rawls's "Difference Principle" focuses on "the least advantaged" and, in Sen's view, identifies "least advantage . . . with having the lowest index value of 'primary goods.'" By contrast, Sen proposes that the focus of moral concern should be on "quality of life, rather than on income or wealth, or on psychological satisfaction." For, as Sen argues, "If the object is to concentrate on the individual's real opportunity to pursue her objectives, then account would have to be taken not only of the primary goods the person holds, but also of the relevant personal characteristics that govern the conversion of primary goods into the person's ability to promote her ends."[32] "Commodities," in short, are merely means for enabling the exercise of human "capabilities."

Sen and other scholars—notably Martha Nussbaum—who have contributed to the development of his approach clearly understand "capabilities" within the framework of Aristotelian thinking about the human person as a social animal. Though Sen's perspective is more emphatic in promoting personal choice than is Catholic social teaching's emphasis on the common good, both of these emphases can be seen as part of a spectrum focused normatively on freedom or, in the U.S. bishops' term, "self-realization."[33] What is distinctively Aristotelian about both perspectives, and the most promising point of convergence between them, is to be found in what the bishops call "participation" and what Sen calls "functionings." Since we have already reviewed what the bishops in *Economic Justice for All* have to say about participation, here is Sen's description of "functionings":

> The concept of "functionings," which has distinctly Aristotelian roots, reflects the various things a person may value doing or being. The valued functionings may vary from elementary ones, such as being adequately nourished and being free from avoidable disease, to very complex activities or personal states, such as being able to take part in the life of the community and having self-respect.
>
> A person's "capability" refers to the alternative combinations of functionings that are feasible for her to achieve. Capability is thus a kind of freedom: the substantive freedom to achieve alternative functioning combinations (or, less formally put, the freedom to achieve various lifestyles).[34]

Sen's description of functionings is more formal and open-ended than *Economic Justice for All*'s description of social participation, for it is meant to make explicit the "space" in which substantive public debate can proceed, over which "particular functionings . . . should be included in the list of important achievements and the corresponding capabilities." *Economic Justice for All*'s theologically grounded perspective on social participation thus would be one proposal for consideration in a larger "evaluative exercise of this kind."[35]

Why a critical correlation between *Economic Justice for All*'s understanding of social participation and Sen's "capabilities approach" is useful for the development of Catholic social thought can be seen from two considerations: (1) the capabilities approach creates the evaluative "space" in which *Economic Justice for All*'s perspective is not only intelligible to economists but also plausible, and possibly persuasive; and (2) the capabilities approach, as Sen develops it, is not simply philosophical but is quantifiable and measurable, at least to some extent.

Summarizing the results of several other studies done by him and his colleagues, Sen observes: "The amount or the extent of each functioning enjoyed by a person may be represented by a real number, and when this is done, a person's actual achievement can be seen as a functioning vector. The 'capability set' would consist of the alternative functioning vectors that she can choose from. While the combination of a person's functionings reflects her actual achievements, the capability set represents the freedom to achieve: the alternative functioning combinations from which this person can choose."[36] As with so many things, here the proof of the pudding is in the eating. In *Development as Freedom*, Sen pulls together arguments made in a number of publications and shows the promising ways in which the "capabilities approach" may be a more effective analytic tool than conventional alternatives in welfare economics.

Because our concern is to understand the ethics of economic inequality, let me review briefly Sen's economic analysis of poverty as "capability deprivation."[37] His description of "capability deprivation" so closely coincides with *Economic Justice for All*'s ethical analysis of "marginalization" that it reinforces my sense of the convergence between the two perspectives. Capability deprivation is not reducible to income deprivation, though they are likely to be interrelated: "Inadequate income is a strong predisposing condition for an impoverished life."[38] Nevertheless, it is important to distinguish them because: (1) the capabilities approach focuses on "deprivations that are intrinsically important (unlike low income, which is only instrumentally significant)"; (2) low income is not the only factor determining capabilities; and (3) "the impact of income on capabilities is contingent and conditional."[39] As Sen goes on to demonstrate in detail, this third point is very important in tracing the patterns by which certain sociological variables (for example, age, gender, education, occupational status, local culture and history) affect the real poverty that people actually experience.

Sen's analysis tends not only to underscore *Economic Justice for All*'s correlation of justice with social participation and injustice with marginalization, but it also allows us to map the economic dynamics of social exclusion:

> For example, the difficulties that some groups of people experience in "taking part in the life of the community" can be crucial for any study of "social exclusion." The need to take part in the life of a community may induce demands for modern equipment (televisions, videocassette recorders, automobiles, and so on) in a country where such facilities are more or less universal (unlike what would be needed in less affluent countries), and this imposes a strain on a relatively poor person in a rich country even when that person is at a much higher level income compared with people in less opulent countries. Indeed, the paradoxical phenomenon of hunger in rich countries—even in the United States—has something to do with the competing demands of these expenses.
>
> What the capability perspective does in poverty analysis is to enhance the understanding of the nature and causes of poverty and deprivation by shifting primary attention away from the means (and one particular means that is usually given exclusive attention, viz., income) to ends that people have reason to pursue, and correspondingly, to the freedoms to be able to satisfy these ends. [40]

Sen's analysis of "capabilities deprivation," in short, implicitly provides a justification for *Economic Justice for All*'s analysis of poverty as the complex phenomenon of societal marginalization, and it broadens the range of empowerment strategies and tactics meant to help overcome poverty. Poverty understood as "capabilities deprivation" may actually be made worse by strategies narrowly focused on increasing incomes or narrowing the "gap" in income-distribution statistics.

One telling example analyzed by Sen that tends to confirm the understanding of poverty in *Economic Justice for All* is the question of the specific deprivation experienced in unemployment and what to do about it. Like the U.S. bishops, Sen prefers enhancing employment opportunities to increasing welfare benefits for the unemployed. When viewed in the perspective of "capabilities deprivation," the marginalization experienced by the unemployed may be a worse catastrophe than their loss of income. Such marginalization may be ignored, if not exacerbated, by simply increasing welfare benefits.[41] Viewed in this light, the U.S. economy's extraordinary recent success in job creation (even if at lower wage levels) may do more to support poor persons' quality of life than the high levels of welfare benefits offered by Western European countries whose policies also favor dramatically high levels of unemployment.[42]

One would have to assess whether the unemployed in European welfare states have lower levels of participation overall than do the working poor in the United States. We know that the percentage of unemployed in Europe who fall below the poverty line is much lower than the percentage of working individuals who fall below a similar poverty threshold in the United States. But income is only one aspect of participation. The assessment would have to account for other aspects of social participation and personal functionings (for example, education, political participation). Moreover, one would have to assess the long-term implications of the European and U.S. alternatives.

The capabilities approach warrants Sen's challenge to the centrality of economic inequality in ethical evaluations of economic justice. The question for Sen (somewhat similar to the question animating this essay) is, "Inequality of what?" Within the capabilities approach, economic inequality is not synonymous with "income inequality," nor with "inequalities in income and wealth" when wealth is understood primarily in terms of marketable assets. (See "The Nature of Wealth" that introduces this volume for a broader description of wealth.) Within the capabilities approach, "economic inequality" must be understood comprehensively. While Sen is reluctant to provide an essential definition, he consistently offers descriptions that suggest multiple and measurable capability deprivations that are neither natural nor inevitable but contingent upon societal arrangements that are subject to evaluation and change.[43] This, in my opinion, is also what *Economic Justice for All* means by marginalization. Sen's economic analyses thus are likely to support *Economic Justice for All*'s perspective precisely because they demonstrate the pragmatic value of these shared ethical criteria.

Conclusion

According to our presentation in this essay, *Economic Justice for All* views economic inequality, considered as an outcome of normal economic activity, as immoral if, and only if, it has the effect of marginalizing persons and communities, that is, of excluding them from, or denying them access to appropriate levels of, social participation. Sen's "capabilities approach," in my view, shares the ethical assumptions—though not the theological presuppositions—that govern *Economic Justice for All*'s correlation of justice and participation and, conversely, injustice and marginalization, and it helps to provide additional philosophical warrants for these assumptions. However encouraging this convergence may be for those committed to Catholic social thought, even more important is the fact that Sen's economic analysis based on these shared assumptions provides us with an opportunity for developing Catholic social thought in a way that could make it a more effective conversation partner in debates over the relationship between ethics and economics. Catholic social thought, in my view, has always been abundant in moral insight but perhaps deficient in economic logic. Connecting it with Sen's capabilities approach may be a way of making up for that deficiency.

As the title of Sen's book, *Development as Freedom,* suggests, his own agenda is constructive and transformative, and not narrowly focused on the injustice of existing patterns of economic inequality.[44] As this volume focuses on wealth creation and distribution in a social and ethical perspective, so, too, does Sen focus on economic development in the fullest sense of the term. This brief excursus into the ethics of economic inequality may contribute to our larger agenda by suggesting that wealth creation and economic development must be aimed at promoting social participation and/or enhancing human capabilities and functionings. When understood only in the narrowly economistic terms of marketable assets, which may well be created at the expense of social participation, "wealth" becomes merely another form of impoverishment.

Notes

1. This phenomenon is known as the "Kuznet curve," named after the economist Simon Kuznet, who noticed this statistical tendency.

2. John Stuart Mill, *Principles of Political Economy* (1848; reprint, Fairfield, N.J.: Augustus Kelley, 1987), Book II.

3. I intend to use the term "economism," and the adjective "economistic," in the same sense in which it is used in *Laborem exercens* and other encyclicals of Pope John Paul II. *Laborem exercens* defines economism as "a conviction of the primacy and superiority of the material, [that] directly or indirectly places the spiritual and the personal (man's activity, moral values and such matters) in a position of subordination to material reality." The pope argues that economism is normally a form of *"practical materialism,* a materialism judged capable of satisfying man's needs not so much on the grounds of premises derived from materialist theory as on the grounds of a particular way of evaluating things and so on the grounds of a certain hierarchy of goods based on the greater immediate attractiveness of what is material" (par. 13). Though the pope's analysis of "economism" is aimed primarily at providing the basis for a critique of conventional understandings of the relationship between labor and capital, it can easily be extended to the question of economic inequality as it is conventionally defined (in terms of the relative abundance or scarcity of existing material goods).

4. The U.S. Catholic Bishops' pastoral letter, *Economic Justice for All: Catholic Social Teaching and the U.S. Economy,* for example, condemns as immoral the existing levels of economic inequality in the United States: "In view of these norms we find the disparities of income and wealth in the United States to be unacceptable." At the same time, the bishops insist that "Catholic social teaching does not require absolute equality in the distribution of income and wealth. Some degree of inequality not only is acceptable, but also may be considered desirable for economic and social reasons, such as the need for incentives and provision of greater rewards for greater risks" (par. 185). The burden of this essay is to offer a theoretical perspective from which the internal consistency of these two statements can be fully appreciated. See National Conference of Catholic Bishops, *Economic Justice for All,* 1986.

5. Dennis P. McCann, *New Experiment in Democracy: The Challenge for American Catholicism* (Kansas City, Mo.: Sheed & Ward, 1987).

6. *Economic Justice for All,* 74.

7. Ibid., 183–85.

8. Ibid., 184 (italics added).

9. Ibid., 185 (italics added).

10. Ibid.

11. In the words of the 1971 Synod of Bishops, "Participation constitutes a right which is to be applied in the economic and in the social and political field" (*Justice in the World,* 18).

12. *Economic Justice for All,* 15 (italics added).

13. Ibid., 77.

14. Ibid., 63–77.

15. Ibid., 64.

16. Ibid., 67.

17. Ibid., 66.

18. Ibid., 65.

19. The form of moral reasoning presupposed in the bishops' consistent appeal to basic "facts" about humans that are both descriptive and normative is rejected by some modern philosophers as an egregious instance of the so-called naturalistic fallacy. Showing how such an accusation involves a serious misunderstanding of Catholic social teaching would involve elaborate arguments over the concept of "nature" presupposed by Catholic social teaching and by its antinaturalistic critics. Because it, too, is ultimately grounded theologically (and biblically), the concept of nature in Catholic social teaching (and in any of its "natural law" arguments) is always already moral and never the abstract of "pure" nature (devoid of intrinsic religious and moral significance) assumed by modern rationalists. Of course, one could ignore the arguments and simply observe that when it comes to committing the "naturalistic fallacy," Catholic social teaching tends to be somewhat Lutheran in its willingness to *Pecca Fortiter!* (Sin Boldly!)

20. *Economic Justice for All,* 71.

21. Ibid., 71–72.

22. Ibid., 79.

23. Ibid. (italics added).

24. Ibid., 77.

25. Jeff Gates, for example, argues that today's economic inequality has been accelerated by an exclusion of capital ownership. "As currently engineered, capitalism is a certifiably poor creator of capitalists. Yet 1998 saw the United States finance $2,531.6 billion—$931.6 billion in new capital expenditures (for plant, equipment and nonresidential structures), plus another $1,600 billion in mergers and acquisitions. We know how to finance; we just don't choose to do that financing in an inclusive manner, even though there are numerous mechanisms adaptable to that purpose." He argues for a variety of inclusive financing mechanisms such as the employee stock ownership plan (ESOP), which can broaden capital ownership, thereby reducing current inequalities. See Jeff Gates, "Reengineering Ownership for the Common Good," in *Rethinking the Purpose of Business: Interdisciplinary Essays from the Catholic Social Tradition,* ed. S. A Cortright and Michael J. Naughton (Notre Dame, Ind.: University of Notre Dame Press, 2002), 264–88.

26. See *Economic Justice for All,* Chapter IV: A New American Experiment: Partnership for the Public Good, 295–325.

27. That this is the conclusion drawn by many Christian social activists can be seen, for example, in the World Council of Churches' 1998 statement (Harare) opposing "globalization" as such. It is also the practical inference of *For the Common Good: Redirecting the Economy toward Community, the Environment, and a Sustainable Future,* by Herman E. Daly and John B. Cobb, Jr. (Boston: Beacon Press, 1994). See Cobb's rejoinder to my own critical endorsement of trade policies designed to facilitate globalization and economic development: Dennis P. McCann, "Serenity, Courage, and Wisdom in the Global Marketplace: How Not to Say No to NAFTA," *The Christian Century* 110 (November 10, 1993): 1129 ff.

28. In any case, Christian strictures against accumulating a large hoard of wealth are far greater than anything the Christian tradition has to say on income or wealth inequality, and they are completely independent from any linkage to the effects that such accumulations of wealth have on the poor. Distribution is a minor concern for the Christian, at least compared to the love of money over the love of God.

29. John Rawls, *A Theory of Justice* (Cambridge: Harvard Belknap Press, 1971), 83.

30. Sen's theories are well summarized in his recent book, *Development as Freedom* (New York: Alfred A. Knopf, 2000). For purposes of this study, his most important earlier works are *On Economic Inequality* [Expanded Edition with a Substantial Annexe by James E. Foster and Amartya Sen] (Oxford: Clarendon Press, 1997); and *On Ethics and Economics* (Malden, Mass.: Blackwell, 1988).

31. Primary goods, in Sen's characterization of Rawls, "are general purpose means that help anyone to promote their ends, and include 'rights, liberties and opportunities, income and wealth, and the social bases of self-respect'" (Rawls, *A Theory of Justice,* 60–65; and Sen, *On Economic Inequality,* 197–98).

32. Sen, *On Economic Inequality,* 198.

33. *Economic Justice for All,* 65.

34. Sen, *Development as Freedom,* 75.

35. Ibid.

36. Ibid.

37. Ibid., 87–110.

38. Ibid., 87.

39. Ibid., 87–88.

40. Ibid., 89–90.

41. Ibid., 94–95.

42. Ibid.

43. Ibid., 92–94, 107–10.

44. A more extended dialogue between Sen's perspective and Catholic social thought would have to be based upon a critical comparison of the philosophical anthropologies implicit in Sen and explicit in Catholic social thought, and how these shape their basic orientations toward moral reasoning and responsibility, human freedom, and the meaning of human life. However urgent such a conversation may be, it is clearly beyond the scope of this essay.

EIGHT # Wealth Distribution in Economic Discourse

Catholic Social Thought and the Individualistic Paradigm

STEFANO ZAMAGNI

The relationship between economics, viewed as a scientific discipline, and a religion-inspired ethics (such as Christian ethics in general and Catholic social thought in particular) is a major issue that today calls into question the problem of the anthropological foundations of economic discourse. It is well known that economic science, with few exceptions, still focuses on the paradigm of axiologic individualism according to which economic action originates from a subject whose features and purposes are those of *homo oeconomicus.* This makes it conceptually impossible for the economic-scientific discourse to meet with that of the truth-searching dimension of faith. Evidence thereof is the absence of any trace of such contact in the wide-ranging economic literature. The economist, even if a believer, does not feel the urge *qua* economist to enter the field and deal with the question of the relationship between science and faith. Although there is a large body of literature on the relationship between economics and Christianity, going back over one hundred years, very little of it has addressed this relationship from the perspective of philosophical anthropology. This is probably because most of the literature is loosely within the Calvinist tradition, which has a view of the person that is closer to the standard economic one than to that of most of Christianity.[1]

Indeed, once one accepts the concept that values and value judgments stand only at both ends of the scientific process and are not to be found in the course of it, one eventually is brought to accept the "thesis of the great division," between knowing and evaluating and between fact (objective) and values (subjective). This is a widely disseminated thesis in contemporary culture whose origin is usually traced back to David Hume, a thesis denying the truth foundation of value judgments by expressing decisions and imperatives as subjective preferences. This thesis, however, cannot be applied to a field of study like that of economics, because economic theories of human behavior, sooner or later and to a greater or lesser extent, change the latter. They are not neutral instruments of knowledge, as some epigone of positivism would have us believe. It is a physicist who reminds us of this, with rare incisiveness: "The movements of the planets preserve a sublime indifference with respect to our earthly astronomy. But human behaviour does not show an equal indifference with respect to the theories on behaviour adopted by man."[2]

Many economists today share the feeling that a radical change is necessary even though it is not clear which is the course that should be taken. It is a fact that the epistemological stances of the past have unduly restricted the ability of the economist to deal with many of the problems of his subject matter. It is time for economists to realize that what is urgent for them is to free intellectual energies from unnecessary shackles. After all, the desertion of old illusions does not coincide with a desire for regression nor with a choice of nihilistic diagnoses. It simply means a recognition of the fact that results of great significance are achieved all the time from "unacceptable" positions. Moreover, a growing number of economists have come to realize that the reality studied by them is not fixed like that of the natural sciences. This implies that more important than the peculiarities of the object under study are those of the scientists themselves. There is no doubt that the cultural background and the "vision" of the scientists have a strong effect on their research activities, and still more determinant are the common ideas and values accepted by the scientific community. Their decrees on the importance of the problems to be studied establish the directions in which solutions should be sought and, ultimately, decide which theories are correct.

The literature dealing with the foundations of the economic discourse in the last two decades clearly reveals how uncomfortable it is to move with a Nessus jacket on, a jacket that demands belief in the alleged neutrality of scientific knowledge. On the contrary, it is obvious to most observers that economic theories are no neutral tools providing knowledge about human behavior, since they are always somehow conducive to specific behaviors in human beings, that is, they do not only convey the results of simulations or experiments but are also directly or indirectly instrumental to the alteration of existing setups. This is why economic science cannot profitably exist if severed from values, as Gunnar Myrdal explicitly recognized some decades ago. The fact is that every epistemological route always ends up on anthropological terrain, that is to say, every question on what of economic reality can be known sends us back inevitably to a new question on the nature of the human person.

In light of the above, the cultural operation I am suggesting is the replacement at the core of economic theory of the notion of the person for that of the individual, thereby substituting the personalist paradigm for the individualistic one. The personalist line of thought I am referring to is the one articulated in modern times by Jacques Maritain, Emmanuel Mounier, Paul Ricoeur, Emmanuel Levinas, and others. As one reads in the Manifesto of the Center for Economic Personalism (CEP),

> Past theories within Christian social thought, as well as free-market econom-
> ics, have tended to be overly rationalistic, unduly collectivist, coldly utili-
> tarian, or lacking intellectual precision concerning the metaphysical struc-
> ture of human existence. These shortcomings resulted in a skewed view of
> human nature.... Economic liberty is only one aspect of the overall autonomy
> of the human person. It is, however, a logical consequence of human freedom.
> Personalists argue that human liberty . . . must always be exercised in relation
> to the truth about the human person.[3]

It is obvious that recapturing the relational or personalistic dimension from within the economic discourse will be well received, or at least not opposed, by the profession if we succeed in proving that while complying with the canons of scientific praxis, it can amend quite a few of the discipline's *aporiai* and shortcomings, thus making possible a closer grip on reality.[4] In other words, it must be demonstrated that the admission into the production process of economic knowledge of the personalistic perspective, as this is rendered by Christian ethics, can broaden the cognitive significance and explanatory function of economic science instead of restricting it.

To be sure, "progress" in science has certainly to do with views, perspectives. Scientific theories are not discovered in the same way that an explorer discovers a new land; they are inventions of the human mind. This is why the "vision" is not merely an expository device. It is of fundamental use if the explorer's task is to understand the whole of the mountain range, not just to climb single peaks. In the following, I will endeavor to apply such a criterion to the intriguing question of wealth distribution. I will not consider the issue of wealth creation, nor the complex question concerning the very nature of wealth. On these matters, I refer the reader to Robert Kennedy's article (chapter 2, this volume), which also contains a thorough discussion of how wealth is dealt with in biblical sources. John Haughey's contribution, on the other hand, addresses the subject of wealth creation as something that God intends. I will not approach my argument from the empirical side. (For such an approach, see the essay by Carlo Dell'Aringa and Claudio Lucifora, chapter 10, this volume.) Rather, I will focus on the theoretical level. Specifically, I will show that the interpretation of our market society that is still dominant nowadays is a major impediment to the solution of the wealth distribution problem in line with Catholic social thought. A discussion of the celebrated thesis proclaiming the priority of the efficiency objective over the equity one will provide a sort of test bed on which to check the robustness of this proposition.

If my aim is the one I have outlined, the spirit in which these pages were written is that of the "culture of engagement," in E. C. Boyer's sense of that phrase,[5] according to which moral commitment and interest in knowledge are linked to each other and influence each other reciprocally. If it is true that all research implies responsibilities and risks, it is equally true that in the social sciences these are, in the first place, moral and political. All the great economists, from Adam Smith onward, whatever school they belonged to, have recognized that economic arrangements are not something that exist prior to the decisions of economic agents, almost as if they were a natural given. They have likewise recognized that market institutions generate (or induce, according to the case) desirable or undesirable traits in people. We have recognized that the antisocial features of economic behavior have reached levels of intensity in our day that must concern us. We need to seek out ways—and they certainly exist—of restoring economics to society. In particular, we need to understand that there is not just one route to economic progress, and that there is a variety of models of the market, each one in tune with a specific cultural matrix. Hence, the choice of market model is a question at least as, and perhaps more, interesting and noble for economic science than research into conditions of efficiency of a *given* market model.

It should not be forgotten that our well-being depends also on the institutions we manage to endow ourselves with, and not only on our capacity to adapt to an institutional setup inherited from a more or less remote past. In this sense, economics must take part of the responsibility for having fostered certain perverse effects of the market mechanism, effects that in their turn have ended up by legitimating, even in recent times, certain forms of neocolonialism and certain practices of exploitation. However paradoxical this may appear, this began to happen precisely when economics was defining itself as a science free from value orientations, as a science that, in order to assume the epistemological status of the natural sciences, especially physics, had to declare the world of life outside of its realms of knowledge. Yet, we need to avoid a new mistake being made today, namely, that economic research ends up by destroying, especially among the younger generation, all hope in a change of intellectual regime, a change that places the human being, the person, at the center of attention. This corresponds to what John Maynard Keynes was alluding to when he wrote: "the economists are the guardians not of civilization, but of the possibility of civilization."[6] Before him, another great economist, Alfred Marshall, after observing that "people are capable of serving an unselfish cause much more often than we may think," had stated: *"the supreme aim of the economist* is to discover how this latent good may be developed more quickly and may be put to good use more wisely."[7]

THE DOMINANT IMAGE OF THE MARKET SOCIETY AND ITS CRITIQUE

Let us consider, even if briefly, the image of our market society that is still dominant in economic studies. This will be useful as a backdrop against which we may see, as if against the light, the serious limitations of the traditional model of individual behavior. According to this picture, the market is a contextualized institution based on a well-defined normative substratum.[8] The existing norms, however, are not able to determine economic decisions fully, nor are they sufficient to regulate economic interaction completely. This is the case insofar as all economic transactions, with the single exception of spot exchanges of goods and services objectively identifiable, offer to the parties the occasion for opportunistic behavior through which one tries to profit at the expense of the other. On the other hand, the expectation that a loss of some kind will be incurred may suggest to the potential participants that they refrain from entering into transactions that would in actual fact be advantageous to both parties. All this adds up to saying that almost all economic transactions necessarily require governance. Within the existing normative framework, therefore, culture and competition fulfill the need of "the two agencies determining the market," in John Stuart Mill's expression.[9]

The specific weight of these "two agencies" is not the same in different historical phases: in traditional societies the predominant agency is culture; in modern societies the forces of competition prevail, to the extent that these forces finish up by gradually eroding those areas of economic activity that stand on conventions and social norms. This picture thus foresees that with the passing of time the sphere of economic relationships will be regulated, almost entirely, only by the forces of competition, as if to say that modernity, intended as a step in the process of cultural evolution, tends inexorably to substitute the anonymous and impersonal laws of the market for interpersonal relationships. Naturally, the supporters of this vision are ready to admit that this substitution will never be complete. "Culture" will never be able to be wholly replaced by "competition," for the obvious reason that there will always be economic activities that cannot be mediated merely through the exchange of equivalent relations. Even in the most modern societies, there will always be a sphere of economic relations that, independently of the fact that they have to do with the market, will be regulated by conventions and social norms of behavior. (One only has to think of the so-called nonprofit organizations and cooperative firms.) But this will nevertheless always be a residual sphere of relations, of slight quantitative importance and in any case unable to affect the logic of the functioning of competition.

There are two unfortunate consequences deriving from this dichotomous mode of representing social reality. On the side of the intellectual division of labor, there has been a crystallization of the separation between economics, as a science that is only involved with the economic sphere and that uses the *homo oeconomicus* to explain human actions; and sociology, the science only involved with the social sphere and that uses the *homo sociologicus* metaphor as its explanatory paradigm. Indeed, these disciplines draw their identities, from the end of the nineteenth century onward, precisely from the presupposition of this division. The fragmentation of social knowledge into disciplines unconnected to each other, when not actually antagonistic, such as economics, sociology, and political science, has ended up by disarming critical thinking. Stephen Toulmin has most effectively described the serious difficulties that the compartmentalizing of scientific knowledge has provoked in the course of the twentieth century, and continues to provoke today, as a consequence of the determined separation of research into disciplines within the socioeconomic sphere. [10]

The second consequence has been the affirmation of a line of thought that identifies the market with the ideal-type place where individuals are motivated to act simply from self-interest, whether egoistic or altruistic (which of the two is operative is of no importance, as we shall see). Through this the conviction has grown that the only value judgment the market can tolerate is the one of efficiency, understood as a judgment on the adequacy of the means to the end and interpreted as the maximum (possible) realization of the interests of those who take part in it. Although the supporters of this line of thinking recognize that there are other values that the market has to take into account, these are a priori, that is, they belong to the premises necessary to the existence and correct functioning of the market. Here we are thinking of values (or moral sentiments) such as honesty and trust—values that shape the so-called code of mercantile morality. These have to exist beforehand and they have to have been already accepted by economic agents for the market to be able to begin to operate.

Nevertheless, standard economic theory does not appear to be afflicted by even the slightest doubt that, as B. Frey has convincingly shown, prices and incentive schemes might, in certain specific circumstances, crowd out the intrinsic motivation to action, which is the real generator of honesty and trust and other similar values without which any kind of market economy would only last a morning.[11] It can happen, in other words, that the external motivation to action, the one based on material or other incentives, crowds out the internal motivation, thus provoking a diminution of efficiency. Think of the case, for example, in which the subjects of a certain community are disposed to pay taxes because of their civic sense. If, in a context of this kind, the state intervenes by threatening sanctions against tax evasion because it adopts as a premise the culture of suspicion, it may well be that those subjects will adjust their sense of civic duty downward (and this is what often happens in reality). And yet, as everyone knows, no market economy could survive for long simply on the basis of external norms, those that produce their effects through opportunities and incentives and whose enforcement is guaranteed only by external sanctions, that is, punishments.

From what I have said, it can be inferred that the pillars supporting the kind of thinking outlined above appear to be pretty wobbly. First, it is not true that the preferences whose satisfaction the individuals try to maximize on the market have exclusively as their object the goods that enter into their choice sets. Also the way in which the objects "chosen" are chosen is important for the agents, because they assign a value to the possibility both of acting on the basis of their own convictions and of forming their convictions in line with their experience. I can certainly judge the option x to be superior to the option y—for example, because x contains a greater quantity of goods than y—but if the choice of x is in conflict with my personal convictions, which are, in their turn, the result of previous experience or of the acceptance of certain values, I might opt for y. As Amartya Sen, more than anyone else, has shown, what the agent chooses is not necessarily what is preferred.[12] And this happens not only and not so much because of the well-known problems of asymmetrical information or errors of judgment (or calculation), but because choices are guided not only by preferences but also by values, that is, by internal norms filtered by the conscience of the subject. Taking this into account means rejecting the well-known postulate of nonsatiety (the idea that more coincides with better) and the postulate of continuity of preferences, with which the very notion of maximizing behavior loses its meaning. As a matter of fact, Nicholas Georgescu-Roegen had already reached this conclusion by introducing into the theory of the consumer the notion of the lexicographical ordering of preferences, to signify that whenever the acts of choosing, and not only the things chosen, are also objects of preference, the ordering is always of the lexicographical kind, with the by-now-familiar analytical consequences.

Generalizing for a moment, the significance of the above paragraphs is that we should expand the grasp of the rationality paradigm in economics, given the paradoxical image of man that this paradigm promotes. On the one hand, *homo oeconomicus* has to exhibit a remarkable ability to analyze and to calculate in order to arrive at a definition of his preferential ordering. On the other, all these abilities are utilized for just one thing: to maximize a utility function under constraints. In other words, there is a great waste of energy and resources, a waste that identifies the nature of the agent as a "rational fool," to use Sen's phrase in what is now a celebrated essay of 1977.[13]

Apart from the doubtful rationality of those who waste resources, the fact is that it is not enough to pay attention simply to the *structure* of preferences, because the *content* of the latter and the motivational system they emerge from are also aspects to take into account for a satisfactory economic theory of human action. An empirical confirmation of this assertion comes from the recent study of E. Fehr and S. Gachter, which discusses the results of an experiment showing that labor contracts including material incentives are on average less efficient, and arouse less effort on the part of agents, than contracts that do not include any incentives.[14] Clearly a result of this kind is in total contradiction to what standard economic theory predicts, even though it is not hard to explain. If workers cultivate a strong sense of equity, it may happen that the introduction of material incentives, in a context in which wages are unfairly distributed, worsens the situation, because the workers cease to practice "reciprocity" toward the firm since only "just wages lead to just levels of effort." This means that an optimal labor contract cannot restrict itself to being "incentive compatible," in the usual meaning of the expression. It also has to be "fairness compatible," in the sense that it has to try to avoid the crowding-out of cooperative behavior within the firm (see Michael Naughton and Robert Wahlstedt, chapter 11, this volume).

Second, the above picture is misleading because, as G. Schlicht shows, law, culture, and competition cannot be seen as alternative instruments to solve the problems of social order and, in particular, of the coordination of individual decisions.[15] They are rather complementary instruments, for the basic reason that if the transactions of the market depend on prevailing social and legal norms, it is equally true that the economic process modifies those norms. Hence the distinction between the paradigms of the *homo oeconomicus* and the *homo sociologicus* is by no means as robust as we believed. In fact, the latest evolutionary game theory has tried to explain the emergence of norms (social and legal) by interpreting them as *routines* adopted because they show themselves to be successful in competitive terms in the solution of problems of coordination or negotiation. By doing this, the theory has claimed to demonstrate that every social relationship can be analyzed, in essence, as an exchange relation, and thus the problem of a social theory consists merely in the problem of the exchange of equivalents. So what at first sight could appear to be a rule-following kind of behavior would in actual fact be a typical problem of rational choice in contexts just slightly more complicated—as if to say that within each *homo sociologicus* there is a *homunculus oeconomicus* always at work.

But it is also true that this instrumentalist conception of norms (social and legal) does not get us very far on the knowledge front, for two reasons. On the one hand, it can explain coordination problems of the type "why do we keep to the right-hand side of the road," while it fails to explain why there are people who respect rules that are individually expensive, despite there being no sanctions, or why there are people who donate anonymously, and so on. On the other hand, the instrumentalist conception of norms can work as long as we are talking about *how* one chooses, but when we try to understand *why* one chooses, it cannot be assumed that values are a given of the problem. As Giacomo Becattini acutely observes, economics appears to be dominated by studies in which it is assumed that "some of the most characteristic or quintessential human properties of economic agents—their ideas of justice, of honor, of loyalty, but also their smallest hopes and illusions [are] pre-economic data, or 'accidental deviations from the rational norm,' reciprocally compensated for in the great mass of data."[16]

John Dewey, the exponent of philosophical pragmatism, observed that human action cannot be fully explained either simply in terms of ends and beliefs, as if the means or the environment counted for nothing, or simply in terms of the environment, as if beliefs counted for nothing at all.[17] The fact is that the environment and the actor are not separate entities, for the obvious reason that while people have transactions with their surrounding environment, they also help to construct that environment. It follows that when G. Stigler and G. Becker claimed that a change in observed behavior should be explained as a response, made by the rational agent, to a change in incentives alone (that is, the set of constraints), they show that they are being led by an ingenuous realism.[18] The incentives (or the constraints), indeed, can never be defined independently of the tastes and beliefs of the agents. Only the latter, while they act to overcome obstacles, can understand the nature and significance of the incentives. We need therefore a synthesis of the sociological approach that places beliefs and cultural aspects first, underestimating the structure of incentives and constraints to which human choice is subject, and the traditional economic approach that emphasizes incentives, whereas it places beliefs and tastes among the given data of the problem of choice.[19]

Third, it is not true that the market is an institution only compatible with the egocentric motivation of its actors. In other words, it is not true that what moves market competition is simply the self-interest of economic agents. This is false, as the mere observation of reality confirms, and it is theoretically unacceptable. In fact, Ronald H. Coase's well-known interpretation that the market is a more-than-perfect substitute for Adam Smith's benevolence—in the sense that the market, arriving where benevolence cannot reach, succeeds in achieving much more than the latter—is, if we reflect for a moment, an aporetic interpretation. In brief, the reason is this: Coase admits (he cannot get out of it) that in order to function, the market presupposes the practice of benevolence and respect of the mercantile moral code by each and every agent. He also argues, however, that the outcomes of the market depend only on the egocentric interest of those who take part in it, as if to say that, to exist, the market requires that certain specific virtues be practiced, but these practices have not the slightest influence on the results of the market process itself, which is simply paradoxical.

Why should rational subjects practice virtues such as benevolence, if the outcomes following on market interactions have nothing to do with those practices? (It should be remembered that, unlike a scarce resource, a virtue increases with use and diminishes when not used.) It is true, on the other hand, that the market, if agents so wish, can become a means for the strengthening of social bonds, with the creation of economic spaces. For example, in the civil economy the interpersonal relation receives a value of its own, the value of bond, as I shall be explaining further on. To sum up, it is the dominant economic interpretation of Smith's thinking that is distorted and off the track. For this interpretation the force of economic reasoning would lie precisely in its knowing how to disregard any consideration of the complexity of human motivations and in demonstrating how the collective well-being can be reached also by a society composed exclusively of rationally egocentric agents (capable of finding unambiguously the choices that guarantee them the maximum welfare and putting them into practice).

That the possibility of interest in others is a redundant hypothesis for economic theory would seem to be confirmed also by the celebrated passage from Adam Smith's *Wealth of Nations*, often invoked as an authoritative legitimization of this position, according to which "it is not from the benevolence of the butcher, the brewer, or the baker, that we expect our dinner, but from their regard to their own interest."[20] This famous maxim seems, however, to be singularly in conflict with the less famous but no less authoritative one that opens his *Theory of Moral Sentiments*: "how selfish soever man may be supposed, there are evidently some principles in his nature which interest him in the fortune of others, and render their happiness necessary to him, though he derives nothing from it except the pleasure of seeing it."[21] We should take careful note of the adjective "necessary": Smith seems to suggest here that attention to others is a fundamental and inescapable component of human nature and hence indispensable to the understanding of individual choices, and of economic ones among others.

This apparent schizophrenia in Smith, which has given rise to a fair amount of discussion (an *Adam Smith problem* arising from it has long been debated by historians of economic thought) can be explained simply: the "incriminating" passage in *The Wealth of Nations* presupposes the theses of *The Theory of Moral Sentiments*, especially the existence of a fundamental system of "norms of civil and economic morality" based on sympathy, which guarantees the orderly and everyday functioning of that complex and heterogeneous system of transactions that is the market, without individuals having to recur continually to violence and coercion to force others to respect the "rules of the game."

In other words, Smith's market is not Thomas Hobbes's arena; his maxim thus affirms in the last analysis that a market economy founded on his premises would be able to function even if the further motivations of all the individuals who take part in it were exclusively of a self-interested nature: it is thus an exaltation of the solidity of the organization of economic activities permitted by the market rather than a negation of the importance of intrinsic motivations. In other words, only within a structure of a relational kind, fed systematically by the practice of "moral sentiments" such as sympathy and benevolence, is it possible for the pursuit of self-interest to produce positive results. Hence, "the gains of both [sides] are mutual and reciprocal," as Adam Smith writes in the chapter "Of the Natural Progress of Opulence" in his *Wealth of Nations,* concerning trade between town and country.[22] Otherwise, it would be inevitable to fall back into a Hobbesian forest in which the economic game becomes a zero-sum game. With time, after the hegemonic influence of the culture of Jeremy Bentham's utilitarianism, as marginalist theory interpreted it, a substantially unilateral and distorted reading of Smith's argument emerged that has transformed the "particular case" of the economy of the selfish agents into a "highly representative case" and has twisted its interpretation, subjecting economic theory to the "hyper-minimalist" anthropology of the *homo oeconomicus,* of a one-dimensional man deprived of his psychological and social complexity. In his essay in this volume (chapter 1), Charles Clark discusses the many ambiguities in the conceptualization of wealth that can be found both in the Christian tradition and in the history of economic thought. Although from a different perspective, Clark arrives at a conclusion similar to the one here indicated.

The Risks of the Current Transition toward a Globalized World: The Importance of Wealth Distribution

I will now consider one of the most serious risks linked to that complex and epochal phenomenon, globalization.[23] (See Simona Beretta, chapter 5, this volume.) Globalization is a positive sum game, a game that increases overall wealth and income but at the same time tends to increase the social distances between countries and inside each country, the distances between one social group and another. In other words, globalization reduces absolute poverty while spreading relative poverty. This is a paradox: something that, according to the Greek etymology of the word, marvels, surprises. While overall wealth increases and absolute poverty (the inability of a person or group of people to attain the threshold conditions of subsistence) decreases, relative poverty is on the rise. According to recent official studies, globalization has reduced absolute poverty over the past twenty-five years: apart from globalization, there would have been approximately 2 billion people living in absolute poverty, whereas currently there are 1.2 billion. This is clearly still a tragic figure, but lower than it would have been without globalization. Many observers, who do not distinguish between people living in absolute poverty and relative poverty, maintain that the existence of 1.2 billion in absolute poverty is a result of globalization. This is not true. However, it is true that globalization increases the gaps, and that is a serious problem. According to recent research by the World Bank, the world Gini coefficient, which is the most widely used statistical indicator to measure inequality, was 62.5 in 1988. In 1993 it went up to 65.9 and in 1999 to 69. An increase of 0.7 Gini points per year is really extraordinary.[24]

It has been shown that when inequalities and relative poverty exceed a certain critical threshold in a given country or region, conditions become ripe for the outbreak of a real, fullscale civil war. There have been forty-nine civil wars in the world over the last forty years, the vast majority triggered by increasing inequality. Therefore, no one who values peace can remain silent in the face of an increase in relative poverty. Moreover, when relative poverty increases significantly, democracy itself comes under fire. This cause/effect relationship has been demonstrated: when inequality in a country exceeds a certain level, those in a position of relative disadvantage stop participating in the democratic community life, which leads the way to varying forms of totalitarianism, the most prevalent at present being technocratic, not military.[25]

It is not true that the maximum extension of the market area improves everybody's well-being. The aphorism according to which "a rising tide raises all boats" is not convincing. As we know, this is the favorite metaphor with the recent liberal-individualistic formulation: since the well-being of people is a function of economic prosperity, which in turn is linked to the spread of market relations, the actual priority of political action should be an effort to ensure all those conditions (fiscal, public administration, optimum allocation of property rights, and so on) that foster a flourishing of markets. In that vision, the welfare state, which redistributes wealth via taxation while keeping itself outside the wealth-producing mechanism, hampers economic growth, all the more so when it is greedy (causing major distorting effects in the market) and when its instruments are submitted to political uses, thus jeopardizing normal democratic dialectics. Whence, the recommendation that the welfare system should take care solely of those whom the market contest leaves on the fringes of society. The others, those who manage to stay inside the virtuous circle of economic growth, will protect themselves via the numerous solutions offered by private insurance schemes.

Where is the weak point in such an argument? It is to be found in the simple reason that the prerequisite of equal opportunities for all is one that must apply throughout the life span of citizens and not just *una tantum*, the moment they enter the economic arena. To put it another way, for all participants to enjoy actual conditions of freedom it is not sufficient to ensure equal opportunities at the start of the economic race. The market contest is indeed different from a sports contest. In the latter, the most gifted or capable wins the prize, but this in no way confers upon him the possibility, or bestows upon him the right, to start the next run with an advantage: all the contestants, with no exception, compete under the same conditions, at any stage or tier of the game. Not so in market contests, where the winner of the first stage is often able to bend to his advantage, in an endogenous way, the rules of the game. (Economic history is rich in examples of this kind. We need only to recollect how monopolies and oligopolies developed in the course of time.) Furthermore, the really alarming news about the *new economy* age, the economy of knowledge and information, is the appearance of a new kind of competition: *positional* competition, as it was called by the late Fred Hirsch. The central feature of positional competition is the generation of "winner-take-all" outcomes, or the "superstar effect," as the American economist Shermin Rose described it. It is easy to see that in the presence of positional competition equating across individuals, initial opportunities are of little or no avail. In a recent paper, Edward Glaeser et al. have proposed a new mechanism by which unfair wealth distributions shape economic and social outcomes: subversion of institutions in the form of corruption, intimidation, and other forms of influence.[26] The fact is that in countries where wealth is inequitably distributed, the wealthy and the politically powerful groups of society tend to subvert the operation of legal and regulatory institutions for their own benefit.

The results are there for everybody to see. Never to the same extent as in the last two decades has one witnessed such an outburst of social inequalities, both horizontal (among different social groups) and vertical (among one subject and another), at the same time as the world's wealth has been growing at a pace never seen before. This is the great *aporia* of the present model of development: extraordinary economic growth (in the sense of sustained increases of wealth) and civil progress (in the sense of ever wider spaces of freedom for people) are unable to keep the same pace. It is therefore easy to understand why, under such circumstances, an increased affluence does not go hand in hand with greater public happiness. Indeed, it may limit or even destroy the ability to partake in the economic game for those subjects who, for whatever reason, are left on the market borders. While it adds nothing to the capabilities of the winners, it produces a rationing of freedom, which is always detrimental to happiness. (See Dennis McCann, chapter 7, this volume, for an interesting discussion of "justice as participation" as a key category in Catholic social thought and for the suggestion of ways that it can become a policy criterion of choice in dealing with wealth inequality issues.)

An important case where the issue of wealth and income distribution stands at center stage is the one regarding the much-debated question of sustainable development. The thesis I defend is that the struggle against poverty and for sustainable development are two sides of the same coin. Let me elaborate briefly.

As is well known, there are three main causes of environmental degradation: inefficient allocation of resources, iniquitous distribution of resources, and disproportion between population and the capacity of the environment to sustain it. Whereas in rich countries the first of these causes is operative, poor countries are mainly afflicted by the other two causes of environmental decay. Through their structural characteristics, these countries tend to specialize in the production and export of goods with a high intensity of environmental degradation. Even now, two-thirds of Latin America's exports are made up of natural resources (Africa's percentage is still higher) that are imported and consumed in the countries of the North. These data, though crude, are already sufficient to have us understand why the question of sustainable development cannot be separated from the reform of the rules of international trade. When we discover that the South exports goods of a high intensity of environmental degradation, though it is not true that the South disposes of higher quantities of these goods compared to the North, we may realize why commercial policies based on the Ricardian principle of comparative advantage are a serious threat to sustainability. If we then consider that most developing countries are located in the region known as the "vital zone," characterized by highly unstable ecological equilibria and by a marked capacity to influence the atmosphere, we realize why, if we continue to force these countries to use their *natural* capital to substitute for an insufficient *physical* and *human* capital, environmental degradation will inevitably suffer a rapid acceleration.

There is more to it. In a document published some years ago, the World Bank thoroughly detailed the relationship existing between some indicators of environmental quality and levels of GNP per head (in 1992). A relation emerged that could be shown through a curve in the form of a U turned upside down: environmental degradation grows with the increase of average income when the latter is at low levels, whereas it decreases with the increase of average income when the latter has gone above a certain threshold. Basing their work on this rich empirical material, G. Grossman and A. Krueger, using econometric techniques, found that the level of the critical threshold of average income, beyond which the above-mentioned curve begins to decrease, stands at around $8,000 per capita annually (in 1985 dollars).[27] The curve in question is known in the literature as the "Environmental Kuznets curve" (EKC) from the name of the Nobel Prize-winner for Economics who first studied its characteristics (with reference, however, to the relation between levels of GNP per capita and variations of an indicator of the inequality of income within a specific population). The empirical evidence in support of the EKC is still today insufficiently robust to recommend its use for the purposes of environmental policy making. It is nevertheless possible to extract from the EKC the following broad indications: some indicators of environmental degradation (emissions of CO_2; solid urban waste) increase, that is, get worse, with the increase of per-capita income; others (the lack of clean water; hygiene indicators) diminish, that is, improve, with the increase in per-capita income; still others (emissions of anidride of sulphur and nitrates) first increase and then diminish with the increase in per-capita income.

What message does this argument send us? Since Northern countries are to the right of the value of the critical threshold mentioned above, whereas most Southern countries are still a long way off this goal, and since the environmental problems that worry us the most today are the global ones, it is evident that we shall have to intervene urgently on the rules of international economic activities. In particular, we must realize that in the context of an increasingly globalized economy, environmental regulation as well as commercial regulation have to be integrated and harmonized, exactly the opposite to what has happened up until now in the World Trade Organization.[28]

It is well known that international trade tends to separate production from consumption. An increase in the demand for tropical wood in the North translates into a corresponding reduction in tropical forest in the Amazon. It is a fact that international trade throws a long, dark shadow over the environment. Without adequate rules and without forms of close cooperation between the agencies that concern themselves with trade and the environment, the growing volume of commercial exchange (in itself positive and a hopeful sign for the future) will translate into increases in environmental degradation.

Another and more important message is that the problem of the sustainability of development, in present-day historical conditions, is intrinsically linked to the problem of poverty, both absolute and relative. It would be naive to imagine that we can solve the former problem separately from the second or, worse still, in opposition to it. Efforts to improve or conserve the quality of the environment in the North will be of very little use unless at the same time there is an urgent and comprehensive program of action against poverty to allow the countries of the South to move beyond the critical threshold identified by the EKC. Clearly, there will have to be a program of redistribution on a global scale, since policies on a national scale are no longer adequate. If we stop and think for a moment, we find ourselves faced with a specific, yet remarkable case in which the defense of justice serves also to improve efficiency (here identified with the sustainability of development), so it is not always true that there is a trade-off between efficiency and justice!

The Idea of the Supposed Trade-off between Efficiency and Equity

The sentence concluding the section above seems to contrast markedly with a well-entrenched idea in economics, according to which there would be a net separation between wealth creation and wealth distribution, whence an unreconcilable trade-off between efficiency and distributive justice. Bentham had already raised the issue with his celebrated dilemma: in order to maximize the total sum of individual utilities, egalitarian wealth-redistribution policies should be promoted. On the other hand, such policies tend to neutralize incentives to produce more wealth. Alfred Marshall would express the same view one century later: "Taking it for granted that a more equal distribution of wealth [is] to be desired, how far would this justify changes in the institutions of property, or limitations of free enterprise even when they would be likely to diminish the aggregate of wealth?"[29] On the other hand, for the economists of the classical school up to Mill, the efficiency objective is coextensive and proceeds along with that of equity. In 1759, Smith writes in his *Theory of Moral Sentiments*: "Justice is the main pillar that upholds the whole edifice. If it is removed, the great, the immense fabric of human society . . . must in a moment crumble into atoms."[30] In Part IV of the same work he adds: "[Men] are led by an invisible hand to make nearly the same distribution of the necessities of life, which would have been made, *had the earth been divided into equal portions among all its inhabitants*, and thus without intending it, without knowing it, advance the interests of the society, and afford means to the multiplication of the species."[31]

Keynesian thought confronts the problem in a peculiar manner. As is well known, in the Keynesian system the state never collides with the market, which it instead supports, since public intervention pursues equity and efficiency at the same time. A situation of unemployment due to a lack of effective demand is in itself a waste of resources and as such is inefficient, but at the same time it is an injustice. What in the Keynesian conceptualization makes the two objectives compatible with each other is the absence of a problem of global, physical, and social shortages of resources. (In the language of game theory, one would say that the situation can be represented by a positive sum game.)

It is a great political achievement of Keynesianism to have evidenced the existence of special historical conditions, such as those dominating Western economies in the 1930s, in which the state can successfully interact as a neutral mediator between classes. A higher level of public investment in a depression not only generates more jobs for the unemployed, whence a higher global wage share, but also helps capitalists to achieve larger profits. This impartial economic role of the state operating to the benefit of all social classes becomes worthless when the game becomes a zero-sum one, that is, when the conditions for the operation of the "cooperative" capitalism model cease to exist. Therefore, it is not surprising that from the late 1960s, at the same time as the appeal of the Keynesian research program was declining, the thesis of a trade-off between efficiency and justice has been spreading again among economists and politicians.

Arthur Okun neatly summarizes the majority's view by stating: "Any insistence on carving the pie into equal slices would shrink the size of the pie."[32] Inefficient interventions on a distributive scale are depicted by Okun with the felicitous image of the pierced pail: "the money must be carried from the rich to the poor in a leaky bucket. Some of it will simply disappear in transit, so the poor will not receive all the money that is taken from the rich."[33] Quite a few economists have tried to quantify redistribution costs. G. A. Browning and R. Johnson, for example, calculated that an income increase of $90 per year (in 1984) for the lower 50 percent of the population costs the upper 50 percent approximately three times as much.[34] This conclusion is opposed by Alan Blinder in an essay aimed at proving that in many important situations governmental interventions can remarkably improve the market process performance in regard to both efficiency and equity.[35] In a similar vein, Robert Kuttner provides numerous real examples of how the government can promote both efficiency and equity.[36] Recently, Kopczuk et al. have addressed the big problem concerning the reasons Western countries are so unwilling to substantially raise their foreign aid to help impoverished regions.[37] One of these reasons has to do with the large efficency cost (that is, waste, corruption, disincentives) that would plague such efforts. On the basis of a robust set of stylized models, the authors reach the conclusion that what limits the cross-country transfers is not the efficency cost of the redistribution.

The antagonism between efficiency and equity is therefore a long-lived concept in economics. Ultimately, it derives from another concept, that of the priority, in economic discourse, of the efficiency over the equity objective. It follows that if we want to criticize the former concept, we have no alternative but to demolish the latter, which rests upon two main arguments. The first argument adopts the process, rather than the final outcome, as a criterion by which social institutions, whatever they are, should be examined. This implies that the process justifies the final outcome, not vice versa, as the end-state perspective asserts. Within the process-oriented perspective two different positions are easily identifiable, both of which were the object of renewed interest in recent years. The first is supported by minimal state theorists, excellently represented by Robert Nozick.[38] The second position is reflected by Friedrich von Hayek.[39] I will examine Nozick first.

For the American philosopher, the market is the only acceptable mechanism for resource allocation because only the market is compatible with the protection and enforcement of freedom in a negative sense, the only idea of freedom that the "good society" can and should pursue for all of its members. This well-known topic of moral philosophy has two important consequences related to the limits of state intervention in distributive matters. The first one declares that no subject can eventually be worse off than it would be in the absence of public intervention. A brief reflection, however, suffices to conclude that this limitation is doomed to remain inactive since in the state of anarchy that would inevitably accompany the absence of government, the levels of individual welfare would be so low that such a condition would always be fulfilled.

The second consequence concerns the refusal by libertarian economists to express any evaluation in moral terms of market results, based on the fact that moral evaluations and assumption of responsibilities are limited to deliberate individual actions. Therefore, since nobody deliberately "wills" the market process outcome, nobody can be held responsible for it. Thus, contrary to what Catholic social thought would maintain, no room is left for any moral speculation.[40]

To shed light on this central point, Nozick uses the following example. If a large number of subjects pay, say, 50 cents each to watch some entertainer's show, they cannot later reasonably object to the distribution of the income ensuing from it, even though these transactions were to generate a remarkably unequal distribution. I will note here that this is a variation of John Locke's famous assertion: "by consenting to the use of money," men eventually consent to any wealth distribution that it produces.

The theory of the market as an end per se lends itself to a fundamental criticism. The fact that no specific agent can be held responsible for the results of market processes does not imply that persons or institutions are relieved of the responsibility for mitigating them. Such results may well be unwanted, but one can always foresee and limit them. Consistently with Nozick's example, all one can say is that many individuals, by independent decisions, would rather pay 50 cents than miss the show. Yet it would be a non sequitur to say that they approve (that is, accept as preferred) also the income distribution it initiates, for the simple reason that this option does not belong to the choice set of the individuals. As an aggregate result, an income distribution pattern can be "chosen" versus a different one only by some kind of collective decision. Nothing can prevent us from modifying, by means of collective action, the results of a myriad of individual actions. Finally, one should never forget that, as noticed by John Waldron, what is a talent and what is not, is at least partly endogenously determined by the social and institutional setting in which the person happens to live. The talents of a rent-seeker and those of an entrepreneur do not flourish in the same institutional milieu.[41]

The other "process-oriented" position as mentioned above is that of the neo-Austrian school, which views the market chiefly as a process of discovery and, more broadly, of progress. For Hayek, the primary moral good is social progress, not freedom as such. "If the result of individual freedom did not show that some life systems are more successful than others, it would lose most of its support."[42] Hayek refers explicitly to the eighteenth-century Scottish philosophical tradition and presents himself as a new interpreter and follower of the same tradition in that he expounds a sort of "generalized proposition of the invisible hand." His central argument is that free interaction among subjects in the market—not only within the limited domain of economic behavior but also extended to the whole context of social conduct—develops behavioral rules and institutional mechanisms allowing the enforcement of political order and the pursuit of society's economic progress.

The generalized proposition of the invisible hand originates from the statement that each economic subject is characterized by an irrepressible peculiar feature: a cognitive background with which man is endowed and which is limited and specific at the same time. According to Hayek, the well-known assumption of the theory of perfect competition, which says that each agent is correctly informed about everything, is misleading. In fact, the primary problem of all economic systems is to distribute to all agents the limited information possessed by each subject, so that it can be utilized to the maximum benefit of society as a whole. The diffusion of scattered information is made possible by the evolution of institutional mechanisms controlling the relationships between economic agents, thereby playing an eminently informational role.

It should be added here that Hayek clearly distinguishes spontaneous order (*cosmos*) as an unsought-for consequence of many individual actions, from the order emerging from organizations (*taxis*) that are guided by human action deliberately pursuing certain targets. Topics such as distributive justice can receive attention only within organizations, yet for Hayek, society is not an organization but a spontaneous order. To think of society as transformed into an organization is tantamount to denying the principle of freedom, seen not only as a shield against coercion but also primarily as individual autonomy.

The main problem that the neo-Austrian position has to tackle in order to become credible deals with the fact that the defense of market order in terms of individual autonomy raises the question of the legitimacy of the initial wealth distribution. The defense of the market as theorized by Hayek would be acceptable only if we acknowledged that it may not only be necessary to redistribute initial endowments to guarantee individual autonomy, but interventions *in itinere* may also be necessary to ensure equal opportunities. The market mechanism is not horizontally fair: similar people may be treated in completely different ways. To cite one example: as Sen has explained on many occasions, an undernourished person has a reduced capability to "function," that is, to be autonomous.[43] Low nutritional levels seriously impair the individual's work potential. For this reason, if under the circumstance the subject were not granted access to income from sources other than work, her vulnerability, even in a perfect labor market, would certainly make her nonautonomous.

Essentially, the point is that, in spite of the due emphasis laid on the category of rights by the individualistic version of liberal thought, its bare rendering of what it means to be a person deprives the concept itself of any practical significance. In fact, according to liberal individualism, a right cannot be fully made use of unless the subject involved is capable of negotiating her own interests with other subjects by unrestricted negotiations. Now, it is certainly true that if contracting parties are somehow equal in their negotiating potential, the most efficient way for them to reach their goals is to be left free to negotiate with one another. But what about those who do not possess the same skills and cannot be "represented" by some gifted subject? The implication is clear: a subject is the holder of rights only as long as she is capable of pursuing her targets, directly or indirectly, as a contracting party in some social pact. It is not difficult to understand the clash of such a position with Catholic social thought, a doctrine that adopts the intrinsic value of the human person as the objective basis for the attribution of rights.[44]

The second argument by which some have tried to give priority to the efficiency goal is the one offered by traditional welfare economics. State intervention should not take place at the outset of or during the market process, but at its end, once economic success has been secured. The basis of ex-post facto distributive policies is the thesis concerning the possibility of including in the list of market failures the fairness of income distribution. For a long time in welfare economics it has been admitted that the distributive results of market processes may not be compatible with the equity standards that society gives itself. What is new is the recognition that income distribution may take the form of a public good, although a peculiar one. The argument runs as follows: the market would not guarantee fair distributions of wealth simply because altruism produces benefits that are internal to society as a whole, yet external to the donors. Therefore, if left to its own automatisms, the market will "produce" less redistribution than would be "efficient," that is, socially desirable, because of the well-known *free-riding* phenomenon. Clearly, this is an application of the general principle that society's welfare, when brought about by individual choices, is in fact a public good, since the contribution given to its realization by the other-regarding attitude of each single member is so small as to cancel the incentive to produce it. (See Helen Alford, chapter 9, this volume, for an inspiring discussion of how the idea of the common good is linked to that of the public good and to the connection between wealth distribution and the common good.)

It may be worthwhile to recall that this approach to fair distribution, which is seen from the public good perspective as against the ethical perspective, had been clearly proposed by Jacob Viner, who remarked that a "distributive justice with which voters are tolerably happy" is a necessary condition for the viability of the market system.[45] The outstanding feature of the market game is indeed its rejection of all upper or lower limits to ex-post results: the upper limit could be represented by all wealth in the hands of one member; the lower limit, a zero wealth for other individuals. Accordingly, one can reasonably infer that there may exist a majority of risk-adverse subjects refusing to stop the market game at the lower level because of bad luck. It follows that in democratic societies the guarantee of an individual minimum-income level becomes a necessary condition to ensure the efficiency of the system itself. Moreover, as clearly demonstrated by recent literature on endogenous growth, markedly unfair income distributions for various reasons threaten economic growth possibilities, whence new space for the planning and legitimization of economic policy interventions.[46]

A twofold criticism can be expressed in this regard. Historical experience has shown the limits of ex-post redistribution. Inasmuch as the pre-intervention situation may be efficient, the adoption of income taxes or transfers for redistribution purposes would distort resource allocations. The magnitude of such distortion may be disputable, yet the perception of redistribution costs may, as indeed it has, represent a powerful factor limiting in practice the use of taxes and transfers. In any case, the more serious criticism is of a theoretical nature. Only in a world à la Arrow-Debreu would it be possible to keep equity and efficiency conceptually separated, a separation based on the two fundamental theorems of welfare economics. It is known that the idea of the moment of production of wealth as distinct from the moment of its distribution was long in use among economists to offer the well-known pragmatic justification of a market which, if objectionable from the point of view of justice, is still the most efficient of all systems of economic activity organization.

The thesis of a separation between efficiency and equity, however, is no longer defensible in all those situations in which unfair wealth distributions generate incentive problems that endanger efficiency itself. On the other hand, any redistributive scheme other than lump-sum transfers is a distorting one and as such is a cause of inefficiencies. Accordingly, a potential trade-off might seem to exist between efficiency and equity. However, this does not imply that redistributive interventionly governments always and necessarily produces a loss of efficiency. This would occur only in a first-best world. In fact, in second-best contexts it is easy to demonstrate that public sector interventions can improve matters both on the efficiency and on the equity fronts, as Blinder, among others, has clearly demonstrated (which shows how certain objections to public intervention have sometimes purely ideological foundations).[47] (See again the inspiring essay by Naughton and Wahlstedt, which is the result of a dialogue between a business leader and an educator.)

CONCLUSION

The main message stemming from the argument developed above is twofold. First, what kind of relationship is there between Catholic social thought and economics? Ignoring the multitude of specific answers, the positions that can be detected may be grouped in two sets. On the one hand, we have those who claim that Catholic social thought should act as a matrix within which economics takes shape as scientific discourse and draws the strength of its theories. On the other hand, we have the position of those, nowadays the majority, who believe that all that Catholic social thought can offer the economist is a twofold support: to suggest selection criteria for those economic problems to be tackled with priority, and to provide guidelines for the practical utilization of the results obtained by the economist. However, during the process of production of economic knowledge, the horizon offered by Catholic social thought is next to irrelevant; indeed, it is jealously kept apart. For example, Catholic social thought may suggest that searching into the unemployment question at one particular time is a priority in the economist's agenda, or it may advise on how to distribute a certain amount of income among different groups. However, how one arrives at a specific theory of the labor market or how one is capable of explaining the level of income produced by a certain economy is totally unconcerned with the value options stemming from Catholic social thought.

Both groups of positions are aporetic and therefore unacceptable, albeit on different grounds. The first one is so because it would disclaim the autonomy of economic science. Yet, at least since *Gaudium et spes,* Catholic teaching has considered such an autonomy a value to be preserved. This principle has been recently reasserted in the encyclical letter *Fides et ratio* by John Paul II. (One should not forget that from Aristotle down to the eighteenth century, economics was treated as a branch of practical philosophy devoid of any independent status.) The second position is also unacceptable since it postulates the well-known avalutativity thesis, according to which knowledge produced by economic thinking is devoid of any practical function. According to such a view, economic science does not accompany, nor does it guide, decision makers' actions, whatever they may be, but it sees and foresees human actions just as the physicist anticipates nature's motions. The acceptance of the avalutativity character as borderline of scientific learning, once combined with the concept that only the latter can be considered rigorously rational, leads one to assume avalutativity as a feature essentially inherent in economic reasoning. This is equivalent to saying that for an economist to be a scientist, he cannot commit himself to value judgments. The gap thus opened between reason and decision making cannot be filled. Ends and dispositions are declared impracticable by scientific reason that has nothing to say about them; hence the spreading of relativistic—not to say skeptical—attitudes among economists, even among those who declare themselves believers.

The uncomfortable condition produced by this lack of orientation is before everybody's eyes. Especially for those economists who are wont to question the significance of their scientific endeavor, this is easy to understand. If we see economics as one way—certainly not the only one—to improve our understanding of the social world and to help modify for the better certain social structures (for example, wealth distribution), the economist cannot limit his range of action to efficiency issues. Above all, he cannot pretend to ignore the fact that the more profound the decisions to be made, the more urgent the need to clarify the value criteria that underlie decision making.

The extent to which this "scientific asceticism" harms the comprehension of the new problems of a postindustrial society and how far it contributes to making Catholic social thought a purely ethical code of conduct is manifest to all. To me, Catholic social thought's proper contribution to a transdisciplinary methodology in the realm of social science is to be found in supplying a hermeneutical horizon promoting a change of those speculative categories that are the basis of today's economic discourse.

The second message is to call for a deep rethinking of the problem concerning the anthropological foundation of economic discourse. This problem has attracted a growing interest among economists, an interest that has been partly motivated by the recognition that a viable and effective strategy to cope with the question of wealth distribution presupposes getting over the reductionist character of a great deal of contemporary economic theory, a reductionism that expresses itself in the fact that in modern economics, relations among human beings are reduced to exchange relations, as if these were the only ones worthy of economic interest. As is well known, the economic universe is made up of various worlds, each characterized by the prevalence of a specific type of relation. Yet, the (ontological) assumption of reductionism in economics requires that all types of social relation can be modelled as some variant or other of exchange relations. In doing so, the discipline is imposing upon itself a Nessus shirt that prevents a thorough investigation of economic relations, which, although they do not appear to be of the exchange relation type, are of great economic relevance to our societies. This is the case with the relations of reciprocity. The compound figure of relational individuality (that is, personalism), as stemming from Catholic social thought, would enable economic theory to be reconstructed on a more solid basis, permitting us to overcome the *aporiai* of individualism, on the one side, and of collectivism, on the other.

It is now a well-recognized fact that market systems, defined as tractable patterns of behavior, are compatible with many cultures. In turn, the degree of compatibility of market systems with cultures is not without effects on the global efficiency of the systems themselves: in general, the final outcome of market coordination will vary from culture to culture. Thus, one should expect that a culture of individuals, although motivated by self-interest, may entertain a sense of society. But cultures are not to be taken as given and beyond analysis. They respond to the investment of resources in cultural patterns, so much so that in many circumstances it may be socially beneficial to engage in cultural engineering. For how good the performance of an economic system is depends also on whether certain conceptions and ways of thinking have achieved dominance, a dominance that is precarious, in any case.

As in all human endeavors, it would be naive to think that radical processes, as those hinted at above, do not entail high rates of conflict. Indeed, the interests involved—both scientific and extra-scientific—are enormous. Not without cause is a sort of distress concerning the future of economic research spreading today in many circles. This concern is being used by some, in the name of a "culture of crisis," as a device to produce a sort of market Machiavellism. It is precisely against this neo-Machiavellism and its underlying ethical relativism that those who, like the Christians, are the bearers of a specific message of hope should put up a fight. In this precise sense, Catholic social thought acquires significance and credibility, even with the nonbeliever, whenever it is expressed through and by means of actual experiences that do not merely represent traditions of moral reflection but turn into laboratories for innovating practices of life.

Notes

1. See M. A. Charles Clark, "The Challenge of Catholic Social Thought to Economic Theory," *Journal of Peace and Justice Studies* (2002): 163–77, for an inspiring discussion of this point and, more generally, of the challenges that Catholic social thought is posing to the mainstream school of economic thought at the "vision" level of analysis.

2. Louis Eisenberg, "The 'Human' Nature of Human Nature," *Science* 176 (1972): 127.

3. CEP, *An Introduction to Economic Personalism: A New Paradigm for a Human Economy* (Grand Rapids, Mich.: Acton Institute, 1999), 5.

4. Here I have elaborated on the issue referred to in Stefano Zamagni, "On the Recent Revival of the Philosophical Dimension in Economic Discourse: Notes on Crossing Boundaries," in Rossini Favretti, G. Sandri, and R. Scazzieri, eds., *Incommensurability and Translation* (Cheltenham, U. K.: Elgar, 1999), where I indicate that the introduction of the personalist perspective into economic discourse does not entail at all the acceptance of methodological holism; rather, it demands going beyond, not against, methodological individualism.

5. E. C. Boyer, "The Scholarship of Engagement," *Bulletin of the American Academy Association* 49 (1996): 7.

6. Robert Skidelsky, *John Maynard Keynes* (Bologna: Il Mulino, 1998), 19.

7. Alfred Marshall, *Principles of Economics* (London: Macmillan, 1949/1980), 9 (emphasis added).

8. The content of this section follows, with many variations and with a different focus, the argument developed in Stefano Zamagni, "Humanising the Economy: On the Relationship between Catholic Social Thinking and Economic Discourse," in J. S. Boswell, F. P. McHugh, and J. Verstraeten, eds., *Catholic Social Thought: Twilight or Renaissance?* (Louvain: Peeters, 2000).

9. G. Schlicht, *On Custom in the Economy* (Oxford: Clarendon Press, 1998), 22.

10. S. Toulmin, *Return to Reason* (Cambridge, Mass.: Harvard University Press, 2001).

11. B. Frey, *Not Just for the Money: An Economic Theory of Personal Motivation* (Cheltenham, U. K.: Elgar, 1997).

12. Amartya Sen, "Internal Consistency of Choice," *Econometrica* 61 (1993): 495–521; and Amartya Sen, "Markets and Freedom: Achievements and Limitations of the Market Mechanism in Promoting Individual Freedoms," *Oxford Economic Papers* (1993): 45.

13. Amartya Sen, "Rational Fools: A Critique of the Behavioural Foundations of Economic Theory," *Philosophy and Public Affairs* 6 (1977): 317–44.

14. E. Fehr and S. Gachter, "Do Incentive Contracts Crowd out Voluntary Cooperation?" University of Southern California, Research Paper, C01.3 (2001).

15. Schlicht, *On Custom in the Economy.*

16. Giacomo Becattini, "Possibilità e limiti dell'economia di mercato," *Economia e Politica Industriale* 101 (1999): 5.

17. J. Dewey and A. Bentley, "Knowing and the Known," in R. Handy and E. Harwood, eds., *Useful Procedures of Inquiry* (Great Barrington, Mass.: Behavioral Research Council, 1973).

18. G. Stigler and G. Becker, "De gustibus non est disputandum," *American Economic Review* 67 (1977): 76–90.

19. For an expansion of the argument, see Lans Bovenberg and Theo van de Klundert, "Christian Tradition and Neo-Classical Economics: Can They Be Reconciled?" in W. Derkse et al., eds., *In Quest of Humanity in a Globalizing World* (Leende: Damon, 2001).

20. Adam Smith, *The Wealth of Nations* (Oxford: Oxford University Press, 1976), 26–27.

21. Adam Smith, *The Theory of Moral Sentiments* (London: Henry J. Bon, 1759), 9.

22. Smith, *Wealth of Nations*, 376.

23. For a synthetic account of the basic features of globalization, see Stefano Zamagni, *Globalization and the New Migratory Question* (Vatican City: Pontifical Academy of Social Sciences, 2001). See also Dani Rodrik, "Feasible Globalization," London, CEPR discussion paper, 3524 (July 2002), according to whom the nation-state system, democratic politics, and full economic integration are mutually incompatible. Of the three, at most two can be had together.

24. See B. C. Milanovic, "How Great Is World Inequality?" *WIDER Angle* 1 (2002), for the details and, in particular, for the important distinction between *world* income distribution and *international* income distribution: the latter being based on differences in mean incomes— weighted by population size—between countries; the former considering also income inequality within countries.

25. See Eric Uslaner, "Trust, Democracy and Inequality," College Park, University of Maryland Working Papers, 2001, for details on the numbers, in particular about the link between inequality and democracy.

26. Edward Glaeser, Jose Scheinkman, and Andrei Shleifer, "The Injustice of Inequality," National Bureau of Economic Research, Working Paper 9150 (September 2002).

27. G. Grossman and A. Krueger, "Economic Growth and the Environment," *Quarterly Journal of Economics,* 110, no. 441 (May 1995).

28. Charles Pearson, *Economics and the Global Environments* (Cambridge: Cambridge University Press, 2000).

29. Marshall, *Principles of Economics,* 41.

30. Smith, *Theory of Moral Sentiments,* 86.

31. Ibid., 185, emphasis added.

32. Arthur Okun, *Equality and Efficiency: The Big Trade-off* (Washington, D.C.: Brookings Institution, 1975), 48.

33. Ibid., 91.

34. It should be noted that the results presented in G. A. Browning and R. Johnson, *Equality and Distribution Costs* (Washington, D.C.: Brookings Institution, 1984), are substantially theory driven, that is, not based on actual examples or cases. Indeed, the period (the 1960s) when the U.S. government intervened the most in promoting economic equity is also the period of its highest growth rates.

35. See Alan Blinder, *Hard Heads, Soft Heart* (Reading, Mass.: Addison-Wesley, 1987). It may be of interest to know that Léon Walras, *Etudes d'économie sociale* (Paris: Pichon, 1888), 44, was very much against the logic of separation as discussed in the text above. In a monograph, almost never cited, he wrote: "When you set about to distribute the cake you won't be able to distribute the injustices incurred to make it bigger."

36. Robert Kuttner, *Economic Illusions: The False Trade-off between Equity and Efficiency* (Philadelphia: University of Pennsylvania Press, 1987).

37. Wojciech Kopczuk, Joel Slemrod, and Shlomo Yitzhaki, "Why World Redistribution Fails," National Bureau of Economic Research, Working Paper 9186 (September 2002).

38. Robert Nozick, *Anarchy, State, and Utopia* (Oxford: Blackwell, 1974).

39. Frederic von Hayek, *The Constitution of Liberty* (Chicago: University of Chicago Press, 1960).

40. For a convincing critique of such a position, see in particular Helen Alford and Michael Naughton, *Managing As If Faith Mattered* (Notre Dame, Ind.: University of Notre Dame Press, 2001).

41. John Waldron, *The Right to Private Property* (Oxford: Clarendon Press, 1988).

42. Hayek, *The Constitution of Liberty*, 85.

43. Amartya Sen, *Development as Freedom* (New York: Anchor Books, 2000).

44. For a penetrating exposition of the personalist view of freedom and the notion of human rights, see Karol Wojtyla, *The Acting Person* (London: Dordrecht, 1979).

45. Jacob Viner, "The Intellectual History of Laissez-Faire," *Journal of Law and Economics* 30 (1960): 68.

46. See Torsten Persson and Guido Tabellini, "Is Inequality Harmful for Growth? Theory and Evidence" (New York: National Bureau of Economic Research, 1991), for showing that societies with serious distribution conflicts have also the lowest growth rates. Refinements of the idea of an equitable distribution of wealth as a public good can be found in Inge Kaul, Isabelle Grunberg, and Marc Stern, eds., *Global Public Goods: International Cooperation in the 21st Century* (New York: Oxford University Press, 1999).

47. Blinder, *Hard Heads, Soft Heart;* Stefano Zamagni, "Social Paradoxes of Growth and Civil Economy," in G. Gandolfo and F. Marzano, eds., *Economic Theory and Social Justice* (London: Macmillan, 1999).

NINE **Equitable Global Wealth Distribution**

A Global Public Good and a Building Block
for the Global Common Good

HELEN ALFORD, O.P.

What we've got is divergence, big time.

—Larry Summers

The increase in global economic inequality is one of the most serious side effects of globalization, as Stefano Zamagni shows in his contribution to this volume (chapter 8), even if it can be difficult to measure exactly how much inequality we have.[1] The nearest relevant statistics, however, brought together by the United Nations Development Program (UNDP) in their Human Development Reports, make striking reading, as the table below shows, using data from the 2001 report:

TABLE 1. Signs that Something Is Wrong

- 1.2 billion people live on less than $1 per day
- 2.8 billion earn less than $2 daily
- Average per-capita income in the OECD (Organization for Economic Cooperation and Development) countries is $22,020 ($26,050 in the high-income OECD), whereas in the least-developed countries it is $1,170
- Highest per-capita income in the world is in Luxembourg, $42,769, and the lowest is in Burundi, $578

- In OECD countries (that is, the high-income countries), 130 million people earn less than 50% of the median income of the country (which puts them below the official poverty line)
- Between 1975 and 1999, per-capita income declined by around 1% in the sub-Saharan African countries, where about 10% of the world's population live, whereas it grew in all other parts of the world
- World inequality* is very high: the data we have for this statistic from 1988 and 1993 indicate that the top 1% of the world population received as much income as the bottom 57%; the top 10% of the U.S. population (about 25 million people) received the same income as 43% of the world's population (about 2 billion people).

Source: UNDP, *Human Development Report 2001,* various pages, available at www.undp.org, see also for more recent statistics.

*World inequality "looks both between and within countries—lining up all the world's people from richest to poorest (in real purchasing power) regardless of national boundaries . . . giving a much more complete picture of world inequality than a simple comparison of country averages would," *Human Development Report 2001,* 33.

Even if these statistics do not measure exactly what we are looking for when we talk about global wealth distribution (GWD), they give us the best indication at the moment that GWD is anything but equitable. What do we mean by "equitable" here? Simply that economic distribution in a globalized society should ensure that everyone has a basic minimum income that grants access to the basics of life (including clean water, health care, sufficient food—especially for children—and education, at least to the high-school level). It does not mean that everyone should have the same income, of course, since this would not only reduce an important incentive to work and produce wealth, but would also be unjust—people who contribute more to the economy should be able to earn more.[2] Access to the basics of decent human living should be quite possible for the world's population, given the level of economic output in the world as a whole. The extremely unequal distribution of global economic wealth, however, militates against this. Zamagni rightly calls the staggering inequality in a world that is generally abundant in economic goods the "great *aporia* of the present model of development."

Why is large inequality in wealth distribution a problem? Zamagni in his contribution offers many useful insights on this point. Even if we leave aside the human and moral arguments for a widely spread wealth distribution and look at GWD from a purely economic point of view, there are many problems associated with glaring inequalities. Widely spread and equitable distribution of wealth can promote competition and participation, tending to increase levels of economic activity, and this can lead, if the activity in question respects the environment and its output is used properly, to greater possibilities for human flourishing. Without other factors intervening to prevent it, such an economic and social situation should promote ongoing development among all sectors of society and in all its dimensions, thus promoting the common good. Equitable and wide GWD would, therefore, promote development of the world economy.[3] Large inequality, then, is an economic problem as well as a human (moral) one.[4] Zamagni cites the work of Edward Glaeser et al. on the distortion that too much wealth in the hands of a small number can produce; in such situations, for instance, we tend to see subversion of regulatory mechanisms on the part of the wealthy for their own benefit.

Widely distributed ownership of wealth, however, is not something that markets alone can be relied on to produce. Wide income and wealth distributions, while good for society, are not generated automatically by market mechanisms. Often governments or other actors have to intervene to ensure sufficient levels of income and asset equity. Since these "wide distributions" are good for society, and since they have to be "produced" (whether or not by means of the market), we could categorize them as "public goods," a concept that has spawned an extensive literature within the discipline of economics. We could call an "equitable global wealth distribution" (EGWD) a "global public good," as it is indeed treated in a recent publication of the UNDP.[5]

The Catholic social tradition uses the idea of the "common good" as the basic principle for guiding economic distribution, but its definition is often left in general terms and, in particular, there is usually little analysis of how to bring about greater distributive equity. The revived and, in some ways, new interest in public goods within economic thought is an opportunity to link thinking on public good to that of the common good, and thus for Catholic social thought (CST) to deal with the question of EGWD in a more practical way. Similarly, it will become clear in the text that follows that there are limitations to the theory of public goods, and that "common good" thinking could provide a stronger basis for "public good" thinking than that of the liberal philosophy, which is based on the idea of the *homo oeconomicus* that underlies most economic thought. Zamagni rightly points out in his article that the theoretical (anthropological) assumptions underlying economic theory need to be addressed if it is to deal with an *aporia* like that of the staggering global inequity in wealth distribution. We will not attempt to make a rigorous comparison between the theoretical underpinnings of the ideas of the "common good" and of the "public good," although we will look at their definitions, compare them, and see what is useful in the "public good" theory from the point of view of a "common good" approach to the EGWD problem. In this essay we want to focus on the more practical level, specifically by examining how the idea of a "public good" is useful in creating effective strategies for dealing with the GWD problem. In a way, then, this chapter can be seen as a follow-up to Zamagni's.

WHAT ARE PUBLIC GOODS?

Public goods have been extensively treated by economists, but a problem we immediately face when dealing with their analysis is the confusion of terms and ideas, with "a dozen different issues, each of which brings along its own idiosyncratic model and relies on its own special set of assumptions."[6] In order to make a short and coherent presentation here, we largely restrict ourselves to the main ideas about public goods presented in the book we have already cited, *Global Public Goods*, which we will refer to from now on by its authors, Inge Kaul, et al. The authors try to simplify this theoretical complexity by focusing on three major issues, which they refer to as nonexcludability, nonrivalry, and externalities.

Nonexcludability means that the benefits derived from the good cannot be limited to the person who pays for it (that is, others cannot be excluded from its benefits). Further, this means that the person who pays for it is also paying for the enjoyment of the good by others. Examples here would include cleaning up and maintaining common land, which is open to the enjoyment of all, or providing infrastructure such as roads (unless they are toll roads, in which case there is a mechanism for excluding people's enjoyment of the good). When a good is nonexclusive, we have the potential problem of "free riding," in which those who do not pay for a good still try to maximize their benefit from it.

Nonrivalry means that if one person benefits from the good, no one else is impeded from benefiting from it. Therefore, clean air or a large, well-kept beach approximates to a good that users enjoy in a nonrivalrous way.

Few public goods are "pure." Peace and equity would be examples of pure public goods since they are perfectly nonexclusive and nonrivalrous (and indeed the opposite—the more people "use" them, the more they are strengthened). Most of the public goods we discuss here are "impure." This means that the goods are partially exclusive (a road leads to only one place or another—it will not be accessible to all) or that enjoying them may involve rivalry (our big beach will start to get crowded). Crucially, however, they are sufficiently nonexclusive, and users are not competing for their use in sufficiently high numbers, that market mechanisms are poor at producing them. Two special kinds of impure public goods are club goods (where enjoyment is exclusive to club members; an example here is that of areas where the residents have pooled together to share security systems, such as entrances protected by gates and security cameras); or goods that are nonexclusive but for which users may compete, such as common land or waters (see table 2 below).

A wide and equitable global wealth distribution is a nonexclusive good insofar as it provides widely dispersed income and asset ownership, thus actively trying to overcome the exclusivity inherent in wealth ownership. It is a club good in organizations

TABLE 2.   Private and Public Goods

	Rivalrous Users	Nonrivalrous Users
Exclusive	Private good (e.g., property)	Network/club good (i.e., mostly nonrivalrous inside the club, e.g., business networks and cooperatives)
Nonexclusive	Subject to congestion or depletion, yet accessible to all; common land	Pure public good; justice, peace, clean air; some global commons (high seas, ozone layer)

Source: Based on the similar table in Kaul et al., *Global Public Goods,* 5.
Note: Public goods, including impure public goods, are in the shaded areas.

such as the European Union, where large "structural funds," for instance, are aimed at redistributing wealth from the richer regions of the union to the poorer ones. EGWD can also involve nonrivalry among users of goods, where ownership of land or other assets is held in common, such as common land on which anyone can walk or, as in medieval England, graze their animals.

A third idea introduced above was that of "externalities." Richard Cornes and Todd Sandler argue that "public goods, notably pure public goods, 'can be thought of as special cases of externalities.'"[7] Externalities are benefits (or costs) that arise from a private exchange but which cannot be confined to those who are party to the exchange, and from which others can therefore benefit (or be damaged, if the externality is negative). A good example would be education. A person who is educated can increase her earning power, so the personal benefit of having been schooled could in theory be calculated by subtracting the earnings anticipated without education from those that she is able to earn after being educated. However, compared to this (relatively small) benefit to the individual arising from her education, the externalities of this transaction, when seen as part of the system of education of the population as a whole, are huge. If people can be relied on to read, then those issuing public warnings or other signs are greatly helped; advertisers can expect the general population to read their publicity, and employers save enormously on training. All of these externalities help businesses to run more efficiently, market their products more effectively, and sell more of their products, since their customers are better educated and therefore generally earning more income. Such externalities therefore contribute enormously to the generation and distribution of wealth. As a result of these large externalities, which dwarf the private benefits of education, there is a big temptation for market actors to "free ride" on others' schooling or to limit their instructional costs by furtively off-loading them onto other market actors. Therefore, markets are often not good "producers" of education, or are only good in a limited way and in the context of a broader system. Other nonmarket mechanisms (usually coordinated by the government) are required.

Near the beginning of their book, Kaul et al. ask, "What is a public good?" they continue: "We know that the marketplace is the most efficient way of producing private goods. But the market relies on a set of goods that it cannot itself provide: property rights, predictability, safety, nomenclature and so on. These goods often need to be provided by non-market or modified market mechanisms."[8] Here we see another way of characterizing public goods in relation to private ones. It is on the basis of a shared set of public goods that the production and exchange of private goods (that is, market mechanisms) are possible. In other words, public goods are what make private goods possible; public goods form the basis of the market mechanism and the "infrastructure" on which the market operates.

One final point: Markets are not good producers of public goods; the non-market sphere (what we could call the cultural—including religious—sphere) is a lot better at "producing" public goods such as a commitment to peace, a clear understanding of justice, and both practical and active solidarity (through, for instance, the churches, nonprofit organizations, and nongovernmental organizations [NGOs]). But since many "impure" public goods, such as transport or health infrastructure, are extremely expensive and there is no government at the global level to raise taxes to pay for these goods, the fact that markets produce them badly means that they tend to suffer from underprovision. According to Kaul et al., this underprovision is largely due to the "free rider" problem as well as to the "prisoners' dilemma." In the latter, people choose a noncooperative solution to a problem because they do not have full information, due to a lack of collaboration and of mutual trust, and thus end up with a solution that is suboptimal both for themselves and for other actors. Underprovision is particularly acute at the international level, where there is no global government to step in and fill the gap left by the market. This is perhaps especially true in regard to global wealth distribution, one might add, where the international institutions set up after the Second World War to oversee global equity in the economic sphere are now operating in a very different environment from the one in which they were initiated.[9]

Kaul et al., however, argue that underproduction is due to policy gaps (rather than to the lack of a global government as such) because "public policy-making has not yet adjusted to present-day realities."[10] They identify three major gaps of this kind: in "jurisdiction," "participation," and "incentive," which we will discuss further below in relation to the public good of EGWD. In brief, the jurisdictional gap refers to the need to provide global goods at a global level, while the main actors in policy making remain the nation-states. What is needed to overcome this gap is "a jurisdictional loop that runs from the national to the international and back to the national—by way of several intermediate levels, regional and subregional."[11] The participation gap refers to the lack of institutional mechanisms for allowing any actors other than governments to take part in deciding global policy. (The International Labor Organization here, with its tripartite representation of governments, employers, and workers is the exception that proves the rule.) New ways need to be found to give voice and power to actors other than governments. The incentive gap, or the lack of incentive to produce global public goods, needs to be addressed by demonstrating the advantages of cooperation at the global level to produce these goods and then to put in place the mechanisms that allow their costs and benefits to be fairly distributed. Kaul et al. suggest that addressing these policy gaps should also address the underproduction of global public goods.

Summarizing what has been said so far, we can say:

1. Pure public goods are nonexclusive in consumption, and their users are not rivaling each other for their use. This is what gives rise to the problem of producing them. Impure public goods have some privatizable aspects, which can mean that their users are not competing with each other but can exclude others from their use (club goods), or that these goods may be nonexclusive but subject to user rivalry (commons). It can also mean that they have "joint products," that is, some outcomes that are privatizable and others that are not.

2. Public goods can be thought of as an "externality," benefits (or costs) that arise from a private exchange but which cannot be confined to those who are party to the exchange.

3. Public goods are what make the market mechanism and the production and consumption of private goods possible. They provide the foundation and infrastructure of the market, but this mechanism does not "produce" enough public goods to maintain the public goods infrastructure on which the market is based.

4. Markets are not able to produce sufficient public goods.

5. Crises are caused by the lack of public goods (either "loud" crises, such as a financial crash, or "silent" crises, such as the daily death toll from famine and poverty).

6. This lack at the global level can be ascribed to three policy gaps: that of jurisdiction (or a global governmental/policymaking gap), that of participation (or a global institutional gap), and that of incentive (or a policy outcome gap).

Points 2 and 3 are, in a way, the inverse of each other. In the first case, public goods are seen to be a by-product or "external product" of the main (private, market-based) exchange. In the second case, public goods are seen as the basis, foundation, or "universe" in which private goods can be produced and consumed. If we try to put these two aspects together, we can see that there is a reciprocal relationship between public and private goods, but that the relationship is not stable. Let us use an agricultural analogy: markets leech out the "nutrients" from the "soil" of the public goods on which they are based and from which they draw "nourishment" and are supported, but they do not return enough nutrients to the soil on which they depend for the public good/private good "ecosystem" to maintain itself. If left unattended, the market mechanism would destroy its own life-support system by sucking it dry, thereby ensuring its own destruction and that of the whole ecosystem.

Thus, welfare systems provided by the state and voluntary or nonprofit organizations are essential in making sure that the economy as a whole, including private market transactions, can function properly.[12] Similarly, as we pointed out above, other things being equal, a genuine EGWD would stimulate and expand the operation of the market. The mutual relationship between the market mechanism and the public goods on which it relies to function must therefore be stabilized by non-market transactions, which fill the gaps left by the market and which supplement the creation and sustenance of public goods. Kaul et al. speak of "policy gaps" and the problems of free-riding and lack of cooperation (prisoners' dilemma) that impede the creation of enough public goods to sustain the market system and the overall ecosystem of goods; hence, points 4, 5, and 6. We can show this graphically (see diagram 1 below), both in general and in regard to a particular public good such as financial stability.

According to the first chapter of Kaul et al., we can split the general category of global public goods into two parts: "final" and "intermediate." Final goods are "outcomes rather than 'goods' in the standard sense," where the "standard" sense referred to is the economic one of a tradable product (only economists could call this the "standard" sense of the word "good"!). Intermediate public goods "contribute towards the provision of final global goods."[13] In Kaul et al.'s conclusion to the book this classification is developed in three categories: natural global commons, human-made global commons, and global policy outcomes. Natural global commons, for example, include the ozone layer; human-made global commons, include universal norms and principles (such as universally recognized human rights) and knowledge;[14] and global policy outcomes include peace, health, financial stability, equity, justice, and so on. In the case of the natural global commons, the main problem that we face is overuse; in the case of the human-made, it is underuse; and in the case of the global policy outcomes, it is underproduction. Underuse of the

DIAGRAM 1.   Public Goods Support the Market Mechanism

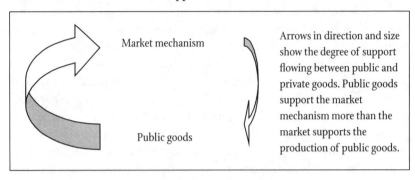

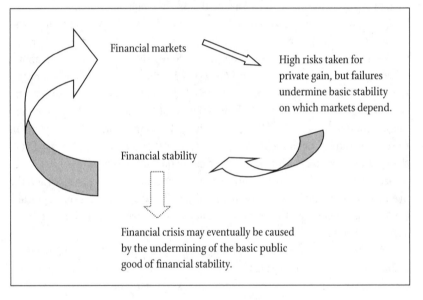

human-made global commons means, for instance, that people are not able to exercise their generally recognized human rights because of repression, or that they cannot benefit from knowledge because of lack of access to it. As a result, these potentially publicly available and accessible goods are not "used" as widely as they could be. All of these goods are relevant to the question of EGWD. First, we need a widely held belief that equitably distributing wealth is a good thing before we can really see efforts being made toward achieving it, as has been the case with the idea of human rights. Second, we need effective (human-made) policies and mechanisms so that the presently excluded poor can be included in a system of equitable wealth distribution. And third, insofar as this is important in obtaining EGWD, we need to work toward the achievement of EGWD as a global policy outcome.[15]

An even more useful way of categorizing public goods is to think of them in a cycle, beginning from generally held values, running through institutions, infrastructure, and policies, and ending up with the state of affairs required by the originally held values. We can illustrate these categories of public goods also (see diagram 2) with respect to EGWD:

> 1st order: Generally held values or beliefs as public goods, such as ideas of justice and equity, of freedoms and rights, including property rights and so on. For these to be *public* there must be some level of consensus over what counts as a value to be held by all. This is where religion and culture can be important in creating and sustaining public goods.

> 2nd order: Social institutions as public goods, which are built upon the first-order public goods and which in turn are needed to maintain or reproduce the same first-order goods. These are of two basic kinds:

>> 2a: This class includes the legal and educational systems, all kinds of regulatory systems to promote predictability and safety, shared systems of nomenclature, market mechanisms, systems of cooperation (OECD, European Union), and international regimes (such as the trade regime).

>> 2b: This class includes physical infrastructure: transport and traffic control and the physical plant of the health, education, and security systems.

> 3rd order: Policies and their effective implementation as public goods: reducing pollution, preventing global warming, eradicating disease, expanding access to knowledge, supervising banks.

> 4th order: States of being (outcomes of the operation of the previous orders), such as peace, justice, equity; development; clean environment, water, air; healthy population; financial stability; preservation of artistic patrimony; preservation of biodiversity.

The first- and fourth-order goods are inherently good (good in themselves, "final" goods, or "policy outcomes" in the terminology of Kaul et al.), while the second and third orders are instrumental goods (or what Kaul et al. call "intermediate" goods). These distinctions bring us close to the understanding of "good" in the common good tradition, and thus we begin to see how thinking and practical initiatives based on the idea of public goods could be useful in promoting the global common good (GCG).

DIAGRAM 2.   Cycle of Public Goods Needed to Produce Equitable Global Wealth Distribution (EGWD)

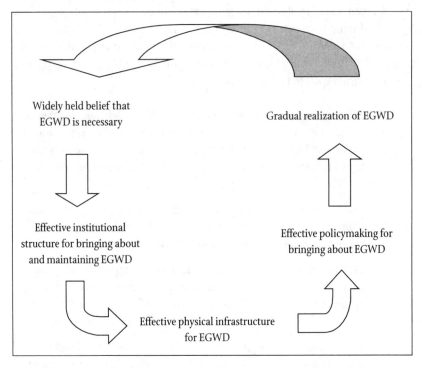

WHAT IS THE COMMON GOOD?

In Catholic social thought (CST), the idea of the "common good,"[16] rather than "public goods," has been very important in dealing with questions such as equitable distribution. It is also like the idea of the public good in that it has been employed in different ways, even if we restrict ourselves to its various usages within CST alone. Philosophically, the idea of the common good within CST is derived ultimately from the Aristotelian-Thomistic tradition. In this worldview, using the language of Kaul et al., the common good is both an intermediate and a final good, providing both the conditions for, and being the outcome of, the action, collective as well as individual, of a community pursuing its good. Clearly, the idea of good here is different from the "standard" one in economic discourse. For St. Thomas, goodness and existence are closely linked (for him, existence is a good, a participation in the existence of God). This also means that what is good for me, and what is good for a human community, depends on the kind of beings we are (or, in other words, the kind of existence we have). Although there may be a gray area where we cannot be sure whether things are good or bad for us, and it may often be difficult to judge whether pursuing something is good or bad, nevertheless in principle we can say that there are (objectively) some things that are good for us, given the kind of beings we are, and other things that are not. Our understanding of what is good and bad may develop over time, but that will be as a result (we hope) of a deepening perception of what human beings are, even if both history and many present-day situations provide examples of how mistaken ideas can be widely spread and distort our understanding of what is good.

Coming back to our definition, then, the common good is the condition and the result of human activity in community. For our purposes, the relevant community is the whole of the human race and the equitable distribution of wealth among its members, belongs to its common good. In order to understand more clearly what we mean by the common good, we need to say more about what is the meaning of "good" and "common" and then put them together. We will subsequently be in a position to grasp how thinking about the common good and the public good can be better used in resolving the EGWD problem.

What Is a Good?

According to Mortimer Adler and Walter Farrell, "Every good can and must be regarded in two ways: as the object of some being's desire . . . and as the perfection of some being's nature."[17] Each (morally significant) action that we undertake is motivated by the desire to attain some kind of good for ourselves and for others; and, if we achieve it, then we can enjoy that perfection of our personhood, that good. As we said above, goodness and being are strongly connected, but at the same time, we can sometimes be mistaken about what is good for us—we do not automatically know what is good, but we have to grow in knowledge and wisdom and follow the advice of trustworthy people. We can therefore distinguish between two types of good: true and apparent. This distinction is necessary to deal with any false assessment of what is "good," either for ourselves or for others. Aquinas believes that no one acts except to try to realize some good that he or she desires, but too often we are mistaken about what is good for us. Dishonest executives make fraudulent statements to fiscal or other authorities not because they want to do something "bad" but because they have convinced themselves that they are going to get something "good" out of doing it. However, what they do *is* bad, certainly for society as a whole and, in the end, also for them. We know through our experience of crime, exploitation, corruption, and so on that people often try to realize a good (money, say) through bad means, or try to realize what is patently a false good (such as the sense of well-being fleetingly obtained from taking heroin).

Thus, only one of the terms, true and apparent, describes a genuine good to be realized. Knowing that such a distinction can be made, we are invited to make a judgment as to whether any good we pursue is a genuine (true) one or not. When our passions are deeply involved, it is often difficult to choose what we know to be the right move, since our strong desire for immediate gratification can dominate our evaluation of a good. We can either judge it to be good for us (when in a calmer moment we might decide otherwise) or to be only an apparent good and yet not stop ourselves from pursuing it. Either way, we can end up doing something that we will later regret. Similarly, sometimes we do not know enough about a good and pursue it when it is doing us harm. An example is tobacco; for centuries, it was not known that tobacco posed major health risks, so people used it widely for its pleasant effects. Much wealth was created out of cultivating and selling tobacco, and this wealth was distributed through wages, dividends to shareholders, taxes, and corporate profits. Now, however, it is clear to us that tobacco is not a true good; its pleasant effect masks some deadly side effects.

Knowing what is truly good is an ongoing process for us. Even though we do not fully understand it, at least as individuals, it is essential for us to strive to distinguish between true and merely apparent goods. Apart from this distinction, some other distinctions are also helpful. Some goods we desire solely because through them we may obtain others; these are what we might call "instrumental" goods, such as all types of technology. Still others we desire, as noted earlier, because they perfect or fulfill us in themselves, such as peace, justice, and self-esteem. These are sometimes called intrinsic or inherent goods. Moreover, goods can be desirable in themselves but also useful. Moral virtues, for example, are desirable in themselves— they perfect or fulfill us as rational agents—and because they fit us for that comprehensive being well and doing well that we call "happiness." Goods of the body are sometimes treated as a separate case, since our bodies are not only instruments for our own use. Health, for instance, is desirable as an aid to all our other desires, but health is also desirable in itself. The proof is that we would choose to be healthy even if health were unconnected to any other good. Goods of the body are difficult to categorize in terms of the extrinsic/intrinsic or instrumental/inherent distinctions since our bodies are at once ourselves and our most immediate instrument. The last set of distinctions we introduce in the next section.[18]

What Is Common?

Some goods are more susceptible to being shared, or held in common, than are others. Examples of "naturally" shareable (or common) goods would be: knowledge, justice, and clean air. Others are more "naturally" private, and we have to organize equitable structures of *distribution* for these to be fairly dispersed among the members of the human community. The classic "particular" goods, as we could call these, are money and land, though we should not forget the tradition of "common land." In the promotion of the common good, both common and particular goods have their role, but the latter, such as property and other assets, need to be directed toward the common good, first, through equitable distribution, and second, through proper use. For example, from the first important encyclical of the papal tradition of CST onward, *Rerum novarum* (1891), the popes have argued strongly that the working poor should be able to gain some economic security by earning enough to save toward the purchase of their own home. Such a position necessarily requires a wide distribution of the housing stock. On the other hand, in addressing the wealthy, *Rerum novarum* reminds propertyowners that they do not have the right to use their property however they please. John Paul II in *Sollicitudo rei socialis* puts this another way by saying that property has a "social mortgage"—it should upbuild community life and the common good. This distinction between particular and common helps us to understand the importance of just structures of wealth distribution. Since wealth is one of those goods that is not shared without diminishment, we actively need to promote fair structures of distribution in society.

How does this analysis enable us to understand better the relationship between our activities, the goods they produce, and the common good? The common good is made up of various goods produced at different levels of the community—goods of the person; goods produced in the family; goods produced in business or schools or hospitals or other institutions in which we work with others; goods of the local political divisions, such as the village, town, rural area, or borough; and goods of more inclusive communities, such as the province, region, state, nation, or international community, including international organizations such as the United Nations. At all levels, there is an ordering: instrumental goods are generated as bases for the development of inherent goods, and, as stated, the use of particular goods needs to be directed toward the common good. In practice, this means that managers, politicians, and others in authority, if they are working out of the common good model, make decisions about resources or people in a way different from those who do not rely on this model as a guide. Since the intrinsic goods must always be respected in every decision that is made, whether in a business or nonprofit organization or in a local or national government department, these goods must be kept in mind "in parallel" when we are thinking about the generation of instrumental goods, such as the generation of profits in a business. So when, for instance, a manager allocates resources or organizes an activity, he should always keep in mind the people impacted by the decision and ensure that the use of these instrumental goods is always ordered toward the development of the intrinsic goods. Intrinsic goods are thus not left to be pursued during afterwork hours in a "sequential" way (along the lines of, "first, we make money, then we try to do something worthwhile with it once it is made"), but are constantly kept in mind and respected in every decision regarding the generation of instrumental goods, so that the proper ordering of the goods is always maintained.[19]

PUTTING THE TWO TOGETHER: PUBLIC GOODS AND THE COMMON GOOD

Having looked at the idea of a "public good" and of the "common good," we can begin to understand how they help us to deal with a single family of problems. Just as Dennis McCann (chapter 7, this volume) has seen an affinity between Amartya Sen's capabilities approach and the ideas of participation and initiative-taking in the Christian social tradition, so, too, we can see an affinity between the idea of the public good and that of the common good. Many of the goods most discussed in the public goods literature would fall into the category of common instrumental goods, according to the common good analysis given above. When we talk about traffic lights or the international trade regime, we are talking about good things that we use to obtain other things. This makes them instrumental according to the common good system of thinking that we have presented. Since they are also shared, these goods are common rather than particular. The public goods literature enriches our understanding of these goods' shared character by dealing with how they are produced, which is important if we want to know more about how to "produce" the public good of EGWD. Kaul et al. give us indications of where the problems are in producing more global public goods as well as what we could do to resolve them.

Another point of connection can be seen when public goods are thought of as the infrastructure that makes possible the creation of private goods. This viewpoint on public goods seems to be close to John XXIII's definition of the common good in *Mater et magistra*, where he refers only to its foundational level: "the sum total of conditions of social living whereby men are enabled to achieve their own integral perfection more fully and more easily."[20] Public goods provide the infrastructure for social living, through which we can strive toward the creation of an ever more genuine and complete common good. The common good here is the framework within which we strive for human development in community as well as the goal toward which that human development and those conditions are aimed. Using the language we have introduced here, we can say that the common good has both foundational and excellent dimensions—it is both a means and an end. This statement is less surprising than one might think, in that all the ideals or goals for which we aim direct our actions and provide the measure by which we evaluate at the end of the day whether we have accomplished what we set out to do. In the same way, the common good is a goal toward which we are striving by promoting the development of all human beings in community, and this goal imposes certain conditions on the development of that community.

When we consider intrinsic goods, the overlap between the two concepts becomes more complex. Insofar as concepts developed within economic theory and the Catholic social tradition (with their very different underlying philosophies) can be similar, pure public goods correspond to common intrinsic goods, whereas "ethnic hatred" and other global "bads" (philosophers would say "harms") fall into the apparent goods category—they are not true goods. The public goods literature finds it more difficult to deal with these "goods" (or "bads/harms") by employing its own concepts and terminology. Ethan Kapstein's paper on distributive justice as a public good in Kaul et al. illustrates the problem; and since distributive justice relates directly to EGWD, it is worth looking at this problem in more detail.

Kapstein shows how an equitable distribution of wealth depends upon values inculcated in the general population, partly through religion or culture and partly through hard experiences such as the Great Depression and the Second World War. Kapstein suggests that, after the Second World War, the redistribution of wealth at national and international levels was pursued through the creation of the welfare state (national) and the adoption of free trade (international). Although at the national level, the welfare state seemed to work, at least for a time, it is no longer doing so, and the international policy of free trade stopped being effective in redistributing wealth a long time before that, if it ever was really effective. As a result, inequality both within and between countries has never been greater. In order to deal with this problem, Kapstein suggests a revision of the Bretton Woods organizations, set up as they were to oversee the international economic system. Migration should be treated as part of the remit of a revised set of Bretton Woods organizations (Zamagni has made important proposals here), and workers should be given a voice within them; an international social minimum income should be agreed upon, depending on the costs of a decent standard of living in different countries; finally, according to Kapstein, "a new Bretton Woods would have to consider capital liberalization, and how mobile capital can best be harnessed in the interests of efficiency and fairness."[21] Coupled with this should be greater integration between trade and labor policies, consideration of a world tax organization, greater investment in health, and more effective aid.

Kapstein's paper approaches the question of distributive justice as we would probably have expected him to do: it gives a historical account of how the postwar order was meant to bring about more equitable distribution but did not, and how one might address this problem today at the policy level. He does not approach his subject with the technical terms of the public goods literature—terms such as excludability, rivalry, or externalities—even though his article appears in *Global Public Goods*, in which the first chapter proceeds to define public goods through the three terms just mentioned. Those who edited that book, therefore, recognize that public good theory is not broad enough to deal with an issue such as distributive justice, even if they want to see it as a public good. Kapstein's paper shows as clearly that public goods such as EGWD need to be seen in relation to an underlying value base and an understanding of human culture, institutions, and history. All of these depend significantly on intrinsic goods, and we have seen that public good theory does not deal with this effectively. However, linked to a kind of cultural history such as the one that Kapstein gives, public good theory could help by applying practical ideas to the resolution of the problems involved in bringing about EGWD.

At a practical policy level, understanding in detail how to promote the global common good would require a political dialogue in order to arrive at a common understanding of what it is or could be in our day, given our circumstances. It would involve setting goals and priorities for action as well as putting into place institutions, infrastructures and policies to enable the global community to move toward achieving these ultimate goals and priorities. The common good tradition that we have been discussing so far sets basic principles and general goals for the realization of the common good, but it leaves open a vast range of choices as to how these basic principles can be put into practice or the goals can be realized. This is why many different cultural forms or historical periods can aim to achieve the common good and yet do it in practice in a myriad of different ways. Any real historical example, of course, is marred by incompetence, lack of knowledge and understanding, prejudice, and human sin and thus can never represent a perfect example of achievement of the common good. But even if there were no weakness or sin, there would still be lots of culturally different ways of achieving the common good (the recognition of which reinforces the importance of subsidiarity and local cultural identity in the creation of the global common good). What the common good model gives us is a basis for discussion and a general indication of the direction that it needs to take and the principles that it needs to respect.

DEALING WITH INEQUITABLE GLOBAL WEALTH DISTRIBUTION

So far, we have seen that EGWD is a worthwhile goal for which to aim, for economic reasons as well as for social and moral ones, and that important agencies such as the UNDP see the concept of "public good" as important in dealing with it. We have also seen that the concept of public good shares much with that of the common good. Both the economic tradition behind the "public good" concept and the philosophical/political tradition behind the "common good" idea can gain something from each other by incorporating some of the insights of the other tradition. For example, one of the economic tradition's main problems in regard to EGWD and other global public goods is its weak anthropological basis, as Zamagni points out very clearly; it is evident that it needs the theoretical reinforcement that the common good tradition can give it.

Before concluding this chapter, however, we cannot ignore the practical issues— that is, what to do about EGWD. The public goods literature can help us, in particular, with how to bring about more equitable global wealth distribution, since it is especially interested in the "production" of good "global policy outcomes" such as EGWD. In order to deal with the lack of global public goods in general, Kaul et al. suggest ways for addressing the global gaps that we mentioned earlier. Going over these and applying them to the urgent EGWD problem, in light of the idea of the global common good, could well help us to deal with the problem.

To remind ourselves, the gaps are, as Kaul et al. tell us: jurisdictional, "the discrepancies between the global boundaries of today's major policy concerns and the essentially national boundaries of policymaking"; participation, "result[ing] from the fact that we live in a multi-actor world but international cooperation is still primarily intergovernmental"; and incentive, "because moral suasion is not enough for countries to correct their international spillovers or to cooperate for the global public good."[22] Systems for international cooperation were set up when "global public goods consisted primarily of 'traffic rules' between countries,"[23] and now they are insufficient to deal with the genuinely global problems that we face, such as EGWD. To deal with the gaps, therefore, we need to create "loops" to fill them: a jurisdictional loop, running from the national to the international and back again; a participation loop, bringing all kinds of nongovernmental actors into the process; and an incentive loop, so that the benefits of cooperation, and not of free-riding on the efforts of others, are properly shared by all. Two points that emerge at a general level are worth mentioning. First, different thinkers in different situations emphasize the role of one kind of actor or another in overcoming these gaps. Some stress the need for governments to act, while others argue that a reinforcement of the United Nations is needed, and still others place the main emphasis on market mechanisms and/or on civil society. Second, it is clear that specific policies in specific situations need to be tailored to those situations and make the most of the strengths that are already there. If, for instance, there exists a strong culture of private enterprise, then one would want to make the most of this cultural variable without undermining the role of other policy actors. Kaul et al. consider these gaps and loops in general; here we will try to apply them to the EGWD problem.

In regard to the jurisdictional gap, Kaul et al. make several interesting suggestions. These include: (1) creating an "externality profile" for each country; (2) internalizing the control of, or costs of, the spillovers created by a country that are identified in the profile; (3) linking national and global policy agendas (such as reorganizing ministries so that they have a "foreign" component rather than a special "foreign office"); and (4) strengthening regional cooperation. Let us look at these in regard to EGWD.

The idea of the externality profile is that it makes clear to governments and to their constituencies what positive and negative effects they are having on other countries and vice versa. Such profiles thus provide information on which international cooperation can be more solidly based. Effective measurements of externalities and their costs have to be made—a form of measurement that is still in its infancy, although much work has already been done. Kaul et al. make a point that is interesting if we try to apply it to EGWD: "If these profiles were to show that all countries have a negative overall balance on their outgoing and incoming externality accounts, it would be clear that the world is caught in a serious prisoner's [sic] dilemma with potentially large implications—be it faltering world economic growth, global warming or the spread of disease and ill health."[24] It is possible to imagine that part of an externality profile could show that low levels of wealth and income in poor countries mean that these countries do not contribute enough to world economic development, given the size of their populations (a negative externality). Meanwhile, it could also be shown that rich countries similarly do not contribute as much to world economic development as they should, given their wealth and their populations (rich people, for instance, spend a smaller proportion of their income than do poor people). This would be another negative externality, thus tending to produce a negative "externality account," as Kaul et al. call it. Knowledge of such a situation could be an important factor in creating incentives to do something about it. Furthermore, as Kaul et al. say elsewhere, "Inequity creates cross-border externalities in the form of social instability, ethnic tensions and environmental damage. . . . [I]t is also an inherently transnational issue and an issue of global, systemic risk. The reason is that inequality has assumed such proportions that policies 'merely' aimed at creating a level playing field no longer suffice. . . . Equal opportunities for *unequal* players produce more inequity."[25] Information on externality profiles would be extremely valuable in convincing governments and their electorates across the rich world of the advantages not only to the poor *but also to themselves* of a more equitable GWD. Even if the application of public good theory and the idea of policy gaps did nothing more than help us at this level, it would already be a major step forward.

Kaul et al. recognize that the major actors are the national ones. National governments, therefore, need to be given the tools (and the incentives) to act globally. These governments participate in international organizations precisely as sole representatives of their countries and not of the global human family. In this respect, the situation at the international level can be compared to that of the small community, where the same people who look after their own homesteads meet together in council to govern the community as a whole. They may be able to broaden their vision so as to promote the good of the community as a whole; on the contrary, focusing on the care of their own homesteads may make it difficult for them to see clearly the good of the entire group. It would seem likely, however, that the homesteader in the community meeting would be more able to envision and promote the common good of his community than would the representative of a national government (which has to respond to the national electorate) be able to do for the international community as a whole. In practice, however, this form of cooperation at the international level is the only realistic possibility we have, and therefore it must be made to work as well as possible. If we can think of what Kaul et al. call the jurisdictional gap rather as a jurisdictional "bridge," helping governments to make the transition from a particular, national viewpoint to a global one, then we can hope, despite the many problems faced by such a system of governance, that progress toward more EGWD can be made.

The second gap involves participation. Two main issues stand out here as important for the prospects for EGWD: the participation of poorer countries in the major international organizations (United Nations, International Monetary Fund (IMF), World Trade Organization, and so on); and the participation of NGOs and civil society in general. Sen points out in *Development and Freedom*, and elsewhere, that countries with democratic governments do not have famines. Those in power have too much to lose by not responding to the basic needs of their people—say, by ensuring that they have enough food—since these same people constitute their electorate and their power base. Similarly, many problems to do with EGWD are not addressed because there is no real democracy at the level of the organizations charged with overseeing international cooperation. Some of the most important of these organizations, such as the IMF, were set up after the Second World War and still are dominated by the influence of their original members, who are largely the wealthy countries of the world. If EGWD is to be addressed, the governments of poor countries need more voice in these major international organizations. Similarly, civil society also needs more structured involvement. An example already exists in the oldest such organization, the International Labor Organization, which, from its inception in 1919, has included representatives of unions and of employers as well as of governments.

Giving people the "incentive" to work toward EGWD involves closing the last gap. It is crucial for people in rich countries to see the benefits to themselves as well as to those in poorer countries of EGWD, if changes to bring it about are to be sustainable. Governments can offer fiscal incentives or subsidies, but no international tax organization exists to initiate these kinds of incentives at the global level. Nonfiscal incentives toward EGWD would be created by the externality profiles we have already discussed, since they would give people the information to see that they also gain from a situation of global economic equity.

We can complement these policy initiatives by drawing insights from the common good tradition. According to this tradition, policies that are technically effective will nevertheless fail in practice if they are not made to work by people who have developed the virtuous disposition or moral character needed to operate them. Indeed, for policies really to work, these dispositions must be widely spread within the general populace as a whole.[26] Policies are not magic; neither can they be effective if we treat them as if they were mechanisms: set them up properly and then let them work like clockwork. Rather, policies have to be put into effect by people with the capabilities, will, character, and good intentions to make them work. Thus, dealing with all these gaps on the policy level has its counterpart on the human and moral level. Technical competence wielded by men and women of virtue is needed to implement effective strategies to promote EGWD as a part of the global common good.

Notes

I would like to acknowledge the very great help that Margaret Atkins has given me in putting this essay together as well as that of Albino Barrera and the editors of this volume, and the comments received from participants in the two conferences that were part of creating this book.

1. We should say at the outset that not everyone agrees that this is a problem, and statistics tend to indicate that absolute poverty is decreasing (as Zamagni also observes), even if *relative* inequality is increasing. Various (anonymous) contributors to *The Economist*, for instance, do not think that global wealth inequality is a problem. Furthermore, we only have certain kinds of statistics for speaking about global wealth distribution (GWD), and some that would be very useful are lacking. In "The Nature of Wealth," the introduction to this book, John Stuart Mills's two definitions of wealth were mentioned: one based on assets, which he suggests is more often the measure of wealth for a country; and the other based on income, or rights to income through capital or property ownership, which is how we usually gauge the wealth of a person. Complete statistics on both these kinds of wealth are lacking at the global level.

2. In practice, actual pay differentials do not always reflect the contribution of people's work to the economy. We are not trying to defend the often inequitable pay differentials that

we see around us today, which are indeed part of the problem when we look at inequitable wealth distribution. The point here is merely that, other things being equal, the principle of differentiating the pay that people receive on the basis of what they contribute is sound and just.

3. See also Box 1.2 on page 17 of *Human Development Report 2001*.

4. However, we should be careful before assuming that more economic growth in poorer nations will "naturally" or "automatically" lead to improved literacy and education in general, better health care, and better life expectancy—all key elements of human development and of the common good. As *Human Development Report 2001* shows, there is no automatic link between improvements in these aspects of human flourishing and increases in income (see figures 1.3 and 1.4 on pages 13 and 15, respectively). It is clear that other factors are important, not the least of which is the distribution of income within the country itself (see pp. 17–18 and figures 1.6 and 1.7 on within-country inequality). See also *Human Development Report 1996*, which was dedicated to looking at the complex relationship between levels of income and levels of human development.

5. Ethan B. Kapstein, "Distributive Justice as an International Public Good: A Historical Perspective," in *Global Public Goods: International Cooperation in the 21st Century,* ed. Inge Kaul, Isabelle, Grunberg, and Marc A. Stern (New York: Oxford University Press, 1999).

6. Stephen Shmanske, *Public Goods, Mixed Goods and Monopolistic Competition* (College Station: Texas A&M University Press, 1991), quoted in Kaul et al., *Global Public Goods,* 3.

7. Richard Cornes and Todd Sandler, *The Theory of Externalities, Public Goods, and Club Goods* (Cambridge: Cambridge University Press, 1986), 5.

8. Kaul et al., *Global Public Goods,* xix–xx.

9. See, for instance, Kapstein, "Distributive Justice."

10. Kaul et al., *Global Public Goods,* 450.

11. Ibid., 466.

12. For more on this, see J. K. Galbraith, *The New Industrial State* (Boston: Houghton Mifflin, 1978).

13. Kaul et al., *Global Public Goods,* 13.

14. The title "human-made" here is somewhat problematic. While it is no doubt true that, if human beings had not existed on the planet, these goods would not have been "used" (if these goods refer to universal norms and rights), human beings only "recognize" them rather than create them. They may create the way in which they are formulated, but not the norm or right itself.

15. I am grateful to Margaret Atkins, who pointed out to me that for this kind of outcome, the most important activity and policy are made at the local level. On the principle of subsidiarity, global policy making should only exist and impact on the local level where the latter is failing or in need of support from a more general, global policy.

16. A different but related way of dealing with the idea of the common good, focused on the business enterprise, can be found in Helen J. Alford, O.P., and Michael J. Naughton, *Managing As If Faith Mattered* (Notre Dame, Ind.: University of Notre Dame Press, 2001). In particular, in this account we use the terms "foundational" and "excellent" for the extrinsic/intrinsic and/or instrumental/inherent distinction. This change in terminology was motivated by considerations of rhetoric. We could thus describe making money as a "foundational"

activity, which sounds much more worthwhile than one that is merely instrumental or extrinsic. It is also true that making enough to live on is foundational to a good life, as all texts on the common good acknowledge. However, the problem with these two terms is that they are already employed in Thomistic thought in different ways from the one we were using, and this has caused confusion. We were not aware of these usages when writing *Managing As If Faith Mattered.* After listening to the helpful critiques of Margaret Atkins and Albino Barrera on earlier drafts of this chapter, and to avoid further confusion, I have decided to revert here to the older terminology and to drop the terms "foundational" and "excellent" for the time being.

17. Mortimer J. Adler and Walter Farrell, O.P., "The Theory of Democracy—Part II," *The Thomist* 3, no. 4 (October 1941): 595.

18. Adler and Farrell have a useful footnote on this point: "The various distinctions can be summarized as follows. The unachieved good is an object of desire. The achieved good is an object of use, enjoyment, or love. As achieved, the good is either the perfection of a human being or of some other (material) thing; and the human perfection achieved is possessed either by the person who desired it, or some other person, *for whom* it was desired. Since the same good may be, at different times or in different respects, both desired and achieved, the triple distinction among goods (as used, enjoyed, or loved) divides them into three fundamental types: extrinsic (the useful), intrinsic and immanent (the enjoyable), intrinsic and separate (the lovable); and the intrinsic is divided against the extrinsic as *bonum honestum* against *bonum utile.* If now we add the subordinate distinction among intrinsic immanent goods according to whether they are possessed by man and brute in virtue of their common generic nature, or possessed by man alone in virtue of his specific difference, we can exhaustively classify every type of finite and partial good (thus excluding temporal happiness and beatitude as immanent complete goods, and God as the transcendent, hence separate, infinite object of love). There are: external goods (extrinsic, useful); bodily goods (intrinsically animal, and either useful as health or enjoyable as sensual pleasure); goods of the soul (intrinsically human, immanent, and enjoyable); social goods (intrinsically human, separate, and lovable)." Ibid., n. 45, 598–99.

19. The definition we have given, however, raises another issue: What is integral human development? To cut a long story short, we argue that it concerns a multidimensional development of the person that involves the bodily, cognitive, emotional, aesthetic, social, moral, and spiritual dimensions of our being. Ordering the creation and use of the different goods in the organization and in society to bring about this shared human development demands intelligence and experience; indeed, it demands a virtuous disposition on the part of all those who are shaping the order of the goods. Although the understanding of human development is core to the idea of the common good, discussion of it here is beyond the scope of this paper. For further development of the connection between human development and the common good, see Alford, "Globalising Human Development: The Key Role of the Common Good" (paper presented at the 11th International Symposium on Ethics, Business, and Society: Ethical Challenges in the Age of Globalization. The Message of *Centesimus Annus* on the 10th Anniversary of Its Publication, IESE Business School, University of Navarre, Barce-

lona, July 5–6, 2001). The paper has been published in English in the journal *OIKONOMIA* (June 2002): 13–23, and is also available at www.oikonomia.it.

20. John XXIII, *Mater et magistra* (1961), 65. John XXIII may have elected to deal only with the foundational level because he wanted to avoid the problems associated with defining what is the shared excellent or final common good of the human community in a pluralist society and to focus on what is more practically attainable in such a society.

21. See Kapstein in Kaul et al., *Global Public Goods*, 105.

22. Kaul et al., *Global Public Goods*, 450–51.

23. Ibid., 450.

24. Ibid., 467.

25. Ibid., 475 (emphasis in original).

26. The literature on the virtues is vast. As a starting point that connects directly with the rest of this essay, I would direct the reader to the third chapter of Alford and Naughton, *Managing As If Faith Mattered.*

TEN

The Role of "Indirect Employers" in Wage Distribution

Economic Data and *Laborem exercens*

CARLO DELL'ARINGA

AND CLAUDIO LUCIFORA

Many economists have long acknowledged that an important aim of economic science is to provide a rigorous, deep, and up-to-date understanding of human behavior in economic activities, looking, in particular, into the effects of these actions on the functioning of markets. What has not been as clear in the field of economics is that the evaluation of the consequences of economic rules on "society" and "human beings" cannot do without referring to those values and principles that can only be found outside the field. The latter is particularly true of those issues that are usually addressed by labor economists, such as wage determination, inequalities, solidarity, and the role of unions. The importance of these themes is reinforced by the fact that they are explicitly addressed also in Pope John Paul II's encyclical *Laborem exercens* (1981).

John Paul II, for example, introduces and discusses the concept of wages in society in *Laborem exercens* by arguing that wages "are still a practical means whereby the vast majority of people can have access to those goods which are intended for common use . . . hence, in every case, a fair wage is the concrete means of verifying the justice of the whole socio-economic system, and, in any case, of checking that it is functioning justly."[1] John Paul, like the popes and councils before him, recognizes that each person will be paid differently depending upon her skill, effort, sacrifice, and other work-related characteristics. However, he is concerned that in a market economy, increases in wage disparities and inequalities present grave challenges to a just economic order. Here we are faced with Dennis McCann's question (chapter 7, this volume), "When does inequality become a moral issue?" For John Paul, inequality becomes injustice when it serves as an obstacle to people having access to meeting their basic needs. It also becomes immoral when it weakens the solidarity of people and creates tensions, divisions, and conflicts among them.[2] Although inequality will always be part of any free-market economic order, there need to be institutional counterweights to market forces that tend toward excessive inequalities. *Laborem exercens* addresses the issue by discussing some of the institutions that could potentially create conditions that promote a more just distribution of wealth in the functioning of the labor market.

Which are the institutions, besides the employer, that John Paul considers as relevant to achieve solidarity, a mutual recognition of the idea of a "fair remuneration," and consequently a more just distribution of wealth? Essentially two appear to be the most relevant, and for which John Paul uses the term "indirect employers": unions, and the state. Both an organization of workers acting collectively and the intervention of the state as regulator are seen in principle as capable of promoting a higher degree of fairness in the labor market. When they function well, unions and the state create conditions that influence the behavior of the employer, whom John Paul refers to as the "direct employer," by determining "in concrete terms the actual work contract and labor relations. This is not to absolve the direct employer from his own responsibility, but only to draw attention to the whole network of influences that condition his conduct."[3]

As an indirect employer, unions are still "an indispensable element of social life . . . a mouthpiece for the struggle for social justice. . . . People unite to secure their rights, their union remains a constructive factor of social order and solidarity, and it is impossible to ignore it."[4] The role of the state can help govern the process of definition and implementation of labor market policies, which can be seen as ethically "fair." *In primis* the state, as regulator, should guarantee and protect workers in the labor market—as components of the "human society"—from any excessive risks deriving from the working of the "industrial society." Labor market policies, a social ethic, and labor laws can be considered as the set of tools that can be used to face these problems.[5] While John Paul sees the employer as an important moral actor in distributing wealth, he also sees a just distribution of wealth as the responsibility of several institutions, none of which alone could achieve a just distribution of wealth. (For the responsibilities of employers see Michael Naughton and Robert Wahlstedt, chapter 11, this volume.)

More than twenty years after the publication of *Laborem exercens,* we investigate whether both these indirect employers—unions and the state—have been able to pursue and achieve those aims set out in the encyclical. In this context, this chapter will attempt a first (partial) evaluation focusing on those issues that, in the encyclical, were associated with the existence of "fair remuneration" and human solidarity as well as the fight against all kinds of poverty. Attention will be devoted, as indicated in *Laborem exercens*, to the analysis of wage inequality, that is, the presence of significant differences in the wages paid to workers, and its effect on a just distribution of wealth. As we said above, there is nothing wrong in paying different wages to different workers, but the existence of large differences, particularly in the lower end of the distribution, are opposed to the principles of solidarity and common use that should permeate the functioning of labor markets (see McCann's analysis of the relation between inequality and injustice). The increase in earnings inequality experienced by most industrialized countries in the Western world has marginalized, in terms of social exclusion and poverty, mostly those individuals located at the bottom end of the earnings distribution. Low-paid, low-skilled, and less-protected groups generally—such as women, young workers, and older men—appear to have borne most of the burden, in terms of lower earnings.[6]

Among the leading explanations offered for these trends, emphasis has been placed on demographic changes, adverse shifts in supply and demand for products and skills, skill-biased technological change, increased globalization of trade, and new forms of work organization.[7] Alternative explanations have emphasized the role of indirect employers, arguing that trade union activity, practices of collective bargaining, and labor market regulations may have played a more relevant role. Institutional pay-setting may alter wage dispersion and the incidence of low pay in various ways. First, legislation on wages may reduce dispersion by gender and by skill. Second, pay standardization policies, by reducing management discretion, may compress pay differences within firms. Third, industrywide bargaining and mandatory extension of the terms set in collective agreements may decrease wage differentials across establishments and reduce the markup of union over nonunion wages. And fourth, when the structure of bargaining is more centralized and negotiations are better coordinated, wage differentials between industries may be reduced.

It has been widely noted that those countries that have experienced the largest increases in inequalities have also been those with the most deregulated and decentralized labor markets. This seems to suggest that centralized wage-setting, institutional constraints, and widespread welfare safety nets may have had a significant role in shaping the distribution of earnings across countries. Heavily regulated labor markets and highly centralized wage-setting mechanisms are characterized by more rigid wage structures and greater wage inertia in the face of economic shocks and business cycle fluctuations. Moreover, in highly unionized labor markets, trade unions have traditionally pursued egalitarian wage policies to enhance worker solidarity and to protect those at the lower end of the earnings distribution. This has been particularly the case in those countries without a statutory minimum wage.[8]

We investigate the role that various institutional features have played in shaping the distribution of wages across a number of countries that are members of the Organization for Economic Cooperation and Development (OECD). Despite the skepticism among economists about the actual role that institutions may play in the functioning of labor markets—on the grounds that the institutional setting is merely a superstructure through which market forces continue to operate—we shall focus on explicit and quantifiable measures of institutional forces to assess their impact. Restricting the scope in this way will avoid excessive arbitrariness in defining the relevant "institutions" for pay-setting, or in interpreting their impact simply as a residual of those features that cannot be otherwise explained. In particular, we shall focus on three specific features: the effects of trade unions, the structure of collective bargaining, and the existence of wage regulation. While by no means the only labor market institutions relevant for wage determination, these three certainly play a central role in explaining differences in the structure and dynamics of wages across countries.[9] This way of proceeding obviously leaves aside the role of social norms and cultural factors as well as business practices, which, though more difficult to measure, are likely also to be important in explaining cross-country differences.

In this chapter, we shall investigate what has been the role of unions and of the state as "indirect employers" in facing the problem of low pay. We shall ask whether in twenty-plus years after *Laborem exercens* these two institutions have been effective in promoting solidarity and reducing wage inequality among workers. In order to achieve this goal we have organized the chapter as follows: in the first section, we review some of the institutional features that characterize the functioning of the labor market and are considered relevant for wage inequality and the incidence of low-wage employment. These fall into two main categories: unionism and collective bargaining practices; and legal regulation of wages. In the second section, we provide an overview of the stylized facts on low-wage labor-markets across a number of OECD countries. In the third section, we investigate the effects that labor-market institutions may have on both the incidence of low-wage employment and the distribution of earnings. In the fourth, we check the robustness of our findings and discuss a number of extensions. The last section contains concluding remarks and discusses some policy implications in the context of *Laborem exercens*.

LABOR MARKET INSTITUTIONS AND WAGE REGULATION: AN OVERVIEW OF INTERNATIONAL DIFFERENCES

Institutional wage-setting may involve direct government legislation on a number of pay issues, such as a minimum wage, legislation against discrimination, or the mandatory extension of collective agreements, or it may operate via the "voluntarist" route, through the activities of trade unions and collective bargaining. While it is largely undisputed that the presence of wage regulation and collective bargaining affects wage formation, the magnitude and direction of the impact that institutions have on the functioning of labor markets and the distribution of wages depend on how far the constraints which they impose are binding. Many institutional arrangements are directed toward a specific portion of the wage distribution or to selected groups of individuals, making it likely that the effects will be concentrated on them.[10] To the extent that the institutional constraint is binding, the wage outcome will differ from that resulting from the operation of market forces. It may be argued that as a general tendency, institutionalized wage-setting, by being targeted at the "average" worker or firm, has the effect of reducing differences across groups. Market forces, on the other hand, by operating at the "margin" (that is, through the "marginal" worker or firm), tend to give rise to a wider dispersion in wage levels.[11] Moreover, we might expect market forces and institutional arrangements to interact in different ways in different parts of the earnings distribution, with a greater impact on the top or at the bottom of the earnings hierarchy, depending on the type of institutions at work.

Figure 1 reports a range of indicators of earnings inequality across OECD countries.[12] We have ranked countries according to overall inequality as measured by the ratio of earnings at the ninth decile to the bottom decile (that is, the D9/D1 ratio). We also report the relative inequality in the top and bottom halves of the distribution (that is, the D9/D5 and D5/D1 ratios). First, significant differences in earnings inequality emerge across countries; in the United States, with the most unequal distribution, the D9/D1 ratio is close to 4.5 while in Norway it is less than 2. Second, in countries where overall inequality is relatively low (that is, those located at the right hand end in figure 1), it appears that earnings dispersion is particularly compressed at the bottom end of the distribution, more so than at the top. Conversely, those countries where earnings inequality is relatively high tend to have a wider dispersion at both ends of the distribution, often particularly at the top end.

The differences in earnings inequality observed across countries are reflected in the existence of similar disparities in the incidence of low pay; those countries characterized by wider dispersion in the bottom part of the earnings distribution also have a larger share of low-paid individuals. The remainder of this section analyzes the factors that might influence the pattern of inequality across countries and, in particular, their effects on the lower part of the earnings distribution and the incidence of low-wage employment. Following a widely used criterion, the definition of low-wage employment will be those workers whose earnings fall below two-thirds of median earnings.[13]

FIGURE 1.   Earnings Inequality: Decile Ratios

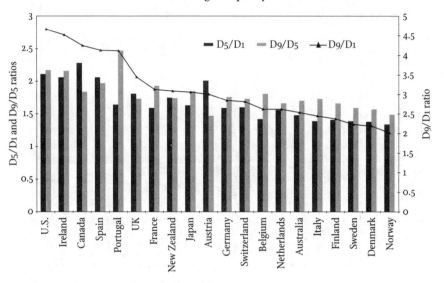

Collective Bargaining and Unionization

The extent of unionization and the practice of collective bargaining are important institutional features in wage determination. As shown in table 1 (columns 1 to 3), different patterns of union presence and activity characterize OECD economies.[14] Moreover, during the 1980s and 1990s, a number of changes occurred in wage-setting institutions in several industrialized countries: notably, declining unionization and progressive decentralization of bargaining. The interaction of wage regulation and union power may therefore have different implications for institutional wage-setting across countries. It has been argued that in decentralized systems with weak unions, such as the United States, the United Kingdom, and New Zealand, a decline in union density produces widespread effects on institutional wage-setting, inequality, and the incidence of low pay. By contrast, in more regulated systems with industrywide bargaining and high union coverage, such as the majority of European countries, the effect of declining unionization barely has an impact. The main explanation for these different outcomes resides in the institutional channels through which unions can influence wage formation: essentially mandatory extension provisions and centralization of bargaining.[15]

Much of the empirical evidence concerning the impact of unions on relative wages suggests that trade unionism can significantly alter the distribution of wages. One route is by raising the pay levels of those workers covered by collective

TABLE 1. Union Presence and Wage Regulations in OECD Countries

	Unionization Indicators			Extension of Collective Agreements*		Wage Regulations		
						Minimum Wage Systems (MW)		Replacement Ratio
Country	Union Density (%)	Coverage (%)	Corporatism index	description	index	description	Kaitz Index	index
	(1)	(2)	(3)	(4)	(5)	(6)	(7)	(8)
Austria	46.2	98	19	almost all agreements	16	nationally negot. MW (*)	0.62	50
Belgium	51.2	90	14	almost all agreements	15	negotiated monthly MW	0.60	60
Denmark	71.4	69	12	by centralization	17	nationally negot. MW (*)	0.64	90
Finland	72	95	16	frequent (minister ext.)	12	nationally negot. MW (*)	0.52	63
France	9.8	95	7	very frequent	14	statutory hourly MW	0.50	57
Germany	32.9	92	17	frequent (small firm)	12	negotiated MW (by industries)	0.55	63
Ireland	49.7	60	7	limited to min. wages	7	statutory MW (only selected industries)	0.55	37
Italy	38.8	85	15	almost all agreements (by ind.)	16	negotiated monthly MW (by industries)	0.71	20
Netherlands	25.5	81	7	frequent (minister ext.)	10	statutory weekly MW	0.55	70
Norway	56	74	18	by centralization	17	nationally negot. MW (*)	0.64	65
Portugal	31.8	71	7	frequent (minister ext.)	16	statutory monthly MW	0.45	65
Spain	11	78	7	frequent by industry	15	statutory monthly MW	0.32	70
Sweden	82.5	89	7	by centralization	17	nationally negot. MW (*)	0.52	80
Switzerland	26.6	50	12	frequent (minister ext.)	11	—	0.50	70
United Kingdom	39.1	47	4	no automatic ext.	3	statutory MW (before 1993, selected industries)	0.40	38
Japan	25.4	21	6	rare (company agreement)	4	statutory daily MW	0.53	59
Australia	40.4	80	5	limited to min. wages	8	negotiated MW	0.45	50
New Zealand	44.8	31	1	limited cases (minister ext.)	10	statutory weekly MW	0.46	60
Canada	35.8	36	1	limited cases	5	statutory hourly MW	0.35	36
United States	15.6	18	1	no automatic ext.	1	statutory hourly MW	0.39	30

Source: OECD, 1996; S. Nickell, "Unemployment and Labour Market Rigidities: Europe versus North America," *Journal of Economic Perspectives* 11, no. 3 (1997): 55–74; for a detailed description of the variables reported, see the text.

* Collective agreements covering most of the labor force

agreements relative to noncovered workers.[16] A second is through "standard rate" policies aimed at reducing inequality among individual workers. In particular, collective agreements seek to fix both the number of job categories in which workers are placed and the rate of pay for each job, thus limiting the ability of the firm to remunerate workers differently according to more individualized criteria.[17]

Some basic factors can be put forward to explain union preferences for a less-dispersed wage structure among similar plants and within the organized sector, although the union's ability to achieve this will necessarily vary with market conditions and the institutional setting. First, worker solidarity requires a relatively uniform wage distribution, as the perception of marked differences in pay may reduce consensus among workers and therefore the strength of the union's "collective voice."[18] Hence, unions tend to resist any decline in low pay relative to the average. Second, given the potential arbitrariness in measuring individual productivity, subject to supervisor evaluation, workers, being risk-averse, will generally prefer narrower wage distributions. Finally, the union can be regarded as a political organization whose consensus depends on median preference. This implies that when the median wage is less than the mean wage, a majority of workers will support a policy favoring the lower paid, thus further reducing dispersion and the incidence of low pay.[19] In this respect, the effects that union presence is likely to produce on the distribution of wages, although indeterminate a priori, tend in practice to result in a marked compression of wage differentials and a lower incidence of low-paid employment.[20] This general proposition will be analyzed in greater detail in the third section.

Wage Regulation

The labor market regulations most relevant for influencing the distribution of wages are probably statutory minimum wages, antidiscrimination legislation, and the mandatory extension of collective agreements (see table 1). These are not necessarily mutually exclusive, since in some countries wage minimums are set by statute after consultation with the unions, while in other cases various aspects of industrial relations interact with legislation in a rather complex way.

Minimum wage legislation, by setting an explicit threshold for the lowest wage rate paid (hourly, daily, or monthly) impacts on the bottom end of the earnings distribution and tends to reduce wage dispersion (see column 6 in table 1). Unemployment benefits also provide a floor to low pay, influencing the search activity of unemployed workers through the effect on the reservation wage. In both cases, the actual effect on the distribution depends on the level of the minimum relative to the median (average) wage—the so-called Kaitz index—or the replacement ratio,[21] and on the number of workers covered (see columns 7 and 8 in table 1). These may differ significantly across countries. Some systems do not have any statutory intervention in setting a minimum wage. Where it is present, the minimum may lose its "bite" over time if it is allowed to decrease both relative to average wages and in terms of coverage of the low-paid. A number of studies have found the abolition or reduction of statutory minimum wages as the main determinant of widening earnings inequality, particularly in the lower part of the distribution, as well as being responsible for the increase in low-wage employment. Obvious examples are the decline (in real terms) of the federal minimum wage in the United States over the 1980s and the abolition of Wages Councils in the United Kingdom. Conversely, in France, where the minimum wage has remained relatively constant, no big changes in low-pay employment have been observed.[22]

Antidiscrimination legislation and fair employment practices, by setting common standards of pay across otherwise different groups of workers, have the effect of reducing overall pay dispersion.[23] The actual impact on low pay, however, will depend on the groups of workers who are affected; if the groups involved are located in the bottom part of the wage distribution, the legislation will move these workers upward. With specific reference to female employment, it can be noted that despite the fact that women are usually overrepresented in low wage jobs and show a greater propensity to experience long spells of low-wage employment, in most OECD economies women's pay has risen relative to that of men in the last twenty years. Moreover, the effects of antidiscrimination legislation have to be evaluated against the contemporaneous massive increase in the participation of women in the labor market. Without institutional constraint this increase could have pushed wage levels downward in the bottom sections of the earnings distribution, further concentrating low pay among women.

Finally, the mandatory extension of collective agreement provisions can have pervasive effects in reducing wage differentials among covered workers, irrespective of their union affiliation. In countries where such provisions exist, the effects of negotiated (minimum) wages are automatically (or de facto) extended to all workers, granting a high coverage to union bargaining activity (see columns 4 and 5 in table 1). The United States and the United Kingdom, on the other hand, provide an interesting example of the absence of any form of mandatory extension. This appears to have been associated with wider wage differentials across groups of workers and firms as well as with larger differences in the incidence of low pay. Conversely, in Continental Europe, the various forms of extension provisions in conjunction with higher union coverage (see below) have had strong equalizing effects, compressing the earnings distribution at the bottom and maintaining a low incidence of low-paid jobs.[24]

LOW-PAID EMPLOYMENT AND THE INSTITUTIONAL SETTING: SOME STYLIZED FACTS

Labor market institutions, such as those previously discussed, may influence the incidence of low-wage employment in a number of ways. Both the "level" and "change" in labor market institutions may influence wage formation and the structure of earnings by altering the impact of market forces. Different institutional settings across countries provide different constraints and incentives for workers and firms involved in wage formation and can limit the impact of economic forces' changes on the wage distribution. Changes in the institutional framework, loosening constraints, and increasing incentives may provide additional freedom to economic agents and favor changes in the structure of earnings. While both the level and the change in institutions are certainly relevant, we concentrate our analysis on the structural differences in labor market institutions across countries rather than changes within countries in considering the effects of the institutional setting on low-wage employment and earnings inequality.

The well-being of individuals at the bottom of the earnings distribution is affected by the general level of real wages, the level and trend in overall inequality, and the degree of earnings mobility that characterizes the wage distribution (see Simona Beretta, chapter 5, this volume). While labor market institutions can influence each of these aspects, their implications for the low paid can be very different and should be distinguished.

Mean Wage

Differences in the level of the mean wage across countries are relevant when low pay is measured with respect to some absolute benchmark. In countries characterized by a higher mean wage and higher living standards, what is classified as low-wage employment may be significantly different from that in substantially poorer countries. In general, a higher mean wage will be associated with a lower proportion of people falling below a fixed threshold. This seems to imply that economic growth can benefit anyone. However, if the variance as well as the mean of the distribution increases, there is no guarantee that everyone will be better off. Some could become worse off in absolute as well as relative terms. International comparisons of low pay face a number of further difficulties arising from differences in productivity levels, definitions of subsistence levels, and purchasing power of each country's national currency. To avoid these, comparisons are most often made in relative terms. As an example of differing low-wage levels across countries, figure 2 reports for a number

FIGURE 2.   Real Hourly Earnings Index (D1) and D1/D5 Ratio (Men)

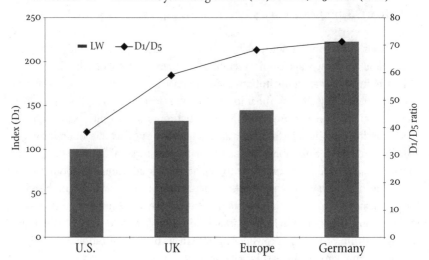

of OECD countries the real hourly earnings of workers located at the first decile of the earnings distribution, and the ratio of this to the mean wage. As shown in the figure, low wages on this definition tend to be notably low in the United States as compared with Europe and in particular with Germany. This suggests that in addition to the differences in overall inequality (see also the D1/D5 ratio), the lowest part of the distribution varies significantly across countries.[25]

Turning to the relationship that might exist between a country's institutional setting and its economic performance, although there is no general agreement among economists on the role that labor market institutions may have on economic growth, a number of hypotheses have been subject to extensive scrutiny.[26] High levels of unionization and centralized bargaining appear to provide an encompassing role, allowing economic policies that are growth-oriented rather than centered on redistributive strategies. By limiting the negative externalities from the wage behavior of self-interested groups, these features lead to a more favorable trade-off between real wages and employment growth from which low-wage employment may benefit. Conversely, when unionization is fragmented and different groups pursue their own interests, the lack of cooperative objectives may prove harmful to the country's performance. Redistributive strategies that favor more powerful groups at the expense of weaker ones may support rent-seeking behavior. Low-wage workers, lacking power as a group, face a worsened trade-off between the real wage and employment. Finally, under decentralized bargaining and weak union power, the functioning of a quasi-market mechanism may adversely affect the relative position of low-wage work-

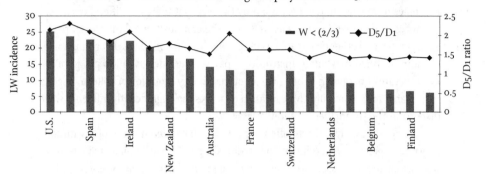

FIGURE 3.   Incidence of Low-Wage Employment and D5/D1 Ratio

ers even in the context of sustained real wage and employment growth. In this context, institutional constraints have a negligible effect and the operation of supply and demand forces can severely affect the earnings of marginal (low-paid) workers.[27]

Wage Inequality

Differences in wage inequality across countries are a further dimension of the low-wage employment problem. Countries with wider wage differentials are often characterized by a larger proportion of low-paid individuals. In figure 3, we have reported for several OECD countries both the proportion of low-paid workers (that is, those whose earnings fall below two-thirds of the median wage), as well as the ratio of the median to the first decile wage. The pattern that emerges, as documented in several studies, shows that countries characterized by a higher dispersion in the lower part of the earnings distribution also have the largest share of low-paid individuals.[28]

International differences in earnings inequality can reflect a wide variety of factors, importantly including differences in measured and unmeasured characteristics (such as educational attainment, skills, and age distribution) and the differing wage returns for those skills; these will be addressed later in the chapter. In the present context, institutional differences in wage formation underline a different set of incentives and constraints that individuals take into account in making their choices. A good starting point in comparing wage inequality and the incidence of low pay across countries is to decompose overall inequality into "between" group and "within" group components.[29] Since labor market institutions can have a pervasive effect both on the distribution of observed characteristics and on the structure of returns to these characteristics, it is important to assess their role in shaping the cross-country pattern of inequality. In other words, differences in the overall inequality and the incidence of low pay may reflect not only the fact that there are differences across countries in unionization rates as well as in the composition of the workforce by skill, gender, and other observable traits, but also that the mode of determination of economic returns may differ. Institutional pay-setting, such as union pay policies, the structure of bargaining, the existence of mandatory extension of collective agreements, and, more generally, the legislation on wages may significantly influence wage dispersion and the incidence of low pay.[30]

An alternative hypothesis, often neglected, is that different types of institutions may induce greater (in)stability in the earnings of people with similar characteristics who belong to the same group. At any moment in time, people may experience different earnings (and employment) patterns with short-term transitory increases or decreases in their earnings. If these fluctuations are larger in one country with respect to another, then both inequality and low-wage employment measured at a given point in time will differ.[31]

Wage Mobility

A further dimension of the functioning of the low-wage labor market and its interactions with the institutional setting relates to the mobility patterns that characterize the earnings distribution. While measures of inequality and low-wage incidence can provide a measure of the diffusion of low pay at a given point in time, they do not offer any perspective on the transitions that occur between the pool of low-wage workers and the rest of the earnings distribution. In particular, when analyzing low-wage employment, it is important to stress that it is not always the same people who are low paid: a person in the lowest percentiles in a given year will not necessarily be in the same percentile a few years later.[32] Differences in mobility patterns both across countries and over time may reflect differences in the covariance structure of earnings for any given distribution. In general, more dispersed distributions are expected to be characterized by higher (short-term) fluctuations in earnings and hence by larger transition flows across the different parts of the distribution. In terms of low-wage employment, the greater dispersion may imply more frequent spells in low pay, while the duration of each spell may be shorter as individuals are also more likely to exit from low pay due to the larger transition flows. To get a rough picture of the relationship that links the extent of low pay to the mobility patterns of individuals located in the lowest deciles of the distribution, in figure 4 we compare across countries an indicator of low-wage incidence with a measure of transitions out of low pay, that is, the proportion of people moving from a low-wage job to a high-wage job.

FIGURE 4.   Low-Wage Employment and Mobility Patterns

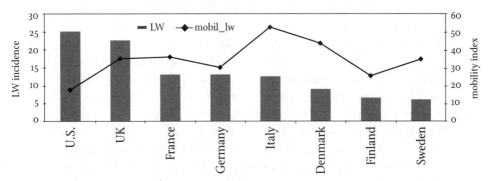

The evidence does not seem to support the hypothesis that countries charac-terized by a larger pool of people earning a low wage are also more likely to have larger flows out of low pay. In particular, contrary to these expectations, in coun-tries where the proportion of low-paid workers is higher, only a small proportion seem to transit to better paid jobs. At the aggregate level, a significant degree of per-sistence in low pay emerges: the same individuals are still found in low pay several years later. Conversely, exiting low pay appears more likely in those countries where its incidence is smaller.[33]

In general, the empirical literature shows that earnings mobility is rather mod-est and not sufficient to override the effects of steady state inequality. In terms of labor market institutions, the fact that the United States has a less regulated labor market and a more decentralized system of collective bargaining as compared to European countries does not translate into greater earnings mobility or into a higher probability of leaving low pay. Likewise, the more centralized wage-setting institu-tions that are present in Germany and in the Nordic countries do not imply a signifi-cantly lower mobility among the low paid.[34] This evidence, even if only sketched, seems to imply that institutions exert their main effects on the permanent compo-nents of pay dynamics, while differences in the transitory components appear to have only marginal effects.

MEASURING THE EFFECTS OF INSTITUTIONS ON LOW-WAGE EMPLOYMENT

The fact that over the 1990s several OECD countries experienced a general ten-dency toward increasing inequality and are still showing considerable differences in the extent of inequality and low-wage employment may be interpreted as evidence that institutional structures under common shocks can produce substantially different outcomes. In this section we shall investigate the extent to which selected institutional features can influence the distribution of wages and the incidence of low-wage employment across a number of OECD countries.[35] In particular, since the impact of institutional features is typically concentrated in specific parts of the distribution, we shall center our attention on those institutions that are most likely to impact on the bottom part of the wage distribution, namely, trade unions and the structure of collective bargaining, and wage regulation. Their main effects, as well as those of selected control variables, measured by simple bivariate correlations and univariate regressions, are reported in table 2 (panel A and B). Alternatively, in figure 5, we report the plots of the same set of labor market institutions against low-pay incidence. The discussion of the main implications follows hereafter.

Unions and Collective Bargaining

There are several routes through which trade unions can alter the overall distribution of wages and in particular the incidence of low pay. Although union pay policies tend to reduce wage dispersion by raising wage floors almost in all countries, the extent to which unions are able to reduce the gap between low and average pay levels appears to be correlated with the degree of unionization (or union density) observed in each country. The empirical evidence, as reported in table 2, shows that where unionization is generally low, a larger pool of low-wage workers is observed.[36] In the United States, where only 14 percent of workers are members of a trade union, the proportion of low-paid workers is over 25 percent, while in Sweden where union density is over 80 percent, less than 6 percent of workers fall below the low-pay threshold (see table 1). Similarly, in Italy, Germany, and Belgium, where nearly one worker out of two is a member of a union (that is, Italy, 40; Germany, 33; Belgium, 51), the proportion of low-paid workers lies between 8 and 13 percent. Hence, at a purely descriptive level, the extent of unionization appears to be negatively correlated (rho = −0.68) with the extent of low-wage employment (see figure 5). However, unionization has been traditionally low in some countries, such as France, which have also experienced a fairly low incidence in low-wage employment. In this context, the existence of mandatory extension provisions for collective bargaining, as previously described, can make the degree of union coverage a more appropriate indicator of the effective "strength" of unions in protecting low wages. When the extension of collective agreements is taken into account, the evidence of a negative correlation between union power and low-wage employment is con-

TABLE 2.   Institutions and Low-Wage Incidence (20 Countries)

Variables	Bivariate Correlations	Simple Univariate Regression dep. variable – log(LWI)		
	$\rho(LW,x)$	constant	x	$R^2(adj)$
(A) Labor market institutions				
Union density	-0.68**	3.23	-0.015**	0.44
Union coverage	-0.60**	3.33	-0.010**	0.33
Centralization	-0.72**	3.20	-0.069**	0.50
Kaitz index	-0.64**	4.07	-0.028*	0.38
Benefit replacement ratio	-0.53*	3.37	-0.021*	0.41
(B) Other controls				
Women employed part-time	-0.30		—	
Proportion of self-employed	-0.36		—	
Test-score ratio	0.58 [#]		—	
Rate enrollment/pop. age (H-School)	-0.23		—	
GDP (per capita)	-0.17		—	
Share (empl. in services/total empl)	-0.22		—	
Share home-ownership	0.05		—	
(C) Competing factors				
Total non-EU trade/GDP	-0.50*	3.05	-0.014*	0.02
Share of "high-tech" empl.	0.10	2.39	0.013	0.09
Skill/unskill labor ratio	-0.32	3.05	-0.511	0.05
Product & labor-market regulation	-0.17	2.72	-0.026	0.00

Source: OECD, 1996
* 5% significance level; ** 1% significance level
[#] based on 11 countries only

firmed (rho=-0.60). In particular, looking at the estimated coefficients from simple univariate regressions, it emerges that an increase of 1 percent in union density or coverage—considered independently—is associated with a reduction of 1 and 1.5 percent, respectively, in low-pay incidence.

In other words, the power of the unions to create a wage floor and reduce wage dispersion at the bottom of the distribution seems to be the result of a combination of factors: on the one side, "pure" union power given by actual membership and, on the other, some form of wage regulation that can extend the power over the outcomes from collective negotiations far above that provided by union presence. In order to see this, we have computed an indicator of coverage extension (measured as the excess of bargaining power over and above union membership) and related it to low-wage incidence. The pattern that emerges, with the exception of some outliers, shows two clusters of points: on the top left (that is, high low-wage employment and low coverage extension), we find countries belonging to the Anglo-Saxon model of industrial relations characterized by limited mandatory extension provisions; conversely, on the bottom right, it is the European model of industrial relations (high coverage and frequent mandatory extensions—see table 1) that predominates.[37]

Finally, the structure of collective bargaining itself might be related to the extent of low pay. In particular, centralization of collective bargaining through the encompassing role played by the unions is shown to reduce significantly wage dispersion in the bottom part of the wage distribution and limit the incidence of low pay. Both table 2 and the graph in figure 5 show a negative (statistically significant) correlation between an index of centralization and the proportion of low-wage workers (rho=-0.72). An upward move in the centralization ranking reduces the percentage of low-pay employment by almost 7 percent.

Wage Regulation

As already discussed, both the existence of a statutory minimum wage and the generosity of unemployment benefits are further labor market institutions that may have an impact on the bottom end of the wage distribution as well as on the propensity of individuals to take up low-paid jobs. In general, a high (low) minimum wage relative to the average wage (the Kaitz index) tends to be associated with lower (higher) levels of low-wage employment. This is confirmed by the negative correlation that emerges between the Kaitz index and the proportion of low-wage workers across countries (rho=-0.64). Alternatively, the generosity of unemployment benefits, as measured by the replacement ratio, appears to be negatively related to the extent of low-wage employment (rho=-0.53). In general, as it emerges from coefficient estimates, a unit increase in the ratio of the minimum to the average wage or in the replacement ratio shows a statistically significant negative impact on the proportion of low pay. The evidence presented thus far seems to confirm the substantial role played by labor market institutions in shaping the distribution of earnings and the incidence of low-wage employment. Different institutions concerned with wage-setting practices, taken one by one, have shown that various forms of wage floors can play a relevant role in alleviating low pay, either by reducing dispersion at the bottom end of the distribution or more directly by truncating the distribution from below.

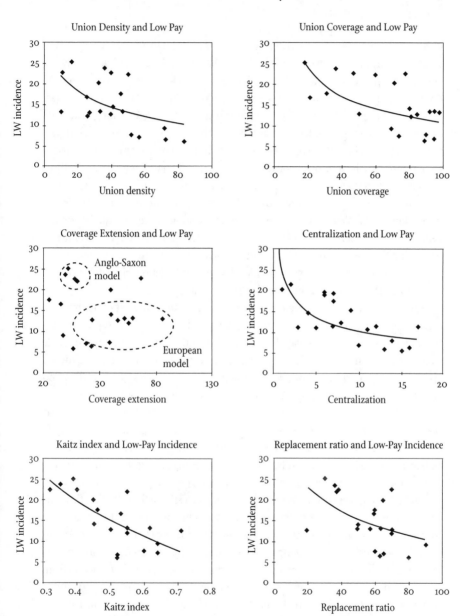

FIGURE 5. Institutional Features and Low-Pay Incidence (20 OECD Countries)

Institutions and Market Forces

Several caveats apply to the above evidence. First, simple correlations between different measures of labor market institutions and the incidence of low pay, across countries, only provide a rough description of the "stylized facts" and do not involve any investigation of the interdependencies among the factors that may generate the observed patterns. Moreover, the exclusive focus on labor market institutions neglects the role that market forces or other factors may play in determining a different incidence in low-wage employment across countries. Some of these (observed) factors are reported in table 2 (panel B and C) and have been further experimented in the empirical analysis below. They range from share of women employed part-time, proportion of self employed, GDP per capita, to share of employment in services and home ownership, on the one side, and share in GDP of (non-European Union) trade, skilled-unskilled labor ratio, and overall regulation in product and labor markets, on the other. All the factors listed above are often indicated as having some role in shaping the distribution of wages and the incidence of low pay. However, simple correlations show that there is no statistically significant relationship between any of the factors listed above and the share of low-pay employment.[38]

Second, when using evidence from aggregate data, compositional effects—originating from a different distribution of observed as well as unobserved characteristics across countries—may distort the observed pattern in an unpredictable way.[39] The obvious factor to be considered is the differing distribution of skill levels, either measured in schooling attainment (number of years or high education enrollment ratios) or, more appropriately, using average test scores. In figure 6, we plot literacy test-score ratios against low-wage employment.[40] This shows a clear positive correlation (rho=0.58; in table 2) between skill dispersion and the incidence of low pay: the more heterogeneous are workers in the bottom part of the skill distribution in terms of skills, the higher are both earnings inequality and the proportion of people falling below the low-wage threshold.

A final point, which applies to all studies that investigate the role of institutions as a potential explanation for differing economic outcomes, relates to the fact that the variety of institutional features of labor markets may be the consequence rather than the cause of the differing incidence of low pay (that is, countries with low dispersion of wages may set a relatively high minimum wage to protect workers from adverse shocks, knowing that very few would be affected). A number of features that have characterized the process of structural change across most industrialized countries, however, appear hard to reconcile with the view that institutions are purely endogenous and therefore should not be considered as one of the key factors capable of explaining the observed differences. One feature that should be consid-

FIGURE 6.   Low-Wage Employment and Test Score

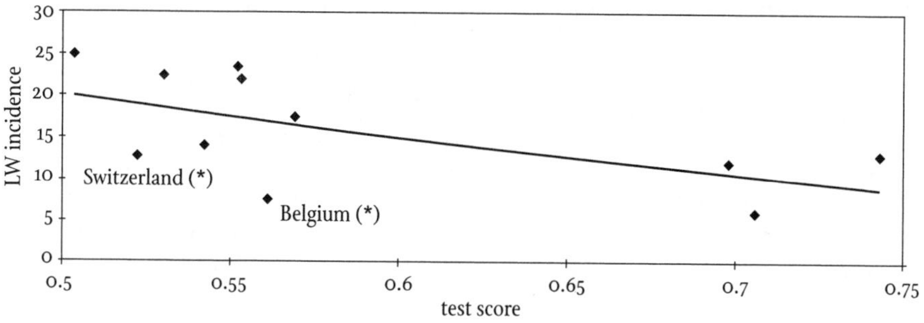

(*) Average of different languages

ered is that pervasive labor market institutions show strong persistence against economic forces. Moreover, common shocks affecting most countries produce very different responses in wages and employment depending on the underlying institutional settings. Countries characterized by similar institutional features share common patterns, as described above, irrespective of the magnitude of the economic changes occurring. If institutional settings were endogenous responses to more fundamental shocks resulting from globalization, technological developments, and organizational change, the pattern of economic effects should have been stronger where institutions proved more sensitive to adjustment. The available evidence suggests that this is not the case. Differences in labor laws and collective bargaining practices, as opposed to demand and supply factors, appear to be the relevant features of the diverging patterns. Also, countries where institutional wage-setting practices are targeted to protect low-wage workers and reduce wage dispersion should exhibit larger employment losses among low-wage or low-skilled workers as compared to countries where wages are set in a more market-oriented fashion. However, the relative employment rates of the low-wage/low-skilled workers evolved in a similar fashion in most countries, which appears in contrast with the view that institutions are endogenous responses to market shocks.[41]

INSTITUTIONS AND LOW PAY: IS THE EVIDENCE ROBUST?

In table 3, we report some evidence drawn from a simple multivariate analysis.[42] The proportion of low-wage workers (in logs) is regressed against a set of institutional features that, as previously described, are expected to affect earnings dispersion in the lower part of the distribution. When we look at the joint effects of

TABLE 3.   Estimates of the Effects of Labor Market Institutions on Low-Wage Incidence (20 OECD Countries)

Variables	Low-Wage Incidence dependent variable – log(LWI)				
	(1)	(2)	(3)	(4)	(5)
Labor market institutions					
Union density	-0.0101*	-0.009*	-0.008**	-0.008**	-0.008**
Union coverage	-0.006°	-0.005*	-0.007*	-0.007**	-0.007**
Centralization	-0.021	—	—	—	—
Kaitz index	—	-0.014**	-0.011**	-0.011*	-0.011*
Benefit replacement					
ratio	—	-0.007**	-0.007**	-0.008**	-0.008**
Other controls					
Test-score ratio	—	—	—	0.003	—
"No score" dummy	—	—	—	0.001	—
Rate enroll/pop.age					
(H-School)	—	—	—	—	0.003
GDP (per capita)/1000			-0.055**	-0.056**	-0.060**
Constant	3.59**	4.45**	5.23**	5.08**	5.07**
$R^2(adj)$	0.61	0.73	0.86	0.84	0.85
N. observations	20	20	20	20	20

Source: OECD, 1996; Nickell, 1997 (see table 1)
°10% significance level;* 5% significance level; ** 1% significance level

unionization, union coverage, and centralization in collective bargaining across countries, we find that they contribute to reducing the incidence of low-wage employment. Coefficient estimates are negatively signed and in general statistically significant (although centralization on its own is not).[43] However, since the institutional wage setting is also strongly influenced by the generosity of unemployment benefits and by a high minimum wage relative to the average wage, we include both of these as additional controls. In line with previous results, our findings also suggest that wage regulations have a significant impact on low-wage employment. Finally, as a further test for the significance of the above results, we experimented with additional control variables, including the proportion of self-employed workers, the share of women employed part-time, and the share of home ownership and GDP per capita.[44] With the sole exception of GDP per capita, none of the above controls seemed to play any role in explaining the distribution of low-wage employment across countries. Conversely, richer countries—for any given institutional setting—seem to be characterized by a reduced incidence in low pay.[45] When considering the distribution of skill levels (as shown in table 3, columns 4 and 5), both the test-score variable and high-education enrollment ratios, while leaving the previous estimates largely unaltered, never achieved statistical significance.

Regression estimates can provide a basis for estimating the potential effects of differences in labor market institutions on the incidence of low wages. For example, if we consider the difference in the incidence of low-wage employment between the United States and Germany (ΔLW=12%), the regression results suggest that 64 percent of that difference ($\Delta LW_{(est)}$=7.7%) can be explained by differences in labor market institutions. Alternatively, in repeating the exercise for the United States against Sweden (ΔLW=19%), the proportion accounted for by differing institutional settings is close to 61 percent ($\Delta LW_{(est)}$=11.7%).

Since many institutional arrangements are targeted toward a specific portion of the wage distribution, we may expect their effects, as previously discussed, to differ between the bottom and the top end of the distribution. In table 4, we evaluate, for the same set of OECD countries, the effects of labor market institutions on various measures of wage inequality. In particular, do the institutional arrangements considered in the previous exercise have an impact on inequality at the top of the wage distribution that is different from its impact at the bottom?[46] In order to do this, we regress different institutional features on various decile ratios (that is, D9/D1; D9/D5; D5/D1). Considering overall inequality (measured by the log of the ratio of the top to the bottom decile), higher union density appears to be associated with lower wage dispersion while no (statistically significant) effect is detected for the coverage or the centralization of collective bargaining. Also, both a higher minimum wage, relative to the average wage, and a more generous benefit replacement ratio result in a lower dispersion. The effect of the minimum wage on the distribution seems particularly strong. When the same set of institutional variables are tested on the top and the bottom of the distribution, respectively, some interesting differences result. First, as one might expect, union density has a mild negative impact on wage dispersion at the bottom of the distribution (column 5, table 4), while it shows no effect at the top (columns 3 and 4, table 4). Interestingly, centralization of collective bargaining plays a significant role in reducing pay dispersion at the top. In other words, it seems that countries with more centralized bargaining systems promote corporatist objectives and worker solidarity mostly by reducing earnings dispersion at the top of the distribution.

When it comes to the role of wage regulation factors, the minimum wage shows a (statistically significant) negative impact on wage dispersion both on the whole distribution and, particularly, on the bottom part. No effect is detected at the top. The benefit replacement ratio also shows a negative impact on the overall distribution and on the bottom end, while no statistically significant effect is detected at the top. Finally, the inclusion of a test score indicator as a proxy for low-skill heterogeneity and as a potential determinant of wage dispersion in the bottom part of the distribution fails to show up statistically significant (see column 7, table 4).

In other words, the results suggest that the main factors that are effective in reducing dispersion at the bottom of the distribution are union power and the minimum wage. In particular, the latter appears very effective in protecting low-wage employment. Conversely, centralized bargaining systems result more effectively in restraining wage differences at the top of the distribution. Finally, the evidence concerning welfare benefits shows that higher replacement ratios also provide a safety net for low wages, reducing dispersion at the bottom of the distribution.

Competing Explanations on Inequality and Low Pay

Most market explanations for the increase in inequality and low-pay incidence focus on factors that affect the demand for and the supply of labor. On the demand side, the role of "skilled-biased" technological change and increased trade with developing countries feature more frequently. The implications of the standard, factor-endowments "Heckscher-Ohlin-Samuelson" model have been widely used as a reference framework to interpret the empirical evidence. In particular, the fact that skill-biased effects are manifested mainly within (rather than between) industries has often been interpreted as supporting the technology explanation.[47] Conversely, on the supply side, it is often stressed that the role of scarce skilled labor is relative to less educated people. Since different groups of workers are imperfect substitutes for each other, it is argued, the existence of adverse shocks or a different structure is reflected on the relative prices of labor and hence on the wage structure. Without going into any further detail, for each of the different explanations, as to the strength of the theoretical implications or the support arising from the empirical evidence, in what follows we shall attempt to complement the evidence presented above by contrasting the role of market forces and that of labor market institutions in explaining cross-country differences in inequality and low-pay incidence.

We shall do the above experiment in a very simple way, that is, by augmenting previous regressions with additional terms that shall be introduced as proxies for competing explanatory factors, namely, trade patterns and the structure of skilled employment. If any of the latter were to be, *ceteris paribus*, a "better" explanation for the existing differences in low-pay employment across OECD countries, one should

TABLE 4. Estimates of the Effects of Labor Market Institutions on the Distribution of Wages (20 OECD Countries)

Variables	Decile Ratio log(D9/D1)		Decile Ratio log(D9/D5)			Decile Ratio log(D5/D1)	
	(1)	(2)	(3)	(4)	(5)	(6)	(7)
Labor market institutions							
Union density	-0.004**	-0.003*	-0.0015	-0.0011	-0.0030°	-0.0011	-0.0010
Union coverage	-0.006**	-0.0022°	0.0002	0.0002	-0.0022	-0.0008	-0.0009
Centralization	—	—	-0.0151**	-0.0165*	0.0013	—	—
Kaitz index	—	-0.011**	—	-0.0019	—	-0.0077**	-0.0080**
Benefit replacement ratio	—	-0.003*	—	0.0010	—	-0.0030*	-0.0031°
Other controls							
Test-score Ratio	—	—	—	—	—	—	0.0898
"No score" dummy (*)	—	—	—	—	—	—	0.058
GDP (per capita)/1000	-0.034*	-0.028*	-0.021**	-0.020**	-0.011	—	—
Constant	1.57**	2.58**	1.08**	1.12**	0.98**	1.17**	1.14**
R^2(adj)	0.55	0.74	0.60	0.63	0.28	0.49	0.41
N. observations	20	20	20	20	20	20	20

Source: OECD, 1996; Nickell, 1997 (see table 1)

* dummy variable that takes value 1 when the test-score variable is missing (i.e., set equal to zero in 9 cases)

* 10% significance level; * 5% significance level; ** 1% significance level

° 10% significance level; * 5% significance level; ** 1% significance level

expect estimated parameters on institutional features to change drastically or at least to lose statistical significance. The main results from this exercise are reported in table 5.

When we include, respectively, the share in GDP of (non-EU) trade, the skilled-unskilled labor ratio (or the share of "high-tech" employment), and an index for the degree of product and labor markets regulation or the share of employment in services, none of them achieves statistical significance while the estimated effects of institutional factors remain mostly unchanged. This evidence partly reinforces the conclusions reached before. Although it ought to be remembered that these results have to be interpreted with care, since they are based on aggregate cross-sectional data and on a limited number of observations, nevertheless they appear to be consistent with the view that labor market institutions do play a relevant part in determining wage inequality and the extent of low-wage employment across countries.

Conclusion

In this chapter, we have investigated a number of issues that are at the core of the research agenda of labor economists and that have also been explicitly addressed in Pope John Paul II's encyclical *Laborem exercens*. The roles of wage determination, inequalities, and solidarity as well as unions have been investigated for a number of OECD countries to assess the impact that the recent evolution in these economies has had (and shall have) on the distribution of wealth. In particular the issue of labor market institutions and low-wage employment has been studied and tested empirically. Since institutional arrangements are typically directed toward a specific portion of the wage distribution or toward given groups of individuals, we have focused the attention on selected institutions that are particularly relevant for low-wage employment. Accordingly, the effects of trade unions, the structure of collective bargaining, and the existence of regulations on wages have been considered.

Labor market institutions, in general, influence wage formation and the structure of earnings by altering the effects of market forces, and they provide a different set of constraints and incentives for workers and firms involved in wage formation. Here the focus has been restricted to the analysis of the structural differences that exist in labor market institutions across countries and the effects that these have on low-wage employment and earnings inequality. Consistent with previous work, our results suggest that institutions are a relevant factor in shaping the distribution of earnings and the incidence of low pay. We have shown that institutional settings differ substantially across countries and that institutional variety in the labor market is able to explain a great deal of the observed patterns in low pay across countries. At

TABLE 5. Estimates of the Effects of Labor Market Institutions and Competing Explanations (20 OECD Countries)

Variables	Dependent Variable – log(LWI)					Dependent Variable – log(D5/D1)			
	(1)	(2)	(3)	(4)	(5)	(6)	(7)	(8)	(9)
Labor market institutions									
Union density	-0.008**	-0.007**	-0.008**	-0.009**	-0.007**	-0.001	-0.001	-0.001	-0.0005
Union coverage	-0.007**	-0.007**	-0.007**	-0.006**	-0.007**	-0.001	-0.001	-0.0007	-0.001
Kaitz index	-0.011**	-0.012**	-0.011*	-0.010*	-0.013*	-0.009**	-0.007**	-0.007*	-0.008**
Benefit replacement ratio	-0.007**	-0.008**	-0.007**	-0.007**	-0.007**	-0.003*	-0.003°	-0.003°	-0.003°
Other characteristics									
GDP (per capita)/1000	-0.055**	-0.067**	-0.053**	-0.060**	-0.040**	—	—	—	—
Competing factors									
Total non-EU trade/GDP	-0.001					0.002			
Share of "high-tech" empl.		0.012					-0.001		
Skill/unskill labor ratio			-0.0004					-0.004	
Product & labor market reg.				-0.018					
Share empl. services/total empl.					-0.009				-0.006
Constant	5.22**	5.24**	5.22**	5.29**	5.76**	1.21**	1.19**	1.17**	1.60**
R²(adj)	0.85	0.86	0.85	0.86	0.86	0.50	0.48	0.50	0.49
N. observations	20	20	20	20	20	20	20	20	20

Source: OECD, 1996; Nickell, 1997 (see table 1)

° 10% significance level; * 5% significance level; ** 1% significance level

a descriptive level, results from simple correlations indicate that union density, collective bargaining coverage, and the structure of wage negotiations jointly contribute to reduce the incidence of low pay across countries. However, the power of unions to create a wage floor and reduce wage dispersion at the bottom of the distribution appears to be the outcome of a combination of union power and wage regulations such as mandatory extension of contracts, statutory minimum wages, and the generosity of unemployment benefits. When the above factors are taken together to explain the pattern of low-wage incidence across countries, the results show that over 60 percent of the cross-country differences in low pay can be accounted for by the different institutional settings. Looking at the effects of institutional arrangements on wage inequality, we show that high minimum wages lower dispersion at the bottom end of the distribution, while a more corporatist system is effective in containing wage differences at the top. The hypothesis that other factors—independent of labor market institutions—might explain the observed patterns in low pay did not prove consistent with the available evidence. Neither the explanation based on the effect of skilled-biased technological change nor the role played by increased trade with developing countries was supported by the data.

While the above evidence is far from providing any conclusive assessment of the complex interactions that exist between labor market institutions and the problem of low-wage employment, it nevertheless provides additional evidence, consistent with other studies, that institutions do matter for the functioning of low-wage labor markets. From a more policy-oriented perspective, the above findings seem to suggest that the state can have a role in supporting or promoting those institutions that have proved effective in dealing with the problem of growing earnings inequalities and low-wage employment.

Our research confirms the importance of John Paul II's notion of indirect employers, which captures the reality that a just wage can only be an *instance* of a *social* achievement founded in cooperation with other employers, employees, and indirect employers, especially unions and governments. While employers can make great strides in paying just wages, they need supporting institutions to make it more reasonable to pay fair wages. For, apart from a comprehensive commitment—a social commitment—to a just wage within a market economy, those who decide unqualifiedly to pay just wages in highly competitive, commodity-driven, price-sensitive markets risk economic disadvantages that cannot long be borne.

As discussed above and in the introduction to this chapter, it should be acknowledged that those institutions referred to in *Laborem exercens* have indeed played a significant role in reducing inequalities (by ensuring a "fair remuneration" to employed workers) and in developing solidarity and fighting poverty in most industrialized countries (see Stefano Zamagni, chapter 8, this volume). Although, it cannot be claimed that those institutions have made possible the elimination of all forms of in-equalities or have greatly reduced the degree of precariousness that characterizes some (weaker) segments of the labor market, nevertheless they have played a signifi-cant role in moderating some of the undesirable effects of the working of the mar-kets. As documented, where the role of those institutions is weaker or their ability to influence economic outcomes is reduced, significant disparities in both wages and working conditions still exist in highly industrialized countries.

Last, we should mention a largely unresolved question that has not been ad-dressed in the present work, although *Laborem exercens* specifically refers to it; the problem of unemployment. Our analysis has focused on wage inequalities among employed workers, neglecting completely the issue of income (or welfare) inequality vis-à-vis those individuals who are jobless. Despite the existence of a widespread safety net for those out of work (in the form of unemployment benefits or other sub-sidies), the presence of a large pool of unemployed people, particularly in some countries, may arouse some concern also for the standard of living and the degree of poverty among the unemployed. In other words, it should be asked whether the same institutions that have proved effective in promoting solidarity and reducing in-equality among workers have been equally effective in reducing unemployment. The issue among economists is highly controversial: some have argued that the presence of those institutions that regulate the functioning of the labor market—by reducing inequality and protecting jobs—also reduce the flexibility needed to adjust to busi-ness cycle shocks and give rise to increasing and persistent unemployment; others believe that employment opportunities, in the long run, are largely unaffected by the presence of such institutions. The empirical evidence is mixed, although it should be noted that the weaker segments of the labor market—young and old people, women, low-skilled workers—are, at the same time, those who experience higher levels of unemployment as well as higher incidences of low pay. Incidentally, the lat-ter are also those less likely to be protected by the unions, which are mainly oriented toward prime-age male workers. In other words, low pay and unemployment are likely to be "the two sides of the coin," as (weaker or marginal) workers might alter-nate spells of unemployment with spells of low-paid employment.

As argued in *Laborem exercens,* trade unions are important actors in the pursuit of both social justice and more equitable distribution of resources; however, in order to achieve these objectives they should be "encompassing" organizations, so as to represent the interests of all workers. What the unions should not do is to rep-resent and protect only "some" groups of workers (those who are well paid and over-protected), in a corporative and egoistic perspective, leaving out the interests and the rights of the weaker groups. Both a "fair wage" and "full employment" should be considered together as the main objectives to be achieved on the labor market.

Social and economic life, as stated in *Laborem exercens*, are closely linked and related, and any member of a group should believe that his interests are duly considered and his rights equally protected. "In this sense, union activity undoubtedly enters the field of politics, understood as prudent concern for the common good."[48]

Notes

A preliminary version of this essay was presented at the 1999 ESPE (European Society for Population Economics) and EALE (European Association of Labour Economists) annual conferences, at the conference on "Unemployment, Poverty, and Social Exclusion" held at the University of Economics and Business, Athens (September 1999), and in seminars at the Università degli Studi di Milano, Università di Napoli, and LIUC (Università Carlo Cattaneo). We would like to thank A. Glyn and M. Gregory for extensive discussion, suggestions, and help on earlier drafts. The usual disclaimer applies.

1. John Paul II, *Laborem exercens*, 19.

2. Ibid., 18.

3. Ibid., 17.

4. Ibid., 20.

5. L. Mengoni, "L'enciclica *Laborem exercens* e la cultura industriale," in G. Lazzati et al., *Lavoro e chiesa oggi. Per una lettura della Laborem exercens* (Milan: Vita e Pensiero, 1983).

6. OECD, *Employment Outlook*, Paris (1996).

7. P. Gottschalk and T. M. Smeeding, "Cross-National Comparisons of Earnings and Income Inequality," *Journal of Economic Literature*, 35 (1997): 633–87; F. D. Blau and L. M. Kahn, "International Differences in Male Wage Inequality: Institutions versus Market Forces," *Journal of Political Economy* 104(4) (1996): 791–836; N. Fortin and T. Lemieux, "Institutional Change and Rising Wage Inequality," *Journal of Economic Perspectives* 11(2) (1997): 75–96.

8. A. Bjorklund and R. Freeman, "Generating Earnings Equality and Eliminating Poverty: The Swedish Way," in R. Freeman, B. Swedenborg, and R. Topel, eds., *Reforming the Welfare State* (Chicago: University of Chicago Press, 1996); D. Blanchflower and R. Freeman, "Unionism in the U.S. and Other OECD Countries," *Industrial Relations* 31(1) (1992): 56–79.

9. See R. B. Freeman, "Labour Market Institutions and Earnings Inequality," *England Economic Review* (May–June 1996), 157–72.

10. Obviously the possibility of spillover effects onto noncovered workers should be taken into account.

11. Since "institutions" arise to represent and insure selected groups of individuals or firms, their focus is on the "average" (median), and they may resist changes that affect the welfare of the "average" worker even if these might be perfectly consistent with an optimizing behavior based on the "marginal" worker, such as that arising from the operation of the market mechanism.

12. Inequality indices are calculated for full-time, full-year earnings. For further details concerning the data used, see OECD, *Employment Outlook, 1998*.

13. Various definitions have been suggested for the earnings cutoff determining low pay. First, this depends on whether an absolute or a relative measure is chosen. "Absolute" measures are defined with reference to a given level of income in real terms, for example, the official poverty line. Conversely, "relative" measures are taken as the earnings level defined as a fraction of mean or median wages, or with respect to some specified quantile of the distribution. Problems arise with any of the above definitions. However, for the purposes of the present study, a "relative" measure, closer to the idea of social distance, was chosen. Despite its apparent arbitrariness, this measure is in line with the Council of Europe's suggested "decency threshold" (defined as 68 percent of full-time average weekly earnings) as well as with the level of the legal minimum wage enforced in several European countries. Other organizations, such as the Trade Union Congress (TUC) and British Low Pay Unit (BLPU), have proposed different pay thresholds. See OECD, *Employment Outlook* (1996), for a thorough discussion of the properties and limitations of the different measures for the low-pay cutoffs. M. Keese, A. Puymoyen, and P. Swain, "Low-Paid Employment in OECD Countries: An International Comparison," in R. Asplund, P. J. Sloane, and I. Theodossiou, eds., *Low Pay and Earnings Mobility in Europe* (Cheltenham, U. K.: Edward Elgar, 1998), also deal with the issue.

14. Information on labor market institutions for the 1990s is drawn from various sources: OECD, *Employment Outlook* (1998); L. Bardone, M. Gittleman, and M. Keese, "Causes and Consequences of Earnings Inequality in OECD Countries," in *Lavoro e Relazioni Industriali: Revista di Economia Applicata* 4(2) (1998).

15. Centralization in bargaining procedures refers to one-to-one union/employer negotiations, while corporatism provides a broader definition encompassing also coordination in bargaining across sectors and/or different levels of negotiations. See also R. B. Freeman, "How Much Has De-Unionization Contributed to the Rise in Male Earnings Inequality?" in S. Danziger and P. Gottschalk, eds., *Uneven Tides: Rising Inequality in America* (New York: Russell Sage Foundation, 1993), 99–164; D. Card, "The Impact of Declining Unionisation on Wage Inequality," *National Bureau of Economic Research*, Working Paper no. 5520 (1998); and J. DiNardo, N. Fortin, and T. Lemieux, "Labor Market Institutions and the Distribution of Wages, 1973–1992: A Semi-Parametric Approach," *Econometrica* 64(5) (1996): 1001–44.

16. The impact on wage inequality will depend on the position of the workers affected by the union markup within the overall wage distribution. Inequality will be reduced if union workers have below-average pay levels, and conversely increased if union workers have above-average pay levels. H. G. Lewis, *Union Relative Wage Effects: A Survey* (Chicago: University of Chicago Press, 1986).

17. In general, unions have been very successful in removing performance evaluations as a factor in determining individual workers' wages. Also, seniority-based pay progression, requiring similar pay conditions to be applied to workers of comparable seniority, tends to reduce wage dispersion. See R. B. Freeman, "Unionism and the Dispersion of Wages," *Industrial and Labor Relations Review* 34 (1980): 3–24.

18. R. B. Freeman, "The Exit-Voice Tradeoff in the Labour Market: Unionism, Job Tenure, Quits, and Separations," *Quarterly Journal of Economics* 94 (1980): 643–73; Freeman, "Unionism and the Dispersion of Wages."

19. R. B. Freeman and J. L. Medoff, *What Do Unions Do?* (New York: Basic Books, 1984); B. T. Hirsch and J. T. Addison, *The Economic Analysis of Unions* (Boston: Allen & Unwin, 1986).

20. Some care should be used in interpreting the impact of institutional wage setting (that is, statutory minimum wages or bargained wages) on earnings dispersion, since it could also be ascribed to a truncation of the earnings distribution resulting from negative employment effects on low-paid work. In general, however, the latter appear to be relatively small (Blau and Kahn, "International Differences").

21. The replacement ratio is defined as the ratio between unemployment benefits and the (average) wage earned by the individual before becoming jobless.

22. S. Machin and A. Manning, "Minimum Wages, Wage Dispersion and Employment: Evidence from the UK Wages Councils," *Industrial and Labour Relations Review* 47 (1994): 319–29; C. Teulings, "The Contribution of Minimum Wages to Increasing Wage Inequality," in C. Lucifora and W. Salverda, *Policies for Low Wage Employment and Social Exclusion* (Milan: Franco Angeli, 1998); Bardone et al., "Causes and Consequences of Earnings Inequality in OECD Countries," 1–25; DiNardo et al. "Labor Market Institutions"; Fortin and Lemieux, "Institutional Change."

23. Since institutions can affect men and women very differently, care should be used in interpreting their overall effects. In particular, while unionization and collective bargaining mostly affect the male wage distribution, female wages are more sensitive to minimum wage legislation.

24. Freeman, "Labour Market Institutions and Earnings Inequality"; H. Joshi, "Gender Equity and Low Pay: A Note Based on Britain," in Lucifora and Salverda, *Policies for Low Wage Employment and Social Exclusion*; C. Dell'Aringa and C. Lucifora, "Wage Dispersion and Unionism: Do Unions Protect Low Pay?" *International Journal of Manpower* 15 (1994): 221–32; OECD, 1997.

25. A consideration of the changes that have occurred over time in various countries can be useful for assessing the relationship between the evolution of mean wages and low pay. In particular, when measured in absolute terms, the increase in real wages in Japan and the United Kingdom has brought a relative fall in the incidence of low pay. In contrast, in the United States the fall in real wages at the bottom of the earnings distribution has brought a rise in the proportion of workers with low real earnings (see also M. Keese et al., "Low-Paid Employment in OECD Countries.")

26. L. Calmfors and J. Driffil, "Bargaining Structure, Corporatism and Macroeconomic Performance," *Economic Policy* 6 (1988): 14–61; R. Brunetta and C. Dell'Aringa, *Labour Relations and Economic Performance* (London: Macmillan, 1990).

27. J. Pekkarinen, M. Pohjola, and B. Rowthorn, *Social Corporatism: A Superior Economic System?* (Oxford: Clarendon Press, 1992); E. Caroli and P. Aghion, "Inequality and Growth," University College London, mimeo (1998).

28. Simple correlations between an index of low-wage incidence *(LW)* and decile ratios measured at different points of the earnings distribution *(W91, W95, W51)* provide additional support to the evidence: $\rho(LW,W91)=0.89$; $\rho(LW,W95)=0.65$; $\rho(LW,W51)=0.83$

29. Inequality differs not only among these different groups but also within groups of workers with the same average characteristics. In terms of the methodology often used, the within group component can be approximated by the dispersion of the residual of the regression, with a wider dispersion of the residuals showing greater inequality within groups.

30. Blau and Kahn, in "International Differences," find that differences across countries in the skill distribution (measured by years of schooling and other relevant worker characteristics) account for only a small part of the differences in the overall dispersion of male wages. Hence, institutional factors could be relevant in explaining the residual (unexplained) variation.

31. P. Gottschalk, "Inequality, Income Growth, and Mobility," *Journal of Economic Perspectives* 11 (1998): 21–40; P. Gottschalk and R. Moffitt, "The Growth of Earnings Instability in the U.S. Labor Market," *Brookings Papers on Economic Activity* 2 (1994): 217–72; Gottschalk and Smeeding, "Cross-National Comparisons."

32. If a large proportion of those earning low wages in one year earn high wages in other years, then the cross-sectional earnings distribution might not be very informative. To get a clear picture of the covariance structure for low-wage workers, it is necessary to have repeated information on the same individual over time, that is, longitudinal data.

33. Care in interpreting these results is necessary for three main reasons. First, given the definition of low pay (relative to the median wage) when earnings are more dispersed, particularly at the extremes of the distribution, the wage gain required to exit low pay might be larger, thus mechanically reducing transition flows. Second, persistence in the aggregate might be due to some specific characteristics of the low-wage pool that are correlated with earnings levels quite independently of pure state dependence (for example, skill as well as unobserved heterogeneity). Third, year-to-year mobility into and out of low pay might also be affected by significant selection effects. Flows of workers out of low pay are often accounted for not only by a move into a higher paid job but also by a move into nonemployment (unemployment or out of the labor force). Similarly, flows into low pay may be associated with an earlier spell of unemployment (OECD, 1997; Bardone et al., "Causes and Consequences of Earnings Inequality in OECD Countries").

34. It is obvious that when a longer accounting period is used, all countries have less inequality, and mobility is in general higher. However, since countries do not differ much in terms of mobility patterns, their ranking in terms of inequality is not significantly altered anyway. R. Burkhauser, D. Holtz-Eakin, and S. Rhody, "Mobility and Inequality in the 1980s: A Cross-National Comparison of the United States and Germany," mimeo (1995); A. Bigard, Y. Guillotin, and C. Lucifora, "An International Comparison of Earnings Mobility: The Case of Italy and France," *The Review of Income and Wealth* (1998): 42–43; R. Dickens, "Caught in a Trap? Wage Mobility in Great Britain, 1975–94," *London School of Economics, Centre for Economic Performance*, Discussion Paper, no. 365 (1997); L. Cappellari, "Wage Inequality Dynamics in the Italian Labour Market: Permanent Changes or Transitory Fluctuations?" Istituto di Economia dell'Impresa e del Lavoro, Università Cattolica, Milan, Working Paper 23 (1998).

35. Earnings inequality indices only refer to private sector full-time, full-year workers.

36. Standard bivariate correlation coefficients are reported in table 2, the only exception being the use of the Spearman rank correlation for the index of centralization.

37. Note that most of the outliers are represented by Scandinavian countries, for which unionization and coverage are both high. In some cases, coverage extension turns out to be negative, that is, union density is higher than coverage.

38. Freeman as well as Bjorklund and Freeman, using U.S. and Swedish data, run a pseudo-experiment comparing earnings inequality between a "treatment" (men of Swedish descent living in the United States and non-Nordic men living in Sweden) and "control" group (native Americans in the United States and persons with Swedish ancestry living in Sweden). Results show insignificant differences in earnings inequality between the two groups, in each experiment, thus suggesting that institutions, more than observed and unobserved characteristics, contribute to shaping the earnings distribution. In other words, Swedish institutional wage setting appears to be more committed to egalitarianism, showing less dispersion in earnings and a lower incidence in low-wage employment, while in the United States there is more inequality because the wage setting system produces higher dispersion in earnings. See Freeman, "Labour Marker Institutions"; and Bjorklund and Freeman, "Generating Earnings Equality."

39. Blau and Kahn, in "International Differences," after correcting for a wide range of worker characteristics, still find that institutional features represent one of the main factors that can account for the observed differences, across countries, in wage inequality and low-wage employment. See also Edwin Leuven, Hessel Oosterbeek, and Hans van Ophem, "International Comparisons of Male Wage Inequality: Are the Findings Robust?" Tinbergen Institute Discussion Paper 97–059/3 (1997) and "Explaining International Differences in Male Wage Inequality by Differences in Demand and Supply of Skill," London School of Economics, Centre for Economic Performance Discussion Paper 0392 (1998) for an alternative explanation.

40. The index is based on the OECD "Literacy Skills Test Scores," and it is the ratio of the 5th percentile divided by the mean (available for eleven countries only). I am particularly grateful to A. Glyn for making the data available to me.

41. S. Nickell and B. Bell, "The Collapse in the Demand for the Unskilled and Unemployment across the OECD," *Oxford Review of Economic Policy* 11(1) (1995): 40–62.

42. Given the limited degrees of freedom, the results reported here should be interpreted with some care. A similar approach, though with fewer observations and fewer control variables, can be found in Freeman, "Labour Market Institutions." The results obtained here are very close to those reported in that study.

43. The centralization index did not result as statistically significant and hence was excluded from subsequent specifications.

44. Note that since earnings data refer to full-time private sector employees, the inclusion of both part-time and self-employment controls is essentially trying to capture a potential underreporting in low-pay employment (since low pay is known to be higher among female part-timers and the self-employed). Results for the other control variables have not been reported in the tables.

45. This result could be interpreted as if earnings "equality" were to be considered a normal good.

46. It should be stressed that the estimation of the effects of labor market institutions on different portions of the wage distribution is particularly demanding with respect to the data used, which is a cross-section of twenty OECD countries. While parameter estimates, both in terms of sign and magnitude, are fairly robust to changes in the specification, the statistical significance on the individual coefficients sometimes weakens when sufficient non-linear terms and interactions are introduced.

47. However, if increased trade occurs by "outsourcing" of low-skilled activities within manufacturing from developed countries to less developed ones, this type of skill upgrading might in fact be the direct outcome of trade factors. Under this hypothesis the two explanations might result as observationally equivalent and their relative effects as quite difficult to discern.

48. *Laborem exercens*, 20.

PART THREE

Two Business Applications

Introduction

The dynamism of the Catholic social tradition rests upon an iterative relationship between thought and action. Without a solid theological and philosophical grounding, this tradition will become unhinged from its deep roots in Scripture and Tradition. It will lose touch with the profound inspirations of its past.

Yet a tradition never relies solely upon its thoughts or ideas. The Catholic social tradition is a lived one. Just as the spiritual life of the Church lives on through liturgical and personal prayer, so, too, her social vision lives on through both the institutional and the personal witness of actions that embody her principles. As John Paul II has noted, "Today more than ever, the church is aware that her social message will gain credibility more immediately from the witness of actions than as a result of its internal logic and consistency" (*Centesimus annus*, 57).

Fortunately, the Catholic social tradition can claim many embodiments, institutional and personal, of its principles for wealth distribution and creation. They can be found in cooperatives such as Mondragón and San Lucas Toliman; in the hundreds of entrepreneurial startups inspired by the Focolare (Economy of Communion) movement; in many individual entrepreneurs and business leaders such as Léon Harmel, Enrique Shaw, and Robert Ouimet; and in the inventive programs, emanating from nonprofits and governments, in microcredit, economic development, training, and so on. These models and witnesses are not perfect, but they set forth practical ways in which the ideas and principles of the Catholic social tradition can be embodied.

While throughout this volume the authors keep their eye on the pragmatic implications of their ideas, these last two essays examine in a more detailed way the local and global implications of the Catholic social tradition as it relates to wealth distribution in light of the demands of wealth creation. They explore the practical dimensions, obstacles, detours, and opportunities faced by practitioners who attempt to found institutions that seek abundance and its just distribution.

The essays of Michael Naughton and Robert Wahlstedt and of Lee Tavis focus on mechanisms at the level of the firm and at the level of international trade for dealing with equitable distribution in the contexts of the local market and the highly competitive international regimes that businesses and business networks must face. At both local firm and international trade levels, what we see in each essay is a thoughtful and careful consideration of the different factors involved in such mechanisms. Economic issues are treated with the seriousness they deserve within a framework that views generating wealth as a means to an end and not as an end in itself.

These two chapters emphasize the *integral connection between wealth creation and distribution*. This connection is clear, in fact, in many of the contributions to this volume, but particularly so in Part III. The Naughton-Wahlstedt dialogue is directed to the firm, one of the mechanisms par excellence for wealth generation. While the issues addressed focus primarily on wealth distribution, the ways of dealing with distribution are discussed within the context of wealth creation and the pressures of profitability, productivity and marketability. Similarly, international contracts for sportswear and related products set the context for Tavis's discussion of just wages and the right to organize, issues that strongly affect the question of wealth distribution. (In the case of the right to organize, Carlo Dell'Aringa and Claudio Lucifora, chapter 10, this volume, make the effect clear.) Tavis maneuvers the reader through the complex factors of apparel manufacture within a globalized economy. He then moves to some practical measures for humanizing the all-too-often inhumane sweatshop-production process in a way that does not undermine the wealth-generating capacity of the developing world.

Both essays highlight the need for the virtue of prudence in economic life. If employers act to pay just wages or to maintain humane factory conditions for humane production of apparel products, but do so in a way that undermines production and the long-term profitability of the firm, they enact not justice but, rather, foolishness. By its definition, justice in the economic order entails the virtue of prudence, which is the capacity to discern the best means for attaining one's morally good ends. Furthermore, prudence applies the right means to good ends—the means of bringing about the concrete realization of justice or right relationships with others. Without prudence, that is, without effective means, justice becomes unrealizable. Without the ability to make effective decisions, we cannot hope to deal fairly with others or to use wisely our capital, property, and material resources.

Yet, without justice, prudence is merely trickery. Paradoxically, prudence is one of the most misunderstood virtues in the Western tradition. Rather than a virtue that embraces goodness, prudence is seen as an evasion of it. It conjures up in the modern mind not human nobility but self-serving calculation. It is often associated with slyness and craftiness—a sort of shrewd knack for satisfying one's particular preferences. The so-called prudent person is often associated with the person who looks after only his own interests in a sea of other conflicting interests. The business manager calculates what his employees will bear in light of this or that inducement and shrewdly plays one against another. He is considered the cunning tactician who, by concealing his real intentions, induces others to serve his self-centered purposes. Prudence, particularly in business circles, is a strategy to weaken the force of justice. These misinterpretations of the classical and Christian understanding of prudence prevent the businessperson from seeing himself as a moral agent. Separating the virtues of prudence and justice from each other is like separating the head from the heart; neither can function without the other. Instead, the prudential businessperson is not a mere calculator, technician, or manipulator, but rather a wiser, practical person who has a grasp of the various disciplines of commerce, perceives situations as they are, and directs his activity toward ends that develop people and encourage right relationships—that is, he promotes justice. The two chapters that follow are attempts to trace creative procedures and policies that promote a more just distribution of resources and actually enhance wealth creation.

ELEVEN # Implementing Just Wages and Ownership

A Dialogue

Michael J. Naughton
and Robert L. Wahlstedt

My own goal is to generate wealth for the people I work with to distribute it in a way that makes the world a better place. It's one thing to want the world to be better; it's another to come up with the resources that let you do it. What I'm trying to do here is raise people's standard of living by showing them how to create wealth and keep it. That's my Big Picture.

—Jack Stack

Business leaders should make their needs for increased capital and profits compatible with requirements of social justice and a working community respectful of its members' personalities and creativities. Educators and opinion leaders should promote and support a view of life in which the criterion for judgment and action would be the transcendental dignity of each person. In synthesis, everyone should be persuaded that a nation, as a community of people, must be built upon sound ethic and moral foundations, and that each and every member must feel responsible for the welfare of all.

—John Paul II

This essay records a dialogue between a business leader and an educator on the distribution of wealth (chiefly ownership shares) and income (chiefly wage rates and policies) within a business organization. The interlocutors seek to clarify, so as to adopt for themselves and communicate to others, the perspective that the Christian social tradition gives on that distribution. Readers of the Scriptures or of other basic documents of the Christian social tradition can hardly escape the sense that distributing wealth is an important part of living a life of faith, so important that the Old Testament (see the prophets Jeremiah, Amos, and Isaiah) and the New Testament alike (see in particular Mt 25:31 ff. and Lk 12:16–21, 16:1–13, 19–31) warn that our salvation may be at risk if we fail to do it well.

Scriptural references to wealth or income often put in readers' minds questions of stewardship: How should I spend the money I earn? Whom should I give my wealth to when I die? Stewardship is, of course, of great personal importance, and disciplined stewardship is a powerful means of addressing particular patterns of inequity. Nevertheless, work organizations in general, and businesses in particular, remain major means for distributing wealth. Business organizations' ownership structures, which distribute wealth, and their compensation policies, which distribute income, have more to do with distributive justice in society at large than private philanthropy or public welfare programs, critical as both are to a just society.

For those "with eyes to see," the multifaceted phenomena of wealth and income inequity demand a deliberately religious response, for the God of the Old and New Testaments demands the praise of justice in human works and institutions. The widening disparity in wealth—for example, stratospheric rates of executive pay (compounded with egregious corruption among some in the executive class), as contrasted with the slow growth of wages on the lower end of the economic ladder; "superdevelopment" of the richest countries of the world, versus the underdevelopment of many others—all indicate prima facie to the religious mind that something has gone radically wrong, within and among the nations, in our current distribution of wealth and income. Moreover, as religious minds contemplate these indices with a view to causes and solutions, they will be drawn to a critical examination of business practices. On the whole, businesses generate wealth with surprising ingenuity; and on the whole, they distribute it formulaically, often with an all-too-mechanical nod to the markets. As wealth is rightly created for the sake of distribution, so ingenuity in producing wealth should be matched by ingenious designs for its more just distribution.

Traditionally, Christian social thought is closely concerned with the just distribution of wealth and income. In general, however, business schools in Christian universities have neglected (as have their secular counterparts) the question of wealth distribution in their professional curricula; they have not thought the question central to the formation of managers. In light of the Christian social tradition, this neglect amounts to failure in a crucial aspect of their mission. Moreover, the schools' omission is a kind of witness: Christian businesspeople and others can be excused if they regard distributive justice as something less than an imperative of sound—that is, religiously and ethically sound—business practice.

For their part, Christian social thinkers often have not effectively incorporated ethical reflection on wealth creation with reflection on wealth distribution. If wealth is to be distributed, it has to be first created, and this is no easy job. Generating customers, making new products, adapting old ones, managing cash flow, financing capital, controlling costs, predicting market changes, and so forth take up much of a manager's day, and if these wealth-generating activities are not done well, the survival of the firm is in jeopardy.

The challenge and opportunity for business practitioners and educators is to devise practices that support a just distribution of wealth and market success, and that help entrepreneurs and managers keep both the bark of conscience and their businesses afloat in the turbulent waters of the present-day economy. The challenge demands that we attend to the moral reflection of popes, bishops, and theologians as well as to the technical advice of economists and business theorists. But it demands no less that we attend to the practical wisdom of women and men who struggle day by day, in the business world, to be faithful to their Christian calling, which includes making an honest profit. The Christian social tradition hands on not only words of wisdom but also the practices—actions, intentions, and institutions—of those who seek to live the tradition. The dialogue form of this essay, therefore, aims to emphasize theorists' and teachers' need to listen to practitioners, and vice versa, if the Christian social tradition is to make progress on all fronts.

The Interlocutors

While both interlocutors in this dialogue adhere to the tenets of the Christian social tradition and try to follow its teachings in their day-to-day lives, each one, by the nature of his work, brings particular strengths (and particular weaknesses) to the dialogue. Bob Wahlstedt is a founding member, chairman of the board, and former president of Reell Precision Manufacturing Corporation, a producer of hi-tech clutches and hinges for the office machine and computer industries. Bob is a member of the Evangelical Covenant Church. Mike Naughton is the director of the John A. Ryan Institute for Catholic Social Thought at the University of St. Thomas, where he teaches courses in the Departments of Theology and Catholic Studies and the College of Business. Mike is a member of the Roman Catholic Church.

The interlocutors share a single dialectic goal: to grasp more clearly Christian social teaching on wealth distribution, so as to discern how it can be operationalized as just wealth distribution within a healthy business. Nevertheless, they approach the goal in different ways. As an entrepreneur, Bob emphasizes problem solving and is more inductive than Mike. His experience as a practitioner leads him to think that the most pressing question is always: "How can it work?" Mike's experience is more theoretical, and therefore he tends to think more in terms of maintaining and applying principles; by comparison to Bob's, his approach is deductive. From his point of view, the most pressing question tends to be: "Is the proposal true to the principles of the Christian social tradition?"

The interlocutors are united in the search for distributively just pay and ownership practices, but they come to this problem from different starting points. Readers will not be disappointed if they anticipate some tension between the interlocutors' positions. To the contrast between an inductive/practical approach and a deductive/principled approach, some political differences may be added. Bob, like many businesspeople, favors a more hands-off government role in economic matters, at least; Mike, like many academics, sees a significant role for government in the economy and civil society generally. Interestingly enough, their theological differences as a Protestant and a Catholic, respectively, generate no discernible tension in this conversation. United by their shared Christian baptism, they both see the importance of a just distribution of wealth in the vocation of a manager.

THE SCOPE OF THE DIALOGUE

The dialogue focuses on two concrete issues of distributive justice proper to business: wages (income) and ownership (wealth). Income and wealth are distinct but interdependent regulative concepts for economic analysis and business practice (see the introduction to this volume, "The Nature of Wealth"). Income refers chiefly to payment for contributions to the economy and business enterprise. Wages and salaries, the major sources of income for most employees (although income also includes interest and dividends), are accordingly the principal subjects of just income distribution within a business. In his encyclical, *Laborem exercens: On Human Work*, John Paul II explains that "[i]n the context of the present there is no more important way for securing a just relationship between the worker and the employer than that constituted by remuneration for work."[1]

Nevertheless, however materially important wages and salaries are to distributive justice in the firm, wages and salaries are also an unstable means for the just distribution of wealth. Centering the question of the just distribution of goods— that is, of material benefits—on wages earned from business is like relying solely on two cyclinders of a four-cylinder engine: with only half the power, the system is driven to breakdown. When John A. Ryan wrote in 1935 that an employee's rise to ownership "relieves him from complete dependence upon his wages," he already understood "relief" to mean relief from bearing an inequitably large share of the market economy's risks and an inequitably small share of its rewards.[2] This is why John Paul II also said in *Laborem exercens* that "recognition of the proper position of labor and the worker in the production process demands various adaptations in the sphere of the right to ownership of the means of production." When capital ownership is connected to labor, it is simply easier, although not guaranteed, to promote "the universal destination of goods and the right to common use of them."[3]

The dialogue, therefore, focuses also on the distribution of wealth, chiefly via ownership of productive assets (with some attention to "human capital" in the form of knowledge and skills). Capital, as a form of wealth, is stored-up economic power. One important element of this economic power is what makes up the "value" of a corporation. Only 25 percent of the assets of the S&P 500 companies take the form of physical capital. Employees sense that what makes up the rest of the value of a company resides increasingly in their knowledge and labor, which they believe is currently undervalued.[4] The interplay among *productivity gains, wage earners,* and *capital owners* helps to illustrate their point. Since 1974, productivity in manufacturing has increased by 68 percent and in the service sector by 50 percent. During this same period, employee wages have stagnated. Between 1989 and 1997, 86 percent of stock market gains flowed to the top 10 percent of households, while 42 percent of these gains went to the wealthiest 1 percent.[5] Since many wage earners are nonowners, the lions' share of the rewards from productivity improvements went to capital owners. Again, since the richest 25 percent own 82 percent of corporate stock in the United States, the clear winners from productivity gains were capital owners, and the consequence was increased income disparity.[6] Louis Kelso, often considered the father of employee stock ownership plans (ESOPs), argued fifty years ago that the percentage of total income derived from labor would decrease and that the percentage derived from capital would increase, one of the main reasons why he advocated wider ownership.[7] If we are going to have a just and sustainable distribution of wealth, we need to devise practices directed toward both wages and capital ownership.

Both parties to the dialogue came to see that they need each other's insights in order to be more effective in what they do. Since our gifts are always limited, we are always in need of the gifts of others. Bob concedes that explicitly articulating the problem in terms of the principles within Christian social thought helps him to solve it more creatively and more comprehensively. Mike has come to discover that listening to someone involved in applying these principles in practice—someone familiar with the attendant tensions and difficulties—can actually help to clarify the principles themselves. Too often academics and businesspeople do not see it as worthwhile to work together on an issue of business organization and strategy, whereas the interlocutors in this dialogue are convinced of the value of such an initiative because of, as well as in spite of, the tension that can arise in its course.

THE DIALOGUE ON PAY

Naughton: Compensation is usually handled by an organization's human resource department. Increasingly, human resource departments describe pay primarily in strategic terms: its purpose is to attract, reward, retain, and motivate employees who best promote the strategic goals of the organization. These strategic goals tend to be exclusively economic in nature: beating the competition, expanding market share, enhancing quality, raising customer satisfaction and retention, increasing efficiency, motivating performance, and maximizing shareholder wealth.

Within the Christian social tradition, there is nothing wrong with viewing pay as strategic or instrumental.[8] The problem arises when pay is seen only as strategic and instrumental, which then results in instrumentalism. The reason for this being a problem comes from the Christian understanding of human work. The fundamental premise of a Christian view of just wages is the following: *work can never be reduced to the pay given, that is, the wage given can never fully account for the labor done, precisely because work is always more than its economic output or instrumental value.* This "something more" can be described in terms of its *subjective dimension*—work not only changes objects but also changes the subject who does the work—and its *transcendent dimension*—through our labor, we participate in the ongoing work of the Creator. Because of these particularly human and spiritual dimensions, pay cannot exhaust the value of the work done.[9] There is always something more to work than its instrumental value, or, to put it another way, work as an aspect of human existence is "incompletely commodified."[10] While one's labor is exchanged for money and can be commodified by the price given for it, it is at the same time forming the personal and social identity of the worker that goes beyond the work itself.

Wahlstedt: I agree with you, Mike, that, idealistically, "pay cannot exhaust the value of the work done" and that the strategic terms in which the market views pay tend to "instrumentalize" human work. However, customers (and all of us are customers) will only pay for the "instrumental value" of work—that is, we will not pay more than the value we receive for the products we buy. As a businessperson I am faced, therefore, with the reality that pay which exceeds that value can lead to dire consequences. First, it may not be sustainable in a competitive situation; second, the worker may not be able to find similar work at a similar pay rate in the event that he must find a new employer. This tends to limit the worker's freedom of employment choice or, worse, to encourage the development of an unsustainable standard of living.

This places us squarely on the horns of a dilemma. Should we, as Christian employers, pay market wages even though they may not support those conditions necessary for human development as stated by Pope John Paul II and other popes throughout this century?[11] Or, on the other hand, should we pay higher wages even in the face of the possibilities identified above? I think that neither is an acceptable response.

At Reell, we have found another alternative. We hire new individuals at a competitive market wage but commit ourselves to raising their pay to a "target wage" within a relatively short period, usually two or three years but never more than five. The target wage could be thought of as the minimum wage that can support conditions that foster human development. The challenge we accept is to structure the work and to teach the individual the skills required to bring the work's "instrumental value" into line with the target wage. This practice has several desirable results:

- It maintains and even enhances competitiveness in the marketplace.
- It accomplishes the principle of "subsidiarity," in that the primary means for upgrading the value of the work is to push responsibility and authority to the lowest possible level.
- It fosters creativity and improves morale.
- It builds positive relationships between co-workers and management.
- It improves mental health and sometimes even physical health.

Naughton: Bob, you put your finger on a critical problem for the principle-based approach to pay in the Christian social tradition. But the tension between your practicality and the principles of the tradition can be resolved, as you've already begun to indicate in your reply. Let me explain further.

Because a wage can never exhaust the meaning of one's work, the Christian social tradition sees wages always in the context of justice, that is, right relationships. It articulates at least three main principles to help clarify what this right relationship between an employer and employee would look like as far as it concerns pay:

- meeting employees' needs (*a living wage*)
- recognizing their contributions (*an equitable wage*)
- sustaining a viable economic order in the business (*a sustainable wage*)

The tension you experience is between the principle of "need" (a living wage) and the principle of "order" (a sustainable wage). The tradition's insistence on the principle of need is at the root of the very notion of a living wage. A living wage rests on the fundamental Christian insight I described above, namely, that because work can never be fully accounted for or exhausted by the wage given, the employer/employee relationship cannot be understood only as a legal contract or a market exchange. Again, there is something more, and what describes this "more" is a moral and spiritual relationship. At minimum for the employer, this entails a living wage, since a wage that fails to meet the needs of the employee cannot carry the weight of a real relationship. As our friend Bob Kennedy has argued, an employee in an ordinary work situation has nothing else with which to earn his living than the work he is giving his employer. The wage is a way, and for many the only way, of providing for human needs that include food, clothing, housing, transportation, insurance, education, leisure, and a pension.[12] An employer who fails to recognize this need of the employee also fails to see the inherent and created dignity of the employee. Yet, a living wage cannot be sustained unless there is a degree of economic order. Or, to put it another way, the *ought* of a living wage always implies the *can* of a sustainable wage. Here we need to attend more carefully to the circumstances and the means.

The circumstances in which Reell finds itself are those of a labor market where the price for labor is unregulated by the state except insofar as there exists a minimum wage, which, however, does not constitute a living wage. Unions are not involved in its labor market, and the current skill level for the work is minimal. When the company first started to wrestle with a target wage in 1996, the nonunion, unregulated, low-skill wage produced a labor rate of $6.80 per hour. These circumstances provided opportunities for and placed limitations on a manager's sphere of action and influence.

Given the circumstances of this competitive price system, and the end that it wished to achieve, namely, provide for employee needs within a sound economic organization, Reell chose the following means: (1) developing employees' skills, making them more efficient, productive, and cost-effective; and (2) redesigning work processes (quality control techniques, Just-in-Time manufacturing, etc.) to take advantage of employees' enhanced skills. These means allow Reell to create organizational conditions that require less supervision, permit faster setup times, and reduce the need for quality inspection. Together, these improvements reduced overall costs, which increased labor rates but decreased labor costs.[13]

If Reell wants to apply Judeo-Christian values in practice, it must pay a living wage. Yet, he who wills the end must will the means: apart from the prudent, concrete means of sustaining them, "just" wages will not be available for long, and it is managers, not popes or theologians, who need to develop these means. In other words, "justice" without prudence (organizing the appropriate means and understanding one's circumstances) is an exercise in moralism (or "justicism") that cannot deliver on its promise.

As Bob mentioned, because we as customers will only pay for the "instrumental value" of work, he is faced with the reality that paying for labor beyond its market value results in organizational decline. While it is critical not to underestimate this instrumental value, the more likely temptation for a manager is to overvalue this instrumental dimension, resulting in a view of labor that can be described as "instrumentalism." Proponents of the strategic view of pay, for example, often acknowledge the importance of a living wage: they know that low-base pay "can cause significant problems in recruiting and retaining the best and the brightest individuals. It can also lead to an internal culture of low self-esteem and to feelings that the organization in general is second best and lacks the resources to do a first-rate job."[14] Yet the strategic logic here, namely, an instrumental logic, still subjects a living wage and the human person to a closed economic system. What happens, for example, when wages are strategically advantageous at a rate that fails to meet the "needs" of employees, such as in developing countries where labor protection is nonexistent, labor unions are suppressed, and labor markets are flooded? Or what happens when "human performance is not a major determinant of organizational performance"?[15] The answer, if we take the logic of strategic pay seriously, is to forfeit the needs of employees. *It is precisely when managers view labor as fully accounted for or exhausted by the pay given that they fall into this instrumental logic.* When the transcendent end of labor is no longer part of the equation of pay, employees become merely one more factor of production.

How does this apply to Bob and Reell? It is difficult to believe that Reell could have developed a target wage on strategic grounds alone, or that the firm's leadership did not first desire the right end, namely, just and right relationships with its employees. Intentions do matter when it comes to organizational life.

Finally, it is this intentionality that helps us to get to the deeper meaning of wealth. When you redesigned your production process, your employees developed their productive capacity through their own knowhow and skills. They became, in a very significant way, "wealthier," because they now "own" the tools (knowledge and skills) that generate the wealth of the business. Like land and capital, their skills and knowledge became a form of "stored-up economic power." This is why John Paul II has argued that the decisive factor concerning wealth—productive capacity—"is increasingly man himself, that is, his knowledge, especially his scientific knowledge, his capacity for interrelated and compact organization, as well as his ability to perceive the needs of others and to satisfy them."[16] Through the target wage, you have not only distributed wages more justly, but you have also distributed knowledge and skills, which further guarantees a more just distribution of wealth.

Wahlstedt: Mike, I like the moral and theological analysis that you provide and really like the three "principles"—need, contribution, and economic order. I have come to realize that the tension between the principle of need and the principle of sustainability could be resolved by the principle of contribution. If employers seek to maximize the contribution of employees, they tend to close the gap between need and sustainability. What jumps out here is the connectedness between just wages and "subsidiarity." Perhaps these two dimensions of Catholic social thought are not meant to be implemented apart from each other. By increasing the skills and responsibilities of employees at all levels, the practice of subsidiarity increases the instrumental value of work. This helps to close the gap between a "living wage" and a "sustainable wage" so that people can be paid enough to live on without jeopardizing the future of the organization.

I further agree that Reell would not have developed its pay system based on economic principles alone. We clearly began "theologically," if you call trying to follow the "will of God" theological, but I fear that we are being naïve if we think that theological argument is going to persuade very many business leaders, many of whom are simply trying to survive in "permanent white water," as Peter Vaill puts it.[17] How can we expect people to ponder all this theology when they are already doing all they can to come up with a workable system, let alone a just one? We are often overwhelmed by trying to balance the bottom line and to keep people sufficiently satisfied so we don't lose them!

You also imply that just pay would be more universal if the state got into the act and set higher minimums, or if we had stronger unions to wrest a bigger chunk of the pie from management. In my opinion, the last things we need are more government interference and more hostility between management and labor.

Although it is true that Reell would not have developed its pay system out of a purely economic model, neither would the Wright brothers have invented the airplane out of purely economic motivation. We always need pioneers—and yes, theologians as well—to blaze new trails, but the fact remains that these new trails will never be followed unless they are economically sustainable.

Finally, however, I must return to the conclusion that theological pioneering in business must, first and foremost, be sustainable and economically successful or it will not survive to be noticed and can never become the "norm" that we would all like to see. It is a matter of *faith* to believe that what is *right* will be successful, and it is an act of faith to put these theological principles into practice before they are proven. It is essential that those who have such faith also have the wisdom and prudence necessary to build economically successful models. *"For the gate is narrow and the way is hard, that leads to life, and those who find it are few"* (Mt 7:14). It is my hope that many will pass through that door when it has been shown that these principles can enhance the material quality of our lives as well as their spiritual quality.

More can be said here on the relationship between success and faith. Faith provides the basis for stronger relationships. These relationships strengthen businesses to be real work communities with a greater potential for economic success. As is the case with many of the Proverbs, this statement is generally true, but in practice, faith does not always create better relationships. Rather, faith will at times strain them.

THE DIALOGUE ON CAPITAL OWNERSHIP

Naughton: The discipline of finance has significantly influenced our understanding of capital and its ownership,[18] and consequently how we understand the distribution of wealth within business. While proponents of the financial model of the firm recognize various goods of an organization, the first and controlling end of the firm lies in maximizing returns for shareholders. Underlying this understanding of corporate property is a philosophical individualism that implies at least two things: (1) exclusivity of ownership: "this property is mine and not yours"; and (2) control: "since it's mine, I alone determine what it is to be used for."[19] While a Christian notion of property would affirm the importance of exclusivity and control, the Christian tradition insists that property, including corporate property, cannot be understood fully unless it is also understood theologically and socially. This calls for a rethinking of property and capital in business.

To understand property within the Christian theological tradition, one must first understand it as a *gift*. Before we own, we are first "receivers" or inheritors of property (see Simona Beretta's essay on this point, chapter 5, this volume). As David Schindler explains, "this receiving disposition remains anterior to and informs every act of human creativity."[20] God, who created the world "and saw that it was very good," gave humanity the gift of dominion over the earth. As receivers versus creators of what we have, our orientation toward property must focus on the *use* of property and not just on its private *possession*.

To illustrate this, it is helpful to recall that when Native Americans first encountered Europeans, they were baffled by their possessiveness. They expected the newcomers to return their gifts because that's how goods continued to circulate in what was then an indigenous gift economy. The idea of maintaining gifts in a perpetual state of exchange equally baffled the Westerners, who negatively portrayed the natives as "Indian givers."[21] Yet, what Native Americans understood, and what we should take heed of, is that when a gift is not shared, it corrupts the holder. The one who makes the gift an occasion for selfish hoarding and who fails to put it "in motion," keeping it only for his private gain, becomes corrupted by the gift itself.

In Western culture, we tend to see property and capital, and our bodies for that matter, as a so-called private matter, and thus we have tended to downplay their social character. Within the financial model, the corporation exists to earn for investors as much money as possible, and then investors decide themselves on what they want to spend it. Yet, this private interpretation of property should give us pause. Augustine pointed out that the word "private" comes from "privation," a certain loss of meaning or substance.[22] To understand property only in terms of privacy is to refuse to recognize its inherent "giftedness" and in particular its social nature—that it is to be shared with others, especially those in need. While Thomas Aquinas was a strong advocate of private property, his advocacy was built upon its proper ordering. He explained that all property should be seen "as common so that, in fact, a person should readily share it when he sees others in need."[23] It is with this disposition toward property that the use of property and capital can be opportunities for growing in virtue. This is why one cannot see wealth distribution as brought about by no more than a mechanistic force determined by market factors, allowing managers and entrepreneurs to excuse themselves from any responsibility. Such a view is contrary to the Christian social tradition. Wealth distribution is a human responsibility because we have been called to be God's stewards of creation—a responsibility that is framed by our sphere of influence. The manager must wrestle with making a fairer distribution of his resources, since, as Thomas puts it, "a man's will is not right in willing a particular good [such as to acquire or use property], unless he refers it to the common good as an end."[24]

Christian thought and teaching on the social and theological dimensions of property are not easy to grasp or accept, but this is the case for much Christian teaching. At the same time, for the businessperson in a corporation, these teachings can constitute an invitation to extend one's thinking as well as a challenge to reflect on one's experience in corporate life so as to see how the social nature of property could come more fully alive. At times, it will become so stretched that it may look impractical and unattainable, but these are moments for hope, where the good to make the world a better place is not yet attained but can be achieved in the future.

Wahlstedt: At Reell, this issue of ownership was first brought to our attention by an insurance agent. He told us that we should purchase life insurance to fund a buy-sell agreement so that, in the event that one of us three should die, there would be funds available to buy out the deceased partner. He pointed out that the failure to do this could result in a forced sale of the company because the estate taxes could easily exceed the liquid funds available. It also would ensure that we would be able to pass on to our heirs the value of our interest in the company.

We foresaw several problems with this approach. First, it would require the purchase of ever-increasing amounts of life insurance as the value of the company rose, and there was no way to be sure that we would remain insurable. Second, it would deal with the death of the first or second of us, but the last survivor—and ultimately his heirs—would end up with the entire company. This seemed like too much of a "crap shoot," and, ultimately, this too would likely result in a forced sale. Finally, it treated the company as nothing more than a financial asset. In the end, the company would be sold to the highest bidder and he would do with it what he pleased. We had established that our fundamental purpose in the business was to be the security and growth of co-workers. In no way did this life insurance approach give us any reason to believe that the purpose and mission of the company would carry on beyond the founders.

We quickly realized that there was no way that we could guarantee that the purpose and mission would survive, but we were determined to do whatever was possible to increase this likelihood. We judged that those who had the most intimate personal relationship with the founders—our children—and those who had the most intimate relationship with the business—our co-workers—would probably have the most appreciation for the purpose and mission and would be the most likely to see that it continue to be developed into the next generation. In 1985, therefore, we established two plans: (1) an annual gifting program to transfer stock to our children; this has resulted in keeping our projected personal estate taxes within the available liquid funds; and (2) an Employees Stock Option Plan (ESOP) to provide retirement income to the participants, our co-workers. These two plans together allow for the control of the company—the ownership of the stock—to pass to our children and to our co-workers after the death of the founders. In fact, two-thirds of the ownership have already been passed: about one-third to the children, and one-third to the ESOP.[25]

Furthermore, the top leadership is now in the hands of a new generation, which does not include members of the founding families, and they are continuing to pursue and develop the mission with even greater vigor. This is in sharp contrast to the experience of several personal acquaintances who sold their businesses when nearing retirement age. In every case those companies were merged into other larger entities with very different agendas, or they have become almost exclusively financially oriented, often to the great disappointment of their founders and employees.

The truth is, whether we like it or not, that the stockholders, by virtue of their right to vote their shares, have the right to choose the purpose and mission of the corporation. When the ownership changes, the purpose and mission will very likely change as well. We may wish that this was not so, but it is—so we must believe that enlightened leaders will choose to follow the higher road described by Mike and that they will be economically successful so that others will be inspired to follow their lead.

Naughton: Bob, what I find particularly interesting in this ownership issue is that you and the two other founders of Reell easily could have undertaken an initial public offering and walked away very rich men, as many entrepreneurs have done. But cashing out somehow did not fit with the mission of Reell, namely, "the operation of a business based on the practical application of spiritual values . . . to advance the common good for the benefit of co-workers and their families, customers, shareholders, suppliers, and community."[26] The company, as you put it, was more than a "financial asset."

As you mentioned above, the impetus for the ESOP was not primarily to share the wealth with employees, but rather to keep the company in friendly hands so that the mission would continue to be honored.[27] Part of the mission includes sharing the wealth, but it is important to examine a couple of questions in more general terms here: Why wouldn't the question of greater wealth distribution motivate you to share capital ownership with your employees? Why did it take an insurance agent to get you to consider an ESOP?

Before addressing these questions as they specifically relate to you and Reell, I want to make some general observations, which I believe provide a helpful context. First, businesspeople in general—and their education encourages this—are somewhat apprehensive of the word "distribution." Influenced by classical economics as well as by their own experience, businesspeople will often see wealth distribution as best handled as a market decision determined by mechanistic forces of supply and demand. Often, they see no relationship between their decisions and their behavior, or between their growth in virtue, on the one hand, and fostering a more just distribution of resources, on the other. The question of distribution is often relegated to the private sphere of individual giving.

Second, businesspeople are often suspicious of the language of justice, and for good reason. Justice has become somewhat politicized both within the wider culture and within the Church in particular, thus making it almost unusable in business. Justice is reduced to a bully club by which the state coerces business to do so-called good things or to a prophetic denunciation by which the Church condemns business behavior. This has generated a certain reservation among businesspeople both toward the Church and the state. In this sense, businesspeople have good cause to be suspicious of a stunted notion of justice and its relationship to distribution. Yet, the unfortunate result is that more often than not, businesspeople do not have a language that can help them personalize their responsibility, as agents of the corporation, to distribute wealth within their own sphere of influence and also help them to understand that they, as "direct employers," cannot by themselves carry the full demands of justice. For example, I was struck by your response to me concerning unions and the state. Any hint of state regulation generates an allergic reaction and is considered to be bad a priori. I would like to add that I was not advocating state regulation above; I was merely trying to describe the company's situation. I do find, however, that Carlo Dell'Aringa and Claudio Lucifora's essay (chapter 10, this volume) offers convincing arguments for the importance of what they call "indirect employers," that is, states and unions, in wealth distribution.

Despite these two observations, which help us to understand the businessperson's reservations with regard to the term "just distribution," Christian businesspeople, on the basis of the insights of the Christian social tradition, must respond to current, problematic patterns of wealth distribution and assume the important role of property and capital in bringing about a more humane distribution of wealth. (For statistical details on the multifaceted dimensions of wealth distribution, see the introduction to this volume, "The Nature of Wealth," Dell'Aringa and Lucifora's essay, and Charles Clark, chapter 1, this volume).

When one takes an honest look at the complexity of our current situation, the question for the Christian businessperson is: "How do I respond to such numbers?" Within the Christian social tradition, the problem is not the magnitude of capital owners' gains, but rather the system's tendency to restrict rather than to promote participation in capital ownership. Another problem is the refusal of those entrepreneurs, managers, and boards of directors to take a serious look at their responsibility for wealth distribution and its impact on the incomes of employees. When the power of the ownership of productive capital is highly concentrated in the hands of the few, the incomes of the nonowning majority grow uncertain;[28] and when capital is disconnected from labor and the communities in which it resides, its uses are determined without regard for the impact on labor or on society at large.

This disconnection is creating a casino-like atmosphere in which investors are increasingly shrinking their time horizons for a maximum return on their investments, resulting in "stock churning." For example, one study found that "76% of the shares of the average U.S. company listed on the New York Stock Exchange turned over last year. That's up from 46% in 1990 and only 12% in 1960. . . . On the Nasdaq . . . shareholder turnover is nearly three times as high."[29] The markets' relentless pressure for maximum investor returns leads corporations to "unleash what the *Wall Street Journal* characterizes as the 'four horsemen of the workplace': (1) downsizing, (2) moving operations to low-wage countries, (3) increased automation, and (4) the use of temporary workers."[30] These "horsemen" can be legitimately used to meet economic and productive challenges in any firm, but to use them as ordinary business practice undermines any attempt to build a community of work where people can genuinely develop. Nevertheless, the "horsemen" have become staples of "disconnected" capital's search for ever-increasing returns, regardless of the social effects.

Don't worry, Bob, I am not advocating that the state expropriate the existing wealth of shareholders, although I am not in principle against a more progressive taxation policy. Like you, I too believe that shareholders have the right to control the destiny of the firm, but the critical question is not simply their right to control but how they should exercise it. The Christian social tradition has promoted the idea of private property not because it allows one the freedom to do whatever one wants—choice is not the highest value here. Rather, private property provides an opportunity for the virtuous person to use his property in a way that respects its social nature. The use of property can be ordered toward the common good and toward the creation of an authentic community of work. Growth in virtue, however, will not come about from the maximizing mentality of the shareholder model of the firm, but rather from reconnecting capital to labor, to communities, and to others who have a stake in the capital.

Finally, this long-winded response brings me to the following answers to the questions I posed above: "Why wouldn't the question of greater wealth distribution motivate Bob to share capital ownership with his employees?" "Why did it take an insurance agent to get him to consider the ESOP?" As we have mentioned throughout this dialogue, the end for Reell is the growth of employees, but the management team did not see capital ownership as an important means toward achieving this end. Or, to adopt a distinction from Helen Alford's essay (chapter 9, this volume), the foundational good of capital was not seen as a means to achieving the excellent good of employee growth. Foundational goods are as necessary to the firm's functioning as are air, food, and water to human functioning: without the latter, we die; without the former, the firm dies. The point is, how do we use these foundational goods, and to what higher or more excellent goods are they ordered? The excellent good here is what people can *become* within a community of work, based on what people *have* through a just distribution of capital.

Precisely because Reell's mission concerns the growth of people, a just distribution is embedded in it. The mission is bigger than wealth distribution, but it still includes it, and because the mission is "big enough" to include this concern, Bob and his co-workers are open to more creative ways to share the wealth when opportunities arise. The ESOP came up in terms of a problem with estate taxes. It did not come up through some grand design on the part of the founders to distribute wealth. Yet this practical problem of transferring ownership provided an opportunity for Reell to express its mission more deeply. Because its vision is grounded in human development or, as Bob puts it, in "the growth of people," Reell has created a generative seedbed of purpose in which practical problems can turn into opportunities for growing in virtue. The failure of so many other businesses to seek these human aims demonstrates why it is dangerous to have narrow and quantitative mission statements that seek only to maximize shareholder price, since a just distribution of wealth only appears on the organizational radar when it is instrumental to greater wealth maximization for the shareholders.[31]

Wahlstedt: Mike, I think that the answer to your questions, "Why wouldn't the question of greater wealth distribution motivate me to share capital ownership with my employees?" and "Why did it take an insurance agent to get me to consider the ESOP?" is simply that our moral and political philosophy does not deem unequal distribution of wealth wrong per se. On the far left of the political spectrum, unequal distribution is considered wrong per se, but it must really be egregious for us to consider it wrong in all cases. We needed a different standard by which to judge it. It was not enough for it to be inequitable; it was not egregious, so we had to consider the concept of a living wage before we could form the basis for judgment. Furthermore, we were focused on our own situation, in which the availability of resources did not allow for the degree of inequality that exists in the broader business context. Finally, these deliberations took place in the late 1970s and early 1980s, culminating in the ESOP being established in 1985. The most glaring examples of inequity that you mention have taken place since then.

In short, we did not see the distribution of wealth within our own company as out of line, and we had no sensitivity to or concern for the broader context. In fact, as a small company, we were well aware that we were not providing our co-workers with even a market level of retirement income. We saw the ESOP as a means of providing a reasonable retirement nest egg for everyone while still retaining most of the funds to finance the growth of the business. So, you see, we were still at a point where we were driven by the need to compete at market levels and maintain a sustainable business.

It may have been unusual that we were thinking about the transition of ownership even before we had established a sustainable business with market-competitive remuneration. This is where the insurance agent came in. He showed us that the tax laws would not allow us to put off the concern about estate planning. We had to establish a plan early or run the risk of being uninsurable or not having the time to set up an effective plan later. You are correct, however, in that we might not have established the ESOP if our value system was to maximize personal (shareholder) wealth. I believe that many business owners find the ESOP unacceptable for this very reason. They are unwilling or psychologically unable to "give away" any of the financial benefits of ownership.

Others, trying to "have their cake and eat it too," establish an ESOP for the tax benefits while doing everything possible to limit or minimize the amount of ownership that they give up. They run the risk of operating at the edge of the law and tend to chafe under the system because it forces them to do what they don't want to do. This is why I think that it is not a good idea to establish an ESOP solely for the tax benefits. Thus, although Reell was not consciously intending to alter wealth distribution patterns, our theological perspective put the sharing of ownership in a positive rather than a negative light.

Now, twenty years later, with the benefit of exposure to more thoughtful, theological thinking on this subject, and with the present explosive increase in the remuneration of top executives, we certainly have a much greater appreciation of the moral implications of employee ownership. Furthermore, we have a greater appreciation of the effect of our ESOP on the relationships within our company. These are indeed more important than the issue of control, although sharing the control is one of the reasons that better relationships develop.

I think that we have again encountered the concept of "foundational" goods and "excellent" goods. Our conscious thinking focused on the foundational good of establishing future ownership that would be sensitive to the excellent good of the development of people. Our conscious understanding of excellent goods was incomplete in that we were not aware of the full effect on wealth distribution. On the other hand, there was an awareness of excellent goods in general as well as of their priority.

This brings us again to an important question: How can people understand how their spiritual values and perspectives apply in the business world and be persuaded to act on that insight? You point out that the ownership of stock gives one the right to determine purpose, but that right should be an opportunity for virtue rather than the freedom to do whatever one wants. It seems to me, however, that the freedom to do whatever I want—or choose—and the opportunity for virtue are one and the same. No act can be considered virtuous if it is coerced. That is precisely why this dialogue is important: business owners must be *persuaded* to act virtuously. I believe that some—perhaps only a few—will begin based on theological understanding. The rest may be persuaded by the economic success of those few. The critical factor is that these few have not only the courage to act on their convictions but also the wisdom and prudence to build morally and economically successful models.

Two Conclusions: Lessons Learned Concerning a Christian Ethic of Distribution

Naughton: (1) *The goal or end of what we are doing is creating a community of work:* The first lesson from this dialogue centers on the importance of creating a community of work within the organization. As stated in many of the essays in this volume, to begin to understand what this means, it is essential to see the goal of an organization as more than just creating and distributing wealth. Pope John XXIII argued in 1961:

> Justice is to be observed not merely in the distribution of wealth, but also in regard to the conditions under which men engaged in productive activity have an opportunity to assume responsibility and to perfect themselves by their efforts. . . . Consequently, if the organization and structure of economic life be such that the human dignity of workers is compromised, or their sense of responsibility is weakened, or their freedom of action is removed, then we judge such an economic order to be unjust, even though it produces a vast amount of goods whose distribution conforms to the norms of justice and equity.[32]

So, the goals of an organization go beyond creating wealth and then distributing it with equity. Since we are social beings, our development is intrinsically related to the development of those around us (interdependence). Our well-being cannot be fully measured by some material standard alone. A more equitable distribution of wealth is not an end in itself, but a means toward the growth of each person within a community of work. A just distribution of wealth is one condition for creating a genuine community of work, one that fosters the growth of people, both inside and outside the organization, according to its specific function and mission. To reduce our understanding of wealth distribution to no more than the portioning out of money and material goods hides from us the ways in which just structures of wealth and income distribution in society form the basis for so much more, in terms of the development of human abilities, character, and personality—indeed, for the "abundance" about which John Haughey speaks (chapter 3, this volume).

This is why the Catholic notion of "participation" examined by Dennis McCann and Lee Tavis (chapters 7 and 12, this volume) is central to determining a more comprehensive notion of justice in the distribution of wealth. These categories help us to understand what a community of work looks like and how organizations can provide participative structures and policies that develop the capabilities of their employees and that in turn serve to strengthen the organizational community. As Bob Kennedy explains (chapter 2, this volume), "To deny someone meaningful work is not only to deny him the means of providing for his own livelihood and that of his family, but it is also to prevent him from fully realizing his humanity."

Managers at Reell knew that sub-living wages that promote excessive income disparity undermine the relationships between the members of a firm. It is hard for people to create a community of work when they cannot support their families. These wages were an indication that in the community of work, all was not well, and that some of its members were suffering as a result. The founders wanted to make a living and have a secure future, but they were not creating conditions for their employees to do the same.

A firm's mission is made clear not only by contemplating great thoughts to put in its mission statement but also, and more important, by struggling with the practical issues and problems of life in business and, through this struggle, discovering how to "incarnate" one's principles in practice. Often problems are of an instrumental nature: how to shorten setup times, how to transfer ownership, how to increase quality, how to expand market share. Reell, for instance, encountered technical problems with faster setup times on new product runs. This technical problem turned into an opportunity for assemblers to become better skilled and for management to provide a target or living wage. The result: development of a new way of thinking about job design on the manufacturing floor, which moved the company from, as they called it, a "Command and Control" system to a "Teach-Equip-Trust" system. The resulting savings in setup and supervisory times and improvements in quality contributed to the economic feasibility of Reell's just-wage policies. What started as the need to deal with a technical problem was transformed into an opportunity for Reell to better express its mission and "incarnate" its principles in practice.

The first necessary condition, then, for a community of work to grow and flourish is that employers, managers, and entrepreneurs promote a rich organizational purpose and culture. Such goals create a seedbed or cultural matrix within which dealing with practical problems can turn into opportunities for expressing in deeper and clearer ways that the organization is a community of work where people can develop as fully as possible. For Reell, "rooted in Judeo-Christian values," their practical application was the animating purpose behind how it did business (see Reell's direction statement in the Appendix to this chapter). This orientation prepared Reell to see financial success in a broader frame and to consider policies that might seem to have put success at risk, for the sake of high ideals. Reell's leadership has had to develop the virtue of prudence: aiming at the highest and most perfect ends possible for a business (human development in community) and employing effective and sustainable means for achieving such ends. Thus, while they may seem to have taken risks with their profitability, these were the prudently evaluated risks of the seasoned entrepreneur who is always trying to find new and more effective solutions to old problems.

The proof that such prudence can work is that, while Reell's management took risks, their spiritual and moral orientation has served thus far not as a constraint on their profitability but as the basis of their success. Not all businesses are, nor do they have to be, so explicitly religious in the expression of their mission as Reell. What is critical for the businessperson is that he or she is cultivated in a moral vision that, negatively, prevents a crass utilitarianism, and, positively, provides opportunities for humanizing the organization in new and yet-unthought-of ways.

A company's mission cannot settle all questions beforehand or have all plans laid out in some strategic grand scheme. Rather, a rich company purpose, embraced by managers and employees, fosters a culture in which people have the ability to respond (respons-ability) to problems and issues in a way that promotes a stronger community of work. Reell managers, for example, did not offload their responsibility for the distribution of wealth in their organization to the operation of market forces, as is too often the case in other companies. The process that led to the taking up of this responsibility started with the creation of high moral expectations within the firm. When practical problems came about, such as production, setup, and ownership issues, these problems became opportunities to develop richer relationships within the firm. When employees in dialogue with their advisers said that they liked everything in the company except the pay, and when setup procedures were causing a productivity slowdown, managers along with employees were able to bring together these two issues and resolve them in a way that was consonant with those antecedent, high moral expectations, Reell's living or target wage. No one initially intended to develop a target or living wage, but as the discussion of these problems developed, this new idea came out under the influence and impetus of their basic values.

As a contrary example, think of a company with wage and ownership issues and problems similar to those of Reell, but whose mission is to maximize shareholder wealth. Such a company would be agnostic in regard to the current situation of wealth and income distribution, believing that ultimately the market is the primary factor in determining distributions. Influenced by this mindset, which absolves them of any responsibility toward employees in this matter, managers' minds are closed to possibilities not yet realized. As Tavis argues in his essay, a major deterrent to better conditions in this [apparel] industry are the pressures for a short-term view of the decision environment and the resulting disconnect in the managerial sense of responsibility toward workers.

(2) The means we need to adopt involve creative policies and programs: While good ends and goals, often expressed in the mission statement of the particular business organization, are important, good intentions are not enough. The strong purpose of Reell, if it is to be sustained, must be embodied in creative distributive policies and programs (means) that foster a stronger community of work. This Reell has attempted to do through a target wage and its ESOP. As we cannot neglect the larger questions of a community of work, neither can we spiritualize the community of work so that we neglect the concrete means of distribution within organizations through which we can distribute wealth justly. Any company that is concerned about Christian social principles on wealth distribution must face the question: "What kind of wage distribution and ownership structure promotes an authentic and engaged community of work?" What is important about Reell's compensation policy is that it both raises the labor rates of employees and aims to develop their capabilities, both of which goals enhance the community of work. Employees are not only able to participate by enjoying the fruits of their labor, but they may also participate more actively through increased skills, knowledge, and decision making. Reell was able to redesign workstations so that employees might become "more capable of acting intelligently, freely, and in ways that lead to self-realization."[33] In other words, Reell was able to move the wage question, as McCann puts it, "from the distribution of 'commodities' to the exercise of human 'capabilities,'" so as to create not only a more just distribution of wages but also a stronger community of work (thus using foundational goods to promote excellent goods). What one sees in Reell's target wage is the concrete working out of Amartya Sen's capabilities approach, discussed in several of the essays in this volume (see McCann, Haughey, and Tavis). In Reell's ownership structure one sees the provision not only of a retirement fund for employees but also an opportunity for employees to participate in ongoing responsibility for the direction of Reell.

Finally, I would like to respond briefly to a possible objection on the part of the reader: Can we treat Reell as a model? Some may read our dialogue, based on a quaint little company in the flyover state of Minnesota, as a nice idea but impractical as a model for other companies. There is some truth to this. An ethic of distribution such as the one we have described in our will be more likely to be operationalized in startup companies, where entrepreneurs can more easily bring their values to bear on their business. Practically speaking, it may be more difficult, although not impossible, to incorporate the ideas of this conversation into larger and, in particular, into publicly traded companies. Such larger companies may adopt an ESOP or skill-based pay, but they may well do it for different reasons, and this will have an effect on whether they promote a community of work through their actions. (Take, for example, the different approaches to employee ownership between United Airlines and Southwest Airlines.)

It is interesting to note that Pius XII was concerned about the impersonal anonymity that tends to be fostered in larger companies. He believed that small- and medium-sized enterprises could better "connect" labor and capital through co-ownership and co-management, and that this could form the basis for a real community of work.[34] Pius XII was keen on the idea that small- and medium-sized enterprises might be easier vehicles through which to incorporate the social teachings of the Church.

This is not to say that larger, publicly traded companies cannot embody principles of the Christian or Catholic social tradition, though it is often more difficult to do so. Furthermore, at least in the United States, recent statistics have demonstrated the dramatically increased impact that entrepreneurship has had on economic growth, something that should give pause to scholars in the area of Catholic social thought. For example, employment in the Fortune 500 companies, as a percentage of the total employed workforce in the United States, dropped from 20 percent in 1980 to about 7 percent in the late 1990s. During that same period, while new businesses represented 77 percent of new jobs created, the Fortune 500 actually lost over 5 million jobs. In the midtwentieth century, about 200,000 new businesses were started each year in the United States. That number is now estimated to be about 3.5 million each year. It's clear that entrepreneurial businesses are now more important than they have been for a long time in the U.S. economy. This set of circumstances may well provide a particularly favorable environment for the adoption of the kinds of means and ends we have discussed in this dialogue.

Entrepreneurial companies such as Reell hold great promise for the future of Catholic social thought. If Catholic business schools, especially those with entrepreneurship programs, would start fostering integration between the Catholic social tradition and the management disciplines, and between faith and work, we could begin to see more businesspeople building their organizations as a community of work that includes a more just distribution of wealth.

Wahlstedt: Mike, I think that the most significant revelation that I have gained from this dialogue is the realization of how important the *dialogue* is. You and your colleagues in the academic community are as comfortable and articulate with the language of *justice* as I and my colleagues in business are with the language of *prudence*. You have pointed out that he "who wills the end must will the means" and that "justice without prudence . . . is an exercise in moralism." I would suggest that prudence without justice is an exercise in egotism. It is the bringing together of these two virtues that produces virtuous behavior in individual lives and in organizations. It seems that there are too few places where the language of justice and the language of prudence are in articulate dialogue with each other.

A second conclusion is that practical challenges can and should be the seeds of virtuous behavior in organizations. I am drawn to think of the Parable of the Sower, where Jesus tells of a sower who spreads the same seed on different kinds of soil with very different results. (Sometimes I think this should be called the Parable of the Soil.) Similarly, the "seeds" of practical challenges can have very different yields depending on the "soil" on which they fall. If work organizations are to be places where managers exercising the virtues of prudence and justice can discover and invent virtuous processes and policies and are to become places where people can grow and develop their true potential, then the "soil" created by the purpose, principles, and values of the organization must be cultivated in truth and with diligence. This is why it is so important for an organization to have *and to use* well-developed and well-articulated statements of belief and of purpose.

Finally, the wisdom in Catholic social thought is the best articulation I know of the "language of justice" for work organizations. This advantage gives Catholic business schools a special opportunity as well as a special obligation to initiate and participate in this "bilingual" dialogue between theologians and business practitioners. Let us pray that this dialogue will be enriched and produce good soil in many organizations, so that the seed of practical challenges will grow into virtuous practices.

APPENDIX. OUR REELL DIRECTION

Reell is a team united in the operation of a business based on the practical application of spiritual values to promote the growth of individuals and advance the common good for the benefit of co-workers and their families, customers, shareholders, suppliers, and community. Rooted in Judeo-Christian values, we welcome and draw on the richness of our spiritually diverse community. We are committed to provide an environment where there is harmony between work and our moral/ethical values and family responsibilities and where everyone is treated justly.

The tradition of excellence at Reell was founded on a commitment to excellence rooted in the character of our Creator. Instead of driving each other toward excellence, we strive to free each other to grow and express the excellence that is within all of us. By adhering to the following four common spiritual principles, we are challenged to work and make decisions consistent with God's purpose for creation according to our individual understanding:

DO WHAT IS RIGHT We are committed to do what is right even when it does not seem to be profitable, expedient, or conventional.

DO OUR BEST In our understanding of excellence we embrace a commitment to continuous improvement in everything we do. It is our commitment to encourage, teach, equip, and free each other to do and become all that we were intended to be.

TREAT OTHERS AS WE WOULD LIKE TO BE TREATED

SEEK INSPIRATIONAL WISDOM by looking outside ourselves, especially with respect to decisions having far-reaching and unpredictable consequences, but we will act only when the action is confirmed unanimously by others concerned.

We currently design and manufacture innovative products for a global market. Our goal is to continually improve our ability to meet customer needs. How we accomplish our mission is important to us. The following groups are fundamental to our success:

CO-WORKERS People are the heart of Reell. We are committed to provide a secure opportunity to earn a livelihood and pursue personal growth.

CUSTOMERS Customers are the lifeblood of Reell. Our products and services must be the best in meeting and exceeding customer expectations.

SHAREHOLDERS We recognize that profitability is necessary to continue in business, reach our full potential, and fulfill our responsibilities to shareholders. We expect profits, but our commitments to co-workers and customers come before short-term profits.

SUPPLIERS We will treat our suppliers as valuable partners in all our activities.

COMMUNITY We will use a share of our energy and resources to meet the needs of our local and global community.

We find that in following these principles we can experience enjoyment, happiness, and peace of mind in our work and in our individual lives.

NOTES

1. *Laborem exercens,* 19. For more information on Reell, see Kenneth E. Goodpaster, Laura L. Nash, and Henri-Claude de Bettignies, *Business Ethics,* 4th ed. (New York: McGraw-Hill Irwin, 2005), 151–66.

2. John A. Ryan, *A Better Economic Order* (New York and London: Harper & Brothers, 1935), 171. Ryan saw three major evils in the U.S. capitalism of his day: (1) sub-living wages; (2) excessive wealth disparity between rich and poor; and (3) concentration of capital ownership. This third evil Ryan saw as particularly problematic: "the narrow distribution of capital ownership is more fundamental than the other two evils because it threatens the stability of the whole system" (Marvin L. Krier Mich, *Catholic Social Teaching and Movements* [Mystic, Conn.: Twenty-Third Publications, 1998], 53). Concern over the narrow distribution of property/capital runs throughout the Catholic social tradition and its various advocates: popes, Josef Pieper, the Distributivists, Catholic Workers, et al. Louis Kelso's two-source theory emphasizes the fact that those who are dependent on their labor alone for income are ipso facto economically vulnerable (Louis O. Kelso and Mortimer J. Adler, *The Capitalist Manifesto* [New York: Random House, 1958], chapter 2). For example, according to figures released by the Bureau of Labor Statistics for the first half of 1994, the average hourly earnings for private workers, adjusted for inflation, declined from $8.03 in 1970 to $7.40 in 1994. In 1995 corporate profits increased 22 percent due in part to a meager 2.9 percent increase in benefits and wages. "'What's going on is a straight redistribution of income from labor to capital,' says James Annable, economist at First National Bank of Chicago" (Bill Montague, "Wages Rose 2.9%; Lowest in 15 Years," *USA Today,* February 14, 1996, 1; see also "For Richer, for Poorer," *The Economist* [November 5, 1994]: 20).

3. John Paul II, *Laborem exercens,* 14 and 19. See also Pius XI, *Quadragesimo anno,* 65; John XXIII, *Mater et magistra,* 119; *Gaudium et spes,* 69–71, 105–7. John Paul II advocates worker ownership not only because it distributes wealth, but also because it serves well as a means of personalization by positively affecting the formative dimension of the person and creating stronger social relationships between worker and employer.

4. Corey Rosen, "Legislative Proposals of the Capital Ownership Group" (unpublished: National Center for Employee Ownership, www.nceo.org.). In a survey reported in *Business*

Week, "most Americans feel as if the New Economy's good-'n'-plenty train is passing them by" and believe that the "benefits of the New Economy have been distributed unevenly" (Michelle Conlin, "Hey, What about Us?" *Business Week* [December 27, 1999]: 52–53).

5. Reported by David Wessel, "U.S. Stock Holdings Rose 20% in 1998," *Wall Street Journal,* March 15, 1999, A6, although it should be noted that the increase in employee ownership and the distribution of stock options are indicators that employees are participating in the access of company profits. For example, the percentage of large companies issuing stock options to at least half of their employees "increased from 17 percent in 1993 to 39 percent in 1999" (Denise M. Rousseau and Zipi Shperling, "Pieces of the Action: Ownership and the Changing Employment Relationship," *Academy of Management Review* 28 [October 2003]: 553).

6. Michael Hout, "Inequality by Design: Myths, Data, and Politics," at www.epn.org/sage/hout.html (these numbers come from *Economic Report of the President,* 1996). "The gains in productivity fueled executive compensation, the stock market, and corporate profits. But not wages." See Corey Rosen, who reports that real wages have dropped 8 percent since 1973: "In the 1990s, productivity is up 7%, but wages and benefits are only up 1%" ("Legislative Proposals"). Richard B. Freeman argues: "That the United States has distributed the gains from economic growth more unevenly than any other advanced country should make every American uneasy about the nation's economic performance" ("The Facts about Rising Economic Disparity," in *The Inequality Paradox: Growth of Income Disparity,* ed. James A. Auerbach and Richard S. Belous [Washington, D.C.: National Policy Association, 1998], 20).

7. See "Ownership News," *Employee Ownership Report* 22, no. 1 (January–February 2002): 1, for a discussion of the point. Peter Koslowski explains that one of the reasons for this increase is tax evasion and the mobility of capital: "The increase of capital income in relation to labor income is enforced by a phenomenon that also results from the globalization and enhanced mobility of capital: increased opportunities for tax avoidance in the advanced economies. This phenomenon results from the fact that capital income can avoid taxation much more easily than labor income, since capital is much more easily moved to locations where lower tax rates prevail. Labor is subject to the necessity of being enculturated and integrated into a community, whereas capital can float relatively freely around the globe" ("The Shareholder Value Principle and the Purpose of the Firm: Limits to Shareholder Value," in *Rethinking the Purpose of Business: Interdisciplinary Essays from the Catholic Social Tradition,* ed. S. A. Cortright and Michael Naughton [Notre Dame, Ind.: University of Notre Dame Press, 2002], 117).

8. For an expanded understanding of a Christian view of wages, see Helen Alford and Michael Naughton, *Managing As If Faith Mattered: Christian Social Principles in the Modern Organization* (Notre Dame, Ind.: University of Notre Dame Press, 2001), chapter 5.

9. John A. Ryan wrote: "Equality between pay and work is nonsense. There exists no third term by which to make the comparison. These incommensurate entities can no more be directly compared, as regards their equality or inequality, than sound and color. Nor does 'equality between pay and the value of work' mean anything, unless we are told how value is to be determined. . . . The sum of the matter is that there can be no equality (nor inequality) between pay and work, but that pay can be equal (or unequal) to the value of the work; but

the value of the work has to be ascertained and determined by some extraneous factor, such as the civil law, the higgling of the market, the decrees of a trade union, or the worker's cost of a decent maintenance" ("The Economic Philosophy of St. Thomas," in *Essays in Thomism*, ed. Robert E. Brennan, O.P. [New York: Sheed & Ward, 1942], 251–52).

10. M. Cathleen Kaveny, "Living the Fullness of Ordinary Time: A Theological Critique of the Instrumentalization of Time in Professional Life," in *Work as Key to the Social Question* (Vatican City: Libreria Editrice Vaticana, 2002), 111–27.

11. John Paul II, *The Dignity of Work*, ed. Robert Kennedy, Gary Atkinson, and Michael Naughton (Lanham, Md.: University Press of America, 1995), 34.

12. Kennedy goes on to say, "The opportunity cost of choosing one employer over another can have drastic consequences which affect not only one's possessions, but potentially one's very life and the lives of one's family" (unpublished). There is also a biblical rationale for this logic: "If ever you take your neighbor's garment in pledge, you shall restore it to him before the sun goes down; for that is his only covering, it is his mantle for his body; in what else shall he sleep?" (Ex 22:26–27). This is why Aquinas, for example, denies that the destitute parent who takes, without paying for it, food to feed his or her starving children is a thief (*Summa theologiae*, IIa-IIae, q. 66, a. 7; see also Ryan, *A Living Wage* [New York: Macmillan, 1920], 69–70). A condition of property that does not provide for people's common needs is structurally deficient and needs radical repair. See Josef Pieper's contrast between Stalin and Pius XI on need and wages, *Leisure: The Basis of Culture* (1948; reprint, South Bend, Ind.: St. Augustine's Press, 1998), 45–47.

13. See Jeffery Pfeffer, "Six Dangerous Myths about Pay," *Harvard Business Review* (May–June 1998): 109–19. Pfeffer distinguishes between labor rates, which are determined as total salary divided by time worked, and labor cost, which is a function of labor rates and productivity. As Pfeffer points out, in many cases a firm with a higher labor rate may nevertheless experience lower labor costs than its competitor, because its employees are significantly more productive than its competitors' employees. For example, General Motors requires 46 employee-hours to assemble a car, Ford 37.92 hours, Toyota 29.44 hours, and Nissan only 27.36 hours (ibid., 114). General Motors' problem is not its labor rate but its labor cost, which is influenced by its culture, quality controls, and production processes. Pfeffer concludes that "only labor costs—and not labor rates—are the basis for competition . . .[and] that the issue is not just what you pay people, but also what they produce" (ibid., 117).

14. Edward E. Lawler, *Strategic Pay* (San Francisco: Jossey-Bass, 1990), 185.

15. Ibid.

16. John Paul II, *Centesimus annus*, 32.

17. Peter Vaill, *Learning as a Way of Being* (San Francisco: Jossey-Bass, 1996), 1–21.

18. For an expanded understanding of a Christian view of capital/property ownership see Alford and Naughton, *Managing As If Faith Mattered*, chapter 6. See also Clive Beed and Cara Beed, "Work and Ownership: Implications of Recent Papal Thought," *Review of Social Economy* 60, no. 1 (March 2002): 47–70.

19. Charles Avila, *Ownership: Early Christian Teaching* (Maryknoll, N.Y.: Orbis Books, 1983), 3.

20. See David Schindler, "Homelessness and the Modern Condition: The Family, Evangelization, and the Global Economy," *LOGOS: A Journal of Catholic Thought and Culture* (Fall 2000): 51.

21. See Lewis Hyde, *The Gift* (New York: Vintage Books, 1983), 3–4.

22. As Augustine explains, "all privation is a diminution" (Avila, *Early Christian Teaching*, 117; see Augustine, *De Genesi*, 11, 15 [from J. P. Migne, ed., *Patrologia Latina* XXXIV, 436]).

23. Aquinas, *Summa theologica*, IIa-IIae, q. 66, a. 2. See also Leo XIII, *Rerum novarum*, 36; and Avila, *Early Christian Teaching*, 45.

24. Aquinas, *Summa theologica*, Ia-IIae, q. 19, a. 10.

25. On the arguments for ESOPs as a way of addressing wealth distribution, see Norman G. Kurland, Dawn K. Brohawn, and Michael D. Greaney, *Capital Homesteading for Every Citizen* (Washington, D.C.: Economic Justice Media, 2004); Center for Economic and Social Justice, at www.cesj.org; Jeff Gates, *The Ownership Solution: Toward a Shared Capitalism for the 21st Century* (Reading, Mass.: Addison-Wesley, 1998); and Shared Capitalism Institute, at www.sharedcapitalism.org. See also John H. Miller, C.S.C., ed., *Curing World Poverty* (St. Louis: Social Justice Review, 1994).

26. From Reell's direction statement. For the full text of this statement and an analysis of its significance, see the Appendix to this chapter as well as Alford and Naughton, *Managing As If Faith Mattered*, 26–29, 35–37, 44–45.

27. It has been pointed out in at least one limited study that ESOP companies are better at "getting more wealth into the hands of employees" than their non-ESOP counterparts: on average, employees have better retirement incomes and higher wages. The study finds that "[t]he average value (per participant) of all retirement benefits in ESOP companies (in 1995) was approximately $32,000, whereas the average value in the comparison companies was about $12,500. . . . The median hourly wage of $14.72 in the ESOP firms was 8% higher than the median hourly wage in the comparison companies" (Peter A. Kardas, Adria L. Scharf, and Jim Keogh, *Wealth and Income Consequences of Employee Ownership* [Oakland, Cal.: National Center for Employee Ownership, 1998], iii).

28. The above study on the relationship between wealth and income "shows that employees are significantly better compensated in ESOP companies than are employees in other companies. The study matched up 102 ESOP companies with 499 companies that were comparable in terms of industrial classification and employment size. The median hourly wage in the ESOP companies was 4% to 18% higher than the median hourly wage in the comparison companies, depending on the wage level. The average value of all retirement benefits in ESOP companies was equal to $32,213, with an average value in the comparison companies of about $12,735. Also, employees in ESOP companies had about as much in diversified (non-company stock) assets as employees had in all assets in non-ESOP companies. This study was the most important research on ESOPs published in the 1990s and remains the most authoritative and objective demonstration of how an ESOP can benefit everyone at a company, not just the corporation itself and its owners and managers who install the plan" (see www.nceo.org/pubs/wealth.html).

29. John A. Byrne, "When Capital Gets Antsy," *Business Week* (September 13, 1999): 72–76.

30. Gates, *The Ownership Solution*, 8.

31. John Paul II, in his Apostolic Letter on this new millennium (*Tertio millennio adveniente*), recalls that the "purpose of the Jubilee Year was precisely to reestablish equality among all the children of Israel, opening new possibilities to families that had lost their goods and even personal liberty." This reestablishment of equality and justice will never be fully accomplished short of God's return. But as stewards and inheritors of His gifts of creation, we are called, with God's grace, to *rethink* our notions of property, since our culture, in its individualism and consumerism, has polluted our vision, making vague the social and spiritual outlines of ownership. We are thus called to *reevaluate* current ownership patterns. We are tempted to rationalize current patterns and reduce them to mere market forces—which are better left untouched—and avoid the critical issues of wealth concentration and wealth distribution. But a Christian manager or entrepreneur can neither capitulate to such an answer nor ignore those who have become marginalized from the economy. Finally, we are called to *reconnect* capital in ways that foster the common good. This will entail wise managers (such as Bob Wahlstedt and his co-workers, who will tolerate compliments only in the footnotes), politicians, planners, and others willing to abandon familiar, cookie-cutter approaches to "business as usual" and to embrace practical daily organizational problems as opportunities for growth in virtue.

32. *Mater et magistra*, 82–83. See also Paul VI, *Octogesima adveniens*, 22.

33. U.S. Bishops, *Economic Justice for All*, 72.

34. Pius XII, "Address to the Catholic Association of Small- and Medium-Sized Businesses, October 8, 1956," in *The Pope Speaks* (Spring 1957): 407–8. See also James V. Schall, S.J., "Catholicism, Business, and Human Priorities," in *The Judeo-Christian Vision and the Modern Corporation*, ed. Oliver Williams and John Houck (Notre Dame, Ind.: University of Notre Dame Press, 1982), 122.

TWELVE

The Problem of Wealth Distribution in the Global Apparel Industry

Locating Responsibilities in the Supply Chain

LEE A. TAVIS

Each of us wears apparel produced mainly in the developing countries and largely under exploitative conditions. Many governmental agencies, nongovernmental organizations (NGOs), and multinational corporations are attempting to relieve these conditions without eliminating jobs, for, although exploitative in practice, sweatshops generate a significant portion of wealth in developing countries and can therefore play a critical role in its more just distribution. Unfortunately, there appears to be little hope that they will move in this direction except under outside pressure. Universities are in a unique position to help. Through the licensing of apparel bearing their trademark, universities can apply some of the required pressure.

This essay addresses working conditions in the global apparel industry and their effect on global wealth distribution; it outlines ways in which a Catholic university is attempting to mitigate these conditions.[1] The initial section will analyze the global pressures toward economic, political, and cultural integration and indicate how this systemic pressure affects the apparel industry. Economic competition and the international division of labor combine to impose intense cost pressure on local apparel producers—pressure that promotes the observed sweatshop conditions. The second section addresses the moral issues associated with globalization, globalization's effect on wealth distribution, and the Catholic social response. The final section addresses the application of Catholic social thought to conditions in apparel production through the University of Notre Dame's monitoring and remediation procedures. If universities, and Catholic universities in particular, recognize their institutional clout, they can influence the way in which wealth is distributed across the globe.

WHY DO APPAREL SWEATSHOPS EXIST? THE GLOBALIZATION PHENOMENON

Globalization is the international integration of individuals and information networks as well as of economic, social, and political institutions, occurring at a rate and depth unprecedented in history. The tight interaction among national economic systems precludes economic isolation as market barriers to trade and investment have been dismantled. Political, social, and cultural systems are subject to the same pressures toward integration and uniformity. As UN Secretary-General Kofi Annan noted, "[globalization's] integrative logic seems inexorable, its momentum irresistible."[2]

Motives and Technology

Globalization is nurtured by two factors: the shift from government-led to market-led development; and technological advancements that enhance production and marketing coordination on a global scale. First, over the past two decades, many national governments have concluded that open markets and competition are a more efficient way of increasing productivity than governmental planning and control; others have acquiesced perforce. "Marketization" has occurred across Asia and Latin America and followed the implosion of the former Soviet Union.[3] Technology, the second factor, contributes dramatic improvement in information flows that facilitate the global coordination of economic networks among suppliers, manufacturers, and consumers as well as within the multinational enterprises themselves. Moreover, production technology allows the separation of component production from final assembly. Transportation efficiency and costs have improved to the point that material produced in one location can be dependably and inexpensively delivered to another site for assembly or sale.

Governmental open-market policies, supported by technological advances, have led to the globalization of mass production. In this process, multinational enterprises search the world for new market opportunities and knowledge. For cost savings, they move production to the sites of immobile, inexpensive, and unskilled labor—the process termed "the international division of labor." New technology is also changing the nature of globalized mass production.[4] This technology is linking computer-aided design and manufacturing to form computer-integrated manufacturing. For those production processes amenable to programmable manufacturing, goods can be produced one at a time at a cost competitive with the long runs of mass production.[5] The emergence of programmable manufacturing has enormous implications for countries that plan on cheap labor for development over the long term.

Globalization's Janus Faces: Creation and Distribution

The sweep of globalization touches each of our lives. Some benefit from it; some do not. There are two faces to globalization: it has contributed to economic productivity and growth, as well as to a significant increase in wealth creation, but the distribution of its benefits is distorted. As Kofi Annan has noted, "The benefits of globalization are plain to see: faster economic growth, higher living standards, accelerated innovation and diffusion of technology, and management skills, new economic opportunities for individuals and countries alike."[6] In the twenty-two years between 1975 and 1997, global real per-capita income increased substantially. Both developed and developing countries shared in this growth with industrialized countries gaining 53 percent (from a base of $12,589 in 1975) and developing countries gaining 51 percent (from a base of $600).[7] In addition to economic growth, other indicators of human development such as infant mortality and life expectancy, education, and access to safe water have all improved. The percentage of people living in absolute poverty has decreased.

Given the dramatic economic performance of our globalizing economy and the benefits associated with this growth, why do we encounter such resistance to globalization as that reflected in the demonstrations at the 1999 World Trade Organization meetings in Seattle and in the meetings of multilateral institutions that have followed? There are at least two reasons: one is the concern over the distribution of benefits; the other is the sense that the process is out of control—that the sweeping power of the faceless market will push aside individual and social concerns.

The dislocation associated with economic globalization is tied to the rate of change of the process. The rapidity with which markets have opened and the intensity of the competition for a place in them, all driven and supported by technological development, create enormous opportunities for those who can access, and cope with, the globalizing institutions, but exploitation and marginalization for those who cannot. National and global distributions of income reflect these differences, particularly in access. In 1960 the wealthiest 20 percent of the world's population received 75 percent of the world's income. The poorest 20 percent received merely 2.3 percent. It is difficult to believe that this gap could widen, but it did. In 1997 the shares were 86 percent and 1 percent.[8] The good news, however, is that overall productivity has improved to the point where the percentage of people living in abject poverty (defined as income of less than $1 per day) has decreased from 28.3 percent in 1987 to 24 percent in 1998 in spite of the greater concentration of wealth.[9] Still, the number of people in poverty increased slightly to 1,198.9 million due to increases in population.[10] (See Stefano Zamagni's essay on relative and absolute poverty, chapter 8, this volume.)

Power Shifts

The change from government-led to market-led development has been associated with changes in national and international governance structures as well as with a fundamental shift in power from the nation-state to the global marketplace. Multinational enterprises are the key implementing institutions in the shift of power from the political system to the economic system, although we must recognize that the two are always intertwined. The upshot for national governments is a loss of regulatory control to the globalizing market (marketization) and to multinational institutions such as the World Bank and regional economic associations. Concomitantly, national governments experience a loss of political and economic policy freedom, particularly those in developing countries who lack a voice in international policy making.

At the same time, systems of global governance are slowly evolving. The United Nations and its sixteen specialized agencies make up a loose framework of global governance. The European Union provides tighter parliamentary-based governance, but on a regional scale. An emerging set of overlapping, global governance networks are assuming a regulatory role. National judiciaries and regulatory agencies are establishing cross-border relationships. Corporations and NGOs, often combined with governmental agencies, are forming to enhance the efficiency of global markets. Examples include the Trade Related Intellectual Property Rights and the International Organization for Standards. Other networks focus on social and environmental issues. For example, the "Responsible Care" initiative of the Canadian Chemical Manufacturers' Program has expanded globally in conjunction with NGOs and governmental agencies to set environmental standards worldwide; human rights groups organized on an international level with close ties to their grassroots counterparts are now challenging the multinational corporations as well as national governments; and the Fair Labor Association is concerned with improving the working conditions in the global apparel industry. This loose web of overlapping networks is gradually imposing constraints on the international marketplace.[11]

In the process of global marketization, the reach and concentration of multinational enterprises (MNEs)—the instruments of economic globalization—have increased dramatically. Foreign direct investment in 1997 was seven times the 1970s level. Between the mid–1980s and 1997 the value added by MNEs increased from 5 percent of world gross domestic product (GDP) to 7 percent, while the MNE share of world exports increased from one-quarter to one-third by 1995. These firms are joining internationally through mergers and acquisitions that more than doubled from 1990 through 1997. Cross-border mergers and acquisitions were valued at $237 billion in 1997.[12] These figures do not include the burgeoning, nonequity strategic alliances among MNEs.

The Apparel Industry

In the apparel industry, highly sophisticated, information-based, supply-chain management presses against production technology that has changed little over the past thirty years. On the one hand, information technology enhances the coordination of components produced in a variety of sites, primarily in the developing world, to be assembled in still other locations. The dependability and cost of transportation ensure product delivery to markets in other industrialized countries. Quality control is enhanced by modern organizational techniques and enabled by the ease of visits by contractors or corporate headquarters staffs. On the other hand, the sewing of garments has defied automation, even though the weaving of textiles is a highly efficient, computer-controlled production process. In footwear, the production of soles and other components of athletic shoes is automated, but their assembly is not.

Retailers, such as Wal-Mart, and brand-marketers, such as Nike, dominate these supply chains. Wal-Mart, for example, which manages its supplier base through information and control networks unsurpassed in any industrial sector, actually schedules production in supplier plants. Developing-country sites are integrated into this system. For example, a typical production process for a Hong Kong manufacturer involves:

- fabrics produced in Taiwan
- cutting and sewing of components (sleeves, collars, etc.) in South China
- components assembled in Hong Kong
- trimming, ironing, folding, and packaging in South China
- finished apparel exported from Hong Kong

Electronically enhanced, information-based control of the supply chain has supported a continued decrease in the cost of apparel at the point of sale. The contrast between this sophistication and the low-skilled, non-automated sewing and assembly processes focuses cost-reduction efforts on direct production. Efficiency gains through team sewing have been unable to stem the flow of production from the United States to low-cost labor sites in developing countries.[13] As cost considerations become the dominant motive for siting production, wage pressure intensifies.[14]

Leaders in developing countries welcome this production, the jobs it creates, and the developmental linkages it provides. Many governments view apparel production as an early step in industrialization. It allows them to use their low-wage comparative advantage. Some, such as Korea, Hong Kong (1960s), and Taiwan (1970s), successfully used low-wage production as an entering wedge into the global economic/financial system.

Industrial Structure: The Supply Chain

Before completed items of apparel finally reach the consumer, the apparel industry supply chain performs a series of functions. Generally, but not always, single companies carry out more than one function.

Retailers: General-purpose retailers such as Wal-Mart, Sears, and J. C. Penney are the dominant outlets for apparel in the United States. There has been a significant concentration in this industry. Four large retailers now account for two-thirds of all retail clothing sales in the United States.[15] These companies often have their own brands, such as Wal-Mart's Kathie Lee Gifford Collection.

Manufacturers/Brand-Marketers: Brand names such as Nike, Adidas, Reebok, Champion, Gear, or Tommy Hilfiger concentrate on pulling their products through the channels of distribution by brand imaging. Some of these manufacturers (for example, The Gap) distribute through their own retail outlets. "Manufacturer," the common term for this category, is not strictly descriptive. While they control the production process, these firms may not own the production facility. Nike, for example, subcontracts all its production.

Contractors, Wholesalers, Agents: The functions of contracting and monitoring are often combined in a single company. The process as undertaken by Ely & Walker, a Western shirt wholesaler, reflects the complexity of these arrangements. "The sequence for a large order is: (1) agreement with the customer about the specifications of the product (quality, color, print, design, delivery times, price); (2) arrangement with an agent to have the textile woven and to reserve time at the factory for cutting and sewing; (3) delivery of material samples to the client; (4) arrangement of bank financing and letters of credit; (5) monitoring of production; (6) delivery free-on-board at shipping port location; (7) arrangement of shipment and U.S. customs clearance through an international freight forwarder; (8) final customer inspection at the Ely & Walker warehouse; and (9) client-directed delivery."[16] Increasingly, retailers and manufacturers are attempting to absorb this "middleman" function.

Producers: The patterns of ownership and control vary widely. Some producers are subsidiaries of the manufacturer/brand-marketer and part of the multinational enterprise network.[17] In other cases, the factory is part of an apparel-producing multinational that is a subcontractor for all of its output, as with Daewoo Enterprises. This massive Korean firm owns and controls numerous production sites across the world. Smaller Korean apparel producers work in close association with one another, while still others are locally owned. These producers then subcontract components, often to individual seamstresses.

Important to these producers is the ease with which a plant can be moved from one location or country to another. Much of the garment production, for example, takes place in warehouses with additional lighting, ventilation, restrooms, and electrical drops for each sewing station. The major investment is in the sewing machines or laser cutters, which can be easily moved. These are the models of what have become known as "runaway" multinationals. The ease of shifting production sites significantly constrains the regulatory power of the hosting nation-state. Developing countries compete vigorously for investment. For most industrial investments, once the multinational assets are committed, there is a rebalancing of the power relationship toward the nation-state. The ease of plant relocation in the apparel industry modifies this advantage, restricting the ability of the host government to increase regulation or to intensify the enforcement of regulations already in effect.

Suppliers: For any producer, suppliers represent a diverse group. They range from the large textile mill to the mother sewing in her own home. Many of these informal-sector workers are beyond the reach of government regulations, monitoring, or safety nets.[18]

Power and Information in the Supply Chain

Global marketization and competition dictate that power increasingly rests with the consumer. With few exceptions, the apparel industry has become hyper-price-sensitive. This sensitivity is exacerbated by the sales mentality encouraged by many retailers and by the "everyday low prices" advertised at stores such as Wal-Mart.

With social conscience as a motivating factor, consumer surveys indicate that 25 percent of potential buyers consider whether clothing was made in a sweatshop and 55 percent indicate that they are willing to pay higher prices to ensure their purchase was not made in a sweatshop.[19] The necessary condition for any kind of activism, however, is dependable information about the conditions to which consumers object or the standards they wish to uphold. The "RugMark" label affixed to Oriental rugs produced in India, for example, certifies that they have not been made with exploited child labor.[20] Advocacy groups such as Campaign for Labor, United Students against Sweatshops, and the National Labor Committee provide information, raise consumer awareness, and propose consumer actions in the apparel industry.

At the present time, however, owing to the limited availability of reliable information and a lack of organization among consumers, most of the power in the apparel value chain is exercised through retailers or manufacturers/brand-marketers. The latter anticipate consumer preferences and plan production either in facilities they own or through contracting middlemen. The contracts tend to be short-term (for a given production run, generally one year or less), although production relationships tend to endure through repeated contracts. Although they expend considerable effort in developing producer efficiency and dependability, contracting manufacturers/brand-marketers have the flexibility to change suppliers, thus controlling the power balance in contractual relationships. The availability of competing producers is, of course, a mitigating factor.

Resulting Production Conditions

The structure of the apparel industry taps the large unskilled labor markets of developing countries. As noted, this production can be an important component of a country's development process and a huge opportunity for those who gain access to those jobs. At the same time, the combination of competitive markets and surplus labor has led to constant pressure on wages and working conditions. The low wages and frequency of deplorable working conditions in these "sweatshops"[21] have been well documented.[22] Workers are paid less in underinvested working environments than their contribution is worth.[23] In spite of exploitation, however, in most countries, sweatshop workers are better off than their marginalized neighbors who have no access to comparable jobs.[24]

Host governments are primarily responsible for protecting the fundamental human rights of their citizens. Given their desire for initiating development based on cheap labor, and in the face of relentless market competition, governmental determination may be lacking. Further, with the abrogation of power associated with marketization, governmental power is often inadequate, even for determined action. Responsibility then falls on the institutions with power in the supply chain— retailers, manufacturers/brand-marketers, and producers. Managers for these concerns are under heavy pressure to take a short-term view of the decision environment. That and the resulting disconnect in their sense of responsibility toward workers combine to deter development of better managerial practices. The notion of developing workers as a means of enhancing their productivity over the intermediate or long term is notably absent (see Michael Naughton and Robert Wahlstedt's essay, chapter 11, this volume, for a counter example). The prevalence of short-term contractual versus ownership linkages in the supply chain precludes long-term relationships among the manufacturer/brand-marketer or retailer, producers, and production employees. For subcontracters, the disconnect is magnified as these firms move from production site to production site to secure low-cost labor, avoid unionization, or escape governmental regulation.

Extensive use of low-cost migrant labor drawn to the production site is also a factor working against sound practice. There is internal migration from central Mexico to the maquiladora plants on the border with the United States. Apparel workers migrate from central China to Guangdong Province bordering Hong Kong and from Mandarin-speaking provinces to Cantonese-speaking Guangdong. Migration across national borders is also a common pattern in the apparel industry: Filipinos work in Taiwan, or Vietnamese in Saipan. Employee turnover is high among migrants at the completion of a contract.[25] Moreover, their different cultures and languages are seldom respected on the plant floor.

The ownership structure of apparel plants can increase risk, shorten the planning horizon, and thus undermine interest in developing workers' skills. In southern China, for example, firms from Hong Kong will share plant ownership with prominent local figures. These local owners arrange for access to land and facilities as well as provide political connections and protection. This is a high-risk strategy, since political influence can shift quickly in China.

In sum, typically neither ultimate employers (retailers, manufacturers/brand-marketers) nor immediate employers (contracting producers) recognize a responsibility for worker development. At the same time, the relatively low-skill requirements of apparel production and a surplus of unskilled labor do little to recommend worker development as a strategic practice.

Contracting retailers or brand-marketers bear no legal responsibility for the welfare of their subcontractors' workers. This legalism was the basis for their denial of responsibility a decade ago. Theoretically, it can be argued that these firms do bear a heavy, if not legal, responsibility since subcontracted workers are stakeholders of the retailer or brand-marketer. The quality of their lives hangs significantly on the activities of their ultimate employer, and they have no other agency, such as an effective local government or union, to protect them.[26] Most retailers or manufacturers/brand-marketers now accept responsibility for the welfare of sub-contractors' workers in developing countries. The change in their stance is due more to public pressure and to concern for the reputation of their brands than to theoretical persuasion. If exploitation is to be reduced, and if fundamental human rights are to be supported, then responsibility must devolve on these institutions, the "powers" in the supply chain.

THE MORAL ISSUES OF DISTRIBUTION AND PARTICIPATION

There are numerous moral issues associated with the impact of globalization. We ought not to confuse the immorality of an unequal distribution of income with the right to subsistence. Whereas subsistence is a threshold concept by which each human being has the right to some minimum level of basic human needs, the distribution of income is a function of each person's efforts, capabilities, and access to the means of enhancing his or her well-being. The discrimination, exploitation, marginalization, and denial of opportunity that are associated with globalization, and that often underlie specific patterns of income dispersion, are immoral. Each person has the right of access to the global economic system, a right to the education necessary for that access, and a right to participate in the decisions that will influence her well-being.[27] The denial of these rights is reflected in inequitable distributions of income. Given continuing uneven access to information, the necessary condition for participation in the modern economic system, we can anticipate an even greater increase in the inequitable dispersion of income, perhaps at an accelerating pace.[28]

In the Catholic social tradition, the response to those exploited by or excluded from the system is uniform and forceful. Relief of poverty itself and redress of the inequity that denies resources for self-improvement to the poor are at the core of Catholic social thought. In their pastoral letter in 1986 on the U.S. economy, *Economic Justice for All,* the National Conference of Catholic Bishops states the Church's well-known position on the preferential option for the poor in terms of three priorities that should govern "personal decisions, social policies, and economic institutions":[29]

- The fulfillment of the basic needs of the poor is of the highest priority.
- Increasing active participation in economic life by those who are presently excluded or vulnerable is a high social priority.
- The investment of wealth, talent, and human energy should be specifically directed to benefit those who are poor or economically insecure.

In this volume (chapter 7), Dennis McCann addresses the Catholic position on inequality in a nuanced analysis of the bishops' economic letter. He emphasizes the inadequacy of wealth and income distributions as measures of inequity, posing instead the bishops' concept of "social participation":

> All people have a *right to participate* in the economic life of society. Basic justice demands that people be assured a *minimum level of participation* in the economy. It is wrong for a person or a group to be excluded unfairly or to be *unable to participate* or contribute to the economy. For example, people who are both able and willing, but cannot get a job are *deprived of the participation* that is so vital to human development. . . . *Such participation* has a special significance in our tradition because we believe that it is a means by which we join in carrying forward God's creative activity.[30]

The bishops' definition of "social participation" is broader than the right of participation indicated here. In its more narrow sense, participation is the right to partake in institutional decisions that affect one's well-being.[31] "Social participation" would include the above right to access and to the education that alone makes access an advantage.

In his essay, McCann's goal is to define the level at which the denial of social participation becomes an immoral inequality, an inequity. Toward this goal, he compares Amartya Sen's notion of the exercise of "human capabilities" with the bishops' social participation requirement, noting their similarity. Since Sen's human capabilities approach is measurable and more comprehensible to economists, it moves us a step closer to McCann's search for the point at which inequality of incomes and wealth becomes culpable inequity.[32]

The distinction between what Helen Alford calls in her essay "foundational" and "excellent" goods (chapter 9, this volume) may aid us in applying Catholic social thought to conditions in the apparel industry. On the level of foundational goods, the concern is to ensure an appropriate standard of living, which is higher than a subsistence minimum for the worker alone or the minimum wage in many or most developing countries. The standard set in Catholic social thought is that each worker should be paid a living wage capable of supporting the dignity of the worker and his family. For virtually all developing countries, this standard exceeds current levels of remuneration.

"Excellent goods" betokens Catholic social thought's concern with more than meeting a minimum standard of living. It aims at human development. Implementing the concept of "social participation" in apparel production would entail "worker participation" in terms both of rewarding work and of workers' right to organize as a means of representing their own interests. The right to organize is strongly supported throughout Catholic social thought (see chapter 10, this volume, Carlo Dell'Arringa and Claudio Lucifora). But so is the right to have a high degree of control over one's work as well as to learn skills and to expand one's knowledge base through one's work. The apparel industry has earned its reputation for treating workers as so many living machines. Still, apparel workers do draw something permanent from their effort. The attainment of excellent goods through social participation is reflected in the enhancement of their quality of life as well as that of their families and communities. They have demonstrated their determination to secure these future opportunities in spite of their current exploitation.

Enhancing one's skills and earnings power is a form of wealth. While we label workers' contributions as "unskilled" when they perform mind-numbing repetitive tasks, we also observe their adeptness, which reflects remarkable discipline and personal skills, thus laying the foundation for more advanced tasks. Given the current production structure, the workers must overcome the employer's short-term view and indifference to providing them opportunities for advancement as well as the lack of governmentally sponsored beyond-the-job training. For the individual worker, the key is a move up to that next, more skilled, job. This has been the experience of many workers in Korea, Hong Kong, and Taiwan, as these national governments have managed to ratchet up their overall economic development.

Achieving a subsistence wage and unionization can also lead to long-term opportunities. Enhanced standards of living in the short term promote the formation of community, which in turn supports personal development. Unionization gives power to workers and can open avenues to self-development and higher wages, although the struggle for union-supported self-development can be as intense as the political struggle for the formation of independent unions. Not surprisingly, the opportunities for long-term self-development and wealth are much greater for local workers than for migrants. The fixed term of a migrant contract or visa discourages whatever long-term view the employer might have. Moreover, migrants start with a large payment to obtain the initial contract; they are not accepted as equals at the job site; in Asia, for example, their savings often go to doweries, which move beyond their control; and for involvement in union organization migrants are simply sent home. Thus, provisions for both a living wage as a fundamental good and the right to organize as leading to the achievement of excellent goods are central to the self-development of the apparel worker. These two components, central principles in the Catholic social tradition, have proven to be intractable aspects of the University of Notre Dame's Apparel Monitoring and Remediation process, the topic of the next section.

How Can Catholic Social Thought Have an Impact on Sweatshop Conditions?

Catholic social thought has a great deal to say about the exploitation of workers in apparel production. Implementing change to meet the strong but general mandates of this teaching, however, calls for considerable prudential judgment. This section addresses monitoring as a means of alleviating worker exploitation, and it discusses the implementation of the Code of Conduct for University of Notre Dame Licensees, with an emphasis on the two issues that call for a particularly sensitive balance—the living wage and the right to organize. The immediate goal of a university monitoring effort is to ensure that items bearing its logo are produced under nonexploitative conditions. Given the competitive cost pressures in the industry, effective monitoring is an absolute necessity if standards reflecting the principles of Catholic social thought are to be achieved.

University Power in the Supply Chain

University power in the apparel value chain is exercised through the retailer or manufacturer/brand-marketer (hereafter retailers and manufacturers/brand-marketers are termed "marketers"). A university enters into licensing contracts with marketers for the production and sale of apparel bearing its logo, for which the university is paid a royalty. As a component of this agreement, the university may require the marketer to meet the provisions of a code of conduct (see the appendix to this chapter, Code of Conduct for University of Notre Dame Licensees). Thus, the power of the university relative to the marketer depends on the market value of the logo. Overall, the value of university logo apparel has decreased in recent years, although sales, concentrated in a few universities, still account annually for about $2 billion. Hence, even though university logo sales are a small fraction of total apparel sales in the United States (about 0.6 percent), they are substantial and provide a wedge for amelioration of the abuse in apparel production.

Monitoring and Remediation

There are several objections to monitoring and remediation on the part of universities.[33] The first has to do with the imposition of codes of conduct. When these codes are required of subcontractors, they create an extra legal responsibility, as noted earlier. There is also a danger that, as they take on this responsibility, marketers relieve pressure on local governments, who have the primary responsibility for guaranteeing social justice.[34] Another set of arguments has to do with the efficiency of the process. There are a vast number of producers to be monitored—two thousand for the University of Notre Dame alone. These numbers mean that many plants will remain unmonitored. Beyond that, producers rely on a broad range of suppliers, of whom many are in the informal sector and are hidden from the control of government regulators, as noted above.

There is a good deal of discussion about disclosure of monitoring results and the responsibility for remediation. Disclosure is evolving. Most marketers now divulge the location of their factories. Beyond that, the Fair Labor Association has developed a "tracking chart" to report the voluminous findings for monitored production sites, including remediation plans and followup.[35] The Global Alliance for Workers and Communities holds promise for disclosure. This group, composed of marketers, the World Bank, and NGOs, surveys worker attitudes and inspects production conditions.[36]

A more serious charge is that workers typically are not involved in the preparation of the codes, in the conduct of the monitoring visits (other than as interviewees), or in the remediation process. According to the principle of subsidiarity, those who are the most proximate to states of affairs are best able to respond to them. Because more remote institutions, representing a higher authority, often do not know the nuances at the local level, their interventions may well have disrupting consequences. Subsidiarity (the word derives from *subsidium* or "aid"), however, does not relieve institutions at higher (that is, more remote or more general) levels of authority of responsibility to support local efforts or, when the issues cannot be resolved locally, to intervene in search of a settlement.

At its core, monitoring is an analysis of a firm's management process. Analysis, feedback, and change are central components of any management system. In many cases, substandard working conditions can be traced to flawed company policies and procedures rather than to intentional abuse. External monitoring is not necessary where ethical intentions, a long-term view, and effective control systems prevail. Thus, an important component of external monitoring is evaluation of both management systems and production conditions.[37]

External monitoring comes in a variety of approaches, sponsored by equally various—often, mutually contentious—organizations.[38] All external monitoring must aim at remediation. The core purpose is to improve the condition of workers, not to terminate production or encourage the factory to relocate. This is the delicate balance of which all monitors must be keenly aware. Furthermore, monitoring is undertaken by both for-profit and not-for-profit organizations. Global accounting firms, for example, have practices devoted to compliance audits, where they audit production sites to ensure compliance with codes established by the firm's clients. The primary expertise of the accounting firm is to audit managerial procedures as well as financial records. These firms also interview workers on site as part of the audit.

Nongovernmental organizations have specific knowledge of local labor conditions and the capability to interact with plant employees. Most NGOs monitor through plant visits. Some, however, oversee working conditions on a continuous basis. Grupo de Monitoreo Independiente en El Salvador (GMIES), for example, has a full-time monitor at the Mandrin International plant in El Salvador—on the shop floor, attending management meetings, and visiting workers at the site. The goal of GMIES is to encourage worker organization, although GMIES tends to serve as a surrogate union in the interim. The distinction between monitoring by NGOs and by global accounting firms is blurring as some NGOs undertake the auditing function.

Notre Dame was the first university in the United States to commission an accounting firm to audit plants where items with its logo are produced. Even though the firm hired accountants from the host country for these audits and conducted confidential worker interviews on site, the University Task Force concluded that more extensive input from the workers was desirable. Thus, the University of Notre Dame adopted a dual monitoring approach in an attempt to draw on the human relations skills and knowledge of local NGOs as well as on the procedural and record-auditing expertise of the accounting firm.[39]

A committee to monitor Central American and Mexican production was established. Chaired at the university, the committee consists of representatives from local NGOs and accounting firms. The monitoring follows two guiding principles: subsidiarity, and building trust through dialogue. At their core, working conditions are the responsibility of factory management. The monitoring procedure first assisted them in revising their policies and procedures. In accord with the principle of subsidiarity, however, when necessary change was not forthcoming through plant management, higher-level intervention was initiated. Noncooperating plants have been barred from producing university logo items.[40] The last resort would be cancellation of the university license for a manufacturer who continues to contract with a banned plant.

To the extent possible, monitoring and remediation are best conducted in an atmosphere of collaboration, not confrontation. Plant visits, for example, should be undertaken jointly by members of the accounting firm and NGO representatives, as equal partners. The same holds for interaction among committee members, plant management, and workers.

Given the advances in monitoring by the Fair Labor Association (FLA), the University of Notre Dame now requires all licensees to join the FLA, which monitors their production sites. There are now 262 Notre Dame Licensees as well as the

2,000 producers of Notre Dame logo materials. Notre Dame is also a member of the Worker Rights Consortium (WRC), which is largely a complaint-based system that intensively investigates alleged labor abuses or WRC code violations. Although no longer responsible for monitoring, the Mexico/Central America committee is still active in policy guidance.

The Living Wage and the Right to Organize

The principle of subsidiarity brings implementation of a living wage and of the right to organize into close association. Those closest to the shop floor—the local plant management and workers—understand in depth what wage levels mean to the enterprise and to its employees and what trade-offs are involved in adjusting them. At the same time, organization offers workers leverage as well as a more equal voice when wages, benefits, and trade-offs with other conditions of employment are determined. In all likelihood, wages and benefits imposed by a remote authority (dictated, for example, by a university code requirement) no more fit unique local requirements than they reflect a valid local negotiation.

When local conditions conducive to fair negotiation are still in development, external intervention may be needed. Given the strong resistance to unionization across the developing world, external intervention is often clearly necessary. Indeed, systematic failure to enforce laws that promote unionization marks an institutional feature of developing countries.[41] Nevertheless, a living wage requirement must be implemented so as not to interfere with workers' ability to organize. Subsidiary intervention by higher authorities should be strictly temporary, since long-term intervention tends to atrophy on-site efforts to deal with the issue.[42]

Implementation of a living wage requirement is an exercise in prudential judgment. No other requirement can have such an immediate impact on costs. While improvements in working conditions tend to be more a matter of managerial determination or capital availability than cost,[43] an externally imposed wage increase goes directly to the bottom line. Beyond the cost impact, implementation is a complex process, involving three requirements: (1) measuring the living wage; (2) allocating the associated increase in cost; and (3) channeling the increased remuneration into the local labor market.[44]

First, there are two methods of measuring a living wage. One is a multiplier approach, exemplified by measurement of the poverty line in the United States; the base is the cost of a subsistence diet for a family. At the initiation of the data series, diet was determined to represent one-third of a subsistence income. Then, over time, the cost of a subsistence diet was recalculated and multiplied by three to determine poverty thresholds. Some minimal adjustment for geographic regions then was made. The advantage of this measure is its simplicity.[45]

The alternative is to study the cost of living in specific locations at specific times. The Center for Reflection, Education, and Action (CREA) ties these costs directly to wages in a Purchasing Power Index.[46] The metric is the number of working minutes it takes to purchase an item at a specific wage level. When combined, the hours of work needed to buy the food, clothing, housing, transportation, and other items necessary for an adequate standard of living indicate the adequacy of the specified wage. The Purchasing Power Index allows for comparison of different wage levels within a country, such as a minimum or a living wage. This approach is also amenable to comparison among locations and over time as a measure of inflation's diverse impact and unique effect on different components of subsistence consumption.[47]

The second requirement is the allocation of increased cost. Given the international division of labor in the apparel industry, production wages are low.[48] Indeed, low wages attract apparel production in the first place.[49] The labor cost component for apparel varies substantially, depending upon the item. Based on ad hoc evidence, a reasonable estimate is that production labor for university logo apparel represents about 5 percent of the sales price.[50] On the 5 percent assumption, a doubling of wages would not increase the retail price dramatically, provided that the wage increase were added directly, unaffected by middleman, producer, or retail markups. For example, the price of a $50 sweatshirt would increase to $52.50 if production wages alone were doubled.

Who should absorb this cost? The market could absorb much of the increase for high-end expensive items sold in college bookstores. While data are limited, the demand elasticity for these items is assumed to be low.[51] For less expensive apparel in discount retail outlets, the elasticity would be greater. In all cases, one would expect the price impact to be mitigated if the consumer were notified of the reason for the increase, particularly for high-priced items in college bookstores. Cost absorption at other points in the value chain would depend on policy and negotiations. Each link in the chain should absorb some portion of the cost. Notre Dame, since it is basing a contemplated wage requirement on Catholic social thought, should be willing to share part of the burden.

The third requirement is raising local wages. Implementing a living wage standard is not simply a matter of paying more to the workers. Indeed, abruptly increasing wages for one segment of a local labor market can be disruptive.[52] The problem for universities is that few factories are devoted exclusively to the production of a particular logo, and sites for contracted production change periodically. The ideal is to have the increased remuneration for the logo-producing workers "ripple" to other workers in the factory and then to other plants. A sudden major change would probably create a high-wage enclave and wage compression with little ripple effect.[53] Given the structure of the apparel industry, it is also possible for manufacturers simply to shift logo contracts to high-wage areas and produce items that carry no living wage requirement in the lowest-cost labor sites. Thus, a living wage standard must be a target to be approached gradually. (For a U.S. example of this gradualism, see the essay by Naughton and Wahlstedt.)

The challenge is to channel the added remuneration so as not to disrupt the local wage balance within the factory or the community. One approach, perhaps the most effective, is to measure the increase in remuneration on the basis of the individual workers but funnel it back to them in the form of group benefits to the plant or the community. Neither wage rates within the plant nor local labor markets would be disrupted. The Catholic social principle of solidarity would support this system of individual contribution to the benefit of the broader group. As to benefits, education or training for all plant employees, on-site child care, transportation, and additional medical care for workers and their families might all figure.[54] With a little moral imagination, the list is long.[55] The difficulty with this sort of program is, of course, management. Who will manage and oversee the diverse services? The NGO that participates in the monitoring/remediation process for the plant is a likely candidate.

As an added advantage, returning the increase in remuneration to the plant or community under management of a local NGO mitigates the remote, clumsy, diktat character of the wage requirement. While the university, a remote and external authority, dictates the amount of the increase via its licensee, the funds would be allocated by a local NGO, a relatively proximate agency whose on-the-scene knowledge and connections can help preserve the principle of subsidiarity during the period of external wage intervention.

Turning now to the right to organize, we find that it is a contentious issue in most developing countries. Both common law and statutory law regimes are marked by a substantial contrast between what the law foresees and what its "implementation" achieves. In formulating and applying a code of conduct, the issue is to determine where to draw the line in the spectrum connecting the content of the law to its implementation. This is an example of Catholic social thought informing prudential judgment.

In some countries, such as China, Iran, Saudi Arabia, and Afghanistan, the law denies workers the right to organize.[56] In others, although the right exists in law, it is not enforced. In El Salvador, for example, the law clearly mandates the right to organize, but its enforcement in the Free Trade Zones, where apparel is produced, is minimal.[57] The lack of enforcement appears to reflect more than an understaffed Labor Ministry. According to a number of respondents, the Labor Ministry is more active outside, than within, the Free Trade Zone. Indeed, there is a sense across a broad spectrum of Salvadorian society that to enforce labor standards within the Free Trade Zone would lose the nation foreign investment and jobs, and so betray the national interest. Furthermore, in most developing countries, if one were to insist on the right to organize, assured by the efficient enforcement of applicable law, there would be precious few acceptable production sites. The Notre Dame Code of Conduct draws the line at the legal right to organize (Section III. D.9.). Apparel produced in China is the most affected.

Labor legislation and policy are at the heart of China's fundamental transition from the paternalism of the self-proclaimed "worker's state" to labor's participation in a market economy. Since the People's Republic of China replaced Taiwan as the Chinese representative to the United Nations, the shift in labor legislation and practice has been undertaken in association with the International Labor Organization (ILO). It has been a fitful relationship.[58]

In the early years of industrialization, Chinese workers were organized in work units of the state-owned enterprise (SOE) where they were employed. The SOE provided housing, ration coupons, and social insurance. Since dismissal from the job meant expulsion from the work unit, firings or layoffs were rare. Much of the employment of the enterprise was devoted to the maintenance of the work unit.[59] The Communist Party was deeply involved in the management of enterprise production as well as the work unit. Now, in contemporary China, marketization involves privatizing SOEs and housing, thus de-emphasizing the role of work units. Control of the workforce is being wrested from the Party and unemployment is increasing rapidly. Chinese officials are deeply concerned about the political implications of an unhappy and unemployed workforce.

The 1989 Tiananmen Square repression was a major setback for the evolution of Chinese workers' right to free association. The Workers' Autonomous Federation, the first independent union movement in the People's Republic, was brutally put down.[60] Chinese authorities state that the freedom of association is guaranteed by the nation's constitution.[61] All workers have the right to form or join the (government-run) All-China Federation of Trade Unions (ACFTU), which does not meet the standards of the ILO. Its role has been described: "Apart from ensuring the maintenance of social services and decent housing, it [ACFTU] was mainly a mechanism to exhort workers to increase production. The worker was expected to obey the rules of the enterprise and accept the guidance of the Party and of management."[62] As stated in the constitution, freedom of association is to be carried out "according to the law," while the law does not specify that a union may be established without state authorization or that a worker may join a union of his or her own choosing, as required by the ILO.[63]

The Chinese response to a complaint lodged in 1998 by the International Confederation of Free Trade Unions maintained that "collective bargaining is practiced in over 90,000 enterprises covering over 40 million employees" and that "the unionization rate of enterprise employees has reached 80 percent." It insisted, however, that the independent organizations of workers referred to in the complaint were not actually unions, but rather groups of individuals who, instead of defending workers' interests, were devoted to illegal activities endangering state security. According to the official line, the prohibition of such groups, therefore, ensures a better defense of workers' fundamental interests.[64] Recent legislation, the 1994 Labor Law (implemented in 1995), confirms the authoritarian control of Chinese officials.[65] The International Confederation of Free Trade Unions is highly critical of the situation in China:

> Currently China is at a crisis point in labor rights that may well have a determining impact on the future direction of the rule of law. The wholesale dismantling of SOEs, downsizing of the bureaucracy announced at the Ninth National People's Congress in March 1988, is creating an unemployment crisis of unparalleled dimensions—a jobless figure of 28 percent by the year 2000. . . . All attempts to organize independent workers' organizations have resulted in the arrest, sentencing, or extended detention without trial of those involved.[66]

A major political and economic event is the Chinese entry into the World Trade Organization (WTO). The entry was temporarily stalled over agricultural protection and China's interest in entering the WTO as a developing country and thus one who can protect her agriculture. There is general agreement that WTO entry will stimulate China's economy, but there is less confidence that it will stimulate the freedom to organize. China's paranoia over the Falun Gong, a spiritual movement aimed at self-realization that caught the government (and, indeed, most of the population) by surprise, reflects the government's determination to bring every organization under supervision and control.

As for the apparel industry, production for export will probably not increase. Wages in Guangdong Province have risen far less than the 3-to-5-times increase in the cost of living over the last fifteen years. It is claimed (although this is not supported by macro data) that apparel production is shifting to the North in search of still lower wages and in an effort to serve the domestic market. The central government seems to be de-emphasizing apparel production. In 1998 subsidies to these factories were dropped, and over one million workers were displaced.[67] The strategic plan to develop western China does not refer to the apparel industry. Furthermore, it is unlikely that production conditions in the industry will improve solely as a result of WTO membership. Thus, the University of Notre Dame's ban on logo items produced in countries that legally restrict workers' right to freely form unions will undoubtedly apply to China for the foreseeable future.

CONCLUSION

This chapter began by describing the intense, systemic pressures that lead to sweatshop conditions in apparel production. Continuing globalization will intensify, rather than soften, these pressures. Business firms across the supply chain as well as numerous associations and NGOs are addressing sweatshop issues with a focus on working conditions, employment practices, and minimum or prevailing wages.

Certain universities are in a unique position to influence the system of apparel production in a modest (but perhaps exemplary) way through their control of licensed products bearing their logos. For one set of these universities, standards for wages and working conditions should be guided by Catholic social thought. While Catholic social thought condemns exploitation in the form of substandard working conditions and employment practices generally, it explicitly raises two issues that expand the envelope of antisweatshop activism—workers' rights to organize and to earn a living wage.

The right to organize is embedded in national law and is realized in the law's enforcement. While most standards do not distinguish between the right of free association and the right to organize, Catholic social thought clearly supports the higher standard of the right to organize. As a legal mandate, the right to organize is relatively easy to measure. Over time, one measure of the effectiveness of the right to organize is the prevailing wage. A living wage standard is far more difficult to assess, to absorb into the supply chain, and to pay. Determination to pay a living wage must be matched by moral imagination and patience.

The Notre Dame Code of Conduct and monitoring/remediation procedures are an initial step in implementing Catholic social thought, which insists on full social/economic participation for everyone. Apparel workers have access to the economic system, but this access is typically exploitative rather than participative. The direct monitoring and followup mandated by the Code and other procedures aim to ensure that standards consistent with workers' human dignity and development are met in both the short and the long run.

The living wage standard—modified to pay increases in real wages in the form of improvements to essential, community-wide services such as education—will directly enhance workers' well-being and improve their access to the economic system. Participation will be enhanced by the counsel and advocacy of concerned, informed local observers who are not dependent on the apparel value chain. In the very long run, workers will gain freedom to form and join unions.

Appendix. Code of Conduct for University of Notre Dame Licensees

I. Introduction: The University of Notre Dame du Lac ("Notre Dame") is committed to conducting its business affairs in a socially responsible manner consistent with its religious and educational mission. Notre Dame expects nothing less of its business partners and licensees. Therefore, Notre Dame will not do business with those who engage in business practices or follow work place standards inconsistent with this Code of Conduct.

II. Application: This Code of Conduct shall apply to all Licensees of Notre Dame. Throughout this Code, the term "Licensee" shall include all persons or entities who have entered a written License Agreement with Notre Dame, as well as their respective contractors, subcontractors, vendors, manufacturers, sublicensees and any related entities throughout the world which produce or sell products or materials incorporated in products which bear the name, trademarks or images of the University of Notre Dame du Lac. This Code of Conduct constitutes a "Guideline" for Notre Dame Licensees pursuant to Paragraph 14 of Notre Dame's License Agreement for national licensees. It is applicable and mandatory with respect to every Licensee of Notre Dame.

As a condition of being permitted to produce and/or sell licensed products bearing the name, trademarks and/or images of Notre Dame, each Licensee must comply with this Code of Conduct. If the University of Notre Dame, in its sole discretion, determines that any Licensee has failed to comply with this Code, then the University may either terminate its business relationship and License Agreement with the Licensee or require that the Licensee implement a corrective action plan on terms acceptable to Notre Dame.

III. Work Place Standards and Practices: Specifically, Notre Dame Licensees must operate work places and contract with employers whose work places adhere to the following minimum standards and practices:

A. **Legal Compliance:** Notre Dame Licensees must comply with all applicable legal requirements in conducting business related to or involving the production or sale of products or materials bearing the name, trademarks or images of Notre Dame.

B. **Environmental Compliance:** Notre Dame Licensees must share Notre Dame's commitment to the protection and preservation of the global environment and the world's finite resources and conduct business accordingly.

C. **Ethical Principles:** Notre Dame Licensees must be committed in the conduct of their business to a set of ethical standards which are not incompatible with those of

Notre Dame. These include but are by no means limited to honesty, integrity, trustworthiness, and respect for the unique intrinsic value of each human being.

D. Employment Standards: Notre Dame will only do business with Licensees whose workers are in all cases present at work voluntarily, not at risk of physical harm, fairly compensated and not exploited in any way. In addition, the following specific guidelines must be followed:

1. **Wages and Benefits:** Licensees must provide wages and benefits which comply with all applicable laws and regulations and match or exceed the prevailing local manufacturing industry practices.

2. **Working Hours:** Licensees must not exceed prevailing local work hours in the country where the work is to be performed, except with respect to appropriately compensated overtime. In any event, Licensees must not require in excess of a sixty-hour week on a regularly scheduled basis.

3. **Child Labor:** The use of child labor is not permissible and will not be tolerated. Workers can be no less than 14 years of age and not younger than the compulsory age to be in school in the country where the work is to be performed.

4. **Prison or Forced Labor:** The use of forced labor and prison labor is not permissible and will not be tolerated. Labor supplied by prisoners working within the United States pursuant to a lawfully authorized work program sponsored by the United States government or a government of one of the fifty states shall only be permissible if the Licensee obtains Notre Dame's prior written consent.

5. **Health and Safety:** Licensees must provide workers with a safe and healthy work environment. If residential facilities are provided to workers, they must be safe and healthy facilities.

6. **Non-Discrimination and Respect for Life:** While Notre Dame recognizes and respects cultural differences, all workers must be employed on the basis of their ability to do the job, rather than on personal characteristics. We insist upon doing business with Licensees who share this value. Workers must not be discriminated against on the basis of their race, ethnicity, religious belief or affiliation, age (except with respect to the child labor requirements set forth herein), disability or gender. The sanctity of human life must be respected in all relations with workers. Specifically, no worker shall be required to undergo pregnancy testing, practice birth control or terminate a pregnancy as a condition of employment or continued employment at any time or for any reason.

7. **Disciplinary Practices:** Licensees must not use or tolerate corporal punishment or any other form of psychological or physical coercion.

8. Human Rights: Products and materials bearing the name, trademarks or images of Notre Dame shall not be manufactured or produced in any country where the human rights environment, as determined by Notre Dame, in its sole discretion, would prevent the conduct of business activities in a manner that is consistent with this Code of Conduct.

9. Legal System: Products and materials bearing the name, trademarks or images of Notre Dame shall not be manufactured or produced in any country where the local legal system would prevent Notre Dame, in its sole discretion, from adequately protecting its name, trademarks, images or other interests or from implementing any provision of this Code of Conduct.

In addition, after June 30, 2001, products bearing the name or other trademarks of the University of Notre Dame shall only be manufactured in countries where all workers enjoy the legal rights to associate freely, form independent labor unions and collectively bargain with their employers concerning wages, hours, working conditions and other terms and conditions of employment.[a] In order to satisfy the minimum requirements of this recommendation, any country where Notre Dame licensed products are manufactured must satisfy one or more of the following: (1) be a signatory to International Labor Organization ("ILO") Convention No. 87;[b] (2) be a signatory to ILO Convention No. 98;[c] or (3) have adopted its own national laws which provide all workers within the country (including but not limited to foreign workers) legal rights to free association and to form and join organizations of their own choosing (including unions) without anti-union discrimination, prior authorization or interference by public authorities or others. Employer created, mandated or sponsored organizations, such as company unions, do not satisfy this requirement.

---

a. For the purpose of this recommendation, the term "manufactured" shall not only include making or processing raw materials into finished products or goods but also screen printing, embroidery, sewing, assembly and any process by which the University's name or other trademarks are applied to a product or good.

b. This international convention is a multilateral treaty which was adopted in 1948. It establishes the right of all workers and employers to form and join organizations of their own choosing without prior authorization, and lays down a series of guarantees for the free functioning of organizations without interference by the public authorities.

c. This international treaty was adopted in 1949. It provides for protection against anti-union discrimination, for protection of workers' and employers' organizations against interference by each other, and for measures to promote collective bargaining.

10. **Political, Economic and Social Environment:** Products and materials bearing the name, trademarks or images of Notre Dame shall not be manufactured or produced in any country where the political, social or economic environment would threaten Notre Dame's reputation and/or commercial or other interests.

IV. Documentation and Inspections: It shall be the responsibility of each Notre Dame Licensee to ensure its compliance with this Code of Conduct and to verify that its business partners, subcontractors and others involved in the production or manufacture of products or materials bearing the name, trademarks or images of Notre Dame are in compliance with this Code of Conduct. Each Notre Dame Licensee shall maintain on file such documentation as may be needed to demonstrate its compliance with this Code of Conduct and shall make the documentation available for Notre Dame's inspection upon request.

A. Monitoring Compliance: Each Notre Dame Licensee shall provide the University and its designated representatives with physical access to all facilities where Notre Dame licensed products are made, in whole or in part, whether by the Licensee or by third parties with whom the Licensee or its agents or representatives contract, in order to monitor and verify compliance with this Code of Conduct. Upon request, and on January 1 of each year, every Licensee shall promptly provide the University with the following information concerning each such facility where Notre Dame licensed products are made: (1) the name, address, telephone number and facsimile number of the facility; (2) the name, address, telephone number and facsimile number of the owner(s) of the facility; (3) the name and job title of a contact person at the facility; (4) a detailed description of the type and quantity of all Notre Dame licensed products made, assembled or processed, in whole or in part, at the facility; (5) a summary description of the Licensee's relationship to the owners and/or operators of the facility (e.g., company owned, contractual); and (6) any other information the University deems necessary to effectively monitor and verify compliance with this Code of Conduct.

It shall be the Licensee's responsibility under this agreement to promptly notify the University whenever it creates or ends relationships with new entities or facilities for the manufacture or assembly, in whole or in part, of Notre Dame licensed products. If the Licensee should fail to do so, and/or the University incurs any expense as a result of the Licensee's failure to notify Notre Dame or provide factory access as required herein, then the Licensee shall reimburse the University for all of its expenses.

Notre Dame Licensees must participate in the Fair Labor Association ("FLA"). Licensees with annual consolidated revenues of $50 million or greater must either join the FLA as a Category A Licensee participating company or as a Category B Licensee and subject all facilities where Notre Dame licensed products are manufactured to the FLA monitoring process. Licensees with annual consolidated revenues of less than $50 million must participate as Category C Licensees or as Category B Licensees if their revenues are less than $1 million and their production facilities are located within 200 miles of a FLA University of which it is a licensee.

Notes

1. The author is a member of the University of Notre Dame Task Force on Anti-Sweatshop Initiatives. Discussion of the University's activities attempts to distinguish between the views of the author, those of the Task Force, and University policy.

2. Kofi A. Annan, *We the Peoples: The Role of the United Nations in the 21st Century* (New York: United Nations, 2000), 9.

3. For an analysis of the shift from government-led to market-led development, see Lee A. Tavis, *Power and Responsibility: Multinational Managers and Developing Country Concerns* (Notre Dame, Ind.: University of Notre Dame Press, 1997), 120–49.

4. Ibid., 52–58.

5. United Nations Centre on Transnational Corporations, *New Approaches to Best-Practice Manufacturing: The Role of Transnational Corporations and Implications for Developing Countries,* United Nations Centre on Transnational Corporations Current Studies Series A, no. 12, bk. 7 (New York: United Nations, October 1990).

6. Annan, *We the Peoples,* 9.

7. These numbers do not include Eastern Europe and the CIS countries; see United Nations Development Programme (UNDP), *Human Development Report 1999* (New York: Oxford University Press, 1999), 154.

8. UNDP, *Human Development Report 1992* (New York: Oxford University Press, 1992), 36; and UNDP, *Human Development Report 1999,* 2.

9. UNDP, *Human Development Report 2000/2001* (New York: Oxford University Press, 2001), 23.

10. Ibid.

11. For a discussion of the shift from national government regulation of the global market to international governance networks, see Lee A. Tavis, "Corporate Governance and the Global Social Void," *Vanderbilt Journal of Transnational Law* 35, no. 2 (March 2002): 487–547.

12. UNDP, *Human Development Report 1999,* 31–32.

13. Peter Berg, "Manufacturing Advantage: The Effects of High Performance Work Practices on Firms and Workers," paper presented at the Higgins Labor Research Center, University of Notre Dame, Notre Dame, Indiana, March 22, 2001.

14. *Women's Wear Daily,* "Let's Talk Shop," January 21, 1999, 2, 3, 5.

15. Richard P. Applebaum, cited in John F. Witte, *Report on the Living Wage Symposium, November 19–21, 1999,* Robert M. LaFollette Institute of Public Affairs, University of Wisconsin-Madison, February 8, 2000, 13; www.lafollette.wisc.edu/publications/otherpublications/economics/1999/LivingWage/report.htm. (bibliography also available).

16. "Case 6, Subcontracting Apparel in Asia: The Ely & Walker Experience," in Tavis, *Power and Responsibility,* 327.

17. These multinational networks are tightly integrated, complex systems. See ibid., 126–29.

18. Ibid., 60–94.

19. MSNBC, *Sweatshops and the Consumer: Reader Responses,* © 1998, http://msnbc.com/Onair/nbc/dateline/sweatshop.asp?cp1=1.

20. Linda F. Golodner, "Consumer Pressure Can Reduce the Use of Sweatshops," *Child Labor and Sweatshops,* ed. Mary E. Williams (San Diego, Calif.: Greenhaven Press, 1999), 55.

21. Laura P. Hartman, Bill Shaw, and Rodney Stevenson, "Sweatshop Ethics: Balancing Labor Rights with Economic Progress" (unpublished manuscript, July 2000), characterize sweatshops as follows: "The Encyclopedia Britannica defines the term sweatshop based on a set of employment practices: 'a workplace in which workers are employed for long hours at low wages and under non-compliance with national labor law.' According to the U.S. General Accounting Office, a place of work with 'an employer that violates more than one federal or state labor, industrial homework, occupational safety and health, workers' compensation, or industry registration law' is a sweatshop. Other groups add to compliance the concept of labor rights. The AFL-CIO Union of Needletrades, Industrial and Textile Employees defines sweatshop as a place of employment with 'systematic violation of one or more fundamental workers' rights that have been codified in international and U.S. law.' Some would say that a variety of substandard labor practices needs to be present before a place of employment can be called a sweatshop. Others, such as the Interfaith Center on Corporate Responsibility, require only a single questionable practice: '[though] a factory may be clean, well-organized and harassment free, unless its workers are paid a sustainable living wage, it's still a sweatshop.' The word sweatshop is emotive and carries prejudicial connotations."

22. From the many sources of information on working conditions in the apparel industry, see www.sweatfree.org; the National Labor Committee (www.nlcnet.org); or Labor Alerts (www.campaignforlaborrights.org).

23. Tavis, *Power and Responsibility,* 415.

24. Of course, not all apparel production takes place under sweatshop conditions (see, for example, *Mattel Independent Monitoring Council for Global Manufacturing Principles: Audit Report 1999* [New York: MIMCO, Zicklin School of Business, Baruch College, CUNY, 1999]. MIMCO is the in-depth monitoring effort of the Mattel Independent Monitoring Committee directed to Mattel-owned and -subcontracted production sites.

25. The South African mines under apartheid represent an exception.

26. For an analysis of extending stakeholder boundaries in developing countries, see Tavis, *Power and Responsibility,* 395–406.

27. For a discussion of the right to subsistence, access, education, and participation, see ibid., 160–64 and 431, n. 7.

28. For measures of access to information, see UNDP, *Human Development Report 1999*.

29. *Economic Justice for All: Pastoral Letter on Catholic Social Teaching and the U.S. Economy* (Washington, D.C.: National Conference of Catholic Bishops, 1986), 89–92.

30. Ibid., 15 (McCann's emphasis).

31. Henry Shue, *Basic Rights: Subsistence, Affluence, and U.S. Foreign Policy* (Princeton, N.J.: Princeton University Press, 1980), 71; Tavis, *Power and Responsibility*, 161.

32. Amartya Sen, *Development as Freedom* (New York: Alfred A. Knopf, 1999). The similarity between the bishops' vision of "social participation" and the writings of an ethicist steeped in Asian religions, and one who refers extensively to that foundation in his work, indicates that we are moving closer to the idea of religiously based *and* universal social norms.

33. For a careful articulation of these critiques, see *Asian Labour Update*, issue no. 26, published by Asia Monitor Resource Center Ltd. (AMRC), Hong Kong. The same kinds of arguments are made by the Workers Rights Consortium.

34. See "Editorial" in *Asian Labour Update*, issue no. 26, 5. The editorial goes on to say, "Therefore, it is a novel way of establishing responsibility, but must go hand in hand with efforts by groups in the South to pressure their governments to implement their own labour laws and improve the plight of all its workers."

35. The Fair Labor Association includes manufacturers/brand-marketers and universities, joined with NGOs, to monitor apparel production of the member manufacturers/brand-marketers. It grows out of the White House Apparel Partnership. The University of Notre Dame is a member of the FLA.

36. The Global Alliance for Workers and Communities is an unusual combination of corporations (Gap and Nike), a multilateral institution (World Bank), universities (St. John's and Penn State), cooperating organizations (Atma Jaya University Research Institute of Indonesia, Center for Economic Studies and Applications in Vietnam, Chalalongkom University Social Research Institute in Thailand), and others to study working conditions in the apparel industry. For more information, see www.theglobalalliance.org.

37. The MIMCO procedure is initiated by a Management Compliance Report. "This document is prepared by the plant manager and provides data on the plant's compliance in considerable detail with regard to all the [200] standards pertaining to the GMP [Global Manufacturing Principles]" (S. Prakash Sethi, Murray L. Weidenbaum, and Paul F. McCleary, "A Case Study of Independent Monitoring of U.S. Overseas Production: Mattel Independent Monitoring Council for Global Manufacturing Principles [MIMCO]—Audit Report 1999," *Global Focus: An International Journal of Business, Economics, and Social Policy* 12, no. 1 [2000]: 139; and at www.stthomas.edu/cathstudies/cst/mgmt/puebla/sethi3.html).

38. Groups concerned with monitoring include associations such as the Fair Labor Association and the Workers Rights Consortium, global accounting firms such as Ernst & Young, nongovernmental organizations such as Verite, the Interfaith Center on Corporate Respon-

sibility (which advises on monitoring efforts but does not provide monitoring), and GMIES, the full-time monitoring of the Mandrin factory in El Salvador.

39. MIMCO also uses dual monitoring with accountants and Verite. Representatives of both institutions jointly conduct plant visits. In the MIMCO case, however, the auditor and NGO are directed by a MIMCO representative. The MIMCO teams consist of eight to twelve people for a plant visit including three or four accounting auditors, three or four Verite interviewers, two or three academic experts in sampling, and one or two MIMCO council members. In 1999, MIMCO conducted eight audits, all in plants wholly owned by Mattel or where Mattel contracts for 100 percent of its output. Given the much larger number of audits anticipated by Notre Dame, plant visits of two to four monitors are anticipated.

40. A plant in Mexico is no longer allowed to produce Notre Dame logo items due to its refusal to stop pregnancy testing.

41. Richard T. De George, *Competing with Integrity in International Business* (New York: Oxford University Press, 1993), 26.

42. The balance between external pressure and local efforts was a major factor in the struggle against apartheid in South Africa. Some of the black unions saw the anti-apartheid movement in the United States as interfering with their purpose.

43. Ivar Aavatsmark, the president of Ely & Walker, noted, "I'm not going to use a factory with unsafe or unclean working conditions. In my experience, these substandard conditions are inefficient with regard to price and quality. I can always get my products at the same price from someone who is a little more attentive and more reliable" (Tavis, *Power and Responsibility*, 333).

44. The Notre Dame Task Force is reflecting on these requirements in considering whether to recommend the inclusion of a living wage clause in the University's Code of Conduct.

45. For information on this measure, see http://www.census.gov/hhes/www/poverty.html.

46. Ruth Rosenbaum, "Applications of the Purchasing Power Index in Haiti, Indonesia, Mexico, and Hartford, CT," CREA Working Paper no. 42 (Hartford, Conn.: Center for Reflection, Education, and Action, 2000); and at www.crea-inc.org/42.pdf.

47. Notre Dame is currently exploring the usefulness of the Purchasing Power Index. The University has sponsored CREA in the study of a region in Mexico where Notre Dame apparel is produced.

48. MIMCO is outstanding in its measurement of workplace standards. As for wage concerns, the focus is on compliance with local law and Mattel's policies on overtime work. An effective component is workers' understanding of pay stubs. There is no evidence, however, of an evaluation of wage level adequacy.

49. The application of a living wage standard would increase the labor costs at virtually every production location and dramatically so at some sites.

50. Applebaum states in Witte, *Living Wage Symposium*, 12: "The wage portion of the cost of clothing is small—about 6 percent of the total cost of an item that is manufactured in the United States and considerably smaller for imports." The data on the production of Disney's "101 Dalmatians" outfits for children sewn in Haiti, as reported by the National Labor

Committee, were far lower—$.06 labor cost for an item selling for $19.99. This appears to be on the low end. A cowboy shirt sewn in China for Ely & Walker would have a labor cost closer to 5 percent. Discussions at a factory in El Salvador indicated about 6 percent labor cost for an authentic basketball jersey.

51. Witte, *Living Wage Symposium*, 33–34.

52. An example of high wages disrupting labor markets occurred at the Dolefil Plantation in the southern Philippines. When the plantation paid higher than the prevailing wages in the community, it drew talent such as schoolteachers and government employees to work in the pineapple fields. See "The Dolefil Operation in the Philippine Islands," Case #1 in Tavis, *Power and Responsibility*, 169–204.

53. See Witte, *Living Wage Symposium*, 33–36.

54. One factory in El Salvador provided family medical care on one Saturday per month by physicians affiliated with the factory clinic.

55. In reviewing the MIMCO audit reports, it is interesting to note how much education and training are taking place.

56. The classification of countries that do not legally allow the right to organize is analyzed and published by the U.S. Department of State, Bureau of Democracy, Human Rights, and Labor, Country Reports on Human Rights Practices.

57. Lee A. Tavis, personal notes from field interviews conducted in El Salvador as a member of the Notre Dame Task Force on Anti-Sweatshop Initiatives, July 26–31, 1999.

58. Ann Kent, *China, the United Nations, and Human Rights: The Limits of Compliance* (Philadelphia: University of Pennsylvania Press, 1999), 117, 145.

59. "In Changchun, for example, First Automobile Works employed only 20 percent of its 60,000 workers in the production of automobiles; the remaining 80 percent were employed in pursuits from barbering to day care to policy work" (Janet S. Adams, "Economic Reform in China: Ethical Issues in Labor Law and Human Resource Management Practices," 7, in paper presented at Second International Society of Business, Economics, and Ethics World Congress on the Ethical Challenges of Globalization, São Paulo, Brazil, July 2000).

60. Kent, *Limits of Compliance*, 128–29.

61. Discussions of human rights between China and the West are fueled by a difference in emphasis. While the individualistic culture of the West stresses civil and political rights, the Chinese communal culture stresses economic and social rights (see Tavis, "Corporate Governance").

62. Kent, *Limits of Compliance*, 32.

63. Ibid., 118.

64. Ibid., 135.

65. The 1999 MIMCO audit report includes worker interviews about harassment by management for union-related activities. The reports on the three audited Chinese plants indicate that "most workers were either not very conscious of, or were reluctant to talk about, the freedom of association or unionization issues" (74, 111). "Workers by and large were reluctant to express opinions on the issues of unionization" (93). Given the contention over unions in China, worker silence is not a surprise. It seems likely, however, that the harassment

occurs through the activities of governmental officials rather than the managers in these two township enterprises and one private enterprise producing on contract for Mattel. This worker reaction in China is very different from the situation in El Salvador, and Honduras, where attempts at unionization have met with substantial managerial harassment and firings, and in Honduras, where they have met with a strong reaction from the Free Trade Zone authorities in Honduras.

66. ICFTU Press Release, April 9, 1997, reprinted in *China Labour Bulletin* (March–April 1997): 35:9. See also edited extracts in "Search and Destroy," *China Labour Bulletin* (May–June 1997): 36:15–16.

67. Alice Kwan, "Don't Turn a Deaf Ear to Workers in China," manuscript draft (Kowloon, Hong Kong: Hong Kong Christian Industrial Committee, April 7, 2000), unpublished.

Postscript

Quis dives salvetur?

When, near the turn of the second and third centuries, Clement of Alexandria asked, Quis dives salvetur?—Who among the rich can be saved?—he was addressing a community that included an increasing number of affluent Christians. No longer virtually an assembly of the poor, it was a community far removed from the religious communism practiced by the first Christians at Jerusalem. Clement addressed his question to Christians for whom the Gospel admonitions concerning wealth had become urgent. His question is even more urgent today, especially in the West, where affluence dominates the minds and desires of many.

Clement's question is a primer for the Christian understanding of wealth. In the first place, its subject reminds us that the Gospel does not treat of wealth in its own right. The Gospel treats of persons, and of wealth so far as it serves persons or thwarts their service to God, enhances or mars their lives, and advances or obstructs their salvific union with Him. While the Gospel treats wealth strictly instrumentally, it sees in it an instrument both of human flourishing and of human ruin.

In the second place, Clement's question reminds us how wary of riches is the Gospel. It echoes the Apostles' astonishment—"Who, then [among the rich], can be saved?"—following Jesus' solemn admonition: "It will be hard for a rich man to enter the kingdom of heaven . . . it is easier for a camel to pass through the eye of a needle." Moreover, like the Apostles' question, Clement's is in the passive voice. It anticipates Jesus' response: "For men this is impossible; for God everything is possible" (Mt 19:23–26). The Gospel bids us to approach the problems of wealth from the viewpoint of faith.

The authors of this volume adopt the perspective of Catholic social thought because its teaching embodies a Gospel perspective on wealth. Traditionally, Catholic social teaching understands the creation and distribution of wealth in terms of its human uses: meeting human needs, promoting the flourishing of each and every person. Certainly, production, prices, and profits cannot be neglected. But Catholic social teaching, like the Gospel, is traditionally wary of wealth.[1] This attitude is evident on many levels. Both the Old and New Testaments note that the wealth of the rich often comes at the expense of the poor and to the exclusion of the needs of the poor. Catholic social teaching follows the Bible in condemning that state of affairs wherever and whenever it occurs. But contrary to what is often claimed, the wariness of the Gospels and of Catholic social thought toward wealth is not rooted in the belief that wealth as such results from a zero-sum game played between the rich and the poor.[2] Rather, it rests on a vivid appreciation of the danger that the love of money will replace the love of God, to the ruin of persons and communities.

The perception of this danger is a function of faith; so, too, is the countervailing prescription that we store up imperishable treasures in heaven through good works here on earth. We are called to "use [our] worldly wealth"[3] toward this end. St. John Chrysostom captures the Gospel view of our right relationship to goods in his comments on the rich fool who took down his barns so that he could store—that is, hoard—even greater wealth: "There is nothing more wretched than such an attitude. In truth he took down his barns; for the safe barns are not walls but the stomachs of the poor."[4] The love of God, supplanting the love of money (as it must also supplant the love of power, pleasure, prestige, and every worldly imposture), is expressed in concrete attention to the poor and marginalized (Mt 25).

Catholic social teaching has always held that the right use of wealth is a spiritual achievement, a triumph of faith. As St. Augustine puts it, for one who understands and observes that this world and its goods are for uses intended by God, no quantity of goods is too great; for all others, any quantity is too great.[5] For the authors of this volume, as for Augustine and the Catholic tradition at large, some essentials of the faith also are necessary for a full understanding of wealth.[6] And as a recent review of the Church Fathers on this topic shows, the essentials of Catholic thought on wealth are constants, substantially unchanged from the Patristic era to the present.[7]

Those essentials include the proposition that all wealth comprises, finally, the gifts of the Creator, resting jointly on the gift of the earth with its natural resources and on the gift of human reason, together with the proposition that God has willed abundance for His creatures and that wealth is the human form of this abundance. Hence, as the gift of God, wealth must be used in a manner that respects the abundance God wills for humankind without discrimination, that is, in a manner that respects (in the language of contemporary Catholic social teaching) the universal destination of goods. Accordingly, wealth is to be used to promote the common good, and especially to ensure that the poor also participate in both the community of goods and the goods of community.

The perception that wealth belongs ultimately to the category of gift has important ramifications for the understanding of private property. While the Catholic tradition has supported the institution of personal ownership or control of goods, it has always completely rejected the ancient Roman idea of exclusive and unqualified property rights. The Church understands owners as stewards who bear responsibilities for the right use of property, that is, for the relief of human need and the promotion of human flourishing. This tradition from Clement of Alexandria to Pope John Paul II holds that private property is justified so far as it promotes the common good. Uses of property that injure the common good, and especially uses that deny the needs of the poor, cannot be justified.

The Catholic tradition thus supports a fundamental distinction between wealth grounded in abundance and wealth grounded in scarcity. On the one hand, wealth—the store of goods—that is created in a manner that respects human dignity and acknowledges God's gift, that is distributed widely so that no one is excluded from its benefits, that is employed to promote the ultimate human objective of union with God, that is, in short, used to "build up treasure in heaven" by promoting the common good, especially in assistance to the poor, is a genuine instrumental good. It belongs to the vital abundance that God has promised us. On the other hand, wealth—the store of goods—that is created through exclusion or by shifting costs onto the poor, that is hoarded by the rich to the exclusion of the poor, that is used to promote consumerism and "super-development"[8] at the expense of the authentic development of persons, especially of their spiritual development, is an instrumental evil. This is a wealth grounded in scarcity, but not in the natural scarcity of limited resources: it rests on the artificial, socially created scarcity of exclusion moved by human vice.

Catholic social thought traditionally addresses economic phenomena in light of their particular social, historical, and cultural circumstances, to which some of the essays in this volume witness. In this connection, the Church's tradition breaks radically with the dominant approach in economic theory, which, for the most part, eschews any treatment of social, historical, and cultural contexts. At the same time, analysis is carried out in terms of Gospel-inspired constants—for example, the primacy of the common good—and the resulting understanding of persons and society perhaps best exemplified in the Thomistic doctrine of eternal, divine, and natural law. For the Catholic tradition, therefore, economic analysis is intrinsically normative, never "value neutral." By the same token, the tradition of Catholic social thought is at odds with postmodernist tendencies toward moral relativism and nihilism. From the perspective of the tradition, in fact, neoliberal economists and postmodernists look rather less like ideological opponents than like one another's complements. The relativist's denial that anyone's view of right and wrong can be denied may be seen as one more affirmation of the "principle" of consumer sovereignty: let each person elect the "brand" of reality to which he or she will agree to be responsible.

Again, from the perspective of the Catholic tradition, neither the "conserva-tive" free-market nor the "liberal" social-democratic approach to handling questions of wealth is quite grounded. While the concept of wealth is unintelligible except in light of an antecedent concept of the human person, conservative and liberal alike treat only of the analytic residue of person, that is, of the individual. Whether taken as an atom in a mechanical equilibrium or a mere organ of the body politic, as a producer-consumer or the end product of class relations, the individual is a material husk, a "shucked" person. Spirit, and with it freedom and responsibility, have been set aside or analyzed away.

The investigations into the creation, distribution, and use of wealth that consti-tute this volume demonstrate that our perception of wealth changes when we adopt the perspective—at once more comprehensive and more concrete—of Catholic so-cial thought. But comprehensiveness and concreteness are achieved at the cost of a certain complexity. Thus, economists typically equate wealth with goods that are de-sired; wealth is either these goods or such goods as can be exchanged for (or yield an income that can be turned into) desired goods. The fact that individuals desire things suffices to classify them "good," since "good" is simply the name for any term of in-dividual action.[9] Doubtless, the economists' account is descriptively true of individu-als, but where persons are concerned, the mere fact of desire opens the question of desirability—*What is worthy of desire?*—and with it a world of complexity. To pursue the question is to go by a short route down the interdisciplinary path that this volume and most of its individual chapters have taken.

Again, dissenters from the typical economist's account note that wealth is a rela-tive concept; that it implies exclusion and that it is thus the basis of exploitation. Doubtless, these dissenters' account is descriptively true to some (perhaps much) of what passes for economic rationality, but where persons are concerned, whatever is thus taken as qualifiedly rational is also subject to the comprehensive evaluation that we call moral. Can an action be economically (that is, qualifiedly) rational as well as morally (that is, without qualification except as a human action) irrational? If not, then wealth is neither unqualifiedly good nor bad; its human value is con-tingent on how it is produced, distributed, and used. In any case, to entertain the question is to go, once again, by a short route down the interdisciplinary path the present volume, and most of its individual chapters, have taken.

Finally, if nothing else, this book makes it abundantly clear that the "question of wealth" unfolds as a tissue of questions that defy any one discipline. One may cite the widening gap between rich and poor both within and between countries and re-gions. One may note the fact that wealth has been growing faster than output, sug-gesting that some wealth "creation" represents exclusion and cost shifting. Nothing, however, rivals the breathtaking cultural impact of wealth, or rather of the cult of wealth: its shrines dominate our cities, its tokens our media, and its acolytes our attention. So it will behoove us to pursue the overriding "question of wealth" that this volume has begun to raise: *Quomodo populus dives salvetur?* "How is a rich people to be saved?"

Notes

1. See Thomas E. Schmidt, *Hostility to Wealth in the Synoptic Gospels* (Sheffield, England: JSOT Press, 1987); and Pheme Perkins, "Does the New Testament Have an Economic Message?" in *Wealth in Western Thought: The Case for and against Riches,* ed. Paul G. Schervish (Westport, Conn.: Preager, 1994), 43–64.

2. The contention is often made that wealth, its creation, and its use are fundamentally different today than in the period of the early Church, thus implying that the views of the Gospel might not hold for our current society. Yet this misses the real objection of the Gospels to wealth: that it replaces God as the object of our devotion. In this sense, the Gospel's hostility to wealth is as valid as ever.

3. Lk 16:9, *The New English Bible* (Oxford: Oxford University Press, 1996). This phrase is often translated as "the mammon of unrighteousness"; see St. Thomas Aquinas, *Catena Aurea,* vol. III, part II (Albany, N.Y.: Preserving Christian Publications, 1993), 531.

4. St. John Chrysostom, *On Wealth and Poverty,* trans. Catherine P. Roth (Crestwood, N.Y.: St. Vladimir's Seminary Press, 1984), 43.

5. See St. Augustine, "Epistle 153, §26" vol. XXXIII, *Patrologia Latina,* ed. J. P. Minge (Paris: N.p., 1845), 665; and St. Augustine, "On Christian Doctrine 1, §4" vol. XXXIV, ibid., 21.

6. One can follow this line of thought, as is done by Charles Clark and Stefano Zamagni (chapters 1 and 8, this volume), and argue that there can be no artificial demarcation between so-called positive and normative issues in economics, that all important issues in economics are based on values, and that all values are ultimately based on faith.

7. Justo L. Gonzalez, *Faith and Wealth: A History of Early Christian Ideas on the Origins, Significance, and Use of Money* (Eugene, Ore.: Wipf & Stock, 1990), chapter 13.

8. For the meaning of "super-development" intended here, see the 1987 encyclical of John Paul II, *Sollicitudo rei socialis,* chapter IV.

9. The only criterion is that all exchanges be voluntary, that is, that they involve no coercion.

Contributors

Helen Alford, O.P., is dean of the Faculty of Social Sciences at the Pontifical University of St. Thomas, Rome. She teaches courses at the interface between ethics and economics/business, with a particular interest in technology. Her most recent book is *Managing As If Faith Mattered: Christian Social Principles in the Modern Organization* (co-author, Michael J. Naughton, 2001). She has served as a research assistant and lecturer in the Engineering Department, University of Cambridge, where she received her master's degree in Engineering and Ph.D. in Management and Engineering. Her dissertation employed central elements of the Catholic social tradition to assess and evaluate the system known as "cellular manufacturing" and the development of "human-centered" technology. She has done significant field research at British Aerospace and among the high-technology manufacturing and subcontracting industries in and around Cambridge, U. K., and has participated in the European Union-sponsored project, "Design of a Human-Centered Computer Integrated Manufacturing Cell," under the aegis of the European Strategic Program of Research in Informational Technology (ESPRIT).

Simona Beretta is a professor of International Economic Policies and Institutions in the Faculty of Political Science and director of the Postgraduate Program in European Studies and Global Affairs at ASERI (Postgraduate School of Economics and International Relations), Università Cattolica, Milan. She is a member of the editorial board of the *Rivista Internazionale di Scienze Sociali* and serves on a task force of the International Association for Catholic Social Thought. She has written numerous articles on international economics, international institutions, economics, and ethics, with special reference to Catholic social teaching.

Charles M. A. Clark is a professor of economics, Tobin College of Business, and Senior Fellow, Vincentian Center for Church and Society at St. John's University, New York. He has authored or edited eight books, the most recent of which is *The Basic*

Income Guarantee: Ensuring Progress and Prosperity in the 21st Century (2002). The most recent of his more than seventy professional publications are "Wealth and Poverty: On the Social Creation of Scarcity," *Journal of Economic Issues* (2002), and a three-part essay on economic equity in Network's *Connections* magazine (2002). He is currently writing a book on the challenges that Catholic social thought presents to economic theory.

S. A. Cortright is professor of philosophy and of the Integral Curriculum of Liberal Arts at St. Mary's College of California, where he has served as chair of the St. Mary's Department of Philosophy and as the founding director of the college's John F. Henning Institute, which is dedicated to the study of the philosophical and theological principles of Catholic social thought. He has edited and contributed to several books on Catholic social teaching, including *Labor, Solidarity, and the Common Good* (2000) and, with Michael Naughton, *Rethinking the Purpose of Business: Interdisciplinary Essays from the Catholic Social Tradition* (2002).

Carlo Dell'Aringa graduated from the Università Cattolica, Milan, in the Faculty of Political Science in 1963 and obtained a Ph.D. in Economics at Oxford University in 1970. Since 1980 he has been a professor of economics at the Università Cattolica. He has been a member of the executive committees of EALE (European Association of Labour Economists) and IIRA (International Industrial Relations Association). He has also been president of AIEL (Italian Association of Labour Economists) and is now president of AISRI (Italian Association for Industrial Relations). His research interests are in the fields of labor market policies and wage determination.

Daniel Finn, an economist and theologian, writes and teaches on the relationship between Christian ethics and economics. He is both a professor of theology and the Clemens Professor of Economics and the Liberal Arts at St. John's University, Collegeville, Minnesota. His writing and speaking around the United States and Latin America have addressed the ethical aspects of economic issues in a variety of ways. He is working on a book entitled, *The Moral Ecology of Markets*, and, as part of a church-based community organization, has been an active leader in a regional, affordable-housing task force developing joint policies for five cities in Central Minnesota. His most recent book is *Just Trading: On the Ethics and the Economics of International Trade.*

Francis T. Hannafey, S.J., is associate professor of Religious Studies at Fairfield University, Connecticut, where he teaches Christian social ethics. He also teaches business ethics in the university's Applied Ethics Program. He received an M.B.A. in Finance and Marketing and a Ph.D. in Christian Ethics from Loyola University, Chicago. His research interests include Roman Catholic social teaching and business ethics. His recent publications have appeared in *Horizons* and *Louvain Studies*, and he has completed an essay that is forthcoming in the *Journal of Business Ethics*.

John C. Haughey, S.J., is from the province of Maryland and has been a professor of Christian ethics at Loyola University in Chicago since 1991. He has published ten books, the most recent being *Housing Heaven's Fire: The Challenge of Holiness* (2002). He has held positions as associate editor of *America* magazine; as visiting chair at Seton Hall, John Carroll, and Marquette; and as senior researcher at Woodstock Theological Center (1974–1984). He has been a Vatican appointee to two bilateral dialogues, one with world Pentecostalism and one with the World Evangelical Alliance.

Robert G. Kennedy is a professor in the departments of Management and Catholic Studies at the University of St. Thomas, St. Paul, Minnesota. He received his Ph.D. in Medieval Studies (with a concentration in philosophy and theology) from the University of Notre Dame and also holds master's degrees in both Biblical Criticism and Business Administration. At St. Thomas, Kennedy teaches courses in Catholic Studies, general management, business ethics, theology, and philosophy, and he has also coordinated the university's required undergraduate course in business ethics. He has been a visiting professor in theology at the University of Dallas and in business ethics at the Instituto Panamericana in Mexico City. Kennedy is the co-author of a book on ethics and management as well as the author of a number of case studies and journal articles on professional ethics and other topics.

Claudio Lucifora, a professor of economics at the Università Cattolica, Milan, earned a B.A. in Economics (Università Cattolica, 1984), an M.A. in Economics (University of Warwick, 1987), and a Ph.D. in Economics (University of Warwick, 1991). He has held teaching and visiting positions at the University of Warwick, London School of Economics–CEP, and Université de Paris II, CEPREMAP. His research interests are in labor economics, and he has published books and articles on wage determination and inequality and poverty as well as on education.

Dennis P. McCann is the Wallace M. Alston Professor of Bible and Religion at Agnes Scott College in Atlanta/Decatur, Georgia, and executive director of the Society of Christian Ethics. Before coming to Agnes Scott College in 1999, McCann taught for eighteen years at DePaul University in Chicago. He received his S.T.L. in Theology from the Gregorian University in Rome in 1971 and a Ph.D. in Theology from the University of Chicago Divinity School in 1976. His publications include *Christian Realism and Liberation Theology* (1981) and *New Experiment in Democracy: The Challenge for American Catholicism* (1987). Along with Charles R. Strain, he authored

Polity and Praxis: A Program for American Practical Theology (1985; reprinted 1990). He has served on the board of directors of the Society of Christian Ethics (1989–1992) and on the editorial board of *The Journal of Religious Ethics* (1981–1996). With Max Stackhouse and Shirley Roels, he edited an anthology of materials for teaching business ethics within an ecumenically Christian perspective: *On Moral Business: Classical and Contemporary Resources for Ethics and Economics* (1995). McCann has had extensive academic experience in Hong Kong, China, and other countries in East Asia. In 1998 he was the Au Yeung King Fong University Fellow at the Centre for Applied Ethics at Hong Kong Baptist University, where he did research on East Asian business ethics within the framework of comparative religious ethics.

Michael J. Naughton is the director of the John A. Ryan Institute for Catholic Social Thought at the University of St. Thomas, St. Paul, Minnesota. He has organized international conferences in the United States, Europe, Asia, and Latin America on the theme of Catholic social thought and management. His most recent books are *Managing As If Faith Mattered: Christian Social Principles in the Modern Organization* (co-author Helen Alford, 2001) translated into Spanish, Russian, and Hungarian, with Italian and Chinese forthcoming, and *Rethinking the Purpose of Business: Interdisciplinary Essays in the Catholic Social Tradition* (co-editor, S. A. Cortright, 2002), translation into Chinese in progress. Naughton is also editor of the series entitled *Catholic Social Tradition,* published by the University of Notre Dame Press. He received a Ph.D. in Theology and Society from Marquette University and an M.B.A. from the University of St. Thomas.

Lee A. Tavis is the C. R. Smith Professor of Finance and the founding director of the Program on Multinational Managers and Developing Country Concerns at the University of Notre Dame. He is a faculty fellow of the Kellogg Institute for International Studies and the Kroc Institute for Peace Studies as well as a member of the faculty advisory committee for the Latino Instituto. He was honored with the university's Faculty Award in 1993 and with the Reinhold Niebuhr award for work in social justice in 1998. With research interests in business planning models and development ethics, his work focuses on the trade-offs between corporate wealth optimization and the corporate contribution to development. He has published numerous journal articles and books in both areas.

Robert L. Wahlstedt is chairman of Reell Precision Manufacturing Corporation, which employs 300 people in the United States and the Netherlands. Reell has become an experiment in the integration of faith and work as employees of the company grow together in faith and professional competence. Many of the innovations that came out of this experiment directly parallel the teaching of Catholic social thought. Reell recently received the national American Business Ethics Award in the small business category for 2002. Wahlstedt serves as an Executive Fellow at the University of St. Thomas and as an investor and adviser with Hi Tempo, a retailer of skis and sailboats.

Stefano Zamagni is a professor of economics and former dean of the Faculty of Economics at the University of Bologna. Educated at the University of Oxford, he serves on several boards and committees, some of which include the Scientific Committee of the L. Luzzatti Institute for Cooperative Studies, Rome; the Pontifical Council for Justice and Peace, Vatican City; the Scientific Committee of the Lanza Foundation, Padua; the Scientific Committee of the E. Mattei Foundation, Milan; and the Scientific Committee of AICCON (Italian Association for the Cooperative and Nonprofit Culture), Forlì. Since 1999 he has been the president of ICMC (International Catholic Migration Commission), Geneva. He is the author of twelve books and the editor of nineteen books, and he has written fifty-five scientific essays for both Italian and international journals.

Index